To Lois for your love of learning, and Mel, the gentle genius.

Acknowledgments

I am grateful to Mike Lawson for his support of this project and to the many people at Thomson who worked to bring this book to fruition. I am also thankful to my editor, Dan J. Foster, who has helped in many ways, and to my wife, Jennifer, who read and commented all of the chapters.

A special thanks goes to my friend and colleague, Dr. Bruce Frazier, for his keen insights as a technical editor. His suggestions helped me to improve and clarify the text immeasurably.

About the Author

Brent Edstrom has utilized music technology as an integral part of an active career as a performer, a composer, an arranger, a transcriber, and a music synthesist for more than 20 years. Highlights of his industry work include hundreds of arrangements and transcriptions for the Hal Leonard Corporation, music for industrial films and television, arrangements for symphony orchestra, and session work for a wide variety of recording projects. In the realm of traditional composition, his pieces have been featured at universities and major festivals such as the International Trumpet Guild. He continues ongoing theoretical work in the area of music notation algorithms in C++. Edstrom currently works as a freelance writer for the Hal Leonard Corporation and does writing and session work for a national production company. He coordinates the music theory and composition program at Whitworth College.

Contents

Introduction

We live in a digital world. E-mail is replacing traditional mail and contracts, and invoices and other business documents bounce from coast to coast in the blink of an eye. In music, digital technology is used in every facet of production from preparation of scores to recording, editing, mixing, and mastering. Musicians often collaborate on projects using network technology, and tracks recorded on the west coast can be uploaded by a producer on the east coast in a matter of minutes. In the realm of music retail, brick-and-mortar record stores are facing competition from online music stores. In short, the digital revolution is here, and an understanding of these technologies should be an essential part of the training of a modern-day musician.

WHY I WROTE THIS BOOK

In teaching music technology to numerous students over the past decade, I have come to the conclusion that, while many textbooks do an excellent job of teaching technological concepts such as sequencing and synthesis, few texts provide insights regarding how to actually use the technology to create music. While a student can learn the basics of sequencing in a few class sessions, these same students often have a difficult time using the technology to sequence and record original compositions. *Musicianship in the Digital Age* focuses on both the technical and musical aspects of computer-based music production. Concepts such as sequencing, synthesis, and digital editing are presented in a holistic way that is applicable to products from a wide range of vendors, and musical concepts such as composition, arranging, and orchestration are presented in a way that can be easily assimilated and applied to a wide variety of projects ranging from traditional acoustic ensembles to synthetic orchestrations.

I have been fortunate to make a living for many years as a composer, arranger, and keyboardist. In my experience, a balance of technical know-how and musicianship has been an essential ingredient to longevity in the industry. I wrote this book in order to share musical and technological concepts that have been useful in many professional situations. To that end, the concepts presented in this book can help you compose, arrange, record, and produce original music using a modest set of tools.

WHO THIS BOOK IS FOR

With the availability of reasonably priced computers and software, many musicians are turning to computers as a primary tool in music production. *Musicianship in the Digital Age* will be useful to musicians from many backgrounds, including students, hobbyists, multimedia specialists, and professionals who wish to use computers and other digital tools to create and record music.

OVERVIEW

This book is organized in three parts. Part I covers the technical aspects of music production such as setting up a project studio, using computers and MIDI, sequencing, digital audio recording, synthesis, loop-based production, and computer-aided notation. Part II covers relevant musical concepts such as chords and scales, the linear process, creating bass and drum grooves, keyboarding techniques, music composition, arranging, and orchestration. The final part features scores and an audio CD with commentary detailing both the musical and technical aspects of each production.

HOW TO USE THIS BOOK

It is not necessary to read this book from start to end, although some chapters build on concepts presented in earlier chapters. Many chapters feature project "starters" and practice techniques that can facilitate the process of composing and arranging music, so I encourage you to explore the book in any order that best serves your creative process. If you are new to music technology, I would suggest reading the first eight chapters in order. If you already have a technical background, I would suggest reading selected chapters in order to fill in any gaps. Most of the concepts presented in the chapters on musicianship can be heard on the CD that accompanies this book, and I encourage you to listen to the recordings to hear relevant concepts such as keyboard techniques, orchestration, the linear process, writing lyrics, and the like.

Part I

Technology

CHAPTER 1

Computers and Software

The computer is, without question, one of the most important tools to a contemporary musician. The computer is at the heart of most modern-day recording facilities and project studios and is used for everything from music typesetting to recording, editing, and processing of digital audio. I often field questions from students and colleagues that can be grouped into two broad categories: questions relating to troubleshooting and system optimization or questions relating to purchasing a new computer or software. This chapter provides an overview of computers, operating systems, software, and hardware that will help you to make good purchasing decisions and keep your system running reliably and efficiently.

Categories of Music Software

This is a wonderful time for musicians: computers are fast and reasonably priced, and there are an amazing variety of software tools from which to choose. However, selecting the right tool for the job is not as easy as it once was: To the benefit of musicians, the lines between software categories are blurring as software products mature and new features are added. For example, most sequencing programs such as Cubase provide at least a rudimentary level of music notation capability, and many loop-based editing tools such as ACID provide support for MIDI recording and editing. (The Musical Instrument Digital Interface is covered in detail in Chapter3, "Introduction to MIDI.")

The following section provides an overview of the common types of software tools available to musicians. This section is not intended to provide a comprehensive list of products in each category but rather to provide an overview so that the reader can evaluate potential tools. Opinions differ as to what constitutes a pleasing and efficient user interface, so when possible I would encourage you to download demos before purchasing new software since this can help you to select a tool that best suits your needs.

SEQUENCING

If your goal is to create music by using a computer and a keyboard to record MIDI data, then you will want to utilize sequencing software. Sequencing programs like Digital Performer (see Figure 1.1) allow you to record MIDI messages transmitted by a MIDI keyboard or other controller and to manipulate these messages in a variety of ways such as transposing a passage, changing the tempo, or cutting and pasting data.

Figure 1.1
MIDI track view in Digital Performer.

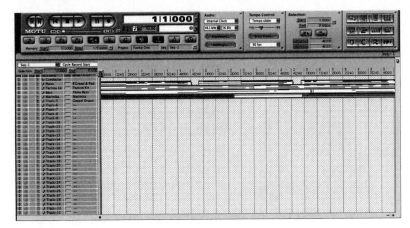

Since MIDI represents a musical performance (not the actual sound), MIDI sequencing is ideal when the utmost editing flexibility is required. Of the categories listed in this section, sequencing is the least processor-intensive application; even complex sequences can be handled by a modest computer system. MIDI files have an added advantage in that they are small and require very little storage space.

DIGITAL AUDIO WORKSTATION

Digital audio workstation (DAW) software and hardware represents a significant category of the music production market. Programs such as Pro Tools typically provide MIDI sequencing and digital audio recording capability in an integrated environment suitable for the production of music for a wide variety of applications (see Figure 1.2).

The major DAW software vendors include Cubase (Steinberg), Digital Performer (Mark of the Unicorn), Logic Pro (Apple), Nuendo (Steinberg), Pro Tools (Digidesign), and Sonar (Cakewalk). Some products (such as Pro Tools) require the use of proprietary hardware, and some products (Performer, Logic, and Sonar) are available only for a single operating system—either Mac or PC.

Figure 1.2
Pro Tools.

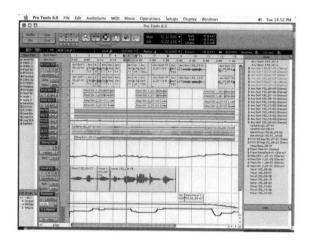

Of all the categories of music software, choosing a DAW system is perhaps the most daunting due to the depth and complexity of these programs, the wide variety of included options such as software synthesizers and audio plug-ins, and varying levels of support for audio hardware and control surfaces. To complicate matters, some products such as Deck by Bias are designed to work solely in the realm of digital audio, while other programs feature various levels of support for MIDI instruments and software synthesizers. My best advice is to consider the intended use of the product: The type and quality of audio plug-ins will be important if you primarily intend to make digital audio recordings. Likewise, MIDI editing capability and support for software synthesizers will be important if you plan to make your own backing tracks.

TWO-TRACK EDITING AND CD MASTERING

Two-track editors are used to edit and process mono and stereo audio files. A common application is the preparation of a master CD, but these tools are also helpful in editing and converting files for a variety of uses. Some mastering programs provide the ability to fix sonic imperfections like clicks and pops that occur when digitizing vinyl albums. Some programs offer *batch processing*, which allows you to conveniently process and convert many files with a few clicks of the mouse. Although some DAW programs provide a full complement of mastering tools, many musicians prefer a dedicated program for this stage of the production process (see Figure 1.3).

Figure 1.3
Peak LE (Bias).

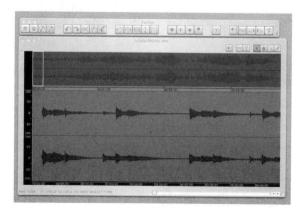

Mastering programs such as Audition (Adobe), Sound Forge (Sony), and Peak (Bias) provide the ability to "rip" audio files from a CD and convert files to a variety of formats. There are even freeware options such as Audacity, a capable editor that can be used to record and edit digital audio.

SOUND PROCESSING

Most DAW programs come with a variety of sound processing tools such as compressors, limiters, EQ, reverb, and delay. Users often expand the functionality of a DAW system by adding third-party plug-ins from a wide variety of vendors. A plug-in requires the use of a host application, and it is important to note that there are a variety of formats—many of which are intended to work with certain host systems. For example, TDM plug-ins are designed for a Pro Tools environment, and MAS plug-ins, a format developed by Mark of the Unicorn, will work only with host programs that support this format. VST is another popular plug-in format developed by Steinberg.

In an attempt to standardize the variety of competing formats, Apple developed the Audio Units format, and Microsoft has developed a Direct X format, but as of this writing plug-in vendors are still developing products in a variety of formats. Clearly, it makes sense to give some thought to this issue before selecting a DAW application. Figure 1.4 shows a typical plug-in—an Audio Unit compressor plug-in.

Figure 1.4
Audio Unit compressor plug-in.

Not all sound processing tools require the use of a host application. For example, the consumer version of Sound Soap (Bias) works as a stand-alone application as do a number of other interesting sound processing tools.

LOOP-BASED COMPOSITION

Loop-based composition tools such as ACID (Sony), Live (Ableton), and GarageBand (Apple) are used primarily to compose music by combining and processing loops of preexisting audio material, but the programs can also be used to record and edit MIDI and digital audio data. These tools are particularly helpful in generating many styles of dance music as well as remixing—creating new music based on samples of preexisting recordings. A typical loop-based project involves importing audio loops and "drawing" these musical phrases and grooves in a timeline view (see Figure 1.5).

Figure 1.5
ACID (Sony).

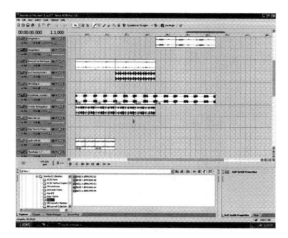

A related category, loop-editing software, is used to prepare audio files for use in a loop-based composition program or sampling synthesizer. These tools will be covered in detail in Chapter 7, "Loop-Based Production." Figure 1.6 shows ReCycle, a tool used to prepare REX files for use in programs such as Reason.

Figure 1.6
Editing a loop in ReCycle.

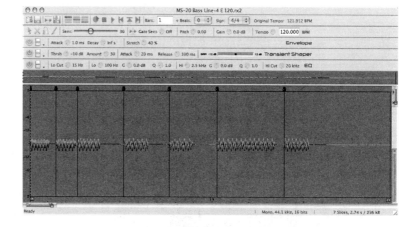

NOTATION

Notation software is used to prepare musical scores for performance or publication. These programs are typically used in conjunction with a MIDI keyboard to facilitate efficient note entry. Although some sequencing applications can be used to prepare scores, these programs typically do not provide enough control over visual elements to produce publisher-ready scores.

Currently, the two primary products are Finale and Sibelius (see Figure 1.7), but some lesser-known products include Igor, Mozart, and Encore. Notion, a relatively new product by VirtuosoWorks, features an interesting blend of music notation capability and sample-playback technology.

Figure 1.7
Sibelius.

REAL-TIME SOFTWARE SYNTHESIS

Many interesting products are available in the realm of software synthesis. These products utilize the processing power of the computer to fabricate a virtual synthesizer that can be played in real time by a MIDI controller or sequencing software. Products range from emulation of analog synthesizers and other "retro" hardware to advanced sample playback and editing systems. As with sound processing software, many software synthesizers function as plug-ins in a host application, while others work as stand-alone programs. Some DAW programs such as Logic Pro provide a number of software synthesizers as a part of the basic installation. Reason, a popular music production tool by Propellerhead, provides numerous synthesizer modules and effects as well as a built-in sequencer (see Figure 1.8). Mach 5, manufactured by Mark of the Unicorn, is another popular virtual synthesizer.

Figure 1.8
Reason.

Software synthesizers have many advantages over hardware synthesizers, such as more convenient editing capability and the ability to utilize the computer for data storage and retrieval. The downside is that software synthesizers can place a great processing burden on the host computer. In order to free up processing power on a primary computer, some musicians elect to run a second computer, connected via a MIDI interface that is devoted solely to running software synthesizers.

The Propellerhead company developed an interesting protocol called "ReWire" that enables ReWire-capable synthesizers to be controlled in real time by a ReWire-capable sequencer. Using this technology, a user can control a rack of virtual synthesizers via a sequencing program such as Digital Performer. This topic will be covered in detail in Chapter 6, "Music Synthesis."

NON REAL-TIME SYNTHESIS AND SOUND DESIGN

Some synthesis programs do not work in real time. These tools "render" an audio file based on a text file or set of parameters entered by the user. One of the most interesting examples is CSound, a rendering language developed by Barry Vercoe in the 1980s. CSound has a loyal user base due in part to the tremendous power of the rendering engine and the fact that open-source front ends are available for most computing platforms (see Figure 1.9).

Figure 1.9
The CSound-OS X front end.

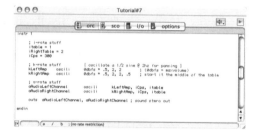

MetaSynth (U & I Software) is another interesting example of a sound design tool. The program functions much like a graphic arts editor but visual elements are used to render complex sounds (see Figure 1.10).

Figure 1.10
MetaSynth.

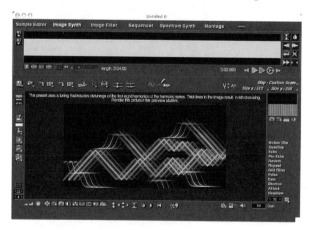

MIDI EDITOR/LIBRARIAN

It can be challenging to edit and program sounds from the front panel of most synthesizers. MIDI Editor/Librarian software provides a convenient way to edit, store, and load sounds from an array of synthesizers (see Figure 1.11). Some programs, such as Unisyn, will even provide an interface to a compatible host sequencing application so that sounds may be selected by name from within the program.

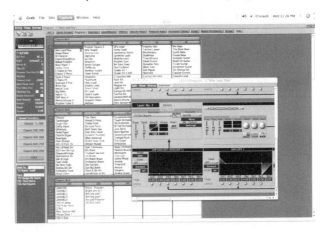

Figure 1.11
Editor/librarian software.

SPECIALIZED SOFTWARE

There are many other categories of music software geared toward specific tasks such as transcription, musical optical character recognition (MOCR), ear training, and algorithmic composition. Trade journals are often a good source of information regarding these products. I would also encourage you to spend some time on the Web; there is an astounding array of specialized commercial and open-source software available for a wide range of specialized applications.

Components of a Computer

It's likely that you are already familiar with the operation of a computer, so this book will not cover topics relating to general computer literacy. However, an understanding of the inner workings of a computer is essential in order to optimize and troubleshoot a system. This section provides a conceptual overview of the components of a computer in a way that is relevant for musicians.

MICROPROCESSOR

The microprocessor is the heart of a digital computer. It is an integrated circuit that contains the "brains" of the computer on a chip. The computational logic of the computer (i.e., how the computer computes using *and*, *or*, and *not* gates) is a key component of the design of the microprocessor. The microprocessor represents the entire *central processing unit* (CPU) of the computer on one chip.

Microprocessors allow digital computers to run at increasingly faster rates. In the days of early computers, large integrated circuit boards were used instead of microprocessors. Today, chip manufacturers such as Intel continue to fit more transistors on increasingly smaller integrated circuits, and the result, from a musician's perspective, is additional horsepower to run software synthesizers and audio effects.

In 1965, Gordon Moore made an interesting observation about the exponential growth of processing power. "Moore's Law" predicts that processing power will double every few years, and, to this point, his prediction has been very accurate. In his book, *The Age of Spiritual Machines* (Viking, published by the Penguin Group), synthesizer pioneer Ray Kurzweil makes some interesting observations about this trend:

"Taking all of this into consideration, it is reasonable to estimate that a $1000 personal computer will match the computing speed and capacity of the human brain by around the year 2020, particularly for the neuron-connection calculations, which appear to comprise the bulk of the computation in the human brain."

In recent years, companies such as Intel have been able to continue Moore's Law by implementing *nanotechnology*—utilizing devices that are less than 100 nanometers in size. (A *nanometer* is a measure of length: 1 nm = 0.000000001 meter, or one billionth of a meter. See http://www.intel.com/technology/silicon/sp/glossary.htm). Robert S. Chau, Intel fellow and director, Transistor Research and Nanotechnology at Intel Corp., states the following ("Nanotech Briefs," May 2005, Vol.2/No.3):

"We crossed the nanotechnology barrier in 2000 (with the 0.13-μm technology node, which has transistor physical gate length of about 70 nm), and are getting ever deeper into nanotechnology space. A very good example of nanotechnology used in our current 90-nm technology note (in production starting 2003) is the gate oxide, which has a physical thickness of only 1.2 nm, about four atomic layers thick."

Another technology, *quantum computing*, has the potential to push computers to unimaginable processing power. A quantum computer utilizes the paradoxical quantum concept of *superposition*. Although we are probably many years from seeing quantum computers, the technology is already being used for encryption in some commercial environments.

It is interesting to note that, though processor speed is an important factor regarding the speed of a computer, the design of the microprocessor also affects speed of operation. Put another way, two computers with the same clock speed may process data at differing rates due to differences in microprocessor design. The speed at which a microprocessor runs is primarily dependent on two factors: the number of bits on the data bus and the internal registers and clock speed. In general, larger data registers and a faster data bus will allow the computer to work more efficiently (e.g., a 64-bit system would, all things being equal, be faster than a 32-bit system).

Clock speed is another important issue regarding the speed of a microprocessor. Microprocessor clock speed is measured in *megahertz* (MHz) or *gigahertz* (GHz). A 1 MHz microprocessor works at a speed of 1 million cycles per second and a 1 "gig" machine works at an astounding 1 billion cycles per second. Though we still use clock speed to compare the speed of computers, the number can be misleading:

Each computer instruction may actually use up several clock cycles, so megahertz is more of a theoretical concept. It is important to note that, in terms of making music, many other factors come into play that affect the perceived speed of the computer. For example, a slow hard drive will have a direct impact on the number of audio tracks, and a poorly implemented device driver may create audio latency (the amount of time it takes for an audio signal to be processed) that is unbearable—even if the underlying microprocessor is fast.

In practical terms, faster processors are better, but, as with most things, there are tradeoffs. Faster processors tend to require more energy, and they tend to generate more heat. These are two issues to consider if you plan to use a portable computer, because they manifest themselves in shorter battery life and potentially more fan noise. Manufacturers such as Apple have utilized innovative techniques such as liquid cooling systems in desktop computers, but it is helpful to be aware of the tradeoffs. Some gaming systems, while extremely fast, are quite noisy because of the cooling fans on the processor and video card, so these systems are not necessarily the best choice for a studio application.

MULTIPROCESSOR COMPUTING

A new trend in computer design is to utilize more than one central processing unit. In a *multiprocessor* computer, two (or more) chips work together to perform computations, resulting in greater processing power. Note that software must be written to take advantage of multiprocessor architecture. Another form of parallel processing, based on *distributed computing* technology, is starting to become available in some audio applications. In such a system, additional computers are connected via an Ethernet network, and processing duties are "farmed" to other computers on the network. Logic Pro is an example of an application that can take advantage of this technology.

CACHE

Modern computers typically utilize a *memory cache*. The cache, a type of fast memory that is used to store recently used data, is located between the CPU and main memory. In some situations, processing will be faster because the CPU can more quickly retrieve "cached" data than data residing in the slower main memory.

BUS

The system bus is used to move data to and from the microprocessor. As with microprocessors, the speed of the bus is dependent on the number of bits that can be simultaneously handled as well as the clock speed of the bus. A 2 GHz machine may actually use a 1 GHz system bus. To understand how the bus is used, it would be helpful to consider how the computer handles a typical instruction such as addition. If the CPU intends to store a number in a memory register, it sends the data down the data wires on the system bus. The CPU also sends a number representing the requested memory location down the address wires. This number is then stored in memory at the requested position. If two numbers are stored in this fashion, it is possible for the computer to store yet another number representing a mathematical operation involving the previously stored numbers. This concept of moving and manipulating numbers is the very essence of modern-day computing.

MOTHERBOARD (SYSTEM BOARD)

The motherboard, or system board, contains the system bus and is used to connect the various components of a computer system. The motherboard includes plugs to connect storage devices such as hard drives and floppy drives, a connection to the power source, slots for RAM (random access memory), ROM (read-only memory) chips for enabling the boot procedure, connections for I/O devices such as a keyboard and mouse, and slots for video and audio cards. You might think of the motherboard like the central nervous system in the human body.

ROM

ROM is the acronym for *read-only memory*. ROM chips are used to store instructions that do not (ordinarily) need to be modified, such as the initial boot-up instructions performed when a computer is first switched on. *Firmware* is a related term that represents software stored in a ROM chip. It is sometimes necessary to update firmware when upgrading an operating system, installing new hardware, or troubleshooting a system.

RAM

RAM is the acronym for *random access memory*. RAM is used for the main memory of a computer as well as in other devices such as samplers and video cards. RAM is used to (temporarily) store data such as text entered on a keypad or numbers representing a digital audio recording. It is important to note that RAM is volatile: Any data residing in RAM will be lost in the event of a power failure or other catastrophic event, so it is a good idea to frequently save your work in order to store the contents of RAM to a nonvolatile medium such as a hard drive or flash drive.

RAM is an essential component of a music-making computer system. Each application, software synthesizer, effect plug-in, and process requires RAM. RAM is used for data buffers when recording digital audio tracks, and RAM is used by the operating system itself. In short, even a fast computer will bog down without enough RAM because the computer will be required to utilize virtual memory (see below).

VIRTUAL MEMORY

Most operating systems utilize a concept called *virtual memory* to simulate additional RAM. In the event of a low memory condition, the operating system stores the contents of portions of RAM to a *swap file* on the hard drive. Although it is not likely you would notice the use of virtual RAM in some applications such as word processing, virtual memory can cause many problems when running time-sensitive applications such as sequencing or digital audio recording software. Frequent disk swapping may be an indication that your computer does not have enough physical RAM.

HARD DRIVE

The hard drive is a storage device containing several disks or platters. Digital data is stored on a hard drive by magnetic means much like a tape recorder uses magnetism to record an audio performance. In fact, early computers used tape drives for storage of data, and digital tape is still a low cost (albeit slow) way to archive data.

Important considerations for digital musicians are the size and speed of the hard drive. With regard to size, it is helpful to remember that a stereo digital audio file requires about 10 megabytes of space for each minute of recording time. Using that figure, it is easy to estimate the amount of space required for a given multi-track recording project.

With regard to speed, one of the first things to consider is the platter rotation speed. Currently, inexpensive drives spin at 4200–5400 rpm, and higher performance drives spin at 7200–10,000 rpm. For most musicians, it makes sense to spend a bit more for a faster rotation speed because this can have a direct impact on the number of digital audio tracks that can be handled by the computer. A related term, *average seek time*, can be useful when evaluating the performance of a hard drive. Seek time refers to the amount of time it takes for the head of the drive to move to the proper position on the disk in order to read or write data. Average seek time is measured in milliseconds, and lower numbers indicate faster performance.

As computer technicians will point out, it is not a matter of *if* your hard drive will fail, it is a matter of *when* the drive will fail, so it is important to make a habit of backing up important work. External hard drives are reasonably priced, so one viable solution is to make regular backups and alternate these backups on several external drives. Data can then be burned to CD or DVD as needed in order to free up space at the conclusion of a project. When saving your work, it often makes sense to save multiple versions because a file can become corrupt in the event of a power failure or system crash as a file is being stored to disk. Although such a procedure may be impractical when dealing with larger digital audio projects, I always make a habit of storing sequential versions of files when saving smaller notation or sequencing documents.

RECORDABLE CD AND DVD

An internal or external CD-R is useful in order to back up data or burn audio CDs. Most CDs store 650 to 700 megabytes of data, which is the equivalent to over an hour of two-track digital audio. In contrast, DVD-R or DVD+R drives can currently store 4.7 gigabytes of data and are a good choice for musicians who do a fair amount of multi-track digital audio recording. For example, the project files for the CD that accompanies this book required about 4 gigabytes of storage space, so I was able to back up all of the files on a single DVD. DVD-R and DVD+R are competing formats, but many newer drives support the ability to read and write both formats.

FLASH DRIVE

For smaller projects, a *flash drive* can offer a convenient way to back up and transfer data. These drives attach to an available USB port. Currently, flash drives up to 1 gigabyte are available for a reasonable price.

PCI

PCI stands for *peripheral component interconnect.* PCI slots are used to connect devices such as sound cards, a SCSI interface, or modem. (The Small Computer System Interface, SCSI, will be covered in the sampling section of Chapter 6). Many professional audio interfaces utilize a PCI card that is installed in the host desktop computer and which is connected, via a high-speed cable, to an external interface. Most consumer sound cards and some professional audio interfaces are contained on a single PCI card, and audio and MIDI connections are made at the back of the card.

FIREWIRE

FireWire, Apple's name for an IEEE-1394 interface, is a high-speed serial interface that can be used to connect devices such as a digital audio interface, video camera, or hard drive. Many professional audio interfaces utilize a FireWire connection because of its fast data transfer rate (currently 400 or 800 megabits per second) and the fact that these devices can be conveniently connected to a variety of machines.

USB

The *universal serial bus* (USB) is similar to FireWire in that devices such as external MIDI or audio interfaces can be conveniently attached via a USB cable. There are currently two variants: USB 1.x is much slower than FireWire and is suitable as a bus for MIDI interfaces or two-channel audio interfaces. USB 2.0 provides faster data transfer (480 megabits per second) and is available on some multi-channel digital audio interfaces as well as many portable hard drives.

HUB

A FireWire or USB hub provides additional *downstream* ports. For example, a computer with a single USB port can be expanded to four (or more) ports by utilizing a USB hub. It is usually necessary to use a powered USB hub because most music interfaces require more power than can be delivered via an unpowered hub.

COMPUTER MONITOR

It is important to invest in a quality monitor if you plan to spend long days working in front of a computer screen. A large monitor is useful for nearly every task, although less important if you rely on an external *control surface.* For many years, CRT (*cathode ray tube*) monitors were most common. Quality CRT monitors are relatively inexpensive but have the disadvantage of being large and heavy. CRT monitors sometimes produce an audible high-frequency sound when running at high resolution.

Many musicians now opt to use a plasma or LCD (*liquid crystal display*) monitor. Although these displays are more expensive, they offer many advantages such as having a smaller footprint and being lighter weight. Most musicians prefer plasma or LCD monitors because they are easier on the eyes.

VIDEO CARD

A video card is responsible for "driving" a computer monitor. Older cards were plugged into an available PCI slot on the motherboard, but most new cards use a special port called an *accelerated graphics port* (AGP). It is important that the card provide sufficient power to run a monitor at the desired resolution and refresh rate. For example, Apple's largest Cinema display requires a special video card. When purchasing a new computer or video card, be sure to see if the unit supports DVI (*digital visual interface*). Some cards provide only analog VGA output, which can be problematic if you wish to utilize an LCD in the future.

AUDIO INTERFACE

In a modern studio, an audio interface provides the link between a computer and the audio subsystem. On the input side, an *analog to digital converter* (ADC) converts analog signals to digital. On the output side, a *digital to analog converter* (DAC) is used to convert digital signals to analog so that the audio interface can be monitored via an analog mixer and speakers. Some interfaces provide digital inputs and outputs to facilitate digital transfers to or from a digital-audio tape machine, digital multitrack recorder, or other device. The common digital formats, S/PDIF and AES/EBU, are covered in Chapter 2, "Setting Up a Project Studio."

Numerous professional audio interfaces are available. A primary consideration is the quality of the converters. As with other aspects of music production, "quality" is a subjective term, so, if possible, it's a good idea to read reviews and get some hands-on time before investing in an audio interface. Another consideration is the connection method: Some high-end interfaces connect to the computer via an internal PCI card. External interfaces typically connect via FireWire or USB. In my own work, I tend to favor FireWire interfaces because these devices can be transported easily and connected to a variety of systems (see Figure 1.12).

Figure 1.12
FireWire audio interface.

MIDI INTERFACE

A MIDI interface provides a link between a computer and the MIDI subsystem. Most current models are connected via a USB port, but serial or parallel models are available for older systems. I would recommend a USB MIDI interface for most users. MIDI, which will be covered in detail in Chapter 3, "Introduction to MIDI," provides 16 channels of data per port. If you own one keyboard, a single-port MIDI interface is sufficient, but a multi-port interface will be advantageous if you have more than one synthesizer or sound module (see Figure 1.13). Note that some interfaces provide timecode data reading and generation capabilities for synchronization with an external device. Some control surfaces require the use of an entire MIDI port, so that is also a consideration.

Figure 1.13
Multi-port USB MIDI interface.

Troubleshooting and System Optimization

To this point, I have covered the primary components of a computer system. In the following section you will see how software and hardware work together to form a functioning music-making environment. I will include concepts that will enable you to troubleshoot and optimize your system for music production.

HOW A COMPUTER WORKS

It is helpful to visualize a computer as a series of hardware and software levels. At the lowest level, *firmware* provides machine-language instructions that bring hardware components to life. In a computer, firmware provides the mechanism for loading, or *booting,* the operating system. In a device such as a synthesizer or control surface, firmware provides the instructions necessary for basic operation of the device. Firmware is an instruction set that resides in ROM chips or EPROM, and it is sometimes necessary to upgrade firmware of a computer or external device to provide enhanced functionality or as a means of fixing bugs in the implementation of existing firmware.

BIOS

BIOS is an acronym for *basic input-output system* and is responsible for the initial boot procedure of a computer. When a computer is first turned on, the BIOS performs several hardware tests to ensure that hardware is functioning properly. The BIOS looks for special programs that actually load the operating system, and once these programs are found on a hard drive or other device, control is passed to a loader program, which then "boots" the operating system. If you have ever added extra RAM to a PC computer, you probably noticed that, during the boot procedure, your computer already recognized the upgrade. This is the BIOS at work.

The term *flashing* is sometimes used to describe the process of updating the BIOS. Remember to make a backup of your data prior to "flashing" a system, because this procedure, while sometimes necessary, is an extreme process that could render your system inoperable should something go wrong.

Device Drivers

A *device driver* is a special type of software that provides a link between hardware components such as a MIDI interface, audio interface, or mouse and the operating system. Device drivers are a key source of troubleshooting for modern musicians: Many crashes and performance issues relate to drivers, so an understanding of the concept will help you to optimize your system.

In general, hardware components are at the mercy of the device driver. A poorly implemented driver will cause timing problems and system crashes, and in a worst-case scenario, a hardware component will not even function if a device driver is not provided for a given operating system.

If you experience crashes or other problems when using a MIDI or audio interface, one of your first steps should be to check the manufacturer's Web site to see if new drivers are available. It is sometimes necessary to remove older drivers prior to installing new device drivers, so be sure to carefully follow the manufacturer's instructions.

A *device manager* is a type of configuration software that allows the user to change the properties of a device driver. For example, most audio interfaces provide a device manager that allows you to select between analog and digital input or to set the size of the audio buffer or other parameter. It is often necessary to make changes via the device manager in order to tune the performance of a given driver for a particular application. For example, a change in the size of the audio buffer can have a dramatic impact on *latency*, an audible playback delay, when using software synthesizers or other types of audio software. Audio device managers are typically available via an "Audio Hardware Settings" menu option in the host software. A device manager may also be available from the System Preferences panel or Control Panel in OS X or Windows (see Figure 1.14).

Figure 1.14
A device manager for an audio interface.

Operating System (OS)

The *operating system* provides the interface between the user and the underlying software and hardware layers. The operating system reserves memory, loads device drivers and other startup programs, provides a user interface, and is generally responsible for the operation of the entire computer system. As with device drivers, the operating system may need to be updated periodically to fix bugs, security flaws, or other problems. In general, it's best to back up your data prior to updating the operating system. When doing a major system update, it is usually preferable to back up your data and initiate a *clean install*. During a clean install, the hard drive is formatted (erased) and a "fresh" copy of the OS is installed. It is also necessary to reinstall application files after a clean installation of the operating system. Unfortunately, modern operating systems tend to build up detritus over a period of months or years. This can result from inadvertent installation of spyware, viruses, or the installation of multiple device drivers and other types of software. A clean install can help a computer to run more efficiently and is sometimes necessary if you are having persistent (and untraceable) system crashes or other problems.

Application Software

Application software provides functionality for specific tasks such as music notation or sequencing. When an application runs, the application reserves memory necessary for input/output buffers and other types of temporary storage. The application will communicate with the operating system for tasks such as determining the dimensions of the screen or querying the type and number of MIDI interfaces. At the most basic level, the application is simply a series of *machine language* instructions that execute on the computer. It is often necessary to upgrade application software to fix bugs or other problems.

In summary, then, a computer system consists of the following hardware and software "layers":

▶ Hardware (microprocessor, hard drive, etc.)

▶ BIOS ("wakes up" the computer)

▶ Device drivers (provide an interface between hardware such as an audio interface and the operating system)

▶ Operating system (provides an interface for user interaction and manages system resources such as memory)

▶ Application software (unique programs that run on a specified OS and handle tasks such as word processing or sequencing)

The conceptual diagram shown in Figure 1.15 illustrates the interconnected nature of a modern computer system.

Figure 1.15
Layers of a computer system.

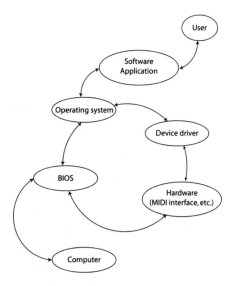

HOW COMPUTERS THINK

The instructions that a microprocessor can perform are defined in its basic *instruction set*. At the most primitive level, *machine language* is used to specify the instructions that a computer should execute. Machine language is a binary language in which each instruction refers to a specific action of the machine. At a slightly higher level, *assembly language* is used to describe machine language instructions using symbolic (text) code that is much easier for humans to read. Thankfully, programmers rarely need to program directly in assembly language anymore. Many higher-level languages such as C++ and Basic provide an easier development cycle. Figure 1.16 illustrates how C++ source code, a text file, is compiled into machine language instructions. The program simply counts from one to ten:

Figure 1.16
A C++ source code example.

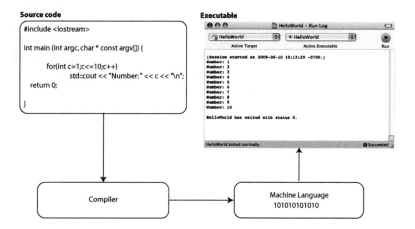

TROUBLESHOOTING

A modern operating system is the result of millions of lines of code. In a very real sense, the user relies on the many programmers who designed the operating system, device drivers, and software applications. Subtle programming errors can lead to bugs resulting from the interaction of these software components. Viruses and spyware can also cause system instability and inefficiency. Consider the following tips:

▶ Make regular backups of essential data. Keep an extra copy of data off-site in case of a catastrophic event such as a flood or fire.

▶ If possible, create a system restore point prior to installing new software or drivers or upgrading your operating system.

▶ Use a firewall to protect against online attacks. This is particularly important for systems with an "always on" connection to the Internet.

▶ Avoid installing unessential software and be particularly careful when downloading software from the Internet.

▶ Use virus protection and anti-spyware software to help guard against installation of malicious programs. Note that virus protection programs can also create system problems, so it is best to back up your data and create a system restore point prior to installing virus protection software.

▶ When installing a major operating system upgrade, back up your data and perform a "clean" installation. A clean installation is almost always preferable for a major upgrade.

▶ Don't install a major upgrade of the operating system or an essential application if you are in the middle of a project—these types of upgrades almost always have a few bugs that need to be tracked and fixed.

▶ Avoid needlessly taxing the system. For example, disk compression is a bad idea for any audio recording system. Similarly, many systems ship with preinstalled troubleshooting and "help" programs that automatically load when the computer boots. Consider disabling these types of applications (but take care not to disable memory-resident programs needed by the operating system).

The following hardware- and software-related tips can be useful in helping you track and fix problems with your music-making system:

Hardware

Hardware issues can be difficult to track. Symptoms might include an inability for the machine to boot because RAM is not seated properly or crashes due to a hard drive that is starting to fail. If you suspect a hardware-related problem, consider the following steps. Note that you may invalidate your warranty if you attempt to open your machine, so proceed with caution. For safety, be sure to unplug the machine prior to opening the case.

▶ Ensure that RAM is properly seated.

▶ Check that wires are properly seated (a CD-ROM drive may stop functioning if the cable jiggles loose, for example).

▶ Make sure SCSI devices are terminated and devices are set to a proper (and nonconflicting) identification number.

▶ Run an appropriate disk repair utility to see if there are problems with the hard drive. A hard drive that suddenly starts making noise may indicate that a failure is imminent.

▶ Try booting in "safe" mode to see if the problem might relate to an issue with a device driver or other software component.

▶ If a USB audio or MIDI interface stops working, exit all applications and remove and replug the device (be sure to first turn off your speakers if unplugging an audio interface).

▶ Unplug external devices such as a MIDI interface or digital audio interface and reboot the system. This may point to a problem with a device driver.

▶ Ensure that the computer has adequate ventilation. Some problems may result from a computer that is running too hot.

▶ It is sometimes necessary to adjust the BIOS settings so that USB or parallel-port devices function properly (but take care, because some changes, such as settings for the hard drive, may render your system unusable).

▶ You may need to adjust the settings in the hardware panel of your operating system. For example, I once had problems with an older parallel-port MIDI interface. The interface would not work with the "ECP printer port" listed in system settings. Updating the port as a "regular" printer port fixed the problem. Similarly, legacy audio cards may need to be disabled via the hardware panel so that a newly installed interface will function properly.

Software

Most computer crashes are the result of a bug, out-of-date device driver, spyware, or a virus. When troubleshooting a software issue, consider the following steps. Be sure to back up your data prior to updating your operating system or attempting any other major upgrade.

▶ Try to replicate the crash. Most "replicable" crashes are the result of an application bug. See if the vendor has provided an upgrade. Alternatively, most vendor forums will address incompatibilities with other software applications.

▶ Remove any unneeded startup applications (but don't remove essential components of the operating system).

► Update application software.

► Update device drivers.

► Update the operating system.

► Try reinstalling application software and drivers. Sometimes crashes are the result of a "corrupt" installation.

► Try restoring the system to a previous restore point.

► One vexing problem called "DLL hell" can occur when updating application software. In some instances, the installation software will overwrite a *dynamic link library* (DLL) used by other applications or the operating system, and the new library creates a system incompatibility. In this instance, a restore point is usually the best fix, although it is sometimes possible to fix the problem by downloading a new version of the dynamic link library. (A dynamic link library contains executable code. Unlike an application, a DLL provides functions that can be used by more than one application. In order to use the functions in a DLL, applications bind *dynamically* to the DLL at run time).

SYSTEM OPTIMIZATION

To keep a computer running efficiently, it may be necessary to perform periodic maintenance. The following paragraphs illustrate several common optimization strategies.

Clean Installation of the Operating System

A clean installation is a drastic step, but I have found it helpful to do a clean install about once a year in order to keep my machines running smoothly. Take note that a clean install will delete all of the files on your hard drive, so it is essential to make a complete backup of all of your data. Consider the following steps when performing a clean installation:

► Back up all of your data to an external hard drive or DVD drive.

► Check that the data is not corrupt (consider making a second copy of all data).

► Make a note of network, e-mail, and other important settings.

► Boot from your operating system CD or DVD and reinstall a clean copy of the operating system.

► Reinstall all necessary applications.

RAM

Frequent hard drive activity may indicate that your system is running low on RAM and is swapping data to the hard drive. As mentioned previously, avoid running unessential memory-resident programs, because this will free up additional RAM. Alternatively, it may make sense to purchase additional RAM.

Macs and PCs provide tools to view system resource usage. For example, I used the Unix "top" command to view system-consuming resources on my Macintosh PowerBook and was surprised to see that several dashboard "widgets" were taking up quite a bit of memory.

```
Processes:  61 total, 2 running, 59 sleeping... 194 threads
16:15:47
Load Avg:  0.17, 0.27, 0.18    CPU usage:  12.8% user, 13.7%
sys, 73.5% idle
SharedLibs: num =  167, resident = 32.7M code, 3.21M data,
4.98M LinkEdit
MemRegions: num =  8197, resident =  206M + 11.4M private,
152M shared
PhysMem:  75.4M wired,  286M active,  143M inactive,  505M
used, 6.55M free
VM: 6.84G +  112M   37678(0) pageins, 11739(0) pageouts
  PID COMMAND      %CPU    TIME   #TH #PRTS #MREGS RPRVT
RSHRD  RSIZE  VSIZE
  258 DashboardC   0.0%  0:03.16   3   100    162   3.42M
7.10M  7.35M   208M
  257 DashboardC   0.0%  0:04.96   3    94    143   2.96M
4.23M  5.37M   199M
  256 DashboardC   0.0%  0:02.40   4   103    151   12.1M
4.18M  14.4M   207M
  255 DashboardC   0.0%  0:00.68   3    97    167   4.83M
7.50M  7.96M   211M
  254 DashboardC   0.0%  0:00.38   3    78    123   2.36M
4.31M  4.89M   198M
  253 DashboardC   0.0%  0:02.43   4    88    166   12.0M
6.67M  15.0M   217M
  252 DashboardC   0.0%  0:00.34   3    94    114   1.98M
4.05M  4.46M   197M
  251 DashboardC   0.0%  0:04.75   3    79    166   3.86M
4.83M  6.58M   201M
```

Hard Drive

As mentioned previously, the rotation speed of the hard drive can directly impact the number of digital audio tracks that can be recorded or played back at a time. Also, as a disk is filled up, the drive will need to work harder to find data on the disk. For these reasons, it is often advisable to dedicate a high-speed external drive devoted solely to audio recording and playback. High-speed external drives have dropped in price in recent years so it might make sense to consider adding one or more drives.

DeFragmentation

Drive fragmentation occurs when files are broken up into small noncontiguous clusters on the disk. Defragmentation software analyzes all of the clusters on the disk and reorganizes the disk so that files occupy contiguous "chunks" on the drive. In theory, the hard drive head will not need to move as much when reading and writing to the disk. However, larger hard drives have made defragmentation less essential. For example, Apple suggests that "you probably won't need to optimize at all if you use Mac OS X" (http://docs.info.apple.com/article.html?artnum=25668). With that said, defragmentation will most likely be advantageous if you frequently make digital audio recordings on your machine. Figure 1.17 shows a defragmentation utility in action.

Figure 1.17
Defragmenting a disk.

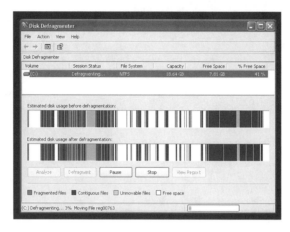

Install Current Drivers

Many performance problems can be traced to outdated device drivers. For example, I experienced timing problems when using a MIDI interface with recently updated sequencing software. New MIDI drivers fixed the problem. Similarly, latency issues with software synthesizers can sometimes be traced to an issue with a digital audio interface driver.

Adjust Buffer Settings

Audio buffers are used to temporarily store data that is going to or from an audio interface. Figure 1.18 illustrates the concept.

Figure 1.18
An audio buffer.

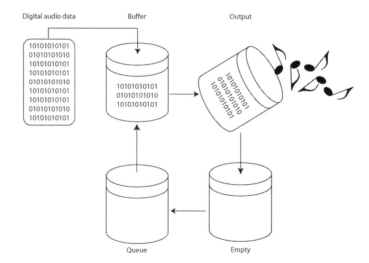

In general, a smaller buffer will cause less latency but will be more taxing on the system because the computer will be required to update buffers more frequently. It is often necessary to adjust the settings of the audio buffer to strike a balance between low latency and system efficiency. There are no hard and fast rules—most users will need to simply experiment with different settings to find an optimum number for the intended application.

The Great Debate: Choosing an Operating System

The selection of an operating system is a big choice for musicians and is a topic that often brings heated debate from proponents of a given system.

MAC AND PC

There are two primary choices: Macintosh computers running OS X or "PC" computers running Microsoft Windows. My intention is not to point you toward one operating system over another (I happen to own both Mac and PC computers; each platform has strengths and weaknesses). What you will learn from this discussion is how to evaluate software and computers and make logical purchase and upgrade decisions tailored for specific tasks.

Before you spend time debating the merits of one operating system over another, you should consider a key issue: software. A computer is only as good as the applications you intend to run on it. Although many outstanding programs are available for both operating systems (Cubase, Sibelius, and Finale, to name a few), some of the most popular programs are written for a single operating system. Logic and Sonar are applications that run only on Macintosh and PC computers, respectively. Similarly, Peak and Sound Forge are digital audio applications that were written for a specific operating system. As you ponder what type of system to invest in, take a hard look at the types of things you plan to do with your computer and make a list of the software that would best serve your needs. After completing your list, the issue of which operating system to choose will probably be moot: If you have your heart set on running Logic or Performer, you need to purchase a Macintosh computer. If you feel that applications such as Sonar or ACID would best serve your needs, your choice will clearly be a PC computer.

It is also a good idea to ask friends and professionals about their choice of computer and software. How often does their system crash? What types of applications do they use, and how is the tech support for those applications? Is peripheral hardware (and more importantly, software drivers) available for their operating system? Is in-house compatibility an issue (i.e., can they easily exchange project files with colleagues)? How stable is the user-base for software applications (e.g., are Web sites and list servers available where users can exchange tips and ideas)? Also, be sure to read current trade magazines (both electronic music and computer-specific publications) to get a feel for the current state of the industry.

Finally, consider the relative price of hardware *and* value-added software. For example, Macintosh computers currently ship with an entry-level sequencing and loop-based production application called GarageBand as well as tools for producing movies and burning DVDs. You would need to spend a fair amount of money to equip a stock PC with similar software tools.

For many years, the choice of operating system meant that a user was making a commitment to a particular microprocessor: the Power PC chip for Macintosh computers or chips based on Intel architecture for PC computers. Apple recently announced that they will start to manufacture computers utilizing Intel chips and, by the time you read this chapter, Intel-based Macintosh computers will likely be available.

LINUX

A few words about Linux are in order. Linux is an operating system at the front of the *open-source* movement. Open-source software is software developed by corporations or volunteers who share source code. Many flavors of Linux (called *distros*, for distributions) are available for a variety of machines. One of the advantages of Linux is that many types of open-source software are available and may be freely downloaded. At the time of this writing, however, none of the major music software vendors are developing Linux versions of music applications.

Figure 1.19 shows a screen shot of "Rosegarden," a popular Linux program running on a prepackaged distribution available from Fervent Software. The package, called "Studio to Go," features an array of music applications including digital editing programs and software synthesizers.

*Figure 1.19
Rosegarden.*

EVALUATING A COMPUTER SYSTEM: WHAT THE NUMBERS MEAN

In many respects, purchasing a computer system can be similar to purchasing a new car. There are numerous things to consider, such as the speed of the processor, amount of RAM, and size and speed of the hard drive. It is also necessary to balance the need for power with a budget and to consider certain tradeoffs such as slower processing power or a smaller screen for longer battery life if you plan to purchase a portable computer.

Students and colleagues often ask for advice when purchasing a new computer and the following section attempts to answer many of the common questions that arise when evaluating a new system. Note that, in most cases, additional hardware such as an external digital audio or MIDI interface will be required. You should also consider a backup strategy, which might include the ability to burn data to a CD or DVD. Finally, not all hardware is of equal quality, so be cautious if you plan to upgrade a system using off-brand components.

Multi-Track Digital Audio Recording

Digital audio recording is one of the most demanding applications for a computer system. Key considerations for such a system include

▶ **Processor/multi-processor:** Processor speed will have a direct impact on the number of plug-ins that can be run concurrently. The speed of the processor will also impact the performance of many editing operations such as time compression and expansion. In order to maximize track and plug-in count, some musicians elect to invest in a multi-processor system.

▶ **Hard drive:** A large hard drive with fast rotation speed is important if you wish to record many audio tracks. In some situations, it makes sense to purchase a high-speed external drive devoted exclusively to digital audio recording.

▶ **RAM:** Adequate RAM is also essential. RAM is required for each track and, if resources are insufficient, the computer will not be able to keep up because the operating system will be required to swap data to and from the hard drive in addition to trying to keep up with multiple tracks of digital audio data.

▶ **FireWire/USB 2/PCI:** Consider the type and number of data ports when selecting a system for digital audio recording. In particular, a FireWire port almost always makes sense because many professional audio interfaces utilize FireWire. Similarly, a desktop system will be necessary if you plan to use a PCI-based audio interface.

▶ **Monitor:** A large monitor can be helpful when dealing with multiple tracks of audio and MIDI data. A dual-monitor setup can be particularly helpful since you can devote one screen to tracks and virtual synthesizers and another screen for a virtual mixing console. Most modern DAW software provides the ability to set up *screen sets*—virtual screens containing visual elements such as a mixer or editing pane that can be called up with a single keystroke. Screen sets make a multiple-monitor setup less essential, although two monitors are almost always helpful from a production standpoint.

▶ **Quiet operation:** Fan noise can be a real problem in a studio environment. Third-party enclosures are available but are expensive, so ideally, you should select a system that is reasonably quiet to begin with.

Software Synthesis

▶ **Processor/multi-processor:** As with digital audio recording, software synthesis requires a fast processor. Faster processing power provides the ability to run more software synthesizers and audio effects.

▶ **Hard drive:** Virtual synthesizers do not require a fast hard drive unless you plan to use a synthesizer such as Gigastudio (Tascam) that *streams* samples from disk. Disk streaming technology provides the ability to play huge samples that would not ordinarily fit in available RAM. In this instance, the requirements are similar to those for digital audio recording: A fast external hard drive may be required to efficiently stream large samples from disk.

▶ **RAM:** Software synthesizers require ample RAM. Consider the amount of RAM required by the operating system and add plenty of extra RAM to run numerous virtual synthesizers and your primary recording application.

Sequencing

MIDI sequencing is one of the least processor-intensive applications. If you plan to sequence MIDI data with an external keyboard and sound module, a system that provides ample power for the operating system should suffice for basic sequencing.

▶ **USB interface:** For convenience and flexibility, I generally recommend MIDI interfaces that connect via a USB cable. If you already own a machine, consider a MIDI breakout cable. A breakout cable can be a cost-effective option for PC computers with the right type of soundcard. If cost is an issue, a second-hand computer combined with an older serial or parallel interface can be a viable option for basic sequencing. For example, I once purchased an older Macintosh G3 computer for $12 at a thrift store. The computer provides ample power to run sequencing software on OS 9 and can even handle a few tracks of digital audio.

▶ **Monitor:** Although processing requirements are minimal for basic sequencing, a large monitor can be convenient when working with multiple MIDI tracks.

Notation

In the past, music notation software was minimally taxing on a computer system. Today, programs such as Finale and Sibelius utilize software synthesizers for playback of scores, so the requirements are more demanding.

▶ **Processor:** The processor should be fast enough to efficiently run the operating system with additional power to handle software synthesizers for playback.

▶ **Monitor:** A quality monitor is one of the primary considerations for a music notation system. The monitor should be large enough to view complex scores at a reasonable view scale. For example, some LCD monitors have a resolution of 1280×854, which provides the ability to view about 15 staves of music at a comfortable scale. Although this is ample for many notation tasks, it may be frustrating to work with a 40-stave orchestral score on such a monitor. A high refresh rate is important if you plan to use a CRT monitor—lower refresh rates cause noticeable flicker that is hard on the eyes.

▶ **Video card:** The video card should be capable of driving a large monitor at high refresh rates. A DVI connection is important if you plan to use a digital LCD or plasma display.

LAPTOP COMPUTERS

For some musicians, a laptop can be a good choice. Laptop computers generally do not provide the same processing power as a desktop computer, but laptops can offer plenty of power for most music making tasks. For example, all of the text, graphics, music, and audio in this book was created or recorded on a laptop computer. An obvious advantage is the ability to take your work with you. For a fixed installation such as a recording studio, desktop computers are generally a better choice since they offer greater processing power for a lower cost.

A WORD ABOUT VIRUSES

An unfortunate reality of modern computing is that computer viruses do exist. Though not all viruses are malicious, any virus is undesirable in that it may cause your system to become unstable. Most viruses propagate by attaching themselves to "healthy" executable files. When an unsuspecting user runs an infected application (often attached to an e-mail message), the virus loads itself into memory and attempts to infect other files. There are two primary ways of avoiding infection by a computer virus. Virus protection software can help to minimize the risk of catching a virus, but note that the software needs to be updated regularly to be effective against new forms of viruses. You can also minimize your risk by avoiding downloads from questionable sources. Unfortunately, even these precautions may not be enough to protect against a virus so, as always, regularly backup your work to avoid a catastrophe.

CHAPTER 2

Setting Up a Project Studio

This chapter looks at the primary components and connections of a project studio: the basic hardware and cabling that forms the backbone of a typical facility. This chapter deals with many of the questions asked by people interested in putting together a project studio and should serve to clarify the function and operation of the primary components. Along the way, you'll discover strategies for setting up a work environment that is ergonomic and fun to use as well as tips to minimize unwanted noise. Many recording engineers will tell you that a recording studio is itself an instrument that must be fine-tuned just like a traditional instrument. The topic of studio acoustics is a deep topic that is covered in several fine books on the recording arts, and I encourage you to supplement this overview with additional readings on related topics such as acoustic treatment and advanced miking techniques.

Mixer/Console

An analog mixer provides inputs for a variety of sources such as 1/4-inch line level signals from a synthesizer or external effects processor or low impedance signals from microphones. Digital mixers provide additional inputs and outputs to connect a variety of digital sources such as a digital audio tape recorder (DAT) or digital multi-track unit. In either case, the function of a mixer is to bring a variety of signals together for mixing and to provide a means of routing, monitoring, and processing the signals (see Figure 2.1).

Figure 2.1
The Mackie Onyx 1640 mixer.

Although a high-end console has many additional features useful to a recording engineer, the basic signal flow remains the same from the lowliest four-channel mixer to expensive consoles costing many thousands of dollars.

CHANNEL STRIP

When visualizing the signal flow of a mixer or console, it is helpful to remember that channel signals flow from top to bottom. A source is plugged into the channel input section of the mixer and the signal flows through several stages until it reaches the channel fader at the bottom of the mixer. Most mixers provide a trim control, which is used to optimize the relative volume of each input source. A channel insert may be provided to enable you to send the signal to an external device such as a compressor or equalizer. Auxiliary sends (see below) are used to route a portion of the signal to an external device. The equalization stage is used to adjust frequencies in order to fix problems in the signal such as adding more "sizzle" to a cymbal or rolling off the bass on a microphone. Pan is used to adjust the amount of signal sent to the left or right output. The signal ends up at the channel fader, which controls the amount of signal sent to its final destination, typically the main bus or a sub bus. Several buttons and switches may also be provided in order to mute or solo a track or turn on phantom power.

More advanced consoles have additional stages to control dynamics and additional buttons to route the signal to various destinations, but all consoles follow this basic flow. Figure 2.2 illustrates the primary stages of a typical channel strip.

BUS

Where channel signals flow from top to bottom, a bus represents a signal that flows from left to right. The main bus is a prime example: In the most basic scenario, each of the channel signals is summed and controlled by the main mix fader. Alternatively, channel signals may be sent to a sub-mix bus. Sub mixes are useful when you want to control the overall level of several signals. For example, you might have five channels devoted to drums. By sending each of these channels to a sub mix, the overall level of the drum kit can be controlled with a single fader.

Figure 2.2
The primary stages of a channel strip.

The *auxiliary send* is another type of bus. Mixers typically have one or more "aux" sends that can be used to route a portion of each channel signal to an external device. Again, the signal flows from left to right, and as you tap into signals on selected channels, the sum of these signals is sent to the auxiliary send, which is, in turn, controlled by an auxiliary send control. The processed signal is typically routed back to the mixer via an auxiliary return. An auxiliary return knob is used to control the amount of processed signal that enters the main mix. Although auxiliary sends are often used to process a signal with outboard gear such as a reverb or delay unit, auxiliary sends can also be used to set up a headphone mix or to feed monitors in a live venue. Figure 2.3 provides a conceptual view of the left-to-right signal flow of an auxiliary send.

Figure 2.3
Conceptual signal flow of an auxiliary send and return.

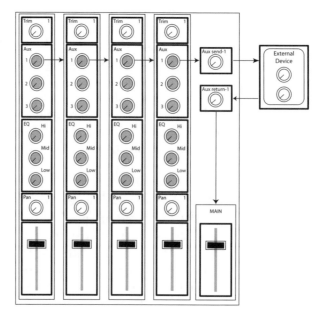

Patch Bay

Although not an absolute necessity, a patch bay can be a great convenience in a project studio. A patch bay provides a convenient way to route signals using patch cables. To take full advantage of the patch bay, all (or at least the primary) audio inputs and outputs are connected to the patch bay. Then, it's easy to route signals for a wide variety of applications. For example, suppose you decide to sample a portion of a groove from an audio CD. Simply connect the output of your CD player to the input of your sampler using a patch bay. Similarly, a main mix could be alternatively routed to the input of a DAT machine, stand-alone CD recorder, or even a cassette deck.

A patch bay consists of two rows of cable jacks. The outputs of audio sources are typically connected to the top row of jacks in the back of the unit and device inputs are typically connected to the bottom row of jacks in the back of the unit. This allows you to patch a connection from a given output (top) to a destination (bottom).

Patch bays come in three varieties: Open (or *de-normalled*), *full normal*, and *half normal*. The scenario I just described illustrates a de-normalled connection—an audio source must be physically connected to a destination via a patch cable at the front of the patch bay (see Figure 2.4).

Figure 2.4
A de-normalled bay.

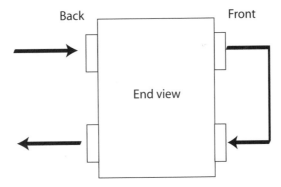

A normalled connection means that the output in the top of the patch bay is "normally" connected to the input of a device attached to the bottom jack. Unless a patch cable is inserted in the front, the connection between output and input is made inside the patch bay. When a plug is inserted into either the top or bottom jack in the front of the unit, the normal internal connection is broken. Consider how a CD player might be connected in a studio: It's likely that the CD player would normally be connected to the two-track tape input of the console. To route an alternate output such as a cassette deck to the console, simply make a new connection from the front of the patch bay and the normal connection between the CD and two-track input is broken (see Figure 2.4).

Figure 2.5
A normalled patch bay.

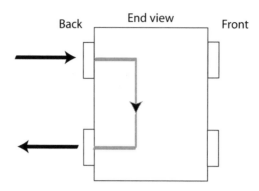

A half-normalled patch bay is similar to a normalled patch bay but the normal internal connection is broken only if a cable is plugged into the bottom jack. This means that the output source at the top of the patch bay can be sent to an alternate destination *at the same time* the signal continues internally to the destination (bottom row). The normalled connection is broken only if a cable is plugged into the bottom jack (see Figure 2.6).

Figure 2.6
A half-normalled bay.

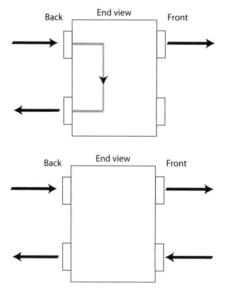

Reference Monitors

Monitors are a key component of any project studio. Ideally, the monitors will accurately reproduce recorded material so that you can mix a project and feel confident that a mix will translate well to other systems. High-quality monitors will not necessarily make your music sound good—they should help you to hear imperfections such as an unbalanced mix, overemphasized frequency, effect artifacts, and other problems. Where consumer-grade monitors tend to color and enhance sound, a mix that sounds good on a pair of "truthful" monitors should sound great on any system.

Professional studios typically utilize both far-field and near-field monitors. Far-field monitors are often built into the facing wall of a control room. The room must be specially designed, and the speakers are tuned to the room so that they produce a flat frequency response. For most project studios, near-field monitors are the best choice. Near-field monitors are placed relatively close to the engineer and have the benefit of minimizing the impact of room acoustics on the sound.

Monitors are either passive or active. In a passive system, the (un-powered) output of a mixer is plugged into the input of an external power amplifier and speaker cables are used to connect the output of the power amplifier to the speakers (see Figure 2.7).

Figure 2.7
Connecting passive monitors.

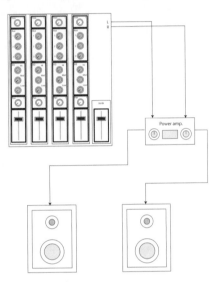

Active monitors utilize one or more internal amplifiers and accept an (unpowered) line-level signal. Active monitors typically utilize an active crossover in which each driver has its own power amp. In this case, the speaker preamp sends frequencies to their respective power amplifiers and drivers such as the woofer, midrange, and tweeter.

Although passive monitors such as the Yamaha NS10 are still used in many studios, my subjective experience has been that the active near-field monitors are used in nearly all smaller studios and as a secondary reference in larger facilities. One of the primary benefits is that active monitors do not require the use of an external crossover network, and the internal amplifiers of such a system are tuned to the speaker cabinet and drivers. In theory, this provides less unwanted coloration of a signal than may exist when routing a signal through an external amplifier. Figure 2.8 shows how active monitors might be connected to an (unamplified) signal emanating from a mixing console.

Figure 2.8
Connecting active monitors to a
mixing console.

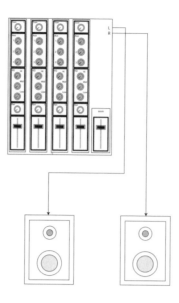

Headphones

Although it is possible (and often necessary) to handle some aspects of the mixing process using headphones, it is virtually impossible to achieve an accurate mix using only headphones since they generally do not provide an accurate representation of lower frequencies. A pair of quality headphones is particularly helpful in tweaking the pan position of instruments and is also a requirement if you plan to record in your control room. If you plan to record acoustic instruments, be sure to buy a set of headphones with a *closed* design so sound does not leak into microphones when the headphones are used in the recording room.

Audio Interface

Although it is possible to record audio using an internal sound card, consumer-grade audio cards generally do not provide a level of audio fidelity necessary for serious recording, so it is generally advisable to invest in a professional-grade audio interface. Thankfully for musicians, many options exist. On the lower end, an internal audio card can be plugged into an available PCI slot in a desktop computer. An external USB audio interface is a good choice if price or portability is an issue and you only need to record one or two tracks at a time. Note that USB 1 does not have the bandwidth to support more than a few tracks of audio at a time. Because USB 2 is substantially faster, newer USB 2 interfaces provide improved performance. Most professional studios utilize an external FireWire audio interface or an external interface that connects to a proprietary PCI card.

Another option is to purchase a hybrid mixer/audio interface. These products, such as the Mackie Onyx or Yamaha 0X1, function as stand-alone mixers but provide (either standard or as an add-on) a FireWire port to connect the unit to the computer.

MIDI Interface

A MIDI interface enables you to connect one or more synthesizers or controllers to a computer. MIDI can also be used to connect a control surface that is used to control virtual synthesizers or a digital audio workstation. On some PC systems, MIDI input and output can be achieved by connecting a MIDI breakout cable to the back of the soundcard. Some MIDI interfaces can be attached to a serial or parallel port, but for most applications, a USB MIDI interface is a good choice because these devices often feature drivers for both Mac and PC systems. Note that if your MIDI needs are modest (e.g., you need only a single MIDI port), you may not need to purchase a MIDI interface; many USB and FireWire audio interfaces feature at least one MIDI I/O port. If you plan to connect more than one synthesizer or controller, then it makes sense to invest in a *multi-port* MIDI interface. Multi-port interfaces typically feature from 4 to 8 discrete MIDI ports, enabling you to devote a full set of 16 MIDI channels to each MIDI device. MIDI will be covered in more detail in Chapter 3, "Introduction to MIDI."

Keyboard

Most project studios feature one or more synthesizers or MIDI controllers. Consider how you will use the instrument: A controller keyboard makes the most sense when you plan to use virtual synthesizers or external sound modules. Controller keyboards usually feature sliders and, a pitch and modulation wheel and often allow you to select patch banks and control parameters on an external module or virtual synthesizer from the front panel of the keyboard. Depending on your keyboarding skill, an 88-key weighted action might be a good choice. If you plan to use a keyboard for playback of sequences, consider the type of synthesis (such as sample playback or analog emulation), flexibility with regard to sound design, and palette of sounds. These topics will be covered in detail in Chapter 6, "Music Synthesis."

Sound Module

Sound modules provide a convenient way to expand the MIDI capabilities of a studio. A sound module is simply a synthesizer sans a keyboard controller. Some sound modules provide sample playback capability and are used primarily to add a bank of function-specific sounds such as orchestral, bass, or drum sounds. Other sound modules are full-fledged synthesizers that feature various forms of synthesis such as physical modeling or analog emulation. These topics will be covered in detail in Chapter 6.

Outboard Gear

Although a digital audio workstation will provide a full array of internal effects such as reverb and delay, many engineers prefer the sound of some external units. One of the most common functions is the use of an external microphone preamp. Although your mixer or console will most likely feature high-quality microphone preamps, engineers sometimes utilize external preamps because they like the way particular brands "color" the sound. Similarly, an engineer may utilize an external compressor or equalizer due to the unique sound provided by a particular device.

Microphones

Unless you plan to make music solely using computers and synthesizers, it will be necessary to invest in at least one or two quality microphones. The topic of microphones is huge and is well covered in several excellent texts dealing with the recording arts. For our purposes, an overview of the primary types of microphones and response characteristics will serve as a good starting point on the subject.

FREQUENCY RESPONSE

The term *frequency response* is used to describe the output characteristics of microphones, reference monitors, and other electronic instruments. With regard to microphones, a frequency response curve is a diagram that reflects the output characteristics of the microphone for a given input frequency. The y-axis represents the average amplitude at the output of the device and the x-axis represents frequency. If the microphone receives a signal of constant amplitude through the entire range of frequencies, then the fluctuation of amplitudes at various frequencies reflects the coloration characteristics of the microphone in question. Figure 2.9 shows a frequency response curve for a Shure SM57 microphone. This particular microphone has an upper frequency boost and bass roll-off and is often used to record guitar amplifiers and snare drums.

Figure 2.9
A frequency response curve
(courtesy of Shure, Incorporated).

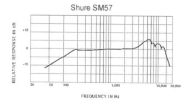

In general, a flat frequency response is good, but there are times when an engineer might select a microphone for its unique coloration—a slight emphasis in the midrange, for example.

DYNAMIC MICROPHONES

Dynamic microphones function through a process called electromagnetic induction. In a moving coil microphone, a diaphragm moves in response to fluctuations of air pressure. Attached to the back of the diaphragm is a coil of wires called the voice coil. Surrounding the voice coil is a fixed magnet. As the diaphragm moves, the voice coil moves against the force of the magnet, creating an electrical current.

Another type of dynamic microphone, the ribbon microphone, functions in a similar way, but instead of utilizing a voice coil, a thin aluminum diaphragm is suspended within a magnetic field. As the diaphragm moves in response to sound waves, an electrical current is generated. It is important to note that phantom power should not be applied to a ribbon microphone because this may damage the microphone.

Moving coil microphones have the advantages of being sturdy and relatively inexpensive (although the cost of some high-end models can rival the price of condenser microphones). They are ideal for close miking but can be used in other situations as well. The venerable Shure SM57 is an example of an inexpensive dynamic microphone found in nearly every studio.

CONDENSER MICROPHONES

A capacitor (condenser) is a type of device that can store energy. In a condenser microphone, a movable diaphragm and fixed back plate are part of a circuit that forms a capacitor. Voltage is applied to this circuit, and as the gap between the diaphragm and back plate increases due to movement of the diaphragm in response to fluctuations in sound pressure, the capacitance of the circuit decreases and voltage increases. Similarly, voltage decreases when the gap narrows and capacitance increases. *Phantom power* (see below) provides the voltage necessary to drive a condenser microphone.

Condenser microphones tend to be more fragile and expensive than moving coil microphones, but they have the advantage of providing better transient response which translates to more "crispness." These microphones are generally used to record acoustic instruments and voice and can be suitable for both close- and far-miking applications.

Phantom Power

A mixer or audio interface will typically provide phantom power on at least a few channels in order to power condenser microphones (sometimes identified by their voltage: +48). Phantom power flows down the same cable that the audio signal flows down but does not affect the signal. Take care when using phantom power: Some ribbon microphones and other equipment can be damaged by phantom power, so it should be turned on only when using a phantom powered microphone.

DIRECTIONAL RESPONSE

Microphones respond to sound sources in different ways. The two overarching types of response are omnidirectional and directional. An omnidirectional microphone is equally sensitive to sounds emanating from all directions (see Figure 2.10).

Figure 2.10
Omnidirectional response.

A directional microphone will be more responsive to sounds emanating from a particular location. A cardioid microphone is one such example (see Figure 2.11). A cardioid microphone, so-called because of its heart shape, will in general, be more sensitive to sounds coming from in front of the microphone, but note that it will respond to low frequencies in an omnidirectional way.

Figure 2.11
Cardioid pattern.

Microphones that exhibit a cardioid response are used to isolate the sound of a given instrument while minimizing room acoustics or the sound of other instruments.

Hypercardioid and supercardioid are two variants of the cardioid pattern. Notice the difference in response in the stylized pickup patterns in Figures 2.12 and 2.13.

Figure 2.12
Hypercardioid pattern.

Figure 2.13
Supercardioid pattern.

Bidirectional ("figure-eight") microphones are sensitive to sounds coming from in front of and behind the microphone but are less sensitive to sounds emanating from either side. One application of a bidirectional microphone is to record or amplify two background vocalists on a single microphone (see Figure 2.14).

Figure 2.14
Bidirectional response.

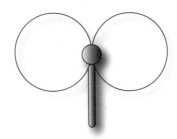

PREAMPLIFICATION

Microphones produce a signal that is relatively weak and must be amplified to a suitable level. Most mixers and some audio interfaces provide microphone preamps in order to boost the signal of a mic prior to its insertion into the signal flow of the mixer. When evaluating a mixer or digital audio interface, the quality of the "mic pres" is a primary consideration. Engineers often elect to use dedicated external microphone preamps costing thousands of dollars in critical situations—particularly on solo vocals and acoustic instruments such as unamplified guitar.

Direct Box

A direct box (also called a direct injection (DI) box) is used to convert a high-impedance signal to low impedance prior to insertion of the signal into a mixer. A direct box is typically used when running an electric guitar or bass directly into a mixing console.

Computer

Computers were covered in detail in the previous chapter but are mentioned here because a computer is an essential component of most project studios. Some studios utilize two or more computers in order to distribute the processing of discrete tasks such as digital audio recording and software synthesis. In such a scenario, one computer might be used solely for digital audio recording and another computer might be used for software synthesis and playback.

An alternative to using a computer is to utilize a dedicated digital audio workstation. Many of these systems feature integrated hard-disk recording and mixing in a stand-alone package.

As I mentioned in Chapter 1, data backup is an important consideration when using a computer. External hard drives are reasonably priced and many musicians elect to use rack-mountable storage and backup drives available from companies such as Glyph. Similarly, an uninterruptible power supply (UPS) is also a good idea. Take care that you only plug essential equipment into the UPS—it should be used to give you time to gracefully save your work in the event of a power failure. It's easy to plug in a rack of gear and forget that amplifiers and other equipment will drain the battery in a short amount of time. Note that a UPS is typically rated for 10 minutes or less.

Power Conditioning

A power conditioner may be used to protect equipment from damage due to brownouts and other power anomalies. Power conditioning may also be useful to reduce signal noise that results from "dirty" power.

Synchronization

There are two primary categories of synchronization to consider in a project studio: synchronization that occurs over a MIDI network such as MIDI Time Code or MIDI Clock, and digital synchronization that is necessary to synchronize the bit rate of digital devices.

Professional model MIDI interfaces typically provide the ability to send or receive *longitudinal time code* (often used in film work) via a specialized audio input, so in most cases, a dedicated time code synchronizer is not required. In such a system, incoming timing data is converted into MIDI time code and distributed throughout the MIDI network via the MIDI interface. Similarly, in order to synchronize the arpeggiator or sequencer of an external sound module or keyboard, a clock master (usually a software sequencer or primary keyboard) is selected to generate MIDI timing information, and other MIDI devices are configured to respond to external MIDI timing messages. This type of synchronization does not require the use of specialized hardware: It is simply a matter of configuring each MIDI device to respond in an appropriate way to incoming MIDI clock messages.

If you plan to utilize two or more digital audio interfaces, an external digital synchronizer may be necessary. In this scenario, a specialized digital synchronizer is used to simultaneously provide word clock to connected digital audio devices in order to avoid clicks, pops, and other problems that result when multiple digital devices are allowed to run out of synch. In many cases, a digital audio interface will provide an in and out port for word clock, so a dedicated digital synchronizer is not needed if you plan to attach a single digital device to such a device. Once word clock connections have been established, configuration is similar to synchronizing MIDI devices: One device is selected as the source, and connected devices are configured to respond to external digital control. Note that, unlike MIDI Time Code, word clock does not encode the passage of time—its purpose is simply to synchronize the bit rate of each connected digital audio device.

Making Connections

To this point, I have covered the primary components of a typical project studio. Although there are many other components to consider, much of the equipment listed in this section will be found in a modest home studio as well as professional facilities, so an understanding of these components will serve as a useful overview.

CABLES AND JACKS

In the following section, I will consider the nuts-and-bolts issues dealing with how to connect the components of a studio as well as some suggestions for minimizing noise and maximizing workflow.

Audio Cables

It is important to purchase quality audio cables and treat the cables with care. Avoid stepping on or otherwise stressing the cable, failing to do so will certainly shorten its lifespan. Quality cables are expensive, so you may want to consider making your own cables. Although a tutorial on soldering is beyond the scope of this chapter, professional-grade cable and connectors can be purchased from many online vendors. I recently started making my own cables and have been very pleased with the results. For example, a quality 30-foot cable can be built for around $15 to $20. Discounting your investment in time and soldering tools, this represents a savings of around $60 per cable.

Unbalanced cables are typically used to connect electric guitars or consumer-grade audio gear such as a CD player or cassette deck. RCA and TS (tip sleeve) are the two most common plugs found on unbalanced lines (see Figures 2.15 A and 2.15 B).

Figure 2.15 A
An unbalanced RCA plug.

Figure 2.15 B
A 1/4-inch tip sleeve (TS) plug.

In an unbalanced line, an internal conductor wire and the cable shield work together to form a circuit. Unbalanced lines are more susceptible to various types of electrical interference such as ground loops, so, cost permitting, it is a good idea to purchase gear with balanced inputs and outputs.

Balanced cables are typically used to connect the audio components in a professional studio. In a balanced cable, two conductor wires form a circuit (see Figure 2.16). The conductor wires carry the same signal, but at any given moment, the polarity is reversed. Any electrical interference that enters the circuit will have the same polarity on both conductors, so unwanted noise is cancelled out at the destination device. Some cables, such as the Star Quad cable manufactured by Canare, use a pair of conductor wires resulting in what might be described as a doubly balanced design.

Figure 2.16
A balanced signal.

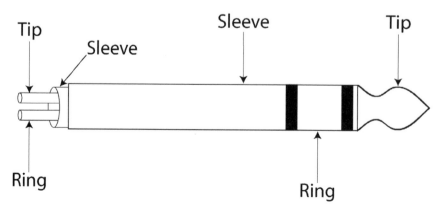

TRS (tip, ring, sleeve) and XLR (Figures 2.17 A and 2.17 B) are the two most common plugs found on balanced cables. Note that the balanced plug in the Figure 2.17 A looks similar to an unbalanced plug except for an extra ring.

Figure 2.17 A
TRS (tip, ring, sleeve) plug.

Figure 2.17 B
XLR plug.

You can plug an unbalanced cable into a balanced jack, but you lose the benefit provided by a balanced line. Similarly, a balanced cable can be plugged into an unbalanced jack, but again, there is no advantage.

MIDI Cables

A 5-pin DIN is used to connect MIDI devices such as keyboards and sound modules (see Figure 2.18).

Figure 2.18
MIDI cable.

Speaker Cables

Speaker cables are used to connect the powered output of an amplifier or powered mixer to an unpowered speaker. It is important to remember that the powered output of such a device should not be plugged into a line-level input jack such as a mixer, patch bay, or powered speaker as this could overload the system and damage the components.

Digital Cables

Digital cables are used to connect devices such as digital audio tape recorders, some synthesizers, and digital mixers. Two common formats are used: The AES/EBU (Audio Engineering Society/European Broadcasting Union) format typically uses XLR connectors. The consumer digital format, called S/PDIF (pronounced "speedif"), is an acronym for Sony/Philips Digital Interface and uses RCA or fiber-optic connections. Take care that digital signals are never plugged into an analog input as this may damage your speakers and/or your ears.

Connecting the Components of a Studio

It can be a complex process to connect the components of a studio—even a modest studio may have dozens of audio, MIDI, and digital connections—so a bit of preplanning can be helpful.

▶ Make a diagram of each component and draw lines indicating audio, MIDI, and digital connections.

▶ Take time to consider the location of each component: Frequently used devices should be easily accessible.

▶ Use a tape measure to determine appropriate cable lengths: It is very easy to underestimate the length of cables. However, cables that are unduly long are undesirable.

▶ When possible, keep audio cables away from power cables and transformers.

▶ Consider labeling or color coding each end of a cable.

CONNECTING AUDIO COMPONENTS

Before I walk through the process of connecting the audio components of a studio, I should mention that there are many ways to set up a studio. The following steps are used to illustrate the concept of signal flow and to acquaint you with a typical configuration, but your setup will undoubtedly vary.

One of my user manuals uses the analogy of water coming out of a faucet to illustrate the concept of signal flow, and I find that is a helpful analogy when visualizing the "flow" of audio connections. It makes sense to use a hose to connect the output of a faucet to an "input" such as a sprinkler, but it does not make sense to connect one faucet to another faucet, nor does it make sense to connect one sprinkler to another sprinkler. The same goes for audio connections—consider the flow and you'll find the process less complex.

To avoid loud pops or accidental feedback loops, it's a good idea to turn off the amplifier or powered speakers before connecting the components of the audio system. Once everything has been connected, turn the volume all the way down on each audio device, power up your system, and slowly turn up the volume on the mixer and monitor system as you begin to check each signal path.

If you're using a patch bay, start by connecting the output of each audio component to the top (back) row of the patch bay and connect the bottom (back) row of the bay to the inputs of the mixer.

For multi-track recording, the direct outs of each input channel are typically wired to the input of a digital audio interface or multi-track recorder. Again, it makes sense to wire these connections through the patch bay—the output of each channel providing a "normal" connection to the input of the recording device. In this scenario, the input channels (1–8, for example) are not assigned to the main output of the mixer— these signals are often monitored via additional channels on the mixer (9–16, for example). Similarly, the outputs of the multi-track device can be normalized to their respective channels on the mixer.

Depending on how you intend to use your mixer, it may be a good idea to route auxiliary sends and returns to a patch bay as well. This provides the flexibility to patch auxiliary sends to an alternate destination such as a headphone distribution amplifier.

Some mixers provide channel inserts that are typically used to route a given channel signal to an external device such as a compressor or equalizer. As you can see in Figure 2.19, channel inserts are connected in a different way than most components in the audio system. Insert cables have a TRS connector on one side and the cable splits into two TS connectors on the other side. One of the conductors, the tip, outputs the signal to a given device, while the ring carries the return signal from the given device.

Figure 2.19
Insert cable.

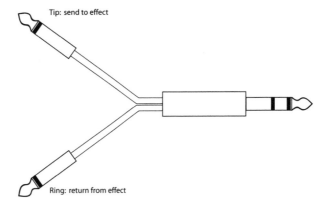

Tip: send to effect

Ring: return from effect

Once all of the audio components have been connected, it would be a good time to turn on the mixer and check to see that signals are flowing as expected. For example, you might patch the output of a synthesizer or CD player to each input channel on the mixer. You might also want to turn up the aux send on a given channel to see if the signal is reaching its intended outboard device and check to see that the processed signal is properly routed to the aux return. Keep an eye on the level meters on the mixer to ensure that you haven't accidentally wired a feedback loop. One way a feedback loop might occur is if you inadvertently patch the output of a channel to the input of the same channel. Note that a tone generator (often set to 1 kHz) is frequently used in testing an audio system. Some consoles are equipped with a tone generator so this can provide a convenient method of troubleshooting your system.

If things are functioning properly, it's time to connect the speakers. If you're using powered speakers, make sure the speakers are turned off. If you are using an amplifier and passive speakers, make sure the amplifier is turned off. In an active speaker setup, connect the appropriate output of the mixer to the input of the speakers. In a passive speaker setup, connect the appropriate output of the mixer to the input of your amplifier and the output of the amplifier to the speakers.

Be sure to turn down the main output of the mixer before turning on the amplifier or active speakers. Some mixers are connected via an output labeled "control room," so be sure to turn that knob down as well. Finally, turn on the speakers or amplifier, send a signal to the mixer, and slowly turn up the main/control room volume to a comfortable level.

A final step involves "trimming" each channel. Consult your manual for specific instructions, but the basic process involves soloing the input of each channel and adjusting the trim control so that each channel is running at a similar level when the channel fader is set to unity. Along these lines, you will want to run a "hot" signal from each device, such as a synthesizer, to avoid adding extra noise into the signal. For example, if an instrument such as a keyboard is running at optimal level, less noise will be evident in the signal. Providing a signal does not distort, a hot signal will provide a better signal-to-noise ratio—the signal will need little boost at the input of the mixer; hence, unwanted noise will be minimized.

CONNECTING MIDI COMPONENTS

Several diagrams of MIDI networks will be presented in Chapter 3, "Introduction to MIDI," but for our purposes remember that the MIDI OUT port of a transmitting device should be connected to the MIDI IN port of a receiving device. In some situations, the MIDI THRU port should be connected to the MIDI IN port of a receiving device. The MIDI THRU port passes any data received at the MIDI IN port so, in that sense, both the THRU and OUT ports are a type of "sender." Figure 2.20 shows a synthesizer and two sound modules connected to a computer via a single-port MIDI interface. I will cover more advanced MIDI networks in Chapter 3.

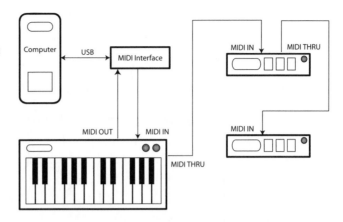

Figure 2.20
A MIDI synthesizer connected to a
single-port MIDI interface.

CONNECTING DIGITAL AUDIO COMPONENTS

The final step is to connect any digital audio components. One such example is to connect a digital audio tape deck to an audio interface. S/PDIF cables are often used for this type of connection. Similarly, some synthesizers provide a digital audio output, which can be connected to the digital input of an audio interface if one is provided. Depending on the device, it may also be necessary to connect a digital audio component via a word clock cable (usually a BNC connector) as well as with a digital audio cable (see Figure 2.21). As mentioned previously, take care that you don't inadvertently plug a digital cable into an analog jack or you may damage your speakers.

Figure 2.21
Connecting a digital sound module
to a digital audio interface.

Putting It All Together

As you can see, there are many possible components in a project studio. Although there are many other items to consider when setting up a project studio, the equipment mentioned in this chapter is found in many studios and should provide a good starting point for an evaluation of your own equipment needs. Variations might include using a FireWire audio interface and control surface in place of a mixer or adding a multiport MIDI interface and additional synthesizers and sound modules. Figure 2.22 illustrates one way the audio, MIDI, and digital subsystems might be connected in a project studio.

Figure 2.22
Cabling overview.

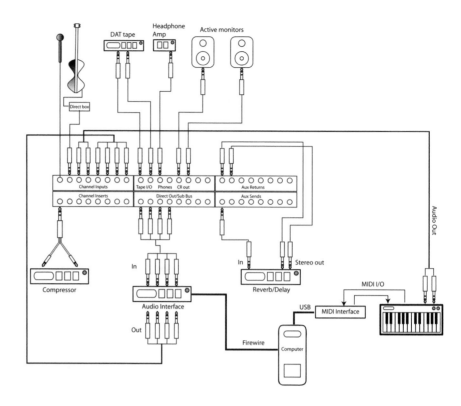

TROUBLESHOOTING

Audio gremlins can be difficult to track. Noise can enter the audio system in a number of ways, including a ground loop, dirty power, and radio transmissions. Here are a few tips that can help you keep noise at bay.

▶ Try to keep audio cables separate from power cables. You might, for example, run audio cables down one side of a rack and power down the other side.

▶ Use balanced cables when appropriate.

▶ Solo each channel on the mixer to see if a particular device is causing the problem.

▶ Consider using a line conditioner.

▶ Check the location of "wall warts" in relation to the position of audio cables.

▶ Avoid using the same circuit as household appliances.

MIDI can be a challenge to troubleshoot because it's not always clear if a given problem has to do with the audio system, software configuration, MIDI driver, MIDI connection, or a faulty MIDI cable. The following tips can help you troubleshoot MIDI problems.

No Sounds Coming from the Keyboard

Turn the local on/off to on and see if a signal is reaching the mixer. If so, the problem has to do with the MIDI subsystem. If not, the problem involves the audio subsystem. In this case, plug a pair of headphones into the main OUT of the keyboard to make sure the problem is not a keyboard issue such as the volume is down, power is off, or no patch is selected.

Problem with the MIDI Subsystem

▶ Make sure the keyboard is set to transmit MIDI and turn local on/off to off.

▶ Check that the MIDI OUT port of the keyboard is connected to the MIDI IN port of the MIDI interface.

▶ See if MIDI messages are reaching the MIDI interface (most interfaces have an LED that indicates MIDI activity). Alternatively, load your sequencing application and see if the software is receiving messages.

No MIDI Messages Received by Interface or Software

▶ Swap MIDI cables to make sure the problem is not the result of a faulty cable.

▶ Exit your software and try unplugging and replugging a USB interface.

▶ Download and install the latest drivers for the MIDI interface.

▶ If the problem persists, talk to your hardware manufacturer.

MIDI Messages Received by Interface or Software but Keyboard or Sound Modules Not Receiving Messages

▶ Check MIDI cables by following the signal flow of each device.

▶ Check that each MIDI device is set to receive MIDI messages.

▶ Check "virtual" connections in your operating system or sequencing application. (See Chapter 3.)

▶ See if a given MIDI device indicates MIDI activity. You may simply need to select a patch or turn up channel volume or main volume on the device.

▶ Check that your sequencing software is properly configured. Is a MIDI track selected and armed for recording?

ERGONOMICS

I found the following tips to be helpful when I set up my own project studio.

▶ Position the reference monitors first. Your manual will suggest the appropriate height, distance, and orientation of the monitors. In most instances, the distance between the monitors should be about the same as the distance between your ears and each monitor.

▶ Position the computer monitor so that it is at a comfortable height and does not unduly interfere with the output of the reference monitors.

▶ Position the primary controller next. For some, this will be a keyboard or synthesizer; for others it might be a control surface. It's usually best to position the primary controller so that you can use the device while sitting in the "sweet spot" between your monitors.

▶ Position frequently used equipment such as a patch bay or synthesizer module so that these devices are within easy reach. Also consider line-of-site for frequently used devices—even a few inches can make a big difference when trying to view a small LCD or LED indicator.

▶ Consider investing in studio furniture that can help facilitate the previous steps. Alternatively, if you are handy with tools, you might want to design and build custom studio furniture. I made the rack shown in Figure 2.23 for the price of one sheet of MDF, trim, four wheels, two rack rails, and some paint. I am really pleased with the rack because it's at a perfect height and angle for my needs.

Figure 2.23
My custom rack.

Summary

At this point you should be familiar with the functions and connections of the primary components of a project studio, including a patch bay, mixer, microphones, bus, auxiliary sends and returns, MIDI interface, and active and passive monitors. The following chapters provide additional information regarding how to use synthesizers and MIDI and audio hardware and software. The sample projects presented at the end of the book will cover the practical application of this technology to create and record original music.

CHAPTER 3

Introduction to MIDI

Of the advancements in music technology over the past century, MIDI is certainly one of the most significant. MIDI is used for many facets of music production from notation and film scoring to automated mixing and lighting. I find it astonishing that, in an age of fast-paced technological change, a technology that was devised in the 1980s is still an integral part of music production. That it is in part due to the extensible nature of the MIDI protocol and its adaptability to changing standards. For example, MIDI fits nicely within newer network technologies such as wireless networks and mLan (a networking protocol for transferring audio and MIDI over a single FireWire connection). That speaks highly of the engineers who devised the original MIDI specification.

This chapter takes a functional look at MIDI—the Musical Instrument Digital Interface. A primary focus will be to develop an understanding of the practical application of MIDI technology as an expressive tool, to learn how MIDI networks are configured and connected, and to consider the type of hardware found in a typical MIDI network. As with many aspects of music technology, an understanding of the inner workings of MIDI, while technical in nature, will provide the best basis for expressive utilization of the technology. This chapter emphasizes the following topics:

▶ How MIDI is used

▶ Performance data

▶ Connecting devices in a MIDI network

▶ MIDI math

▶ MIDI structures and messages

▶ Timestamps and running status

▶ Status and data bytes

▶ Channel voice messages

▶ Control change messages

▶ "Fine" and "Coarse" controllers

▶ RPNs

▶ Channel mode messages and system messages

▶ General MIDI

▶ Case studies: MIDI as a creative tool

What Is MIDI?

MIDI is an acronym for Musical Instrument Digital Interface. In pre-MIDI days, keyboard and synthesizer manufacturers competed in an environment without well-defined standards. To be viable in the marketplace, each synthesizer had to function as a stand-alone machine (usually in the form of a keyboard controller, sound source, and several modifiers). In order to add a new instrument to his or her setup, any synthesist of this period had to purchase (and lug around) another self-contained synthesizer. Although communication protocols existed, no standards were in place. Each manufacturer provided proprietary communication protocols. This all changed in the 1980s with the advent of MIDI.

MIDI is a communications protocol. Through MIDI, a keyboard manufactured by one company can communicate with a synthesizer manufactured by another company. This same keyboard can also send or receive data from a computer or any other type of MIDI device. You could make a comparison to a standard phone line. When you call a friend, you don't care who manufactured the phone on the other end of the line or what carrier is used—all that's important is that the conversation be audible. The same goes for MIDI; MIDI allows for complex networks of synthesizers, computers, and other devices to communicate seamlessly with one another.

Performance Data

A key concept with regard to MIDI is the idea of *performance data*. When a musician records a MIDI performance using a MIDI sequencer, nearly every nuance of the MIDI performance is recorded: which notes were played at what time, how hard each key was struck, when a note was released, the exact points in time at which the damper pedal was pressed and released, and so on. The MIDI specification provides for a wide variety of performance messages. Some of the messages are standardized (the damper pedal, for example); other messages are available for the performer to define.

Unlike a traditional tape recorder, a sequencer does not record the *sounds* of a MIDI performance—the sequencer records *numbers* that represent a musical performance. In this way, a sequencer is similar to a player piano. Just as a piano roll can be used to "play" a different instrument, so can MIDI data be used to control any number of MIDI instruments. For example, you might decide to change the playback sound from an acoustic piano to an electric piano. In this case, the performance data remains the same, but the sounds you hear will depend on the configuration of the receiving instrument. Performance data can also be manipulated with appropriate software to fix mistakes or edit a performance in much the same way that a word processor is used to edit or manipulate words and characters.

Figure 3.1 shows a list of MIDI events representing a C-major scale. This particular view, called an *event list*, is found in most sequencers and illustrates the concept of performance data. As you can see in this example, the scale is represented by a series of numbers signifying the name (data 1 column), velocity (data 2 column), and length of each note as well as the starting and ending position of each event. (Event lists and other types of editing views will be covered in Chapter 4.)

Figure 3.1
An event list view of a C-major scale.

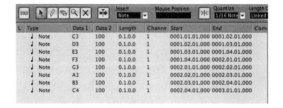

The MIDI Network

Although MIDI is often used to create music with a complexity that rivals or even surpasses that of the modern symphony orchestra, it is interesting to note that MIDI is a *serial network*. That is to say that performance data (the numeric messages that represent a performance) travel down a MIDI cable one message at a time. How then is it possible to record and play back chords (two or more notes played simultaneously)? Technically speaking, it is not possible to play a chord through

MIDI. In practical terms, the transmission rate of MIDI is sufficiently fast that delays are rarely audible except in extremely dense passages.

CONNECTING MIDI DEVICES

MIDI instruments typically have three MIDI ports labeled IN, OUT, and THRU that are used to connect each device in a MIDI network, and a 5-pin DIN cable is used to connect a port on one instrument to a port on another instrument or MIDI interface. Unlike many computer messages that utilize two-way connections such as a modem or serial cable, MIDI messages travel in one direction. A common scenario involves connecting a master controller keyboard to a synthesizer or sound module. (A sound module is essentially a synthesizer without a keyboard. Sound modules are used to generate sound but must be controlled via an external keyboard or other controller.) As you can see in Figure 3.2, the MIDI OUT of the controller is connected to the MIDI IN of the sound module.

Figure 3.2
A controller keyboard connected to a single sound module.

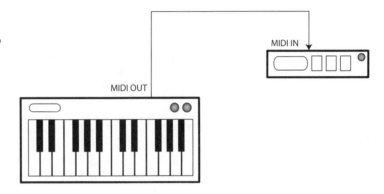

The THRU port can be a source of confusion: This port sends an exact copy of any data that arrives at the IN port. Although the THRU port doesn't send data on its own, you can think of the THRU port as a type of OUT port. It is used to chain several MIDI devices together. Imagine that you would like to connect a master keyboard to two sound modules: Connect the master to the first sound module as usual using an OUT to IN connection. Connect the first sound module to the second module using THRU to IN (see Figure 3.3). In this case, any data sent to the first module will be passed along to the second module (remember that the THRU port sends an exact copy of any data that arrives at the IN port).

Figure 3.3
A controller keyboard connected to two sound modules.

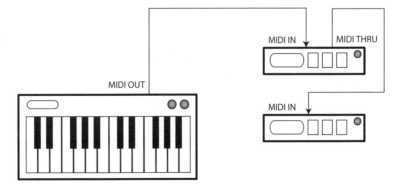

What would happen if you connected the OUT of the first module to the IN of the second module? Nothing—module two would not receive any messages from the master keyboard. The THRU port is the only way for the first sound module to pass a copy of incoming data to the next module in the chain (see Figure 3.4).

Figure 3.4
A controller keyboard improperly connected to sound modules.

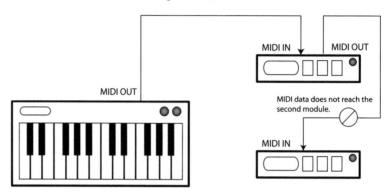

Some synthesizers provide only an IN and OUT port. These types of instruments usually allow you to specify whether the OUT port functions as a true OUT port or as a THRU port. It is rare to find only two ports on a modern MIDI device.

Another common setup involves the connection of multiple sound modules and a master keyboard to a sequencer or computer. In this example, the modules must be able to respond to real-time messages generated from the keyboard as well as to messages sent by the sequencer. The master keyboard will also need to respond to sequenced messages unless it is a *keyboard controller*: Most "controller" keyboards do not provide any internal sounds—they are used to control other MIDI instruments. In this case, it is not necessary to connect the output of the sequencer to the input of the controller. Figure 3.5 illustrates how a master keyboard (with sounds) can be connected to a computer and two or more sound modules with a single-port MIDI interface.

Figure 3.5
Hookup of master keyboard, modules, and computer with sequencing software.

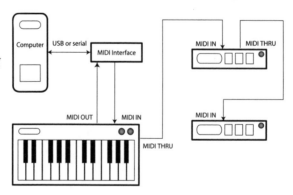

In this example, a message initiating from the master keyboard travels to the computer, where it is processed (and recorded if the software sequencer is set to this mode). Depending on the configuration of the sequencer, the message will be sent via the OUT port (a form of THRU that can be turned on or off from the sequencer). The message will return to the IN port of the master keyboard. A copy of this incoming message will be sent to the modules via the THRU port on the master keyboard.

There are many variations on the previous examples. If you plan to develop an extensive MIDI network, you might want to consider investing in a *multi-port* MIDI interface. A multi-port interface provides from two to eight discrete MIDI ports so each instrument can have its own port without the need for daisy chaining. Figure 3.6 illustrates how a multi-port interface can be used to connect multiple devices. Note that the MIDI OUT port of each sound module is connected to an IN port on the interface to facilitate the use of MIDI editor/librarian software. For example, the computer can request a bank of sounds from the sound module and the module can respond via its MIDI OUT port.

Figure 3.6
Hookup of a multi-port MIDI interface.

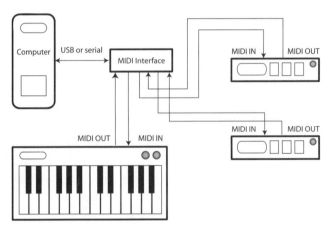

Local On/Off

In Figure 3.5, the master keyboard is used to play notes into the sequencer, but the instrument is also used as sound source for playback of data from the sequencer. In this instance, a key press would trigger a sound on the keyboard, and depending on the configuration of the sequencer, the sequencer would pass the note back to the keyboard, resulting in two note-on messages for a single key press (see Figure 3.7).

Figure 3.7
Two note-on messages (local on).

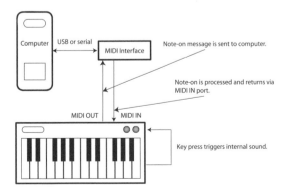

A setting on the master keyboard called *local on/off* is used to fix this problem. When local is turned to off, the connection between the master keyboard and the internal sound generator is turned off. In this way, the keyboard will respond only to notes received at the IN port. Of course, you will need to turn local to on should you want to use the keyboard in a live setting without a computer or sequencer. One type of MIDI instrument, called a MIDI controller, is used to generate MIDI notes and other types of messages but does not have any onboard sounds. These devices are useful if you primarily use software synthesizers or external sound modules. In contrast, a synthesizer includes two MIDI devices: a controller and an internal sound module. The local on command makes an internal connection between the controller and sound module but is not needed when a computer or hardware sequencer is used in the system.

Channels and Tracks

The MIDI specification allows for transmission of 16 discrete channels of data on a single MIDI cable. For example, you could set a keyboard or sound module to play piano sounds on channel one, bass sounds on channel two, and so forth. You might think about this like the channels on a cable television set: The TV can respond to any number of channels through a single cable. However, unlike a TV set, a MIDI instrument can simultaneously respond to 16 channels of data. MIDI instruments that can play back more than one sound on different MIDI channels are said to be *multitimbral*.

If you're new to MIDI, the relationship between channels and tracks can be a source of confusion. A sequencer track represents a collection of MIDI or audio data. Hardware or software sequencers provide from 16 to dozens of tracks, and each MIDI track may be configured to output data on a single channel. Why would anyone need more than 16 MIDI tracks then? One reason is that a multi-port MIDI system can handle more than 16 MIDI channels. Another reason is that additional tracks can offer flexibility and convenience. You might, for example, record the right hand of a piano part on track one and the left hand part on track two but assign the output of both tracks to the same MIDI channel. Similarly, it is often convenient to utilize multiple tracks when sequencing drum parts: You could use one track for hi-hat, another for shaker, and a third track for bass drum and snare. In Figure 3.8, multiple drum tracks are configured to play back on a single MIDI channel.

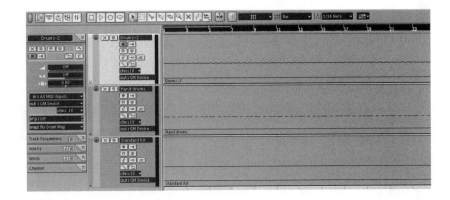

Figure 3.8
Multiple drum tracks assigned to the same channel.

MIDI Math

You have already learned that MIDI involves the transmission of digital performance data. What types of numbers are actually transmitted? Before delving into the intricacies of MIDI messages, let's look at some math. For MIDI musicians, there are three types of numbering systems that are relevant: decimal (what you and I are used to), hexadecimal, and binary. It is not necessary to be able to count or perform mathematical calculations in "hex" or binary in order to use MIDI technology, but you will run across these numbering systems when configuring a sequencer or MIDI instrument. In particular, a conceptual understanding of binary is helpful in understanding MIDI messages, digital audio data, and many other music-related technologies.

BINARY

The base-2 binary number system is well suited for use with computers because of the simple on/off mechanisms associated with logic gates and other electrical devices. The term *bit* stands for a *binary digit*. A binary digit can be only a 1 or 0, but you can represent large numbers providing you use enough digits. Let's count from 0 to 4 using two-bit binary numbers to see how this works (see Table 3.1). As you can see in this example, an additional bit is required to count past 3.

Table 3.1. Counting from 0 to 4 in Binary

Binary	Decimal
00	0
01	1
10	2
11	3
_____	
100	4

Table 3.2 illustrates how a 4-bit binary number can represent decimal numbers in the range of 0 to 15. The important thing to learn from this illustration is that "ones" and "zeros" can represent large numbers if enough bits are used. This concept comes into play with MIDI messages, digital audio, and other aspects of music technology.

Table 3.2. Counting from 0 to 15 in Binary	
Binary	**Decimal**
0000	0
0001	1
0010	2
0011	3
.	.
.	.
.	.
1111	15

As you can see, the greater the number of bits used, the greater the numeric range. A range of 0–127 is common in MIDI because seven bits are used to encode most MIDI messages.

HEXADECIMAL

The hexadecimal numbering system is often used with MIDI. Many sequencing applications allow you send special *system exclusive* messages by entering hexadecimal numbers in a configuration window (more on system exclusive messages later in the chapter). Figure 3.9 is a screenshot of a configuration dialog box in Digital Performer and shows how hexadecimal numbers are entered in order to customize a virtual fader.

Figure 3.9
Entering system exclusive data in Digital Performer.

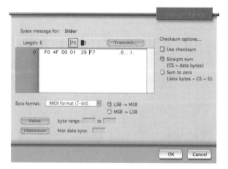

It is interesting to note that, in the hexadecimal system, the numbers from 0 to 15 can be represented using only a single character. Table 3.3 illustrates how this works.

Table 3.3. Counting from 0 to 16 in Hexadecimal

Hex	Binary	Decimal (base 10)
0	0000	0
1	0001	1
2	0010	2
3	0011	3
4	0100	4
5	0101	5
6	0110	6
7	0111	7
8	1000	8
9	1001	9
A	1010	10
B	1011	11
C	1100	12
D	1101	13
E	1110	14
F	1111	15

10	10000	16

Hexadecimal notation is useful because it provides a convenient shorthand for representing binary numbers. By looking at binary numbers four digits at a time you can easily convert between binary and hexadecimal. For example:

```
Binary number (one byte)      1111      1011
Hexadecimal equivalent        F         B

1111011=FB
```

Though hexadecimal notation may look strange at first, just remember that in this numbering system, the letters A through F are equivalent to decimal numbers 10–15.

Although it is not necessary to be able to count in binary or translate from decimal to hexadecimal, an understanding of the underlying numbering schemes will be helpful. For example, advanced users often enter system exclusive information in hex in order to customize and expand the functionality of a software sequencer, and hexadecimal and binary notation is often used in MIDI instrument manuals.

Most modern operating systems provide a calculator that can be configured to translate decimal numbers to hexadecimal or binary, and you will find these calculators helpful for developing a better understanding of alternate numbering systems. Figure 3.10 shows one such example. In this screenshot, it is evident that the number 127 is the largest number that can be represented with seven bits of data. As you will see in a moment, the decimal range of 0–127 is frequently used in MIDI.

Figure 3.10
The scientific calculator in OS X.

BITS, BYTES, AND NIBBLES

In computer jargon, a grouping of 8 bits is termed a *byte*. To be more precise, a byte refers to the amount of memory space needed to store a single character (typically 8 bits) on a given system. A related term, *nibble*, appropriately describes half of a byte.

In a MIDI network, streams of bytes flow down a MIDI cable. These bytes fall into one of two categories: status bytes or data bytes. If the first bit (called the most significant bit) is set to 1, the byte is a status byte. Conversely, if the first bit is 0 then the byte is a data byte. Status bytes are used to encode a particular type of message such as a note-on message, while one or more data bytes provide additional information about the message such as which key was pressed and how hard the note was struck. Notice how the most significant bit signifies a data byte (the leftmost bit equals the most significant bit—zero in this example).

```
0100        0000
|   |

first nibble    second nibble
```

MIDI Structures and Messages

Let's look in greater detail at one of the most common MIDI messages: a note-on message. A note-on message is comprised of an 8-bit status byte and two 8-bit data bytes (see Table 3.4).

Table 3.4. A Note-On Message		
Status Byte	**Data Byte 1**	**Data Byte 2**
1001 0001	0011 1100	0111 0000
Status/Channel #	**Note #**	**Velocity**
Note on, ch. 2	MIDI note # = 60	Velocity = 112

Since the most significant bit is used to determine the type of byte (status or data), only seven bits remain to encode status or data information. Because of this fact, data values will fall in the range of 0–127 (the largest number that can be represented using 7 bits of data). Exceptions to this rule are pitch bend messages in which two data bytes are combined to yield a 14-bit number.

You can think of the status byte as a description byte: It alerts the receiving device as to the type of message and to which MIDI channel the message relates. Note that the second nibble of the status byte provides a channel range of 0–15, but sequencers and MIDI instruments always present this in a more user-friendly range of 1–16. The two data bytes refer to the note number and attack velocity, respectively. It is helpful to remember that middle C on the piano is equal to MIDI note number 60.

TIMESTAMP

It is interesting to note that the note-on message does not include timing information. Timing is handled by the sequencing application in conjunction with a system timer. When a sequencer receives an incoming MIDI message, the message is stored with a timestamp indicating when the message was received. On playback, the sequencer uses a system timer to determine when each message should be sent to the OUT port. When you edit the position of a MIDI note in a sequencer, you are essentially altering the timestamp of the note. This is one of the reasons MIDI data can be edited with such ease—each performance event provides its own timestamp.

RUNNING STATUS

Since MIDI is a serial network, slight timing errors can occur because of a data bottleneck in very dense passages. *Running status* is used to combat this problem. Consider a situation where ten notes occur near the same beat on the same channel. It would be inefficient to send ten separate status bytes. With running status, only one status byte needs to be sent prior to transmitting the required data bytes for each note-on message. This is significantly more efficient since only 22 bytes are required instead of the 30 bytes required to send ten notes without running status. Figure 3.11 shows how fewer bytes are needed to transmit note-on messages when running status is used.

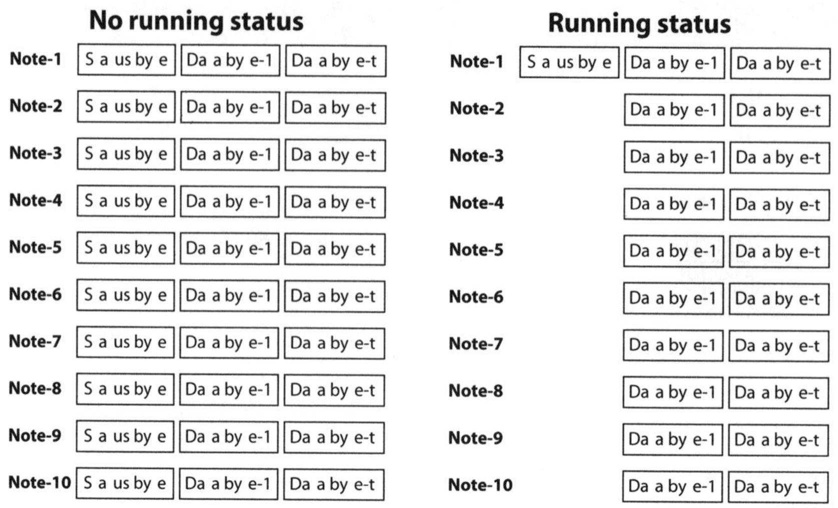

Figure 3.11
Note-on messages with and without running status.

No running status

Note-1	S a us by e	Da a by e-1	Da a by e-t
Note-2	S a us by e	Da a by e-1	Da a by e-t
Note-3	S a us by e	Da a by e-1	Da a by e-t
Note-4	S a us by e	Da a by e-1	Da a by e-t
Note-5	S a us by e	Da a by e-1	Da a by e-t
Note-6	S a us by e	Da a by e-1	Da a by e-t
Note-7	S a us by e	Da a by e-1	Da a by e-t
Note-8	S a us by e	Da a by e-1	Da a by e-t
Note-9	S a us by e	Da a by e-1	Da a by e-t
Note-10	S a us by e	Da a by e-1	Da a by e-t

Running status

Note-1	S a us by e	Da a by e-1	Da a by e-t
Note-2		Da a by e-1	Da a by e-t
Note-3		Da a by e-1	Da a by e-t
Note-4		Da a by e-1	Da a by e-t
Note-5		Da a by e-1	Da a by e-t
Note-6		Da a by e-1	Da a by e-t
Note-7		Da a by e-1	Da a by e-t
Note-8		Da a by e-1	Da a by e-t
Note-9		Da a by e-1	Da a by e-t
Note-10		Da a by e-1	Da a by e-t

OVERVIEW OF MIDI MESSAGES

MIDI messages fall into two primary categories: *channel voice messages* and *system messages*. You have already seen an example of a channel voice message: The note-on message is one such example. These messages are used to transmit performance data intended for a particular channel. System messages, as the name implies, relate to the MIDI network itself and do not contain actual performance data. Two other categories of messages, *system exclusive messages*, and *channel mode messages*, will be covered later in the chapter.

Tables 3.5–3.9 show the possible MIDI status bytes. Notice how the first bit of each byte is equal to one (denoting a status byte).

Table 3.5. Channel Voice Messages

Status Byte	Type of Message	Number of Data Bytes
1000cccc	Note off	2: Note and release velocity
1001cccc	Note on	2: Note and attack velocity
1010cccc	Polyphonic aftertouch	2: Note and pressure
1011cccc	Control change	2: Controller ID (0–120) and value
1100cccc	Program change	1: Program (patch) number
1101cccc	Channel aftertouch	1: Pressure value
1110cccc	Pitch bend	2: Pitch bend *LSB and MSB
cccc = channel number, xxx = three-bit numeric value		
*LSB = least significant byte, MSB = most significant byte		

Table 3.6. Channel Mode Message

Status Byte	Type of Message	Number of Data Bytes
1011cccc	Channel mode	2: Controller ID 120–127 and value

Table 3.7. System Exclusive Message

Status Byte	Type of Message	Number of Data Bytes
11110000	System exclusive message	?: Variable number of data bytes

Table 3.8. System Common Messages

11110xxx	Type of Message	Number of Data Bytes
11110010	Song position pointer	2: Song position pointer LSB and MSB
11110011	Song select	1: Specifies song to be played
11110110	Tune request	0
11110111	End of exclusive	0

Table 3.9. System Real-Time Messages

11111xxx	Type of Message	Number of Data Bytes
11111000	Timing clock	0
11111010	Start	0
11111011	Continue	0
11111100	Stop	0
11111110	Active sensing	0
11111111	Reset	0

CHANNEL VOICE MESSAGES

All channel messages consist of a status byte and one or more data bytes. There are seven possible channel voice messages: *note-off*, *note-on*, *polyphonic aftertouch*, *channel aftertouch*, *program change*, *pitch bend*, and *control change*.

Note-On

The note-on message is the most common MIDI message. As you saw in the previous example, a note-on message consists of a status byte and two data bytes. The first data byte contains the MIDI note number. The second data byte is used for attack velocity (see Table 3.10).

Table 3.10. A Note-On Message		
Status Byte	**Data Byte 1**	**Data Byte 2**
1001cccc	Note number (0–127)	Attack velocity (0–127)

Note-Off

The note-off message complements the note-on message. Like the note-on message, this message consists of a status byte and two data bytes (see Table 3.11). The first data byte represents the MIDI note number, and the second data byte indicates release velocity. Though release velocity is rarely implemented in synthesizers, this parameter can potentially be very expressive. Because of running status, it is common for sequencers to send a note-on message with a velocity of zero instead of sending separate note-off messages for each note.

Table 3.11. A Note-Off Message		
Status Byte	**Data Byte 1**	**Data Byte 2**
1000cccc	Note number (0–127)	Release velocity (0–127)

A "stuck" note occurs if a MIDI device receives a note-on message but no corresponding note-off message. This can easily occur if you happen to stop recording prior to releasing a key. Most sequencers include a panic button that will fix a stuck note. You can also try playing a chromatic scale on the offending channel to find the stuck note—this will send a note-off message that should fix the problem.

Aftertouch

Aftertouch is used to alter a note after it has been played but before the note is released. Aftertouch is usually added by applying additional pressure to a key after the note has been played—the message is typically used to add expressive nuance such as a crescendo or vibrato. You can also configure most synthesizers to send aftertouch via a modulation wheel or data slider, but not all synthesizers can respond to or transmit aftertouch messages.

There are two forms of aftertouch: *polyphonic aftertouch* and *channel aftertouch*. With polyphonic aftertouch, each note of a chord can respond to differing amounts of aftertouch pressure. Polyphonic aftertouch is the least common form of aftertouch. Channel aftertouch affects all notes on a given channel.

Polyphonic Aftertouch

Polyphonic aftertouch messages consist of the usual status byte and two data bytes. The first data byte denotes the note number. The second data byte denotes the amount of aftertouch pressure (see Table 3.12).

Table 3.12. Polyphonic Aftertouch		
Status Byte	**Data Byte 1**	**Data Byte 2**
1010cccc	Note number (0–127)	Amount of pressure (0–127)

Channel Aftertouch

Channel aftertouch is the most common form of aftertouch. With this message, an increase in aftertouch pressure on any key will increase the amount of aftertouch for all notes currently playing on the given channel.

As you can see in Table 3.13, the channel aftertouch message requires a status byte and a single data byte. The data byte provides the amount of aftertouch pressure for the entire channel.

Table 3.13. Channel Aftertouch	
Status Byte	**Data Byte**
1101cccc	Amount of pressure (0–127)

Program/Patch Change

Program change messages (sometimes referred to as patch change messages) are used to call up a given sound on a MIDI instrument. For example, in live performance you might want to send a program change message from a controller keyboard to call up a new sound on an attached sound module. Similarly, sequencers will usually send a program message for each track when you load a sequence, alleviating the need to manually select sounds on an attached MIDI instrument.

Program change messages can be a source of confusion if a sequencer is not configured for a particular MIDI device. Although most software sequencers allow a user to select sounds by name, the name is just a pretty face for an underlying program change message. Depending on the configuration of the sequencer, the onscreen name may not match the sounds coming out of the synthesizer. For example, a piano patch might be located at program change 1 on one instrument and program change 50 on another. One exception are General MIDI instruments: "GM" instruments utilize a standardized patch scheme (more on this later in the chapter).

A program change message has a status byte and a single data byte with a range of 0–127 (see Table 3.14). Earlier in the chapter I mentioned that sequencers and MIDI instruments always show MIDI channels in a range of 1–16 (even though the actual value is 0–15). Not all MIDI instruments show patch or program changes in the same user-friendly fashion, so you may experience "off by one" errors. In most cases, a setting can be made in either the sequencer or the MIDI instrument to alleviate the problem.

Table 3.14. A Program Change Message	
Status Byte	**Data Byte 1**
1100cccc	Program (patch) number

Pitch Bend

If you have ever listened to a great blues guitar player, you know how important fluctuations in pitch or "bent" notes can be. The pitch bend message allows a performer to adjust the pitch of a note in real time. This message requires two data bytes (see Table 3.15). Both bytes, taken together, provide a number that is greater than our usual seven-bit data byte. By combining two data bytes, the pitch bend message has a resolution of 14 bits (±8191). The terms *most significant byte* and *least significant byte* refer to the two "halves" that make up a larger word. Note that the shorthand MSB and LSB are often used in MIDI manuals.

Table 3.15. A Pitch Bend Message		
Status Byte	**Data Byte 1**	**Data Byte 2**
1110cccc	Least significant byte	Most significant byte

Pitch bend values are relative: The amount of bend will be determined by settings on your synthesizer. I find that I can better control pitch bend by setting my instruments to respond +/- a major second, although some people prefer to use +/- an octave. In any case, you may need to adjust the settings on a MIDI instrument to suit your playing style or when transferring sequences between instruments. (See also "Registered Parameter Numbers (RPN)" later in this chapter.)

As with a "lost" note-off message, synthesizers may sound out of tune if you record a series of pitch bends and end the recording before the lever is reset to zero. Also note that pitch bend levers generally transmit a flood of information into the MIDI stream, so it may be wise to filter some of these messages after recording a passage with many pitch bends. Data thinning is analogous to a comb—you could remove every other tooth on a comb and the comb would still work. Most sequencers provide options for filtering and thinning data, and it is helpful to use these functions if you plan to post a MIDI file on the Web—small files are always an advantage for Web-based delivery.

Control Change

The term *control change* refers to a large subset of messages contained within the overarching category of channel messages. Many control change messages are called *continuous controllers* because these messages are sent in response to real-time control of a data slider, foot pedal, or other expressive controller. Some control change messages, called *channel mode messages*, are used to configure the operating mode of a MIDI instrument.

"Coarse" and "Fine" Controllers

Control change messages come in two types: coarse and fine. A coarse control change message requires a status byte and two data bytes (see Table 3.16). The first data byte refers to the controller number, and the second data byte specifies the value of the controller message. For example, the identification number for channel volume is #7, and this controller has a range of 0–127. If finer resolution is needed, coarse controls can be combined with an additional control change message specifying the least significant byte (LSB). Control changes in the range of 32 to 63 provide the LSB in these instances. Bank select 0 (MSB), when combined with bank select 32 (LSB), is an example of a common "fine" controller (see Table 3.17)

Table 3.16. A Control Change Message

Status Byte	Data Byte 1	Data Byte 2
1011cccc	Controller ID number	Value

Table 3.17. A Fine Controller (MSB and LSB)

Status Byte	Data Byte 1	Data Byte 2
1011cccc	Control #0	Value = MSB
1011cccc	Control #32	Value = LSB

Unlike messages such as a note-on or program change message, the function of a control change message is dependent on the value of the identification number: Control change 1 is used for modulation, control change 10 is used for panning, and so on. Although there are 128 possible identification numbers, I will focus on the control change messages used in most sequences (see Table 3.18).

Table 3.18. Control Change Message Functions

Control Change Number	Function
0	Bank select (MSB)
1	Modulation wheel
2	Breath control
7	Channel volume
10	Pan
11	Expression
32	Bank select (LSB)
64	Damper pedal on/off (sustain)
?	Registered and non-registered parameters

Bank Select

In the early days of MIDI, a program change range of 0–127 was sufficient for most instruments, but with the advent of more powerful synthesizers, a limitation of 128 sounds would be considered inhibiting. Bank select, when combined with a program change message, makes it possible to gain access to hundreds of sounds stored in most modern synthesizers. Manufacturers have implemented bank select in different ways, so you will likely need to check your owner's manual, but the following scenarios are common.

Control Change #0 = MSB, Control Change #32 = LSB
With this "standard" method, two control change messages are required to select a bank of sounds. The most significant byte is contained in control change #0 and the least significant byte is contained in control change #32. Once a bank has been selected, a program change message can be used to select a particular sound within the bank.

Control Change #0
Since most synthesizers do not have more than 128 banks of sounds, some instruments will respond to a single coarse control change message. In this instance, the data byte of control change #0 corresponds to the bank.

Two Program Changes
Some instruments, such as older Kurzweil synthesizers, reserve a range of program change messages (typically above program change #100) as a form of bank select. The first program change calls up the bank, and the second program change calls up a sound within the bank.

I have found the following trick to be helpful when configuring a sequencer to send bank select messages to a synthesizer: Press the record button on your sequencer and then select a series of banks from the front panel of your synthesizer. Since most synthesizers send bank select messages when choosing banks in this way, the sequencer will record the bank select messages, and you can view this information in the sequencer event list. I have found this to be a convenient way of configuring my sequencer when I don't have access to a user manual for a particular device.

Modulation

Control change #1 is used for modulation. Modulation, which is usually performed via a modulation wheel, is often used to add vibrato to a performance. A modulation wheel might also be used to control another expressive parameter such as filter cutoff or resonance.

Breath Control

Control change #2 is used for breath control. Some keyboards feature a special port for connecting an external breath controller, and these messages are typically used to control volume, pitch, or another expressive parameter in real time. As the name implies, a performer uses breath velocity to control the level of control change #2 with an appropriate device.

Channel Volume

Control change #7 is used to set the overall volume for a channel. In addition to setting the main volume of the channel, this continuous controller can be used to automate a mix. For example, a series of decreasing control change #7 events could be inserted at the end of a tune to effect a fadeout. It is helpful to know that once you start automating a track in this way, it is necessary to automate an entire track because the given channel will stay at the volume of the most recently received control change #7 event. Put another way, if you fade a channel to zero at the end of a sequence, you will not hear that channel again unless you add at least one volume change event at the start of the sequence. It is a good idea to insert the desired channel volume setting (such as 127) after a fade and beyond the last note-off message.

Pan

Control change #10 is used to pan a given instrument from left to right in the stereo field. Values less than 64 move the instrument to the left and values greater than 64 will move an instrument to the right. A related controller, balance (CC#8), is used for stereo sounds. The balance controller will adjust the left-to-right balance of a stereo sound but does not affect its pan position.

Expression

Although the expression controller #11 is another form of volume control like controller #7, expression is typically used to add crescendos and decrescendos. In most cases, you will want to use channel volume (#7) to control the relative balance of instruments in a mix and use expression (#11) for transitory volume changes such as might occur when phrasing a melodic line. In this way, volume changes made during the mixing phase do not alter the dynamic phrasing of a track. Figure 3.12 will serve to clarify the concept.

Figure 3.12
The relationship between volume and expression.

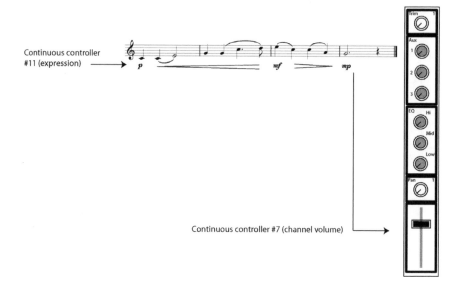

Damper Pedal

The damper pedal is one of several *switch controllers*. Values greater than or equal to 64 indicate that the pedal is on, and values less than 64 mean the pedal is off. Pianists will also want to experiment with other switch controllers such as CC#66 (sustenuto) and CC#67 (soft pedal).

Registered Parameter Numbers (RPN)

Registered parameter numbers provide a mechanism for expanding the number of controllers beyond the 120 functions available with a single control change data byte. For example, the pitch bend sensitivity of a keyboard can be set via an RPN. Inserting such an RPN in a sequence provides a great opportunity to automate bend settings so that a keyboard will play back with the expected pitch-bend range.

Two control change messages are sent in order to identify an RPN function. Control change #100 supplies the least significant byte, and control change #101 provides the most significant byte. Once the RPN function has been identified, control change #6 (data entry) provides the coarse setting for the function. This message may be combined with control #38, which provides the least significant byte. Relative adjustments to the value of the RPN can be made with the data increment and decrement controllers (#96 and #97). It is customary to send a *null RPN* after executing an RPN function. To send a null RPN, controller #100 and #101 are sent with a data byte of 127. Figure 3.13 illustrates the process of sending an RPN message.

Figure 3.13
Sending an RPN message.

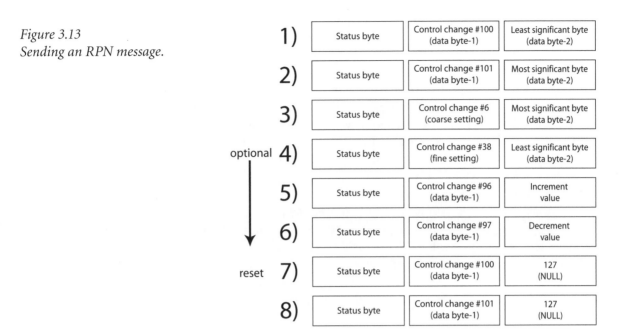

Table 3.19 lists the currently registered RPN functions. It is likely that new functions will be registered as the MIDI standard evolves.

Table 3.19. Registered Parameter Numbers				
Decimal	**Control 101 Value (MSB)**	**Control 100 Value (LSB)**	**Parameter Function**	**Data Entry Value**
0	00H = 0	00H = 0	Pitch Bend Sensitivity	MSB = +/- semitones, LSB =+/- cents
1	00H = 0	01H = 1	Channel Fine Tuning	Resolution 100/8192 cents, 00H 00H = -100 cents, 40H 00H = A440, 7FH 7FH = +100 cents
2	00H = 0	02H = 2	Channel Coarse Tuning (formerly Coarse Tuning) Only MSB used, Resolution 100 cents, 00H = -6400 cents, 40H = A440, 7FH = +6300 cents	
3	00H = 0	03H = 3	Tuning Program Change	Tuning Program Number
4	00H = 0	04H = 4	Tuning Bank Select	Tuning Bank Number
5	00H = 0	05H = 5	Modulation Depth Range	

Non-Registered Parameter Numbers (NRPN)

Manufacturers implement *non-registered parameters* in cases where the MIDI specification does not provide a control message for a particular function. Non-registered parameter numbers function exactly like registered parameters except that control #98 and control #99 are used to set the LSB and MSB respectively.

Although it is likely that you will not need to use RPN and NRPN functions in a typical sequence, RPNs can be particularly useful in establishing a default setting for pitch bend and modulation. Also, most sequencing software provides the ability to map a hardware or software slider to a given MIDI message. NRPN functions can provide a useful way of using a hardware or software slider to control a vendor-specific parameter.

Channel Mode Messages

Channel mode messages represent a subset of control change messages in the range of 120–127. You can think of these messages as mode-of-operation commands. These messages are used to configure a MIDI device to function in a particular way or to set the state of the device. Here are the commonly used channel mode messages.

Reset All Controllers (#121)

This message is used to reset controllers such as pitch bend and modulation to a default state.

Local Control (#122)

Local control, in the off state, disconnects the keys of a synthesizer from the sound source of the instrument. The most common reason for doing this is when using a keyboard in a sequencing environment. Local-off ensures that the sequencer, not the keyboard, will drive the sound source of the instrument.

Omni Mode On/Off (#124 and #125)

A MIDI instrument will respond to all channels when omni is set to on. (Omni-on is the most common value.) Omni-off is useful when you want to daisy chain several synthesizers. In this case, each synthesizer can be configured to respond to a single channel and ignore messages on other channels. For example, you could set a drum module to respond to channel 1, a bass module to respond to channel 2, and so on.

Mono On (Poly Off) (#126)

When mono mode is on, an instrument will play monophonically (one note at a time). Simultaneous notes can be played when a MIDI device is set to polyphonic mode.

Receiving Modes

The omni mode and mono/poly messages are combined to form one of four receiving modes. In practical terms, you shouldn't need to worry about setting modes: Most synthesizers default to a setting of omni-on/poly mode (usually termed *multitimbral mode*). Mode 3 is used for percussion when multiple instruments are used on a single channel. Mode 4 is commonly used for guitar controllers where each string is assigned its own mono channel. Table 3.20 lists the four possible receiving modes.

Table 3.20. Receiving Modes

Omni Setting	Poly	Mono
Omni On	**Mode 1**, Omni On, Poly	**Mode 2**, Omni On, Mono
Omni Off	**Mode 3**, Omni Off, Poly	**Mode 4**, Omni Off, Mono

As you can see, there are a wide variety of control change messages. Although I didn't cover every message, the discussion will provide a good basis for using control change messages in a typical sequencing environment. Of course, once you know how control change messages work, it's easy to incorporate new messages as the need arises. Table 3.21 will provide a helpful reference as you begin to explore control change messages. Note that the most common messages are listed in bold.

Table 3.21. Control Changes and Mode Changes (Status Bytes 176–191)

Adapted from "MIDI by the Numbers" by D. Valenti, *Electronic Musician* 2/88, updated 1995/1999/2002 by the MIDI Manufacturers Association. Used with permission.

Control Number (2nd Byte Value)			Control Function	3rd Byte Value	
Decimal	**Binary**	**Hex**		**Value**	**Used As**
0	00000000	00	Bank Select	0-127	MSB
1	00000001	01	Modulation Wheel or Lever	0-127	MSB
2	00000010	02	Breath Controller	0-127	MSB
3	00000011	03	Undefined	0-127	MSB
4	00000100	04	Foot Controller	0-127	MSB
5	00000101	05	Portamento Time	0-127	MSB
6	00000110	06	Data Entry MSB	0-127	MSB
7	00000111	07	Channel Volume (formerly Main Volume)	0-127	MSB
8	00001000	08	Balance	0-127	MSB
9	00001001	09	Undefined	0-127	MSB
10	00001010	0A	Pan	0-127	MSB
11	00001011	0B	Expression Controller	0-127	MSB
12	00001100	0C	Effect Control 1	0-127	MSB
13	00001101	0D	Effect Control 2	0-127	MSB
14	00001110	0E	Undefined	0-127	MSB
15	00001111	0F	Undefined	0-127	MSB
16	00010000	10	General Purpose Controller 1	0-127	MSB
17	00010001	11	General Purpose Controller 2	0-127	MSB
18	00010010	12	General Purpose Controller 3	0-127	MSB
19	00010011	13	General Purpose Controller 4	0-127	MSB
20	00010100	14	Undefined	0-127	MSB
21	00010101	15	Undefined	0-127	MSB

Control Number (2nd Byte Value)			Control Function	3rd Byte Value	
Decimal	Binary	Hex		Value	Used As
22	00010110	16	Undefined	0-127	MSB
23	00010111	17	Undefined	0-127	MSB
24	00011000	18	Undefined	0-127	MSB
25	00011001	19	Undefined	0-127	MSB
26	00011010	1A	Undefined	0-127	MSB
27	00011011	1B	Undefined	0-127	MSB
28	00011100	1C	Undefined	0-127	MSB
29	00011101	1D	Undefined	0-127	MSB
30	00011110	1E	Undefined	0-127	MSB
31	00011111	1F	Undefined	0-127	MSB
32	00100000	20	LSB for Control 0 (Bank Select)	0-127	LSB
33	00100001	21	LSB for Control 1 (Modulation Wheel or Lever)	0-127	LSB
34	00100010	22	LSB for Control 2 (Breath Controller)	0-127	LSB
35	00100011	23	LSB for Control 3 (Undefined)	0-127	LSB
36	00100100	24	LSB for Control 4 (Foot Controller)	0-127	LSB
37	00100101	25	LSB for Control 5 (Portamento Time)	0-127	LSB
38	00100110	26	LSB for Control 6 (Data Entry)	0-127	LSB
39	00100111	27	LSB for Control 7 (Channel Volume, formerly Main Volume)	0-127	LSB
40	00101000	28	LSB for Control 8 (Balance)	0-127	LSB
41	00101001	29	LSB for Control 9 (Undefined)	0-127	LSB
42	00101010	2A	LSB for Control 10 (Pan)	0-127	LSB
43	00101011	2B	LSB for Control 11 (Expression Controller)	0-127	LSB
44	00101100	2C	LSB for Control 12 (Effect control 1)	0-127	LSB
45	00101101	2D	LSB for Control 13 (Effect control 2)	0-127	LSB
46	00101110	2E	LSB for Control 14 (Undefined)	0-127	LSB
47	00101111	2F	LSB for Control 15 (Undefined)	0-127	LSB
48	00110000	30	LSB for Control 16 (General Purpose Controller 1)	0-127	LSB
49	00110001	31	LSB for Control 17 (General Purpose Controller 2)	0-127	LSB
50	00110010	32	LSB for Control 18 (General Purpose Controller 3)	0-127	LSB
51	00110011	33	LSB for Control 19 (General Purpose Controller 4)	0-127	LSB
52	00110100	34	LSB for Control 20 (Undefined)	0-127	LSB
53	00110101	35	LSB for Control 21 (Undefined)	0-127	LSB
54	00110110	36	LSB for Control 22 (Undefined)	0-127	LSB
55	00110111	37	LSB for Control 23 (Undefined)	0-127	LSB
56	00111000	38	LSB for Control 24 (Undefined)	0-127	LSB
57	00111001	39	LSB for Control 25 (Undefined)	0-127	LSB
58	00111010	3A	LSB for Control 26 (Undefined)	0-127	LSB
59	00111011	3B	LSB for Control 27 (Undefined)	0-127	LSB
60	00111100	3C	LSB for Control 28 (Undefined)	0-127	LSB
61	00111101	3D	LSB for Control 29 (Undefined)	0-127	LSB
62	00111110	3E	LSB for Control 30 (Undefined)	0-127	LSB

| Control Number (2nd Byte Value) | | | Control Function | 3rd Byte Value | |
Decimal	Binary	Hex		Value	Used As
63	00111111	3F	LSB for Control 31 (Undefined)	0-127	LSB
64	01000000	40	Damper Pedal on/off (Sustain)	<63 off, >64 on	---
65	01000001	41	Portamento On/Off	<63 off, >64 on	---
66	01000010	42	Sustenuto On/Off	<63 off, >64 on	---
67	01000011	43	Soft Pedal On/Off	<63 off, >64 on	---
68	01000100	44	Legato Footswitch	<63 Normal, >64 Legato	---
69	01000101	45	Hold 2	<63 off, >64 on	---
70	01000110	46	Sound Controller 1 (default: Sound Variation)	0-127	LSB
71	01000111	47	Sound Controller 2 (default: Timbre/Harmonic Intens.)	0-127	LSB
72	01001000	48	Sound Controller 3 (default: Release Time)	0-127	LSB
73	01001001	49	Sound Controller 4 (default: Attack Time)	0-127	LSB
74	01001010	4A	Sound Controller 5 (default: Brightness)	0-127	LSB
75	01001011	4B	Sound Controller 6 (default: Decay Time– see MMA RP-021)	0-127	LSB
76	01001100	4C	Sound Controller 7 (default: Vibrato Rate–see MMA RP-021)	0-127	LSB
77	01001101	4D	Sound Controller 8 (default: Vibrato Depth–see MMA RP-021)	0-127	LSB
78	01001110	4E	Sound Controller 9 (default: Vibrato Delay– see MMA RP-021)	0-127	LSB
79	01001111	4F	Sound Controller 10 (default undefined – see MMA RP-021)	0-127	LSB
80	01010000	50	General Purpose Controller 5	0-127	LSB
81	01010001	51	General Purpose Controller 6	0-127	LSB
82	01010010	52	General Purpose Controller 7	0-127	LSB
83	01010011	53	General Purpose Controller 8	0-127	LSB
84	01010100	54	Portamento Control	0-127	LSB
85	01010101	55	Undefined	---	---
86	01010110	56	Undefined	---	---
87	01010111	57	Undefined	---	---
88	01011000	58	Undefined	---	---
89	01011001	59	Undefined	---	---
90	01011010	5A	Undefined	---	---
91	01011011	5B	Effects 1 Depth (default: Reverb Send Level– see MMA RP-023) (formerly External Effects Depth)	0-127	LSB
92	01011100	5C	Effects 2 Depth (formerly Tremolo Depth)	0-127	LSB
93	01011101	5D	Effects 3 Depth (default: Chorus Send Level–see MMA RP-023) (formerly Chorus Depth)	0-127	LSB
94	01011110	5E	Effects 4 Depth (formerly Celeste [Detune] Depth)	0-127	LSB
95	01011111	5F	Effects 5 Depth (formerly Phaser Depth)	0-127	LSB
96	01100000	60	Data Increment (Data Entry +1) (see MMA RP-018)	N/A	---
97	01100001	61	Data Decrement (Data Entry -1) (see MMA RP-018)	N/A	---

Control Number (2nd Byte Value)			Control Function	3rd Byte Value	
Decimal	Binary	Hex		Value	Used As
98	01100010	62	Non-Registered Parameter Number (NRPN) - LSB	0-127	LSB
99	01100011	63	Non-Registered Parameter Number (NRPN) - MSB	0-127	MSB
100	01100100	64	Registered Parameter Number (RPN) - LSB*	0-127	LSB
101	01100101	65	Registered Parameter Number (RPN) - MSB*	0-127	MSB
102	01100110	66	Undefined	---	---
103	01100111	67	Undefined	---	---
104	01101000	68	Undefined	---	---
105	01101001	69	Undefined	---	---
106	01101010	6A	Undefined	---	---
107	01101011	6B	Undefined	---	---
108	01101100	6C	Undefined	---	---
109	01101101	6D	Undefined	---	---
110	01101110	6E	Undefined	---	---
111	01101111	6F	Undefined	---	---
112	01110000	70	Undefined	---	---
113	01110001	71	Undefined	---	---
114	01110010	72	Undefined	---	---
115	01110011	73	Undefined	---	---
116	01110100	74	Undefined	---	---
117	01110101	75	Undefined	---	---
118	01110110	76	Undefined	---	---
119	01110111	77	Undefined	---	---
120*	01111000	78	[Channel Mode Message] All Sound Off	0	---
121	01111001	79	[Channel Mode Message] Reset All Controllers		
(See MMA RP-015)	0	---			
122	01111010	7A	[Channel Mode Message] Local Control On/Off	0 off, 127 on	---
123	01111011	7B	[Channel Mode Message] All Notes Off	0	---
124	01111100	7C	[Channel Mode Message] Omni Mode Off (+ all notes off)	0	---
125	01111101	7D	[Channel Mode Message] Omni Mode On (+ all notes off)	0	---
126	01111110	7E	[Channel Mode Message] Poly Mode On/Off (+ all notes off)	**	---
127	01111111	7F	[Channel Mode Message] Poly Mode On (+ mono off +all notes off)	0	---

* Note: Controller numbers 120–127 are reserved for channel mode messages, which, rather than controlling sound parameters, affect the channel's operating mode.

** Note: This equals the number of channels, or zero if the number of channels equals the number of voices in the receiver.

SYSTEM MESSAGES

Up to this point we have concerned ourselves with channel messages—performance data that applies to a specific MIDI channel. MIDI also provides for a number of system messages that apply to the entire MIDI network. These messages can be organized into three groups: *system common*, *system exclusive*, and *system real-time messages* (see Table 3.22). It is interesting to note that the first nibble of any system message is 1111 in binary, 15 in decimal, or F in hexadecimal.

Table 3.22. List of System Messages		
Status Byte	**Number of Data Bytes**	**Type of Message**
11110000	Variable	System exclusive
11110xxx	0 to 2	System common
11111xxx	0	System real-time

System Common Messages

Where channel messages are used to transmit information specific to a single channel, system common messages relate to the entire MIDI system. The following section provides an overview of system messages and how these messages are used in a MIDI network.

MIDI Time Code

SMPTE (an acronym for *Society of Motion Picture and Television Engineers*) time code is used to synchronize video, audio, and MIDI. Although MIDI does not directly support SMPTE time code, SMPTE can be translated to its MIDI counterpart, *MIDI Time Code* (MTC), via a specialized MIDI interface. An interface such as the Mark of the Unicorn MIDI Timepiece AV can generate MTC based on incoming SMPTE time code (as well as other forms of synchronization).

SMPTE time code, which represents the passage of *absolute time*, is given in hours, minutes, seconds, frames (a division of the second into 30 parts), and optionally subframes. The example below represents a frame 65 seconds from the start of a film. In this context, the term *absolute* means that the given frame will always occur at 00:01:05:00, regardless of the tempo of the sequence.

```
00:01:05:00
hh:mm:ss:ff
```

MIDI time code messages are used to translate each of the "quarters" of SMPTE code (hours, minutes, seconds, and frames) throughout the MIDI network. A separate MTC event is required to transmit each of the four components of a SMPTE position.

End of Exclusive

Another type of system common message, end of exclusive, or EOX, signals the end of system exclusive data transmission. We will explore system exclusive messages in a moment.

Song Position Pointer

The *song position pointer* (SPP) message is used to synchronize the starting positions of devices such as a MIDI drum machine and a sequencer. The song position pointer is an incremental counter: This message increases by a count of one for every six MIDI clock messages. Since 24 timing clock messages are sent on every beat, SPP messages have a resolution of four 16th notes per beat.

Song Select

The primary use of the *song select* message is for live performance. It is similar to a program select message, but instead of selecting a sound, the song select message requests a specific song from an external sequencer or drum machine. Song select would be useful in the following scenario: A performer might use a hardware sequencer to prepare backing tracks for a number of songs. The performer could elect to program drum patterns for each of the songs using a drum machine. Onstage, the performer would simply need to send a song select message to cue up a given song on *both* machines.

Tune Request

This message is rarely used in modern MIDI networks. In the days of analog synthesizers, the synthesizers would sometimes float out of tune as the oscillators heated up. The tune request message is an attempt to combat this problem. A tune request message asks MIDI devices to initiate their internal tuning routines. Such a message would be moot to a digital synthesizer since digital oscillators can't float out of tune.

System Real-Time Messages

System real-time messages are used to synchronize MIDI devices such as a drum machine or hardware sequencer. These messages are unique in that they can occur at any time, even in the midst of other MIDI messages.

Timing Clock

The timing clock is used to synchronize the clocks of MIDI devices throughout the MIDI network and is transmitted at a rate of 24 *pulses per quarter note* (ppqn). For many modern musicians, the timing clock is important when synchronizing an external synthesizer arpeggiator to a sequencer. For example, a software sequencer can be configured to send timing clock to each device in a MIDI network. An external sound module can be configured so that the tempo of an internal sequencer or arpeggiator is controlled by the external clock source. Since timing clock messages are dependent on the tempo of a song, these messages provide a *relative* time reference.

Start, Stop, Continue

As the names imply, the start, stop, and continue messages are used to control playback of a MIDI device that is being synchronized with song position pointer messages. When such a device receives a start message, it will begin playback as soon as it begins to receive song position pointer messages.

Active Sensing

Some MIDI devices send active sensing messages. While in Stop mode, such a device will send a message every 300 milliseconds. If an active sensing keyboard is attached to the input of a sequencer, it is possible for the sequencer to determine that there is a problem with the device if more than 300 milliseconds elapse without receiving an active sensing message. My experience has been that this message is not very helpful, since not all manufacturers have implemented active sensing and I have never received such an alert message from a sequencer stating that a MIDI device has stopped sending active sensing messages.

System Reset

System reset is used to reset a MIDI device back to its power-up settings (i.e., local-on and channel volume to a default value).

System Exclusive Messages

At the beginning of this chapter I mentioned that much of the success of MIDI has to do with the extensible nature of the MIDI protocol. *System exclusive* messages are a great example: These messages provide a way to transfer data that is unique to a particular MIDI device. Examples of "SysEx" data might include banks of sounds, sample data, tuning tables, or many other types of information. Unlike other MIDI messages, SysEx messages can contain any arbitrary number of data bytes, which is why they are helpful in transferring such a wide range of data.

System exclusive messages, like all MIDI messages, start with a status byte. The status byte (11110000 in binary, F0 in hexadecimal) alerts the network that system exclusive data is about to be transmitted. A unique manufacturer ID is included in the SysEx header. If the receiving device "understands" the manufacturer ID (i.e., the message is intended for this device), it will know what to do with the remaining data bytes. If a given device does not recognize the manufacturer ID, the remainder of the system exclusive message will be ignored. The *end of exclusive* (EOX) message signals that a SysEx message is complete.

An example of a typical SysEx message follows. Note that, other than the status byte (F0), ID byte, and end of exclusive byte (F7), any number of data bytes may be transmitted. Additional data bytes are used to describe the specific product (i.e., what model of synthesizer), and a device ID number (in case you have more than one of these same devices connected to your MIDI network). Table 3.23 provides an overview of a system exclusive message for an E-MU synthesizer module.

Table 3.23. A System Exclusive Message (Hexadecimal)

F0	system exclusive status byte
18	E-MU ID byte
04	product ID byte (i.e. Proteus synthesizer)
dd	device ID byte (if more than one is connected to MIDI network)
.	
.	any number of data bytes that mean something to this synthesizer
.	(patch dump, program map, etc.)
.	
F7	(EOX—end of exclusive)

In plain English, the above message might read as: *"Transmitting a system exclusive message. This message is intended for a device manufactured by E-MU. This message is intended specifically for an E-MU Proteus Synthesizer that is set to the given device ID number. This message will be complete when you receive an end of exclusive data byte."*

One caveat: Large SysEx messages can take a long time to transfer over the MIDI network (a few seconds to several minutes). It is almost always a good idea to avoid transmitting these messages during time-sensitive playback of a sequence or timing errors will likely occur. However, small SysEx messages may be sent without worry, and some manufacturers implement these messages as a way of controlling device parameters in real time.

Although SysEx messages are often used in conjunction with MIDI editor/librarian software, these messages can be very helpful even without dedicated software. For example, most synthesizers can perform a *bulk dump* in which all of the editable parameters such internal sounds and patch names are sent as one large system exclusive message. In many cases, you can simply press Record on a sequencer and initiate a bulk dump from the front panel of an attached synthesizer. The sequencer will record the bulk dump, which can provide a convenient method of backing up custom sound designs and other types of data. To reset the synthesizer, simply "play back" the sequence and the bulk dump will, in most cases, restore the synthesizer to the state it was in when the bulk dump was recorded.

General MIDI

General MIDI provides a means of translating a sequence prepared on one synthesizer to another synthesizer or sound module in such a way that playback will sound similar on each device. A General MIDI-capable synthesizer provides a standardized selection of sounds and control change assignments. If you record a GM sequence with a fretless bass on channel 1, any GM compatible synthesizer will play back with a similar sound (some version of a fretless bass) on the same channel. General MIDI is not very helpful for MIDI musicians who like to program their own sounds; the general MIDI palette of sounds is somewhat limited. It does, however, provide an easy, organized way to distribute sequences. A GM synthesizer or sound module may be a good choice to support the process of computer-aided music notation since customized sounds are not needed for playback of traditional scores. A newer form of General MIDI, General MIDI 2 (GM2) is backward compatible with GM1 but provides a larger palette of sounds as well as support for RPNs and universal system exclusive messages.

General MIDI sounds are grouped by families such as piano, guitar, strings, and brass. Each family contains eight sounds (see Table 3.24).

Table 3.24. General MIDI Instrument Family and Patch Maps

PC#	Family	PC#	Family
1-8	Piano	65-72	Reed
9-16	Chromatic Percussion	73-80	Pipe
17-24	Organ	81-88	Synth Lead
25-32	Guitar	89-96	Synth Pad
33-40	Bass	97-104	Synth Effects
41-48	Strings	105-112	Ethnic
49-56	Ensemble	113-120	Percussive
57-64	Brass	121-128	Sound Effects

PC#	Instrument	PC#	Instrument
1	Acoustic Grand Piano	65	Soprano Sax
2	Bright Acoustic Piano	66	Alto Sax
3	Electric Grand Piano	67	Tenor Sax
4	Honky-tonk Piano	68	Baritone Sax
5	Electric Piano1	69	Oboe
6	Electric Piano2	70	English Horn
7	Harpsichord	71	Bassoon
8	Clavi	72	Clarinet
9	Celesta	73	Piccolo
10	Glockenspiel	74	Flute
11	Music Box	75	Recorder

PC#	Instrument	PC#	Instrument
12	Vibraphone	76	Pan Flute
13	Marimba	77	Blown Bottle
14	Xylophone	78	Shakuhachi
15	Tubular Bells	79	Whistle
16	Dulcimer	80	Ocarina
17	Drawbar Organ	81	Lead1 (square)
18	Percussive Organ	82	Lead2 (sawtooth)
19	Rock Organ	83	Lead3 (calliope)
20	Church Organ	84	Lead4 (chiff)
21	Reed Organ	85	Lead5 (charang)
22	Accordion	86	Lead6 (voice)
23	Harmonica	87	Lead7 (fifths)
24	Tango Accordion	88	Lead8 (bass+lead)
25	Acoustic Guitar (nylon)	89	Pad1 (newage)
26	Acoustic Guitar (steel)	90	Pad2 (warm)
27	Electric Guitar (jazz)	91	Pad3 (polysynth)
28	Electric Guitar (clean)	92	Pad4 (choir)
29	Electric Guitar (muted)	93	Pad5 (bowed)
30	Overdriven Guitar	94	Pad6 (metallic)
31	Distortion Guitar	95	Pad7 (halo)
32	Guitar harmonics	96	Pad8 (sweep)
33	Acoustic Bass	97	FX1 (rain)
34	Electric Bass (finger)	98	FX2 (soundtrack)
35	Electric Bass (pick)	99	FX3 (crystal)
36	Fretless Bass	100	FX4 (atmosphere)
37	Slap Bass1	101	FX5 (brightness)
38	Slap Bass2	102	FX6 (goblins)
39	Synth Bass1	103	FX7 (echoes)
40	Synth Bass2	104	FX8 (sci-fi)
41	Violin	105	Sitar
42	Viola	106	Banjo
43	Cello	107	Shamisen
44	Contrabass	108	Koto
45	Tremolo Strings	109	Kalimba
46	Pizzicato Strings	110	Bagpipe
47	Orchestral Harp	111	Fiddle
48	Timpani	112	Shanai
49	String Ensemble 1	113	Tinkle Bell
50	String Ensemble 2	114	Agogo
51	Synth Strings 1	115	Steel Drums
52	Synth Strings 2	116	Woodblock
53	Choir Aahs	117	Taiko Drum
54	Voice Oohs	118	MelodicTom

PC#	Instrument	PC#	Instrument
55	Synth Voice	119	Synth Drum
56	Orchestra Hit	120	Reverse Cymbal
57	Trumpet	121	Guitar Fret Noise
58	Trombone	122	Breath Noise
59	Tuba	123	Seashore
60	Muted Trumpet	124	Bird Tweet
61	French Horn	125	Telephone Ring
62	Brass Section	126	Helicopter
63	SynthBrass1	127	Applause
64	SynthBrass2	128	Gunshot
©1991, 1994 MIDI Manufacturers Association. Used with permission.			

In General MIDI, channel 10 is always used for drums. Table 3.25 lists the key assignments for each percussive instrument in a General MIDI drum kit.

Table 3.25. General MIDI Percussion Key Map

Key#	Drum Sound	Key#	Drum Sound
35	Acoustic Bass Drum	59	Ride Cymbal 2
36	Bass Drum 1	60	Hi Bongo
37	Side Stick	61	Low Bongo
38	Acoustic Snare	62	Mute Hi Conga
39	Hand Clap	63	Open Hi Conga
40	Electric Snare	64	Low Conga
41	Low Floor Tom	65	High Timbale
42	Closed Hi Hat	66	Low Timbale
43	High Floor Tom	67	High Agogo
44	Pedal Hi-Hat	68	Low Agogo
45	Low Tom	69	Cabasa
46	Open Hi-Hat	70	Maracas
47	Low-Mid Tom	71	Short Whistle
48	Hi Mid Tom	72	Long Whistle
49	Crash Cymbal 1	73	Short Guiro
50	High Tom	74	Long Guiro
51	Ride Cymbal 1	75	Claves
52	Chinese Cymbal	76	Hi Wood Block
53	Ride Bell	77	Low Wood Block
54	Tambourine	78	Mute Cuica
55	Splash Cymbal	79	Open Cuica

Key#	Drum Sound	Key#	Drum Sound
56	Cowbell	80	Mute Triangle
57	Crash Cymbal 2	81	Open Triangle
58	Vibraslap		
©1991, 1994 MIDI Manufacturers Association. Used with permission.			

Case Studies: Using MIDI as a Creative Tool

Modern sequencing software typically provides many options for capturing, routing, and transforming MIDI messages in new and interesting ways, so an understanding of these messages can provide opportunities to enhance the creative experience. The following case studies represent just a few of the things that can be done to take advantage of the flexibility that MIDI has to offer. I elected to demonstrate each of these examples in Logic Pro because its "Environment" view offers many powerful tools for manipulating MIDI messages.

EXPRESSIVE MULTI-CONTROLLER
Musicians often add vibrato at the end of a crescendo or to emphasize a note. In this example, a virtual fader is configured to simulate this effect by adding modulation as expression values (CC#11) increase. The virtual fader is set to respond to incoming expression messages. The messages are routed to a virtual synthesizer, and a copy of each expression message is sent to a transformer that transforms them into modulation messages (CC#1). Figure 3.14 shows the basic signal flow.

Figure 3.14
Transforming a MIDI message.

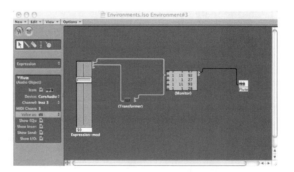

The transformer tool is a powerful tool that enables MIDI messages to be transformed and altered in many ways. In this example, expression messages are transformed into modulation messages, and the data byte representing the amount of modulation is scaled so that modulation is subtly added as expression values increase. Figure 3.15 shows the transformer in action: The top half of the dialog represents the incoming message, and the bottom half represents the transformed message. Notice how a value of 65 is subtracted from the second data byte in order to reduce modulation to a natural-sounding level.

DAMPER PEDAL AS KICK DRUM

In the next example, incoming damper pedal messages (CC#64) are transformed into note-on messages so that the pedal can be used to play bass drum parts. The damper pedal, when combined with hands playing the hi-hat and snare, provides a natural approach to keyboard-based drum sequencing. For a more authentic sound, the velocity of the bass drum is randomized within a small range. Figure 3.16 shows the signal flow of the damper pedal transformer.

Figure 3.15
The MIDI transformer.

TWO-DIMENSIONAL MIDI CONTROLLER

Logic Pro provides an interesting two-dimensional controller that can be configured to output separate events on the horizontal and vertical axes. A mouse is used to "draw" fader moves in two dimensions, and the movement can trigger any number of MIDI events. In this example, expression (CC#11) is generated by movement on the vertical axis and panning (CC#10) is generated by movement on the horizontal axis. The signal is then split, and a transformer adds modulation if the expression level is greater than 100. A cable splitter is used to trigger sounds on another software synthesizer if velocities reach a predefined threshold (see Figure 3.17).

Figure 3.16
The kick drum transformer.

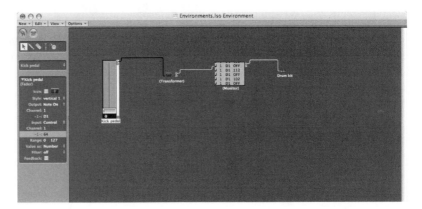

Figure 3.17
The two-dimensional controller in
Logic Pro.

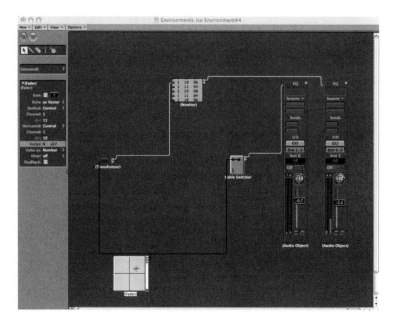

The previous examples provide a look at some of the interesting things that can be done in a sequencing environment. At the very least, you will find that an understanding of MIDI technology will enable you to configure your MIDI network and enjoy greater expressive control of your electronic instruments. As you continue to experiment with MIDI, you will undoubtedly discover new ways of using the technology to support your style of work and creative vision.

MIDI Manufacturers Association

Many of the tables in this chapter have been adapted from information available on the MIDI Manufacturers Association Web site. You can purchase *The Complete MIDI 1.0 Detailed Specification* from the MMA for about $50. Although the MMA encourages the dissemination of this information, the MIDI specification is periodically revised, so you may wish to contact them to purchase a current version of *The Complete MIDI Detailed Specification*.

MIDI Manufacturers Association
P.O. Box 3173
La Habra, California 90632-3173
www.midi.org/

CHAPTER 4

Sequencing Concepts

The lines have blurred between MIDI sequencing software and digital audio recording software to the point that very few MIDI-only applications exist. This chapter focuses on the sequencing capabilities of most modern digital audio workstations. You will look at the production process, from setting up MIDI devices in a host application to creating and editing MIDI sequences. The chapter takes a holistic approach to the process that does not focus on a product from a single vendor. With this approach, concepts are applicable to software from most vendors. Along the way, you'll discover techniques that can help you enhance your production process. This chapter emphasizes the following primary objectives:

▶ Configuring MIDI devices and patch names

▶ Troubleshooting MIDI and sequencer settings

▶ Setting up virtual synthesizers via ReWire

▶ Setting up a metronome

▶ Using a conductor track

▶ Recording a MIDI clip

▶ MIDI entry methods

▶ Markers and navigation

▶ Editing and quantifying MIDI data

▶ Real-time MIDI effects

▶ Editing views

▶ Track automation

▶ Enhancing workflow

▶ Using a control surface

Choosing a Sequencer

It can be challenging to select a sequencing or DAW application. An interface that works well for one user may be awkward for another user. Over the years, I have used most of the major programs and have found that some programs suit my work style better than others. For this reason, it's a good idea to spend some time with product demos and user manuals prior to investing in a sequencing application. Most vendors provide entry-level products (with an upgrade path to professional versions), so for some users it may make sense to purchase a less expensive version in order to get a feel for the interface and gauge the reliability of the product prior to upgrading to an expensive high-end product. Note, though, that initial ease of use is not necessarily the best criterion for which to evaluate a product. Modern sequencing and DAW applications are "deep," and though it may take some time to become fluent, the robust nature of these products will, after an initial learning curve, provide many features that can enhance your productivity.

Configuring Patch Names

Most sequencing and DAW programs default to general MIDI patch names. Unless you plan to sequence with a general MIDI keyboard or soundcard, a helpful first step will likely be to configure your workspace so that device names and patch names reflect the physical components of your MIDI system.

MACINTOSH OS X

In previous versions of the Macintosh operating system, MIDI devices were configured using one of two third-party options: OMS or FreeMIDI. Thankfully, OS X now provides system-level support for MIDI devices. To set up a MIDI network, first install any necessary drivers for your MIDI and audio interface. In most cases, you will want to visit the vendor's Web site to download the most recent drivers and install the drivers according to the manufacturers instructions. Once drivers have been installed, run the Audio MIDI Setup (AMS) program, which is located in the Utilities subdirectory. AMS provides several helpful functions such as the ability to auto-detect MIDI instruments.

Connect all MIDI devices according to the instructions in Chapter 3, power up each MIDI instrument, and click the "Rescan MIDI" option. The program will then attempt to determine which MIDI devices are attached. If a device does not show up, check the cabling and power status. The "Add Device" option can be used to manually add any instruments not detected by AMS. Double-click on the newly added device to edit its properties (see Figure 4.1).

Figure 4.1
Audio MIDI Setup: configuring a MIDI device.

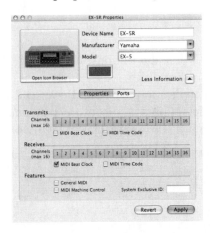

After adding a MIDI device, drag the arrows to reflect the physical setup of each MIDI port. Figure 4.2 shows a Yamaha DX 7 being connected to one of the ports of a two-port MIDI interface.

Figure 4.2
Connecting devices in Audio MIDI Setup.

Configuration of patch names will vary depending on the host application. For example, Digital Performer provides patch lists for many devices. In many cases, the "Auto Configure MIDI Devices" command, available in the Setup menu, can be used to automatically configure devices and patch names. These patch lists are stored as XML documents with a ".midnam" extension in the Library\Audio\MIDI Devices\MOTU subfolder. (XML stands for "Extensible Markup Language" and is similar to an HTML file in that XML documents are plain text documents containing special formatting characters). Since ".midnam" files can be loaded and edited with a text editor, a custom patch list can be created by editing a ".midnam" file with a text editor. (It's a good idea to create a backup copy of the file prior to editing.) For example, in order to update a patch list for a Yamaha sound module, I located its associated ".midnam" file in the Yamaha subdirectory and edited the names of patches using a text editor. Changes made to the patch names in this file were reflected in Digital Performer the next time I loaded the program. Following is the relevant portion of an XML document. The edited patch names are shown in bold type.

```
<PatchNameList>
    <Patch Number="1" Name="Organ" ProgramChange="0" />
    <Patch Number="2" Name="Mono synth" ProgramChange="1" />
    <Patch Number="3" Name="Clav" ProgramChange="2" />
    <Patch Number="4" Name="Warm Bass" ProgramChange="3" />
```

Other applications, such as Logic Pro, store patch names within each document. In this case, patch names can be pasted from a MIDI librarian application like SoundDiver and stored as part of a default template. In lieu of librarian software, patch names can also be typed directly into a "multi" device, such as in Figure 4.3.

Figure 4.3
Typing patch names in Logic Pro.

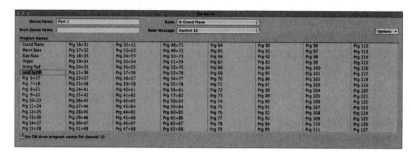

To gain access to banks of patches, it is necessary to configure the bank select method for each device. As I mentioned in Chapter 3, one common method is to use MIDI controller 0 with a data byte specifying the bank. Another common method utilizes a combination of controller 0 and controller 32 specifying the most significant and least significant bytes. Figure 4.4 shows bank select messages being configured for a new device in Logic Pro. If you are unsure of the type of bank select method to use, try the bank select tip mentioned in Chapter 3.

Figure 4.4
Setting up bank select messages in Logic Pro.

WINDOWS XP

To install a MIDI interface on a Windows XP machine, download the latest drivers from the interface vendor. The drivers will typically be downloaded as part of an installation program called "Setup.exe." In most cases, the MIDI interface should not be attached to the computer until the setup program has installed the drivers. The computer may need to be rebooted in order for the new drivers to take effect.

To troubleshoot a MIDI device, right click on My Computer and click Properties. Select the Hardware tab and click Device Manager. Open the "Sound, video and game controllers" submenu to see if the interface has been installed and if there are any problems reported by the device manger (see Figure 4.5).

Figure 4.5
Viewing device manager properties in Windows XP.

If you experience problems with a newly updated driver, the Roll Back Driver button, available under the Driver tab, can be a real lifesaver.

Patch lists and bank select are configured in a host application such as Cubase or Sonar. Most applications ship with numerous instrument definitions, which can be loaded via a device manager. Of course, custom definitions can also be created. In Figure 4.6, bank select and patch change messages are being added to a newly created instrument definition in Cubase SE. When creating instrument lists in this way, I always create definitions for several banks with just a few sounds in each bank. This way, I avoid wasting time if I happen to select the wrong bank select message. Patch selection may appear to work properly but can "break" when a new bank is selected.

Figure 4.6
Creating a custom instrument definition in Cubase SE.

Most applications store instrument definitions in a plain text or XML file. A text editor, such as Notepad in the Accessories menu, can provide a convenient way to edit instrument configuration files. It often saves time to make a copy of an instrument definition that is similar to a given device and manually type patch names. A more convenient method is to use a compatible editor librarian such as Midi Quest by Sound Quest Inc.

Using Virtual Synthesizers with ReWire

The Propellerhead Software company, maker of Reason and several other popular MIDI and audio applications, developed a useful protocol called *ReWire*. The company describes ReWire as an "'invisible cable that streams audio from one computer program into another." With ReWire, two applications that support the protocol can stream MIDI and audio data to one another. In a typical setup, a software sequencer or DAW might be used to control virtual synthesizers in another application such as Reason.

To establish a ReWire connection, the host application must first be launched. Then, the client application is launched, and a ReWire connection is automatically established between the two applications. The client application provides a virtual audio and MIDI connection to the host application so that sounds can be monitored and processed by the host application. In this way, a DAW program such as Digital Performer can play "ReWired" tracks just like any other MIDI/Audio track.

By way of example, here are the steps to establish a ReWire connection between Digital Performer and Reason. The steps will be very similar for other ReWire compatible software. For example, in Logic Pro it is necessary to make one or more ReWire objects in the environment window after establishing a ReWired audio connection as described below.

1. Launch the host application (Digital Performer in this case).

2. Create an auxiliary track in the host application with the client application as the input source (Reason in this instance).

3. Ensure that the output of the auxiliary track is set to a valid audio device.

4. Run the client application.

5. Load devices such as a virtual synthesizer or sampler in the client application.

6. Create a MIDI track in the host application and select a ReWired device such as the newly created virtual sampler.

7. Arm the track for recording. MIDI data can now be recorded on the track, and audio output from the ReWired synthesizer can be processed just like any other audio track.

Figure 4.7 shows the selection of a virtual ReWire device in Digital Performer.

Figure 4.7
Selecting a ReWire instrument in
Digital Performer.

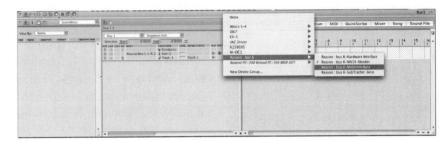

Troubleshooting

It is often necessary to troubleshoot a newly installed sequencing environment. Problems may occur as the result of any number of issues. Consider the following steps in order to find the source of the problem:

▶ **Setup:** In OS X, launch the utility called Audio MIDI Setup and select the Test MIDI Setup option to see if MIDI data is being sent and received by each connected device. Most PC sequencing applications include a similar setup screen that can be accessed within the application.

▶ **Input:** Make sure the OUT port of the MIDI controller is connected to the IN port of the MIDI interface and that, if necessary, the device is selected as an input device in the sequencing application.

▶ **Track settings:** Most programs require that a MIDI device be selected for input and output. Select a valid device and see if the software receives input by playing a few notes on the controller. (Sequencing programs usually provide visual feedback when MIDI messages are received.) Alternatively, press Record and play a few notes to see if messages are recorded in the track.

▶ **Interface:** If the previous steps do not produce MIDI messages, it may be necessary to update or reinstall the MIDI interface driver. Check the Audio and MIDI Setup program (in OS X) or the Sounds and Audio Devices application (available in the control panel of Windows) to see if the interface appears to be properly installed. In some instances, device drivers may have not loaded properly. Try exiting the program and uplugging and replugging the USB interface.

▶ **Output:** If the program is receiving MIDI input but no notes are heard, check the MIDI track destination to see if a valid MIDI device is selected and the track is armed. Also make sure that the input of the destination device is physically connected to the output of the MIDI interface.

▶ **Audio:** Check that the audio output of the destination device is properly connected to a mixer or amplifier and make certain that all components are powered up.

▶ **Local:** If you are having trouble with a synthesizer, it may be helpful to turn local to ON in order to check that the problem does not relate to the audio system. If the synthesizer produces sound when local is on, that indicates a problem with the MIDI interface, software setting, or MIDI connection between the synthesizer and interface. You may want to swap MIDI cables to determine if the problem has to do with a defective cable.

▶ **Bank select:** Improper bank select setup is the cause of many problems. Some instruments may default to an "empty" user patch. In this case, it may be helpful to manually select a sound on the instrument to aurally check whether MIDI messages are reaching the instrument.

▶ **MIDI Clock:** Some keyboards have built-in sequencers and arpeggiators that may conflict with MIDI Clock produced by sequencing software. Check that your sequencer is functioning as the clock source and that any instruments are set to respond to external clock. On some synthesizers, arpeggiated sounds will not play back unless the sequencer is in Play mode.

Getting Started

The following section details the primary steps necessary to record MIDI into the track view of a sequencer or DAW. Since most modern applications function in a similar way, a familiarity with these concepts will be applicable to any number of applications.

TRACK VIEW

The track view is the heart of most sequencing and DAW programs. MIDI and audio data is presented as a series of "clips" on each track, and these clips can be edited and reordered to form a musical composition. Musical clips are analogous to words in a word-processing program— these "words" can be cut, copied, pasted, and otherwise manipulated (see Figure 4.8).

Figure 4.8
Track view.

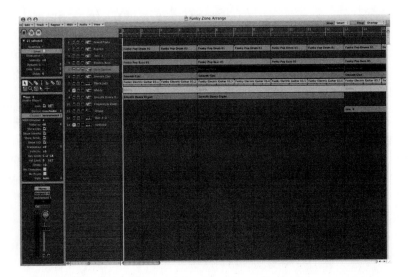

When pasting musical clips, it is usually necessary to align the left side of the clip with a measure boundary so that the music stays in synch with a click track. When pasting multiple copies of a clip, an offset of a few ticks will, over time, cause the phrase to drift out of synch. Most sequencers provide a "Go To" command that can be used to quickly set the insertion point to the start of a measure as in Figure 4.9. An adjustable snap-to-grid feature may also be available to facilitate the alignment of MIDI clips.

Figure 4.9
Aligning an insertion point using a "Go To" command.

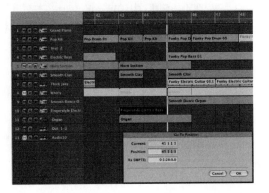

Each MIDI track must have an output destination, usually in the form of a MIDI port and channel assignment or ReWire connection. When assigning sounds, remember that it is not possible to have more than one concurrent patch on a given channel, so in most cases, each track should have a unique MIDI channel assignment. However, there are times when it makes sense to assign multiple tracks to a single MIDI channel—drum parts are one such example. It is often convenient to record the hi-hat or ride cymbal on one track and bass drum and snare drum on another track. Some synthesizers and sound modules allow a single MIDI channel (usually channel 10) for drums, so it is necessary to assign multiple tracks to the same channel to separate percussion instruments when using this type of MIDI instrument.

SETTING UP THE METRONOME

It is necessary to record to a metronome if you wish to quantize a performance (see "Quantization" later in this chapter). Selecting a metronome sound is largely a matter of personal preference, but sounds such as a woodblock or triangle will tend to cut through dense passages better than sounds like a hand drum or bass drum. Most sequencers provide the ability to assign a separate MIDI note and velocity for the primary and weak beats, and it is a good idea to differentiate the primary beat in case you decide to notate a performance. Other metronome options will be available to specify when the click will play such as during countoff, recording, or playback. Since it is less likely that you will experience latency issues with an external MIDI device, an external keyboard or sound module may be a better choice as a metronome than a software synthesizer or sound card. After installing new software or MIDI drivers, it is a good idea to record a series of quarter notes in synch with the metronome. I once experienced problems recording MIDI tracks in a new sequencing application and realized that latency was causing the metronome to sound slightly late—updated drivers fixed the problem.

CONDUCTOR TRACK

Most sequencers provide a conductor track that is accessible from the main track view. As the name implies, a conductor track is used to "direct" a sequence, but it does not store note data. The conductor track is responsible for establishing tempo, key, and time signature changes and provides a sort of road map for the sequence. You may not need to worry about editing a conductor track if your sequences generally consist of a single meter and tempo, but conductor tracks are useful in many situations. For film work, you can create a road map of tempos and meters that best complements scenes in the movie. If you plan to convert your sequence to traditional notation, it is also advisable to insert appropriate key and meter changes into the conductor track. Figure 4.10 shows a series of tempo changes in a typical conductor track.

Figure 4.10
Editing tempo events in a conductor track.

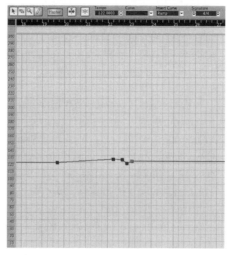

Conductor tracks can also be used to map a preexisting performance to bars and beats in a sequencer. For example, a recording of an acoustic piano or guitar (recorded without a click track) could be imported and aligned to bars and beats in the sequencer using a series of tempo changes. Once beats have been aligned to the audio recording, the metronome will follow changes in tempo on the original recording. The process varies depending on the sequencer, but in most cases, the software will analyze transients in the recording to determine beats. This works well for tracks that are percussive and have a well-defined rhythmic pulse. For nonrhythmic tracks, it is often possible to record a MIDI beat track in order to "teach" the software how beats should align with preexisting material. Figure 4.11 shows a recently created beat map in Logic Pro:

Figure 4.11
Mapping beats using a beat track.

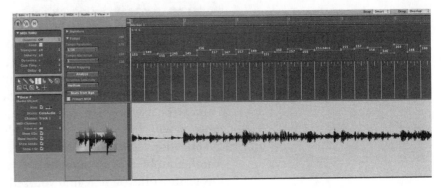

RECORDING A CLIP

There are three primary methods of recording MIDI data: real-time, step-time, and real-time quantization. Of the three common entry methods, recording a real-time performance generally yields the most musical results. I find that, even if a passage is difficult to play in real time, it is better to record it slowly than resort to step-time entry, which tends to sound mechanical.

It is usually necessary to "arm" a track prior to recording a MIDI clip. Most sequencers provide an arming button for the purpose. If you experience doubled notes when recording, check to see that local is turned to off on the master keyboard. If you plan to use the modulation wheel, pitch bend, or expression controller, be sure to record a fader move prior to recording the first note. This will ensure that the controller will have a predictable starting level each time the clip is played back. Otherwise, the clip will jump to the level of the first controller event found within the clip. Similarly, it is a good idea to record or insert a volume (controller 7) setting for each track if you plan to automate your mix. A value of 64 (*mf*) can provide a good point of departure. It's a good idea to also insert a patch change, particularly if you plan to distribute a MIDI file or import the file into another application.

With step-time entry, a rhythmic value such as an eighth note is first selected, and then notes, rests, and chords can be entered via a MIDI keyboard at the given "step" value. Step-time can be useful for any passage that is difficult to play in real time, such as drum fills, harp arpeggios, or repetitive "techno" passages. To experiment with this concept, try using step-time entry to insert a measure or two of 32nd-note tom and snare notes. If you vary note velocities and insert an occasional rest, you can easily come up with many interesting fills. Step-time entry can also be useful for recording drum rolls, which are notoriously difficult to execute on a keyboard in real time. Rolls will sound most natural if a variety of note velocities are used. Figure 4.12 shows notes being entered in step-time.

Figure 4.12
A step-entry dialog box.

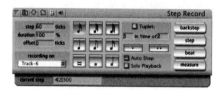

Some MIDI musicians prefer to record real-time tracks with input quantization on. The benefit of this method is that tracks such as a drum part will be rhythmically "fixed" at the same time they are recorded. This can be useful when layering drum parts using loop recording. The problem with this method is that, unless you are sure to pick the correct quantization value, your performance will not be accurately recorded. Another problem with input quantization is that, if you forget to turn this feature off, you may find yourself inadvertently quantizing a real-time performance.

I find input quantization to be particularly helpful when creating drum loops. For example, configure the sequencing software to loop a region of two or four bars and turn on the input quantize or auto-quantize function. If the record mode is set to merge MIDI data, it is then possible to record a drum groove by adding a layer at a time such as hi-hat on one pass, snare drum on the next pass, and so on. Most sequencing applications provide the ability to edit MIDI data while in record mode, so this can provide an intuitive way to develop drum grooves. Figure 4.13 shows a drum loop being recorded with auto-quantize function turned on in Cubase SE.

Figure 4.13
Establishing a loop in Cubase SE.

USING MARKERS

Markers are a useful in most production situations. Markers can be inserted to indicate important structural points such as a verse or chorus, or they can be locked to a specific video frame when scoring a film.

Since markers can facilitate navigation of a long sequence, it's almost always a good idea to take the time to insert markers. An added benefit is that markers can be used to experiment with formal structure. You could, for example, play back a sequence and select markers in real time to see how the sections of a sequence might sound in a new order such as verse, chorus, bridge instead of verse, bridge, and chorus.

NAVIGATION

Sequencers provide many predefined key commands to facilitate navigation of a composition, but I have noticed that new users tend to use the mouse. However, most people agree that key commands are faster than using a mouse, so it is advantageous to learn a few essential commands in order to become fluent in navigating through a project. In addition to standardized commands such as cut, copy, paste, and undo, I find that the following commands are the most helpful to memorize:

▶ Go to measure

▶ Play

▶ Stop

▶ Record

▶ Quantize

▶ Transpose

▶ Insert marker (round to nearest measure)

▶ Go to next marker

▶ Go to previous marker

I have found these commands to be so helpful that I always assign the same keystrokes in each program so that I can work efficiently in any of my primary sequencing applications. In particular, the "Go to measure" command provides an efficient way to move throughout a sequence. I prefer the '.' key (on the numeric keypad) for this purpose. This command makes it possible to move to any measure with just a few quick keystrokes. Of course, advanced users will utilize many other key commands to "nudge" or quantize clips, zoom in on a region, or call up a screen set, but the commands listed above, in consort with standardized commands such as cut, copy, paste, and undo, will provide a reasonable level of facility with most applications.

Manipulating MIDI Data

In this section I will explore many of the common editing functions available in a modern sequencing environment. Along the way I will present a number of tips that will allow you to manipulate and experiment with musical data in new and interesting ways.

QUANTIZATION

One of the most helpful (and sometimes overused) editing functions is quantization. Quantization can be used to "fix" rhythmic inaccuracies in a MIDI performance. In simple quantization, a user selects a value for note attacks and/or durations. The software analyzes a selected region or tracks and adjusts the timing of notes to reflect the selected note value. For example, when recording a series of quarter notes, if one of the notes is a 16th early, quantization can be used to adjust the inaccuracy to the nearest quarter note. Figure 4.14 shows a rhythmically inaccurate passage, and Figure 4.15 demonstrates how quantization can be used to fix the rhythm.

Figure 4.14
Rhythmic inaccuracy.

Figure 4.15
Quantizing a rhythmic inaccuracy.

Use quantification judiciously; many programs destructively edit MIDI data and, unless multiple undo is available, your original performance may be lost forever! If you are using a destructive mode sequencer, be sure to listen back to the entire quantified region before continuing your work. A performance inaccuracy might result in notes being quantified in the wrong direction in a later region of the sequence, so be sure to check this out. Often, a clip might sound good except for one or two misplaced notes. Editing views such as an event list or piano roll view (see below) can be useful for selecting just a few MIDI events to quantize. If your sequencer supports it, a track quantization insert is often preferable to destructive quantization (more on this later in the chapter).

Some programs allow you to select a sensitivity value (see Figure 4.16). If a note is close to the quantification grid (i.e., a specified number of ticks before or after the quantization value) the software will not alter its rhythmic position if you define a sensitivity or strength value. Swing sensitivity values may also be an option and can be useful in selectively quantizing a series of swing eighth notes.

Figure 4.16
Setting quantization sensitivity level.

GROOVE QUANTIZATION

One of the problems with traditional quantization is that it may make your music sound mechanical. Although this is desirable for some styles of music such as "dance" or "techno," sequencing-software vendors have developed several new forms of quantization that may be more suitable. Another problem with simple quantization is that only note attacks and/or durations are quantified. Good grooves are often the result of a combination of rhythmic placement and dynamics or accents. Groove quantization provides a means of manipulating both of these characteristics. Although there are many ways of implementing groove quantization, most programs provide a number of built-in groove maps that represent specific styles such as "shuffle" or "laid back" (see Figure 4.17). In general, design of groove maps involves analyzing digital audio performances (e.g., a groove recorded by a great drummer). Timing and velocity data are extracted, and users of the software are able to apply these groove maps to their own sequenced data. Some applications even provide the option of using an existing MIDI clip as a quantization template. This can be a great way to adjust the feel of supporting tracks to an existing groove such as a clavichord performance or MIDI drum track.

Figure 4.17
Applying groove quantization.

HUMANIZE

"Humanizing" (sometimes included as a strength adjustment in a quantification dialog box) is used to add an element of imperfection or randomness to a passage of music. As I mentioned earlier, if a performance is quantified it will tend to sound mechanical or rigid. Humanizing is used to add slight timing imperfections to a passage of music. The user can select an adjustment range of, say, a 32nd note, and the software will analyze a selected region and add some slight rhythmic inaccuracies (within the specified value range) to the performance. However, I have found humanizing functions to be less helpful than, say, traditional or groove quantization because computer-generated inaccuracies tend to sound, well, inaccurate. The performance inaccuracies most musicians use tend to be slight variations that enhance the given style of music (e.g., natural rubato that might result from "laying back" during the climax of a melody). I have noticed that notation applications such as Sibelius have developed "humanizing" playback routines that go beyond simple randomizing features found in some sequencers. Consider importing a MIDI file created with such an application in order to explore a more natural-sounding version of the "humanizing" technique.

SWING QUANTIZATION

Most software synthesizers provide the ability to adjust a swing percentage when applying quantization to a range of notes. Although it is certainly possible to have swing 16th notes, the most common scenario involves applying a swing percentage to a passage of eighth notes. In general, you will want to select a large swing percentage for slower tunes and a small swing percentage for faster tunes. For example, the eighth notes for a fast bop tune are usually played very close to even notes (i.e., very little swing). The eighth notes in a slow swing blues will tend to be very "wide."

One of the problems I have experienced with swing quantization is that, in most implementations, the swing feel is applied to every eighth note. In jazz, an eighth note that is combined with sixteenths (or smaller) rhythmic value is usually not swung. An alternative is to selectively apply swing quantization to sections of music that include eighth note (or higher) durations.

DURATION

The duration of notes can also be quantified. Use duration quantization to change a legato passage to staccato or vice versa. Note that many programs include options to adjust the duration of notes as a part of a quantification dialog box—there may not be a specific duration function provided (see Figure 4.18). I almost always turn off the duration function when applying quantification to a passage of music. In many cases, quantifying the release of notes in a phrase will make it sound even more mechanical than simple quantification. Even if a musician has good time, he or she will probably use note durations that fluctuate widely, and this can be an important musical aspect of a MIDI performance.

Figure 4.18
The duration option in a
quantization dialog box.

VELOCITY SCALING

It is often helpful to adjust the velocities of a group notes. Software sequencers employ a number of functions to adjust velocities. In most cases, velocities can be scaled by a percentage, limited, or compressed. Percentage scaling is useful for retaining the original character of a passage but increasing or decreasing velocities by a specified percentage such as 80% of the original value. Compression and limiting are used to emphasize or limit velocities that fall beyond a specified threshold. It is also possible to specify a value for each of the notes in a selected region. This method works best for techno and dance styles of music where you intend for the music to sound artificial or computer-generated. Figure 4.19 shows a typical velocity scaling dialog box. Since instrument patches respond differently to velocity messages, scaling the overall velocities of a track can be helpful when changing to a sound other than the one used to record the data.

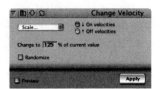

Figure 4.19
Velocity scaling.

TRACK OR CLIP SHIFTING

Most sequencers allow you to adjust a track or clip by a specified range of "ticks" (see Figure 4.20). This can be a great way to experiment with variations on a rhythm section groove. Some bass players, for example, tend to play a bit behind the beat. By offsetting a bass or other track by a few ticks you may find some interesting variations to an existing groove. I sometimes find it helpful to adjust percussion tracks in this manner—a repetitive hi-hat pattern can sound very interesting when offset in this way.

Figure 4.20
Setting a track offset.

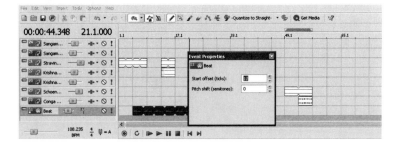

TRANSPOSITION

One of the more straightforward sequencing operations is transposition. Simply select a region of notes and transpose up or down by a specified amount (see Figure 4.21). One caveat to keep in mind as you use a transpose function: Drum tracks can also be transposed. In most situations, transposing drum tracks will result in strange or unusual results. This is due to the fact that, on most synthesizers, each key is mapped to a specific drum sound. Transposing a drum track has the effect of remapping the entire track. Of course, transposition can be combined with cut and paste operations to quickly create modulations in a last verse or chorus. Transposition can also be helpful when creating parts for transposing instruments: Though most sequencers do not support transposing part extraction, it is easy to temporarily transpose a saxophone or other transposing instrument track prior to printing parts for your band.

Figure 4.21
Transposing notes in a MIDI clip.

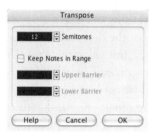

SEARCH AND REPLACE (INTERPOLATE)

Interpolation involves searching for and changing or inserting a specified element en masse. A search and replace function is valuable when you need to change one type of MIDI data to another. You might, for example, decide that a sequence that utilizes a drum sound on C4 would sound better using another drum sound that resides at D4. By replacing all of the C4 notes in a selected region it is easy to make this type of change (see Figure 4.22).

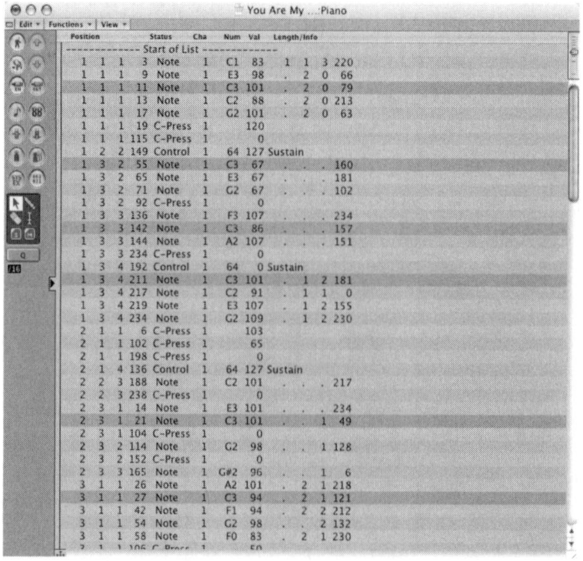

Figure 4.22
Search and replace in Logic Pro.

EVENT STRETCHING AND SHRINKING

Stretching and shrinking functions are most helpful when doing film and commercial work. You may decide that the first 15 seconds of music in a 30-second radio spot needs to be 18 seconds to better complement a voice-over. Event stretching allows you to change the timing of your sequence without the need to re-record each part to a different tempo. Some programs will even let you specify a graph or ratio to effect a natural-sounding accelerando or ritardando (see Figure 4.23). Most modern sequencers can also time stretch audio (see Chapter 6, "Music"), but audio quality will suffer if an extreme tempo change is required.

Figure 4.23
Time scaling.

Using and Editing Controller Data

Although it is possible (and sometimes desirable) to edit continuous controllers using an event list, most software sequencers allow you to make these edits visually using a graphical editor. This approach is more intuitive: It is much easier to "draw" a smooth crescendo than it is to insert a number of expression messages into an event list! In most cases, a controller such as expression, panning, or channel volume can be selected to overlay a MIDI clip. In this way, it is easy to see where controller messages should be inserted in relation to an underlying musical phrase. Figure 4.24 illustrates graphic editing of expression data. In most programs, data points such as the ones shown can be inserted by double-clicking with the mouse. In some graphic editing views, continuous controller data can be drawn in freehand with a virtual pen or line drawing tool.

Figure 4.24
Using a clip overlay to edit a continuous controller.

EXPRESSION AND CHANNEL VOLUME

Volume change messages are one of the more helpful continuous controllers, but they can also be tricky to handle. Unlike note velocity (which simply represents how loud or soft a given note was played), channel volume is used to affect the dynamic level of an entire channel. These messages can be problematic in that you may find yourself in a "tail wagging the dog" syndrome: Volume or expression changes you make at the end of a sequence will affect volume levels earlier in the sequence unless you insert these events throughout a track. The best way to avoid this problem is to record at least one expression level (by moving a data slider) or insert a continuous controller 7 message at the start of each clip. In this way, each MIDI clip will have its own "automatic" expression level. As discussed in Chapter 3, use channel volume to control the overall volume of a given channel and use expression for phrasing dynamic contour within each MIDI clip. Figure 4.25 shows channel volume (CC#7) being edited in a hybrid editing view (note the data in the lower part of the screen.)

Figure 4.25
Editing channel volume.

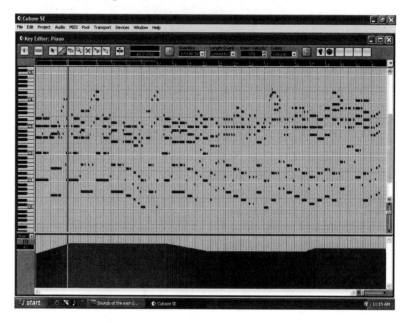

If you listen to a wind player such as a flutist, clarinetist, or saxophonist, you will hear that these players rarely play statically. Put another way, it is rare to hear a wind player play a whole note that does not subtly change in dynamic level. I find it helpful to use a MIDI volume pedal or keyboard data slider to record expression changes as I record a passage of notes. With this approach you will find that your music breathes and sounds much more natural. Even if you primarily use synthetic sounds, a melody that has a dynamic contour will sound much more musical to the listener.

MODULATION

Most keyboards provide modulation and pitch bend wheels or data sliders. Although these controls can usually be programmed for any number of functions, modulation is typically used for vibrato effects or control of a synthesizer parameter such as filter cutoff or resonance. Modulation can be applied using onscreen sliders, the modulation wheel, or an event list. To achieve a very expressive playing style you may want to consider recording expression and modulation as you record a passage of notes. Most professionals will control volume changes using a foot pedal while the left hand is free to control the modulation wheel. You may even consider using a breath controller to control expression or other parameters for a truly expressive style of playing. Most often, modulation is used to enhance a climactic point of a melody, but it can it be used effectively in a rhythmical fashion to control filter cutoff, resonance, or another parameter. For example, you might alter the cutoff frequency of a low-pass filter in synch with the tempo of a sequence.

PITCH BEND

Real-time control of pitch can add an expressive dimension to a sequence (just listen to any good blues guitarist or saxophonist). Unfortunately, pitch bend can be very difficult to implement in a natural or musical way. Some tips that I have found to be helpful include the following:

▶ Set your pitch wheel to a range of a major second or third. Most acoustic instruments can only bend pitch in this range. Although it is possible to set your pitch wheel to a larger interval such as an octave, a large interval is very hard to control.

▶ Use pitch bend in the same way acoustic instrumentalists do (e.g., to create a blue third in a blues sequence).

▶ Practice continuous controller etudes (e.g., arpeggiate a series of major triads and bend the top note of each triad up a half or whole step as in Figure 4.26). If you can get to the point where the pitch wheel is an extension of your body (as your hands are when you input notes), pitch bend can add a wonderful dimension to your sequences.

Figure 4.26
A pitch bend etude.

I will repeat a caveat from Chapter 3: When sequencing, if you press stop before the pitch wheel has had a chance to reset to the unity position you will find that your synthesizer will sound as if it has drifted out of tune. The reason for this is that pitch bend messages are similar to volume change messages in that they affect the state of the channel. If the synthesizer never receives a message to reset pitch on a given channel, it will continue to play back at the wrong pitch. The solution is simple: Record or insert a pitch bend movement to reset the synthesizer.

Real-Time MIDI Effects

Real-time MIDI effects are used in much the same way as outboard gear in a traditional recording studio: A MIDI track may be processed with a MIDI effect, and the resulting sounds are output from the MIDI OUT port. Figure 4.27 shows a real-time effect being applied to a MIDI track via a mixer view.

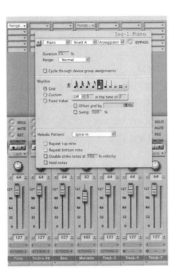

Figure 4.27
Selecting a real-time MIDI effect.

There are many benefits to real-time MIDI effects. For example, some sequencers provide quantization options such as groove quantization and humanizing as a real-time effect. When used in this way, original performance data is not destructively quantized as is usually the case when these routines are applied from the Edit menu. Also, not all keyboards include arpeggiators, so the ability to arpeggiate such an instrument is beneficial.

MIDI DELAY

Although MIDI delay can be used as a traditional delay effect, I find that it can also be a helpful composition tool. Unlike traditional delays that fade out over time, many MIDI delay processors can repeat a group of notes for a specified number of repetitions with no fade. This type of effect can be an asset when composing minimalist sequences or other styles of music that rely on a great deal of repetition. Most implementations also provide the option of transposing each repetition—this can yield some interesting special effects such as cascading "sheets" of chromatic tones.

ARPEGGIATION

I remember salivating over an early arpeggiator in the 1970s. This unit allowed a person to arpeggiate up to a total of 16 notes! Electronic music seems to have come full circle, and arpeggiation is a big part of some styles of computer-based music. Note that the goal of using an arpeggiator is not usually to re-create "pianistic" arpeggios. An arpeggiator is a tool that is more along the lines of a synthesizer's low-frequency modulator. Most sequencers allow you to arpeggiate a group of notes in real time. The arpeggiation may be down, up, random, or some user-defined pattern. Most computer musicians use arpeggiation to repeat the notes of a chord at a specified rate, such as 16th notes at the same tempo as the sequence. Arpeggiation can also be useful when sequencing repetitive bass lines. These types of "mechanical" sounding lines are appropriate for many styles of modern electronic music. Incidentally, arpeggiation can also be useful when applied to drum tracks. For an interesting drum fill, hold down the snare, kick, and hi-hat keys as you apply virtual arpeggiation at a value such as a 1/24 or 32nd note.

VELOCITY SCALING AND COMPRESSION

Many sequencers provide real-time dynamic processors that can be useful in tweaking a track. For example, compression, when applied with channel volume, can be used to "beef up" a track that is dynamically too extreme. Velocity scaling is helpful in situations where a patch responds too aggressively to note attacks—a secondary sample might be triggered by velocities greater than 100, for example. Velocity scaling can be used to tone down such a performance so that the sound responds in a more convincing way.

Editing Views

In this section I will explore common editing views. I elected to include this section in the book for two primary reasons. First, I have noticed that many musicians who are new to sequencing tend to focus on a single editing view. In my case, I happened to focus on a notation view because this was what I was most familiar with in other musical settings. However, I eventually realized that a notation view is not a very efficient view for many types of editing tasks. Second, a familiarity with the primary views will allow you to be reasonably comfortable in nearly any sequencing environment.

Most popular sequencing programs provide at least five ways of viewing MIDI data, and each of the views facilitates specific types of editing operations.

► Event list

► Piano roll (matrix view)

► Notation

► Graphical (usually used for editing tempo, note velocity, or continuous controller data)

► Mixing

If your software supports macros or key assignments, you may wish to assign a keystroke for each of the primary views. This will help you quickly bring up a window that is most relevant for the type of editing you need to do.

EVENT LIST

An event list is the heart of your sequencing environment (see Figure 4.28). The event list simply displays a sequential list of MIDI data found in one or more tracks or clips. The event list is most helpful when you need to edit MIDI data numerically—as is the case when inserting or deleting program changes, tweaking the timestamp of a note, or deleting extraneous controller messages such as a "stuck" damper pedal or pitch bend. An event list is also helpful when importing and exporting standard MIDI files because it provides an opportunity to view track data in its "raw" form.

Figure 4.28
Editing data in an event list.

Most software sequencers allow you to set up a filter to facilitate editing. By setting a filter you can filter out unnecessary data from the current view. Let's say you would like to find and delete a channel volume message (continuous controller #7). By filtering note-on and note-off messages you will be able to view only controller or system messages. This can be a godsend when you are searching through a complex event list or doing multiple edits such as deleting all continuous controller data. Note that most applications also allow you to "scrub" musical data in the event list. Scrubbing involves using the mouse to play a region of notes—the faster you move the mouse, the faster the playback. Scrubbing can help you quickly find a wrong note in an event list. Figure 4.29 shows a typical event list.

Figure 4.29
Using an event list filter.

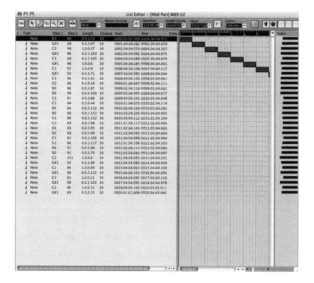

If your software supports it, a "find similar" data function can be very useful when working with data in an event list. With a find or search function you can quickly find all instances of one type of data in a sequence. I have found this function to be helpful in removing specific types of events such as pitch bend or panning.

PIANO ROLL (MATRIX)

The piano roll or matrix view lets you view and manipulate MIDI notes in a graphical fashion. The term piano roll suggests the similarity to piano rolls from the early part of the 20th century: Pitch is represented in the y-axis (i.e., higher notes will appear near the top of the screen, lower notes near the bottom). Time (both attack and release) is represented on the x-axis. Although the piano roll view can be helpful when transposing or quantifying notes, I find that the piano roll view is perfectly suited to editing note durations. Music notation is notoriously inaccurate at representing durations of notes—it is very hard to tell if a staccato quarter note is really an eighth or a 16th, for example. A matrix view is well suited for this type of editing. Most sequencers allow you to select a grouping of notes and edit the pitch or duration of the entire group with a single mouse drag, as shown in Figure 4.30.

Figure 4.30
Piano roll editing: changing the duration of a group of notes.

In general, the piano roll view is well suited to any type of pattern editing. For example, when combined with cycle or loop playback, a matrix view provides one of the best ways to create and edit drum patterns. Individual notes can easily be dragged to new pitches or rhythmic locations in order to create derivative patterns in real time (see Figure 4.31).

Figure 4.31
Using a matrix view to edit a drum pattern.

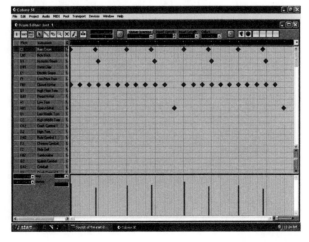

NOTATION VIEW

If you have a traditional music background you may find that the notation view best serves your needs when editing a sequence. The primary advantage of this view is the familiarity of viewing MIDI data as a musical score. Though real-time transcription algorithms are steadily improving, most software applications provide only a rough approximation of a real transcription in the notation view. The reason for this is simple: The goal of any sequencer is to provide accurate and rock-steady playback of MIDI data. A program that spends too much time analyzing MIDI data for the purposes of accurate transcription might result in inaccurate playback. The notation view is most helpful when you need to find and edit a wrong note. Most programs will allow you to simply drag a wrong note to a new line or space on a musical staff in order to correct the pitch (see Figure 4.32).

Figure 4.32
Fixing a wrong note using a notation view.

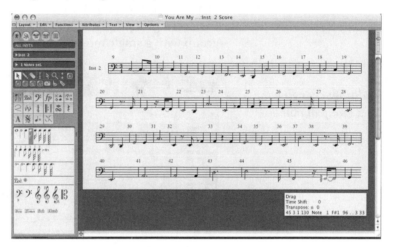

Some of the more sophisticated sequencers allow you to edit and create complete scores using a notation view. If you plan to use sequencing software in this way, I suggest spending some time in the notation view of a program demo before making a purchase. Many sequencers provide only minimal score-editing and formatting capabilities in this view.

If your software supports it, a combination of notation and graphical editing views can be very helpful. With this type of setup, you can view notes in a familiar notation format while utilizing the benefits of graphical notation to edit note velocity or continuous controller data (see Figure 4.33).

Figure 4.33
Combining notation and graphical editing views.

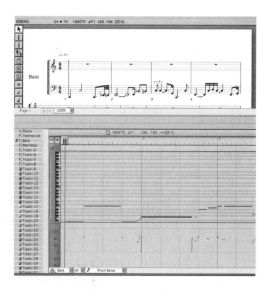

GRAPHICAL VIEW

Many years ago I used sequencing software that was devoid of many of the bells and whistles found in a modern sequencing environment. I will never forget the frustration of trying to edit a ritardando using only a series of tempo changes in an event list. Graphical editing views have evolved to provide a comfortable means of manipulating MIDI data. These views are primarily used for editing data that fluctuates (e.g., tempo change, modulation, or pitch bend). Figure 4.34 shows a typical graphical editing view.

Figure 4.34
Using a graphical editing view to edit continuous controllers.

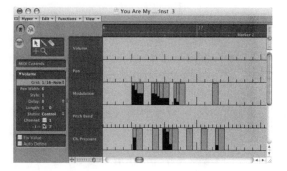

Most sequencers provide a virtual pencil or pen for drawing data changes, and you will probably want to memorize the keystrokes for zooming in and out. I find it most helpful to zoom in for detailed editing and to zoom out to see how my edits relate to the surrounding musical content. You may also want to consider setting up multiple graphic editing windows to view the relationship of several types of data. Pitch bend and modulation are often related, so viewing and editing this data at the same time can be very helpful.

MIXING VIEW

Modern sequencers provide a virtual mixing console that can be used to set and automate parameters such as channel volume, panning, real-time MIDI effects, and input and output sources (see Figure 4.35).

Aside from channel volume, panning is one of the most useful mixing tools. If you have not yet experimented with panning you are in for a real treat: Careful use of panning can help your sequences to sound much more professional. If each of the instruments in a sequence is panned "straight up" the tracks will tend to fight one another. Panning provides a way to create a pleasing stereo image by moving, say, the guitar slightly to the left, keyboard to the right, and bass in the middle.

Figure 4.35
A virtual mixing console.

When working in a mixing view, the following track-related concepts often come into play.

Track Freezing

Software synthesizers can place a large strain on computer processing resources. Many sequencers provide the ability to "freeze" such a track to free up additional processing power. In a frozen track, an audio file is rendered based on current track data and the settings of the virtual synthesizer. Since it generally takes less processing overhead to play an audio track than to render real-time synthesized sounds, frozen tracks can provide an excellent way of achieving greater track count when using virtual synthesizers.

Track Automation

Track automation provides a way of recording mixer "moves" such as a fade out at the end of a piece or increase of volume during a solo. In most sequencing environments, track automation must be armed separately from the regular record arming button, but once track automation is armed, fader moves may be recorded whether the sequencer is in record *or* playback mode. Figure 4.36 shows a typical track arming button.

It is typical for tracks to provide the following automation options:

▶ **Off:** Tracks will ignore automation on playback

▶ **Touch:** Automation data will be recorded when a virtual knob or slider is selected. Automation data will stop being recorded when the knob or slider is released.

▶ **Latch:** Automation data will be recorded when a knob or slider is touched and will continue to be recorded even when the control is released.

▶ **Overwrite:** Useful for creating a "fresh" mix. Automation is recorded at the current setting regardless of whether a controller is activated.

Figure 4.36
Turning on track automation.

Track Grouping

Track grouping is a powerful feature that can aid the process of mixing many MIDI or audio tracks with a mouse. For example, an orchestral sequence might utilize five separate tracks representing the instrument groups in the string choir. These tracks could be grouped so that a single fader controls the overall level of the entire string choir. Creating a group is usually just a matter of selecting tracks or faders from a list. Bussing to a group can be helpful when applying plug-ins or effects since less processing power is required to apply an effect to a bussed group than to apply the effect to each individual track.

SUMMARY OF EDITING VIEWS

Although there are a few other types of views that I didn't cover (such as drum and pattern views), a familiarity with the primary views listed above will help you to function efficiently in almost any sequencing environment. One way to develop facility with the editing features of various views is to record a short passage such as a major scale and play a mistake such as a wrong note or a note that is too soft. Practice fixing the mistake in each of the views to develop a sense of which view works best for a given editing task.

If your software supports it, be sure to assign hot keys to the editing views you most frequently use. This will allow you to view and manipulate data easily. If you find that you use more than a few mouse clicks or keystrokes you are probably using the wrong view for the task at hand.

Workflow

I have covered many sequencing concepts such as recording modes, navigation, quantization, and editing views. With this information, it is possible to feel reasonably comfortable with programs from any of the primary vendors. The following discussion relates to workflow: concepts that will enable you to work more efficiently.

WINDOW SETS

Nearly all modern DAW applications support the concept of window sets (sometimes called screen sets). A window set represents a virtual collection of windows such as an event list, track window, and marker view that work together to facilitate editing. Multiple window sets can be configured for activities such as mixing, digital audio editing, arranging, or film scoring. A window set can be associated with a key command, and the combination of powerful editing views with simple key commands provides the ultimate in efficient editing. Consider associating views with function keys—for example, F2 event list, F3 notation view, and so forth.

TEMPLATES

Templates can be a big help when the muse strikes you. Nothing is more frustrating than searching through thousands of patch names when you have an idea for a new sequence. Most professional electronic musicians create templates for common ensemble groupings such as an orchestral ensemble or small combo. With this type of approach you can start work on a new composition with only a few mouse clicks. Most sequencers provide the ability to set a user-created template as the default workspace. I find it helpful to take the time to create a default template that includes all of my patch names, favorite screen sets, metronome settings, and key commands. Since virtual synthesizers can take a long time to load, I usually prefer a more streamlined template that provides four to eight tracks for each MIDI instrument as well as several audio tracks. If you plan to do commercial work, it is a good idea to create additional templates for orchestral and other types of ensembles since these types of virtual ensembles take a long time to set up by hand.

KEY COMMANDS

I talked about the importance of learning the primary key commands at the start of this chapter. As you become fluent in a sequencing environment, take the time to view and edit your sequencer key command preferences. Since it is not uncommon for a sequencer to provide more than 600 user-configurable commands, a visit to the key commands preferences page will provide many opportunities to enhance workflow. I am always surprised to find commands and functions that I was unaware of. Most of us will use a small subset of these commands, but each user will likely use a different subset. Tailoring key commands to support your style of work is one of the best ways to enhance workflow and is almost always preferable to using a mouse.

CONTROL SURFACE

Control surfaces such as the Mackie Control Universal (see Figure 4.37) can be useful for many production tasks. Some musicians prefer to use a keyboard and mouse while sequencing, and for many years I preferred to use that approach. With that said, I have come to embrace the use of a dedicated control surface. Motorized sliders are a great help in the mixing process, and the physical connection a control surface provides can offer a more intuitive approach to tasks such as arming tracks, setting levels, inserting markers, and adjusting parameters of software synthesizers and the like.

Figure 4.37
Mackie Control Universal.

CHAPTER 5

Digital Recording Concepts

This chapter explores digital recording and editing concepts. The discussion will include an overview of the digitizing process, sample rate and bit depth, "lossy" and lossless audio, ripping and burning, as well as editing and processing concepts that will help you get the most out of a digital audio workstation (DAW).

Anatomy of a Digital Sample

When an analog signal is converted to digital, a series of numbers are used to represent the fluctuations in amplitude that comprise the original signal. To determine the amplitude at a given point in time, an *analog to digital converter* (ADC) takes periodic *samples* of the incoming signal. The rate at which samples are taken is called the *sample rate* and is represented on the x-axis in the waveform illustrated in Figure 5.1.

Figure 5.1
Sample rate.

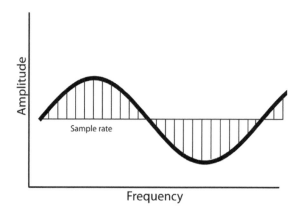

CD recordings use a rate of 44.1 kHz, or 44,100 samples per second, which is slightly higher than twice the range of human hearing of about 20 hertz to 20 kHz. The *Nyquist Theorem* suggests that a waveform may be accurately sampled and reproduced if the sample rate is twice the rate of the highest frequency, which is why that particular sample rate was chosen. The reason that a slightly higher number is used is that frequencies above the threshold of hearing may become truncated and enter the signal in the form of unwanted digital *artifacts*. Although this number seems high, it is interesting to note that modern studios often run at a rate of 96 kHz (or higher).

Purists sometimes say that analog recordings have more "warmth" and that digital recordings can sound "sterile." One of the reasons people may hear a difference in analog and digital recordings has to do with the fact that, by definition, the sampling process is leaving out some data. To illustrate the concept, it may be helpful to visualize a line drawn with traditional pen and paper with a line drawn on a computer screen. The "analog" line is continuous and, unless you were to look at the line under an electron microscope, the line represents a continuous flow of ink. The digital line, on the other hand, is represented by a finite number of pixels on the screen. It is not hard to see that such a line does not flow in the same sense as its analog counterpart. Similarly, analog tape, while it may add more noise to a signal, is a form of continuous recording that may provide a more natural-sounding representation of the original signal.

A related term, *bit depth*, refers to the number of bits used to represent a given amplitude. An 8-bit number provides only 256 discrete amplitude levels, whereas a 16-bit number provides 65,536 amplitude levels. Today, 24 bits (or more) are typically used in music production. (See Chapter 3 for a review of musical math terms such as *bit* and *word*.) To continue the analogy of a line, consider bit depth as it relates to color. If only 8 bits are used, colors will look primitive because the 256 colors provided by an 8-bit number are not sufficient to accurately represent subtle shades. Since a 16-bit number will provide thousands of shades of any one color, in the same way, an audio signal can be more accurately represented with additional bits. Common delivery formats include commercial CD (44.1 k sample rate/16 bit depth) and DAT tape (48 k sample rate/24 bit depth).

Data Compression

Uncompressed or raw audio files are large, so data compression is sometimes used to produce files that are smaller in size. Data compression can produce files that are *lossless* or *lossy*. With lossless compression, the original uncompressed data can be *exactly* reproduced through the decompression process. "Lossy" compression leaves some data out, and the uncompressed version is different than the original raw data. For this reason, uncompressed or lossless formats are always used for audio production. Lossy formats (such as MP3) are most appropriate in situations where file size and bandwidth are an issue, such as delivery of music over the Web or storing music in a portable player such as an iPod. Depending on the type of compression and other factors such as bit depth and sample rate, compression ratios of 10:1 (or higher) are possible.

To understand how compression works, it might be helpful to visualize the process of compressing a digitized picture. The picture in Figure 5.2 could be stored in a raw format where a number is used to represent the color of each point or pixel.

Figure 5.2
Compressing a simple picture.

If the dimensions of the picture are 1,000 × 1,000 pixels, and an 8-bit number is used to represent the color of each pixel, then 8,000,000 bits would be required to store this picture to disk. This particular picture could be efficiently stored with lossless compression. One way to achieve this would be to store a number representing the color and another number representing the number of consecutive pixels of the given color. In this way, the picture could be stored with just four numbers: white * 500,000, black * 500,000. Although this compression scheme is too simplistic to handle more complex types of photos, it demonstrates the basic concept of how lossless compression works. "Lossy" compression algorithms are very complex, and in the case of digital audio, these algorithms attempt to discard data that the listener would be unable to hear. Since the uncompressed version of a "lossy" file does not accurately represent the original data, the fidelity of these files will degrade as edits and data transfers occur.

Digital Audio Recording

The digital audio recording process involves several primary steps. First, the audio interface hardware is configured to the desired sample rate and resolution. Prior to tracking, a record path is established and input levels are optimized. The final steps involve editing and processing tracks. This section will look at the process of recording and editing digital audio tracks.

HARDWARE SETTINGS
A first step will likely be to use a device driver interface to establish settings such as sample rate and bit depth for the project at hand. This is not always a straightforward process since many variables come into play such as the available disk space, speed of the computer and hard drive, sample rates supported by digital audio hardware, and delivery format

required by a client. Figure 5.3 shows the type of settings available on most digital audio interfaces:

Figure 5.3
Device driver interface.

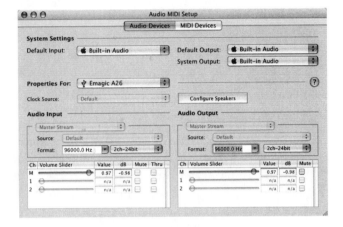

It is a good idea to avoid *up-sampling,* which means that a project is recorded at a sample rate such as 44.1 kHz and then converted to a higher rate such as 96 kHz. On the other hand, *down-sampling* may also be a consideration. In theory, a project recorded at a high sample rate is less susceptible to digital artifacts that result from the analog to digital conversion process. However, the process of down-sampling from a sample rate such as 48 kHz to 44.1 kHz can, in itself, add digital artifacts. In a sense, music that has been recorded and processed in this way undergoes the sampling process two times. In most cases, though, good results can be achieved by using a high sample rate throughout the production process and down-sampling to the destination format (such as CD-quality 44.1 kHz) when bouncing the final master to disk. To avoid up-sampling or down-sampling, it is important to use a consistent sample rate and bit depth throughout the production process.

It is often necessary to adjust the audio buffer settings in order to balance track count with latency. Since smaller buffer settings can cause the computer to work harder, take time to test buffer settings before the start of a session. If the computer is pushed too hard, it will simply stop recording and prompt the user with an error message—clearly not helpful in the middle of a session!

SETTING THE AUDIO PATH

It is important to develop a consistent file management and backup strategy when doing digital audio recording. It is very easy to import files from several sources and end up with a project that references files in a number of different folders scattered throughout a hard drive. This can make for a time-consuming process to reorganize project files so that a project can be archived or moved to a new system. Most programs provide the option of selecting a project folder for audio files, and it is a good idea to set the path to an appropriate location at the start of a new project. When importing files from alternate locations, it is a good idea to copy the file to the current project directory so that all project data is stored in the same place. Some programs provide an archive function that can be used to automatically copy externally referenced files the project folder. It is important to know that most DAW programs do not store audio files *within* a document file, so it is important to back up both the document file and any referenced audio files.

OPTIMIZING INPUT LEVELS

Once an audio interface has been configured and the software is set up to record audio to a predetermined location, it is time to optimize input levels. When recording a line-level source such as an analog synthesizer, it is best to turn up the volume on the instrument and then adjust the input trim on the mixer and/or audio interface. When an instrument sends a "hot" signal, the signal will need less amplification at the input stage, resulting in a better *signal-to-noise ratio*. Signal-to-noise ratio can be visualized in this way: consider a weak instrument signal that is outputting at 10% of its optimal level. At 10%, there is a greater percentage of noise to good signal. When a noisy signal is amplified using a trim control or fader, both the noise and clean signal are raised, resulting in unwanted noise. If the same instrument is sending a signal of 90% of its optimal level, there is a much lower percentage of unwanted line noise, and when the overall signal is increased at the input stage, the signal to noise ratio stays at an appropriate level (see Figure 5.4).

Figure 5.4
Signal to noise ratio.

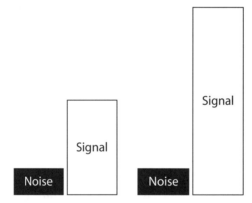

It's also a good idea to make sure an input signal isn't running too hot; some keyboards and other instruments may cause clipping when their output level is set to maximum.

POSITIONING A MICROPHONE

The position of a microphone is crucial to attain the desired sound and minimize unwanted noise and other problems. For many years, I was apprehensive about doing my own audio recording because I felt that I lacked the pedigree to achieve professional results. After all, how could I hope to compete with a well-trained audio engineer equipped with a pristine recording room and an arsenal of high-end microphones? In a word, it is not possible to compete under those circumstances, and I never hesitate to hire the services of a professional facility when necessary. As a matter of practicality, however, it is often necessary to record homespun tracks, and I have found the process to be both enjoyable and liberating.

One thing I have noticed in working with many good engineers is that there is often no best way to position a microphone. Technical concepts can help to narrow the choices, but at the end of the day, the microphone should be positioned where it sounds best for the task at hand. This is a big part of the *art* of recording science that a good engineer brings to the table. I have found the following concepts to be a helpful starting point when experimenting with microphone placement (note that common microphones and pickup characteristics are covered in Chapter 2, "Setting Up a Project Studio").

Distance from the sound source. Increasing the distance between a microphone and a sound source will result in more room ambiance and a less present sound. Jazz and classical recordings are often recorded in this way in order to achieve a natural acoustic sound. Distance miking is also useful in preserving the natural balance of instrumental ensembles and choirs or to record ambient sounds such as when placing a pair of microphones a few feet over a drum kit. In contrast, close microphone placement will minimize the effect of room acoustics and maximize the presence of the sound source. The advantage of this method is that the engineer maintains more control over the process: Varying amounts of reverb, delay, and other types of processing can be added as necessary. Close miking is also useful for minimizing bleed from other instruments when simultaneously recording several instruments.

Position. Each acoustic instrument has unique sound-producing characteristics, and there are usually a number of ways to effectively record these sources. Consider an acoustic guitar: Sound resonates in the body of the instrument and emanates from a sound hole. The fretboard provides another important sound component. For this reason, many engineers place one microphone near the sound hole and another near the fretboard. (Some engineers recommend the 12th fret as a good starting point.) In a similar way, an engineer, when recording a flute, may elect to place a microphone close to the head joint in order to pick up both the sound of the flute and the sound of air passing over the mouthpiece.

Proximity effect. Directional microphones exhibit an increase in bass response when placed very near to a sound source (about an inch away). The effect can be useful for creating a bigger or more robust sound when recording vocals. For other sources, it may be necessary to turn on a low-frequency filter or use an omnidirectional microphone.

Orientation of the microphone. Microphones respond differently to *off-axis* sounds (sounds that hit the microphone from the side) than to sounds that are placed in front of the diaphragm. It can be advantageous to experiment with off-axis positions when recording some instruments such as an electric guitar. The combination of microphone distance and orientation provides a wide range of sonic possibilities.

Avoiding pops. When close-miking a voice, it is usually necessary to place a *pop screen* between the microphone and the vocalist in order to avoid pops that result from singing words such as *people*. To see how this works, hold your hand about an inch away from your mouth and say the word "people" and then say the word "hello." You can actually feel the *plosive* on your hand. A pop screen prevents the burst of air from directly interfering with the microphone diaphragm. Off-axis microphone placement can also help with plosive sounds.

Stereo techniques. It is often desirable to record sources such as an acoustic piano in stereo, but care must be taken to avoid *phase* issues when using two microphones on a source. If identical signals are out of phase, the signals effectively cancel each other out (see Figure 5.5).

Figure 5.5
Out-of-phase signals cancel each other out.

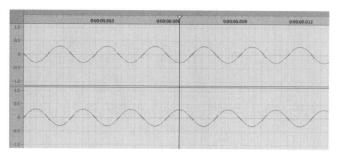

To see how phase issues can be problematic, import a mono wave file into your DAW software. Create a copy of the clip on an adjacent track but edit the second clip so that it is inverted (most programs provide an inversion function). Play back both tracks and you will hear that the clips effectively cancel each other out! Although it is unlikely that two identical signals would be perfectly out of phase as with this example, problems can result when two similar signals are slightly out of phase. Symptoms are a sound that might be described as thin or "phasey." These problems can result when two microphones are placed such that the signal arrives at one of the microphones with a substantial time delay. Phase issues can also result from differences in the *polarity* of microphones. For example, if the polarity of two microphones is reversed, the signals can cancel each other out. Fortunately, in digital audio recording these types of problems can usually be fixed by using an inverse function as described above.

Several common stereo recording techniques are frequently employed by engineers. In a *coincident* or *X/Y* setup, two matched directional microphones are placed on top of one another so that each diaphragm points to an alternate side of the sound source. The width of the stereo image can be controlled by varying the angle between the two microphones (see Figure 5.6).

A similar technique called M-S (middle side) uses two microphones, but the output is routed through a *sum and difference* matrix. As David Miles Huber describes in his book, *Microphone Manual: Design and Application* (Hayden Books, 1988), the output of the two signals are processed by the network into a conventional X/Y stereo signal (M + S) and (M − S). The primary advantage of this setup is to avoid phase problems associated with converting coincident microphones to mono: the sum of the signals $(M + S) + (M - S)$ is 2M.

Figure 5.6
Coincident miking.

Another technique, called *near coincident* placement, is useful in some situations. Here, a matched pair of microphones are placed close together but with enough separation so that some delay is evident. Unlike coincident placement, the microphones are oriented away from the centerline (see Figure 5.7). Many variations can be achieved by adjusting the separation and angle of the microphones.

Figure 5.7
Near coincident miking.

One other technique, called *spaced microphone* placement involves placing two microphones perpendicular to one another in front of a sound source (see Figure 5.8). In most instances, it is desirable to place the microphones so that three units of separation are used for every unit of distance from the sound source. This "three-to-one" rule can help avoid the phase problems mentioned in the previous section.

Figure 5.8
Spaced microphone technique: 3-1 ratio.

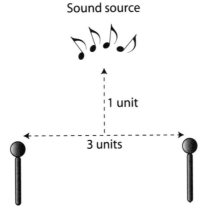

Because it can be tricky to place microphones properly when recording in stereo, many musicians elect to purchase a dedicated stereo microphone. These microphones offer many benefits such as optimal orientation of the capsules and, in many cases, the ability to adjust the width of the stereo image. With that said, a pair of matched microphones offers greater flexibility and can also be used when recording a variety of mono sources.

TRACKING

The recording or tracking phase involves arming tracks and recording a performance to disk. When tracking, it is a good idea to keep notes about placement of microphones and other details such as the mic type and polar pattern should you need to re-record a section at a later date. It is also important to adjust the input gain to avoid distortion should a performer hit a particularly strident note.

During the tracking process, it is common that a musician may want to *punch in* a few bars of an otherwise good take. All digital audio workstations provide the capability to punch in a region, and the process is nearly identical on all of the primary DAWs: First, left and right locators are set to an appropriate location in the song. Next, the punch-in mode is enabled. This means that, even though the record button is pressed, recording will only occur in the punch-in zone as determined by the locators. Finally, the recording process is started and the software will record audio or MIDI in the punch-in region (see Figure 5.9).

Figure 5.9
Setting up a punch-in location.

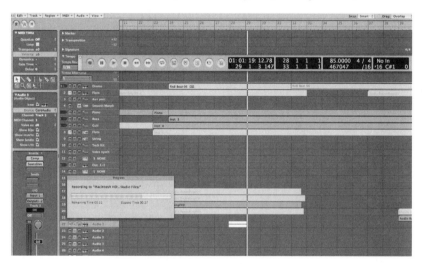

A *composite track* is often used when recording vocals or instrumental solos. The idea is that the musician records multiple versions of the same solo. Each version is placed on a separate track, and a composite track is created by cutting and pasting the best phrases from each take.

SIGNAL FLOW

I talked about the concept of signal flow in Chapter 2, but a brief review will be helpful for visualizing the flow of signals in digital audio software.

In a traditional analog console or virtual mixer, a signal enters at the top of a channel strip and flows downward until it becomes a part of the *main bus*. A channel fader controls the amount of signal added to the main bus. When the signal first enters a channel strip, a *trim* control may be used to optimize the level of the incoming signal. Next, inserts provide an opportunity to tap into the signal in order to apply compression, equalization, or another type of processing.

As you learned in Chapter 2, the term *bus* reflects signals that flow from left to right, and most virtual mixers provide the ability to send the incoming signal to a sub bus or auxiliary send. In Figure 5.10, channels one and two are sending a signal on sub-bus one. Processed sound is routed back to the mixer via the sub-bus return. In this instance, since a reverb is inserted into the signal path of the sub bus, tracks one and two will be processed with reverb, and the subfader is used to adjust the amount of processed signal added to the main mix. This technique can provide a good way to conserve computer-processing power since a single effect can be used for more than one channel.

Figure 5.10
Using an auxiliary send and return for reverb.

Separate sends may be provided for routing a signal to a subbus. For example, it is often useful to control multiple tracks with a single sub-bus fader (see Figure 5.11). In this instance, the output of tracks one and two is routed to a sub bus so that a single fader can be used to control the volume of two or more tracks. One way that a sub bus can be useful is for routing several drum tracks to a single bus. Once the relative level of the drums have been mixed, a single sub-bus fader can be used to control the level of the entire drum kit.

Figure 5.11
Routing multiple tracks to a single sub bus.

PRE/POST SENDS

Sends can generally be configured as "pre" or "post" fader. The post-fader setting is most common. When a send is configured as post fader, the amount of signal sent to the send is proportional to the level of the channel fader. For example, if a post fader is used to route a signal to a reverb unit, the effect disappears as the channel level is turned down. The pre-fader setting is useful for monitoring purposes. It would make sense to configure a headphone mix using pre-fader sends so that adjustments in channel volume (such as a fade-out at the end of a tune) do not have an effect on the amount of signal heard in the headphone mix.

Signal Processing

Modern DAW software provides many useful signal processing tools. Some processors such as *vocoders* are useful in creating special vocal effects, while other tools may provide the ability to model various types of amplifiers or microphones. The tools listed in the next few paragraphs are the ones most commonly used in audio production.

When selecting a tool such as a compressor or reverb, you need to decide how to route a signal to and from the processing tool. Dynamic processors such as compressors, limiters, and noise gates should always be inserted directly into a channel, a pre-fader sub bus, or at the main output so that the processor can work with the entire signal. Effects such as reverb or delay are typically configured to work on a portion of one or more signals. Auxiliary sends and returns are used for this purpose. (Note than an auxiliary is a type of subbus, so this term might be used depending on the audio application.) Take care that effects or other types of processing are not recorded to disk during the tracking phase. In most cases it's best to record a clean sound so that effects and equalization can be adjusted during the mixing phase.

COMPRESSION

At first glance, compressors may seem counterintuitive. These devices are used to "pump up" a single track or an entire recording, but they work by reducing or attenuating a signal. When dynamics are controlled with compression, the result is that less contrast exists between loud and soft signals and overall track gain can be increased or more easily controlled. Compression is often helpful on vocal tracks. A singer may sing in a full voice at one point in the song and whisper or coo at another point. Assuming that backing tracks are of a similar level and density in each section, it will be impossible to bring a whispered part to the front of the mix. Compression, when applied to the vocal part, enables a whispered section to be closer in dynamic level to a section in full voice.

A *threshold* setting is used to determine when a signal should be attenuated. If the signal exceeds the threshold, the compressor will reduce the signal. The amount of reduction is determined by the *compression ratio.* The compression ratio is the amount of input signal required to cause a 1 dB increase in output. If a ratio of 4:1 were used, a 6 dB increase in input would result in a 2 dB increase in output. Larger ratios provide more aggressive compression and might be suitable for a drum or vocal track. Smaller ratios are typically used to subtly enhance a recording during the mastering phase.

Compressors provide an *attack* and *release* setting to determine the speed at which compression is applied and released to a signal. There are no hard and fast rules, but the attack and release settings should be set to enhance the musical material in a natural-sounding way. For example, if the release time is too short, *pumping* may be heard. Compressors may have a hard or soft knee. With a hard knee, the full amount of compression is applied when the threshold is reached. In contrast, a soft knee gradually increases the amount of compression based on incoming signal level. For this reason, a soft-knee compressor will provide a more subtle application of compression to an audio signal. Figure 5.12 shows a compressor in action.

Figure 5.12
Applying compression to a track.

A compressor is one of the most helpful audio tools, but compression has become a source of contention in the music industry. When compression is overused, music loses dynamic contrast, and many people suggest that overly compressed tracks are tiresome to listen to. In popular music recordings, engineers may compress many individual tracks, and compression may also be applied to an entire song during the mastering phase. There is no question that compressors can help to give a track that "in your face" sound, but, as with all things musical, you will want to experiment and use the technology judiciously.

LIMITER

A limiter provides an extreme form of compression, usually with a ratio of 10:1 or higher (see Figure 5.13). Consider a piano part that is relatively soft but contains a few distortion-causing peaks: A limiter can be used to attenuate those peaks so that they do not cause distortion. An alternative is to turn down the input level of the signal, but that is not always an ideal choice since more signal noise would be evident if the overall input level is turned down.

Figure 5.13
A limiter.

EXPANDER

Where a compressor decreases dynamic range as determined by the threshold setting, an expander increases dynamic range. An expander can be used to emphasize transients in a track that has been compressed. Depending on the settings of the unit, an expander can also function as a noise reduction tool where unwanted noise below the threshold is reduced. As you can see in Figure 5.14, an expander has the same primary controls as a compressor.

Figure 5.14
An expander.

NOISE GATE

A noise gate can be used to clean up a track that suffers from background noise such as a fan or noisy guitar amp. Signals that fall below a defined threshold are muted, while signals above the threshold are allowed to pass. In general, the attack and release parameters should be set to match the musical material. For example, a short attack and release is more appropriate for a snare drum, and a slower attack and release would work better for a slowly evolving synthesizer pad. A *side-chain filter* can be useful in isolating a particular frequency component of the signal. A hi-hat will tend to bleed into a snare microphone and may inadvertently trigger a noise gate on the snare channel. A low-pass filter could be used to isolate the sound of the snare so that the gate is triggered only by the lower-frequency snare sounds.

EQUALIZATION

Equalization (EQ) is the process of fixing or enhancing the frequency response of one or more signals. EQ can be used to fix problems with a microphone, room, or instrument or to provide a better blend when mixing instruments that share the same portion of the frequency spectrum. EQ can also be used to fix problems with bleed between microphones (rolling off the low end of a hi-hat channel, for example). Of course, equalization can also be used for purely artistic reasons such as to add more "sizzle" to a hi-hat part or emphasize the midrange of a lead vocal.

When adjusting settings on an external equalizer or EQ plug-in, it is helpful to remember that adjustments will affect frequencies on each side of the selected frequency. The term *Q factor* is often used to describe the width or *bandwidth* of the resulting bell curve (see Figure 5.15). In this example, a bell curve is centered around 500 Hz. Frequencies near the center of the bell are moderately affected, while frequencies near the ends of the bell curve are minimally affected.

Figure 5.15
An equalization curve.

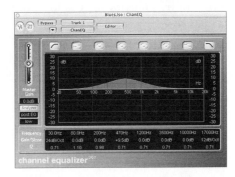

One of the most common equalizers, a *parametric EQ*, provides several selectable frequency bands in which the center frequency and bandwidth can be adjusted for each frequency band. Parametric equalization allows bands to overlap, producing a smooth response curve between each band (see Figure 5.16). In this example, a bell curve is centered around 290 Hz, and another bell curve is centered around 3,600 Hz.

Figure 5.16
Parametric equalization: multiple
response curves.

In contrast, a *graphic equalizer* provides numerous bands that can be cut or boosted with a series of sliders (see Figure 5.17).

Figure 5.17
A graphic equalizer.

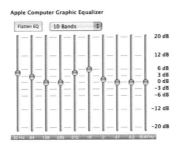

A special type of equalization is provided by *high-pass, low-pass, band-pass,* and *notch* filters. Filters will be covered in more detail in Chapter 6, "Music Synthesis," but the terms are presented at this point because filters can be useful in the equalization process. As the name implies, a high-pass filter allows higher frequencies to pass while removing lower frequencies. A low-pass filter works in a similar way but is used to remove high frequencies. A band-pass filter, a combination of high- and low-pass filters, can be used to allow only a specific range of frequencies to pass and will provide settings for adjusting both the low and high frequency cutoff. Notch filters are used to remove a specific range of frequencies such as to minimize problems with 60-cycle hum in a live recording.

As with all things musical, using equalizers is largely a matter of using your ears to make adjustments, but the following tips may provide a useful starting point.

▶ It is generally best to avoid adding equalization during the recording process. In the days of analog recording, equalization was required to minimize tape hiss, but in a digital world it's best not to commit to a particular equalization setting until the mixing phase.

▶ Be aware that boosting EQ can increase the loudness or intensity of a sound source. This will usually require level adjustments.

▶ Consider turning up the level of a given band and use the frequency setting to sweep through the spectrum to zero in on a problem frequency.

REVERB

Reverb is used to simulate the effect of sound waves as they interact with the physical characteristics of a room. Reverb units provide the ability to control the length of reverberation as well as the mix between dry (unprocessed) and wet (reverberant) sound. Many plug-ins can be edited to simulate a variety of room shapes and sizes and may provide options to control early reflections.

When using reverb, it is helpful to consider that different styles of music require different approaches. By way of example, classical recordings often utilize longer reverberations than popular music recordings. One way to approach adding reverb to a classical recording (such as a string quartet) is to use a single reverb plug-in on the main bus. In this way, reverb can be used to simulate the effect of having multiple instruments in a large performance hall. (I used this approach on the composition titled "Lullaby for Emily" on the accompanying CD.) In contrast, a different approach is often used for pop or rock recordings. One approach is to use an auxiliary send for reverb so that differing amounts of signal can be sent from each channel—a snare drum might require less reverb than the lead vocal, for example. Another approach is to use a dedicated reverb unit on each channel. Although this approach was impractical in the days of analog recording (most studios do not have an unlimited number of external reverb units), this type of approach is viable with modern DAW software. Keep in mind that multiple reverbs can have a tendency to muddy a mix, so it is often best to use multiple reverbs judiciously. I often find it useful to assign a reverb on an auxiliary send for use in sweetening backing tracks and another reverb dedicated to sweetening a lead vocal or horn part.

DELAY

A delay unit is used to create echo effects, although shorter delay times can be used to simulate the sound of multiple sound sources for effective doubling. For example, it is possible to mimic the sound of a choir by recording a few singers and running the signal through both a delay and reverb unit.

Delay can also be useful for positioning of instruments. One of the ways we can determine the location of a sound is the slight difference in time it takes a sound to reach each ear, and, as such delay can be useful in mimicking this effect. An interesting way to explore this phenomenon is to record or import a sample of a percussive sound such as a clave. Loop the track and listen with headphones as you add a delay to either the right or left channel. In this way it is possible to position the sound in the stereo field without using panning. When combined with reverb, delay can help to produce a three-dimensional mix.

The Mixing Process

Many books have been written on the topic of mixing and mastering, but it is probably safe to say that there are as many ways to mix as there are to perform. It is also true that each project may require a slightly different approach, and the success of a project is dependent on many factors such as the selection and placement of microphones and quality of the performance. For these reasons, mixing and mastering is truly an art that requires time and attention to develop.

Having taught ear training for many years, I feel confident in saying that our ears can be developed through attentive practice. In my own case, I have developed the ability to transcribe complex music by performers such as Oscar Peterson and Art Tatum—something that would have been well beyond my ability level in college. In a similar way, I have noticed that most of my mixes are better than they were five years ago (and I hope they are much better five years from now)! I freely admit that my skills as a mixer and producer are not as advanced as engineers who spend the majority of each day mixing music. However, I have noticed that as I concentrate on evaluating subtleties in a mix, my ears have begun to improve in this regard. My best advice is to develop the habit of listening critically so that your ears develop a sensitivity to the subtle nuances of a mix.

I find the following concepts to be useful during the mixing phase of a project.

▶ In general, instruments that share the same frequency range should not be placed on top of one another.

▶ Equalization can be useful in cleaning up a muddy mix. For example, equalization can be used to tone down low frequencies in a boomy bass, or a subtle emphasis of mid range frequencies can bring a lead vocal to the front of a mix.

▶ Use a combination of panning, volume, and equalization so that each instrument or voice has "its own space."

▶ If an instrument is too far in the background, consider turning other tracks down instead of necessarily increasing the volume of a given track. Panning can also have an effect on the perceived loudness of a track.

▶ Consider using compression in situations where one or more instruments tend to occasionally drop out of a mix—this is particularly true for commercial recordings.

▶ Frequently mute and solo tracks in order to determine how each track fits within the mix as a whole.

▶ Always trust your ears over visual slider or knob settings when adjusting volume, pan, or equalization.

▶ Mix at a low volume. A mix that sounds good when played quietly usually translates to a mix that sounds good at higher volume, but the reverse is rarely true.

▶ Take occasional breaks; ear fatigue is a reality and can undermine the mixing process.

▶ Listen to your work in a variety of rooms on professional and consumer playback systems.

▶ Solicit feedback from friends and professionals.

▶ Know when a mix is finished. It is easy to tweak a mix to death, so keep an ear open to the possibility that a mix is finished. If a project sounds great then it's time to move on.

Digital Audio Editing

The next few paragraphs will explore common editing techniques available on most digital audio workstations and two-track editors. Although modern DAW software can be very complex, the majority of editing tasks involve simple procedures that are akin to the process of creating and editing a word processing document. With a little practice, you will feel comfortable using any digital audio editing program.

RIPPING AND BURNING CDS

Most programs provide an "Import" option to rip audio from a CD. Be sure to select an appropriate file format before ripping a track. For example, you will probably want to select the same sample rate and bit depth as the CD (16-bit, 44.1 kHz) unless your goal is to create a "lossy" version of the file such as an MP3 for delivery over the Web.

A number of methods are used to burn audio CDs, but a common method is to use your DAW to bounce a master mix to disk (typically in the form of a stereo .wav file). Once files have been bounced to disk, the files can be imported into specialized CD burning software such as CD Architect (Sony) or WaveBurner (Apple). These types of tools offer the flexibility of adjusting the amount of time between tracks, control over the relative volume of each track, and many other options. An optional intermediate step is to edit each stereo master in a dedicated two-track editor such as Peak (Bias) or Sound Forge (Sony) in order to tweak the start and end of a file or to normalize or otherwise process the final master.

PLAYBACK AND LOOPING

Nearly all DAW programs use the spacebar to toggle between playback and stop modes. A loop button, usually located near the playback controls, can be used to loop a selected region (see Figure 5.18). This can be useful when preparing a file for use in loop editing software (see Chapter 7, "Loop-Based Production") or to zero in on an audio defect. Along these lines, audio "scrubbing" can usually be achieved by dragging the insertion point marker with the mouse. Scrubbing is useful for finding a specific spot such as a click or pop that is evident in a recording. The process is similar to playing back and rewinding a tape machine in slow motion.

Figure 5.18
Audio looping.

ZOOMING

It is often necessary to zoom in on a portion of a file in order to cut or paste a region. Most programs provide a button in the form of a magnifier or telescope that can be used for zooming, but key commands are more efficient. Since most digital audio editing requires a fair amount of zooming, it's a good idea to learn the key commands for these important functions.

SELECTING A REGION OF FILE

Click and drag to select a region in an audio file. The selected region can then be normalized or otherwise processed (see below). Most programs default to loop playback mode when a region is selected, and this can be a convenient way to check that you have selected an appropriate region (see Figure 5.19).

Figure 5.19
Selecting a region prior to truncating the file.

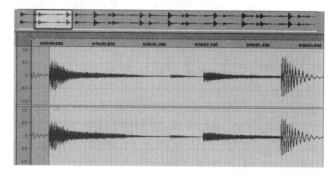

COMMON PROCESSING OPTIONS

Once a region has been selected, many processing options will be available. Common functions include fade-in or fade-out (which are self-explanatory), normalization, inversion, time stretching, equalization, and effects such as reverb and delay.

Normalization

Normalization, which is usually applied to an entire file, is used to optimize signal levels. When a file is normalized, the software searches the file for the highest peak and increases the level of this peak to a maximum value as determined by the user. All other amplitude levels are raised a proportional amount. Normalization is typically used to adjust the level of one or more tracks prior to burning a CD master. For example, the difference in levels between a tender ballad and an up-tempo number might be too extreme, so normalization can be used to bring up the level of a track that is too quiet.

Invert

As mentioned previously in the chapter, waveforms can be inverted in order to fix phase problems. If a stereo track sounds "phasey" or too thin, consider inverting one of the channels as a possible solution.

Time Stretch

Time stretching can be used to fit an existing track into a specified amount of time. For example, a 32-second clip can be made to fit within the time parameters of a 30-second jingle. In most cases, extreme time (or pitch) stretching will cause audible artifacts, so the function is generally useful for subtle changes in the length of a clip.

Applying Effects

Unlike effect inserts that are used with multi-track editors, most two-track editors destructively apply effects such as reverb and delay. *Destructive* editing means that the underlying file is changed. Often, only one level of undo is provided, so use destructive functions judiciously. Some programs, such as Apple's Soundtrack Pro, provide editing "layers" that leave the underlying data intact. Layers can be undone at any time unless a file is stored with "flattened" layers, in which case the edits are destructively applied to a file.

CUT, COPY, DELETE, PASTE, AND MERGE

As I mentioned previously, cutting and pasting works in the same way as editing a word processing document. Simply select a region and choose the appropriate option from the Edit menu. One difference is that, when pasting data, clips can be inserted or merged. When inserting a clip, data to the right of the insertion point is moved to make room for the clip. When merging a clip, the source and destination clips are blended by a percentage as determined by the user (see Figure 5.20).

Figure 5.20
Selecting a merge ratio.

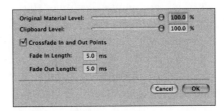

CROSSFADES

It is usually desirable to create a seamless fade between overlapping audio files to avoid an audible click. The term *crossfade* is used to describe the process of fading one clip out as another one fades in. Crossfading is one of the most useful digital editing functions because it can be used for many types of detailed editing such as seamlessly inserting a single note. In most cases, the fade-in and fade-out envelope can be independently adjusted. Figure 5.21 shows a typical crossfade overlay.

Figure 5.21
Crossfade overlay.

Mixing Tips

I asked two professional engineers if they would respond to a series of questions about the mixing process. The following tips come from audio professionals who write, record, and produce music for a living.

BILL BYRNE: COMPOSER/PRODUCER

For the last 22 years, Bill Byrne has composed and produced memorable music for clients around the world. Included in that list of clients are the ABC, CBS, NBC, FOX, and UPN television networks. Some shows that his work has been heard on include *Home Improvement—Backstage Pass final episode, The Oprah Winfrey Show, Regis and Kathy Lee, Major League Baseball, The Tony Danza Show, Switched!, Nick and Jessica,* the opening to *Monday Night Football*, and many other ads, show openers and theatrical trailers.

From 1997 through 2005, Byrne, with partner Brock Walsh, has created the main Network Image music campaigns for CBS Television, and countless other promotional scores for all of CBS's hit shows.

Byrne has won many awards for his work, including the International Monitor Awards, PROMAX Gold and Silver Medallions, Addys, the Northwest Regional Emmy, and Media Inc.'s Hall of Fame Award.

My approach to mixing over the years has remained quite a bit the same in some ways, and in others, changed quite radically. Early on in my career I was lucky enough to study a bit under a Grammy nominated engineer, who stressed the importance of getting a great sound from the room, players, and microphones first, before ever turning to EQ and outboard processing. (This was also born out of necessity in that the console I owned at the time had EQ that was designed for "sweetening" with high, mid, and low knobs at fixed frequencies and no Q.) I've been lucky enough to be at some wonderful film and TV sessions where this concept really hit home. These sessions were set up with 20- to 30-piece groups, or full orchestras, the studios sounded great, the mic selection and placement was fabulous, and done with all top-flight players. The conductor starts, the engineer presses record, and more often than not the live two-track master would be what aired in the show or film, with the 24-track being made only for safety and archival purposes. Great recording rooms, excellent mic technique, and wonderful players.

On a smaller scale, recording the drum kit is a good example of the importance of this concept. When I first started recording it was on a two-track reel-to-reel, then 4, 8, 16, and eventually 24 tracks. (It wasn't because the technology didn't exist, I just couldn't afford it and had to slowly buy my way up!) With the smaller tape track count we would combine the bass, drums, guitar, etc. on one channel, and the vocals on the other. You had to get it right going down, 'cause that's the way it was gonna stay! As we got more tracks, we would try to isolate the instruments on separate tracks. This led to using 8 or more channels for drums; kick, snare top, snare bottom, hi-hats, stereo toms, and stereo overheads, room mics, etc. It also led me to forget what I had learned. I was so into the idea of being able to process each individual track that I lost sight of what really mattered: the sound of the room, the tuning of the drums, which is absolutely critical; the mics and placement, and how they are played. I've spent many a wasted hour in mixing trying to make a kick or snare drum sound great, when it never did in the first place.

Eventually I got tired of twiddling and wasting mix hours and went back to the basics—record in a room that sounds good; if it doesn't, work on making it sound better. Hang some blankets or foam to get rid of bad reflections, try positioning some reflective surfaces to liven it up if it's dead. Then spend the majority of time on the kit (or whatever source you're recording), listen to the sound of the drums in the room. Do they sound great? Is the snare right for the track, do the toms ring, etc.? Make the drums sound great first, then put up a stereo pair or even a single mic. In the control room, do the drums sound like they did when you were in the studio? Adjust the placement of the mics, or the type of mic you use. Great cables make a big difference too. Get it to sound the way you want it in the room, then set up the rest of the close mics (making sure to check the mics to make sure they are in phase). Nowadays I find myself using the overhead mics much more than I ever used to. (Led Zeppelin is a good example of a great "big drum" sound, many times using only three mics.)

These principles apply to any live source. Got an acoustic guitar that doesn't sound the way that you want it to? Same principles: listen to the room; does the guitar sound better in the corner, the middle, with gobos, etc.? Listen to the guitar, maybe you need to get a different one for the session? Got the guitar sounding the way you want in the room? Listen to the sound in the control room; does it sound like it did in the room? Move the mic, change the mic, don't just reach for the EQ or processor. Consider using these only after things are sounding great. (Of course if you can afford it, a great mic preamp can only make things better.) Remember, GIGO—garbage in, garbage out—the time you spend mixing is in direct proportion to the recording quality—great recording, quick mix.

Another concept that I've tried to keep over the years is whenever possible lay out your tracks in the same place every time. For example:

Channel 1	*Kick*
Channel 2	*Snare Top*
Channel 3	*Snare Bottom*
Channel 4	*Hats*
Channel 5	*Toms L*
Channel 6	*Toms R*
Channel 7	*OH L*
Channel 8	*OH R*
Channel 9	*Bass*
Channel 10–14	*Guitars*
Channel 15–19	*Keys and extra Percussion*
Channel 20–24	*Vocals*

This will help you get quickly through mixes by generally being instantly familiar with where things are all the time. I also lay out my tracks in my DAW this way so they match the console. I have templates set up so the tracks are laid out this way, and in folders so that you can easily mute, solo, and edit, etc. similar groups of tracks.

For me this was also born out of necessity. I have to get so much music out quickly, that more often than not I don't have the time to make proper track sheets (which is a very bad habit!). Always laying things out the same leads to familiarity, especially important in the heat of battle with tight deadlines. This method was also extremely important when I used to own a fairly large commercial music house with four composers working in different studios at the same time. We were always able to go into each other's studio to collaborate, track, and mix quickly without spending a lot of time getting familiar with the layout of the tracks because they were generally always the same.

Another mix technique that has remained with me is to first cut EQ before boosting. If you're having trouble with the low frequencies, don't turn up the highs, roll back the lows first. Get the sound close to the way you like it using EQ cutting, then add a bit of high or mid EQ to finish. Remember to regularly check your mix in mono—this will help you detect any phase problems and get a good sense of the balance. I also keep a decibel meter next to my board at all times. I try to keep under 85 dB for the most part, though at times I do crank it up (never past 95). The louder it is when writing and tracking during the day, the less effective I am late in the day at getting the final mix out. Whenever I try to fool myself into thinking it's not too loud, a quick check of the dB meter puts me in my place. Try to step out of the room regularly to clear your ears. Also, listening from down the hall, outside the control room gives a whole new perspective to the mix balance as well. Make a temp CD, play it in the car, on a boom box, TV, or computer, etc.

For me, digital brought about the most change in my technique. I started as an analog guy, before personal computers, MIDI, and digital recording and editing. Automating a mix meant gathering up your friends to grab a set of faders, then using masking tape and colored pencils to mark the various level changes. With tape rolling and all hands flying we'd give it our best. We'd practice a few times and hope to get it right. We would record the various passes or sections on two-track tape, then later go back with the razor blade and edit the various sections together. Many times we would get some wonderful mixes by sort of "playing the board" like a musical instrument and capturing the results on tape. Sometimes I do miss this spontaneity.

The next step up was basic automation on the console with Voltage Controlled Amplifiers, VCAs, or Flying Faders. Then came total recall of console parameters. This was followed by affordable small-format digital consoles such as the Yamaha O2R and Mackie D8b. They are wonderful tools for getting great mixes, however with one small drawback—the resolution of the faders. Because they are digital, there are limited amounts of measurements or "steps" built into to the software to tell the computer how far the fader has moved. If you put a 1 kHz test tone through a channel and then move the fader, you can hear this "zippering" effect, which is certainly not that musical.

This led to the greatest change in my mixing technique. As computers grew more powerful, so did the ability of the DAW software. Now I generally do all my mixing inside the DAW and just use the console as a big router for all my various digital cards, and some analog stuff. With computers now running at 2+ GHz, the powered software plug-ins from companies such as UAD and TC now sound nearly as good as the original equipment they are emulating. Also they are far cheaper than the originals and do not require a full-time tech guy to keep them working. Of course as you add more plug-ins, it increases latency, the time it takes to process the task. The program I use most frequently, Cubase SX 3, has "plug-in delay compensation" built into the program. It goes through the various channels and automatically adjusts the timing to compensate for the latency of the plug-ins. For me this is absolutely essential! Uncorrected, the timing differences introduced by latency are for me musically unacceptable.

Initially I didn't like the automation built into DAWs, due to their limited resolution and editing. Also, using the mouse to mix with didn't excite me that much. However, now with the ability to use MIDI control surfaces and the improved editing features, I am comfortable writing and editing my automation in the DAW. Also, for my projects, time is of essence, and the ability to have everything recalled with one file is great. It also makes multiple revisions much easier.

Sometimes I still miss the 'old school' way, but the demands of today's projects just don't allow the time. I think through all of this though, the single most important lesson that I've learned is: Make the composition and the arrangement great, and you'll spend a lot less time on "fixing it in the mix." Fancy production tricks can certainly help, but they are not a substitute for great melodies and orchestration, performed by real people.

STEVEN HELLER: COMPOSER/PRODUCER

Steven Heller is a three-time Grammy-Award-winning producer and composer whose work has spanned the full spectrum of audio and video production—from CDs and live concerts to television and movie scores. He has received numerous national awards for his music and recordings, including the American Library Association's Notable Children's Recording Award, various Parent's Choice Awards, and Grammys for his production of David Holt's CD of the popular children's story, *Stellaluna*, and most recently for engineering and production of Legacy, featuring Doc Watson and David Holt.

I like to do all the technical tasks during the first session. Set up the busses, clean the tracks, etc., so I won't have to deal with mindless chores when I am in the groove. I usually set up the same for every piece, so I know where to look for the bass or the chorus vocals. I will set up groups, bus EQs, reverb sends, etc. I click out the reverb lengths to the metronome markings so I don't smear the material with out-of-time-reverb.

EQ and compression is always specific to the material—that is, if the project is acoustic or "organic," I will want the dynamics to be natural, so I will allow for a wide dynamic range. I will do a quick mix before I start over thinking the song. Like a live to two-track. I save it.

If there is time (money), I will listen to all the tracks in the project, do a quick mix of each before I get down to the real mix. If I don't get a quick feel for the material, I will bounce it to my iPod and listen to the roughs a few times in a few days, so that when I approach the mix, I am familiar with the material.

I use EQ to fix problems in the mic technique, instrument, or room. As subtle as possible. Ring out the EQ to find the trouble spots, then reduce as little as possible. I will also use EQ to make room for lead lines or layers— that is, when an overdub or layer is in generally the same range as other instruments in the mix, I will either pan away from the like tones or I will EQ the substrates during the lead sections.

Mixing mono in the beginning is a great technique to locate problem areas in the arrangement. Plus, when you switch back to stereo you feel alive again!

I keep the decibel level down at first, or I listen through a boom box. This is hard if there are clients in the room who want the satisfaction of hearing their material at 110 dB. If they want that, put up a rough mix, turn it up, and leave it playing while you get a drink or make a call.

Save your ears. After a few hours, depending on your sleep deprivation, you will have to stop mixing or fly blind.

If I am expected to "work" the material, I will try to bare bones the mix, taking everything out but the most essential instrumentation. I then add back tracks, and when it starts to sound cluttered I will listen to the last added track to see if I can mute it entirely or partially, bringing it in only where it is most effective. Of course if I am the producer or I recorded all the tracks to begin with, I am already familiar with the arrangement.

You can sometimes tell who was in charge of a mix. Their instrument will be the loudest. If you want to fix that with aplomb, pan their instrument to the side they are sitting on during the mix so it will sound louder.

I keep the mic away from the air being pushed out of an acoustic instrument. I try and mic the sound of the instrument in the room. If the room sucks, I will bring the mic close but avoid the "phump." Other than that, I will wear good headphones and fish with the mic for the sound I want while the musician is playing. I think mics are important, but the player and the instrument can make an inexpensive mic sound great! On the other hand, a $5,000 mic will not improve a lackluster performance. Of course, if you have a great artist and great equipment, when you listen back you think, "So that's how they do it!"

I save my mixes as I hit new plateaus. Sometimes, I am painfully aware that I overmixed. There are moments when it all comes together, and I will hit the Save As button right away. I will have several versions of a mix saved by the end.

When I am in a mix, I try and save every change so that when things freeze or the power goes out I have not lost a productive hour. In a 4- to 6-hour mix session, there is probably 90 to 120 minutes of golden time where things elevate out of the chore dimension and it really goes somewhere. When I feel like I am "forcing it," I will take walks, stretch, rest my ears, answer e-mails, whatever, during a session. A 10-minute break will improve your chances.

In my opinion, distortion in the monitors is the true enemy of the ear. It fatigues me far more than volume. Going to clubs, or running FOH, *distortion in the speakers will damage my ears. Invest in custom ear protectors and don't be ashamed to wear them. They look a lot better than hearing aids. You can put a 6 dB to 25 dB broadband attenuator in the device.*

If you decide to use your ears for a living, protect them! If you are setting up drum mics, ask the drummer to stop playing while you set up. If they won't stop (or can't hear you ask), wear your earplugs or in-ear monitors into the drum room.

Lack of money can cause there to be a stressful clock-watching buzz-kill vibe. If you can afford it, turn off the meter and take your time. You are only as good as your last project! When an unfamiliar client wants to control your every move, or asks you to do something you know won't work, try it anyway. Sometimes they are smarter than they look. (If it doesn't work they may quiet down).

▶ *Subtlety is amazingly effective. Panning slightly out of the norm will wake a sleepy track up.*

▶ *A mix is never really finished, it is simply abandoned (Orson Wells paraphrase).*

▶ *A mix is finished when you run out of time (money).*

▶ *A mix is finished when anything else you attempt makes it sound worse.*

▶ *A mix is finished when everybody wants to hear it again and again.*

▶ *A mix is finished when the client loves it.*

▶ *If you keep turning it down, it's probably out of tune.*

▶ *If you are not the producer, keep your mind open and your mouth on the shut side.*

▶ *There are many ways to do something right.*

▶ *Keep everyone's secrets. It is a small world.*

▶ *Burn incense after lunch.*

Summary

In this chapter you have learned about lossy and lossless audio, bit depth and sample rate, microphone placement concepts, signal flow, signal processing, and digital audio recording, mixing, and editing concepts. You will find that, once you familiarize yourself with these concepts, most digital audio software will be fun and intuitive to use.

CHAPTER 6

Music Synthesis

Hardware and software-based synthesizers are an important component of modern-day music production. Although these instruments are often used to mimic traditional acoustic instruments in films, on television, and on CD recordings, synthesizers offer a virtually limitless array of sonic possibilities to a contemporary musician. In this chapter you will learn about the ins and outs of music synthesis: the components, signal flow, and editing techniques that will allow you to feel at home with vintage analog gear, complex software synthesizers, or digital hardware synthesizers. This chapter will cover the following topics:

► Brief history of synthesizers

► Components of a synthesizer

► Sound source

► Waveforms

► Modifiers

► Filters

► Amplifier

► Control voltage and signal flow

► Envelope generator

► Low frequency oscillation

▶ Navigating around a synthesizer

▶ Creating sounds from scratch

▶ Digital synthesis

▶ Synthesis methods

▶ Sampling concepts

▶ Taking a sample

▶ Archiving and loading samples

▶ Sound design tips and practice techniques

A Brief History of Synthesizers

In the 1920s, Leon Theremin designed what was to be one of the first viable electronic instrument. The pitch and volume of the Theremin were controlled by proximity of the performer's hands to an antenna and loop. The Theremin proved to be one of the first electronic instruments to find favor with composers of the day. Composers who wrote for this instrument include Edgar Varése and Percy Grainger. Although the technology is over 80 years old, it is interesting to note that some modern synthesists still use synthesizers based on the original Theremin design. Companies such as Moog Music still offer commercial versions of this singular instrument.

By the 1950s and 1960s, many composers of art music were exploring exciting new sounds available on early synthesizers. Composers such as Stockhauzen and Babbitt were attracted to the synthesizer's many sonic possibilities. These composers were also interested in utilizing the synthesizer's capabilities to realize compositions that were unplayable by human performers.

Early synthesizers were plagued by two major deficits: They were very large and expensive to produce, so only a select few composers had the luxury of using them. The advent of the transistor changed all of this. By the 1960s, synthesizer pioneers such as Robert Moog and Donald Buchla had created the first voltage-controlled synths. The Minimoog was one of the first synthesizers designed and manufactured for the mass market. Though these first synths were monophonic (able to produce a single note at a time), the relatively small size and low cost made synthesis available to a generation of musicians. One of the results of this development was that the synthesizer came into vogue with many popular musicians of the day. Groups such as Pink Floyd and Emerson, Lake & Palmer utilized the sonic possibilities of the synthesizer in their music. Other musicians such as Wendy Carlos used these early synths to realize new orchestrations of traditional classical literature. If you have not yet listened to *Switched-On Bach,* find a copy of Carlos's version of J.S. Bach's *Brandenburg Concertos.* This milestone recording is a gem of synthesizer prowess: As you listen, keep in mind that the entire recording was produced, one phrase at a time, using *very* primitive synthesis and recording techniques.

You have learned a bit of the history of electronic music and synthesis, but what exactly is a synthesizer? A synthesizer is an instrument that produces and modifies sound entirely by electronic means. Although early analog synths provide just a few ways of generating sounds, modern hardware and software synths are capable of producing complex waveforms and often include emulations of traditional acoustic instruments. If you have ever used or listened to an analog synthesizer, you probably noticed how synthetic the sounds were. The reason for this is that analog synthesizers could only produce simple waveforms such as sine, square, triangle, and sawtooth waves. Although the palette of waveforms is limited on classic analog synthesizers such as those made by Moog, Arp, and Korg, many musicians prefer the "real thing" because these instruments provide a distinctive sound that is difficult to emulate using digital *modeling.* (Physical modeling involves using complex mathematical formulas to emulate the physical characteristics of an instrument.)

In addition to hardware-based analog and digital synthesizers, many musicians use software-based synthesizers. Some software synthesizers function as a stand-alone application, while others require the use of a host application. Software synthesizers that require the use of a host application may use one of a number of plug-in formats such as VST, TDM, Direct X, or Audio Units. Most stand-alone synthesizers provide ReWire capability for virtual connection to a host application (see Chapters 1 and 4).

Components of a Synthesizer

I will begin the discussion of synthesizer architecture with a look at a typical analog synthesizer (see Figure 6.1). Where digital synthesizers use numbers to represent sounds, analog synthesizers use electronic oscillators. These electrical oscillations are *analogous* to sound produced through a loudspeaker; hence the term *analog.*

Figure 6.1
A classic analog Korg MS-20 synthesizer.

Even though newer digital synthesizers often provide more options for manipulation of sound than the early analog ones did, an introduction to analog synthesis will provide a solid foundation for understanding the components and signal path of even the most advanced digital synthesizers. Synthesis architecture and options for manipulation of sound have evolved over the years, yet most hardware- and software-based synthesizers still use a modular design very similar to the transistor-based synths developed in the 1960s.

An analog synthesizer consists of three primary components: *sound source*, *modifiers*, and *control voltage*. In the early days of synthesis, sounds were created by connecting with a patch cord various controller, sound source, and modifier modules. Though few modern synthesizers require the use of patch cords, we still refer to a particular sound on a synthesizer as a *patch*. It is interesting to note that some modern software synthesizers such as those found in Reason still use a virtual patch cord architecture for routing controllers and modifiers (see Figure 6.2).

Figure 6.2
Using virtual patch cables in Reason.

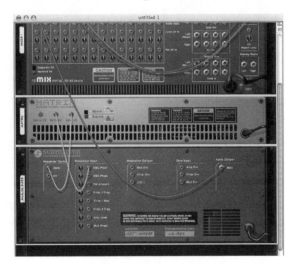

SOUND SOURCE

The primary sound source of an analog synthesizer is the *voltage- controlled oscillator* (VCO). The output frequency (or pitch) of a VCO is controlled by application of control voltage. A control-voltage keyboard is typically used to control the frequency of an oscillator, but other types of control may be used, such as an envelope generator. Most analog oscillators provide several types of waveforms. I will not go into the math behind each type of waveform; what is important to understand is that the combination of fundamental frequency and the relative amplitude of overtones is what provides the unique timbral quality of each waveform. A sawtooth wave, for example, provides a brilliant timbre because the summative amplitude of the first three overtones is greater than the amplitude of the fundamental. In contrast, a sine wave has no overtones and provides a timbre that might be characterized as "mellow."

Figures 6.3–6.6 represent waveforms available on most analog synthesizers. Note than when viewing a waveform, amplitude is represented on the y-axis and frequency is represented by the x-axis.

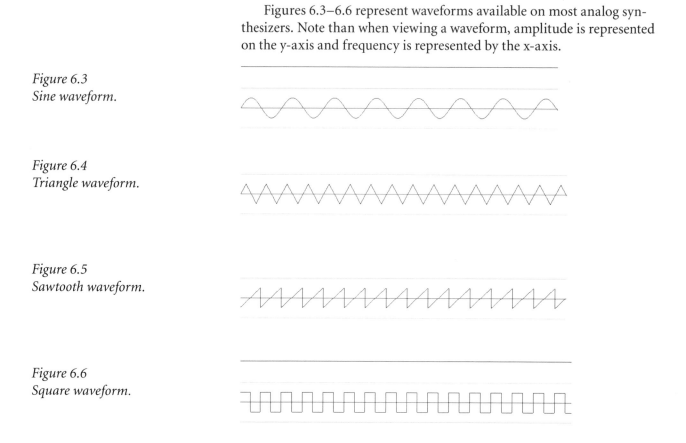

Figure 6.3
Sine waveform.

Figure 6.4
Triangle waveform.

Figure 6.5
Sawtooth waveform.

Figure 6.6
Square waveform.

It might be helpful to visualize a guitar string as you view a waveform graph. On a stringed instrument such as a guitar, thicker strings produce a slower rate or *frequency* of vibration. The length of the string also has an effect on frequency: Shorter strings produce higher frequencies than longer strings. A guitarist effectively changes the length of a string when fingering a string on the fretboard. If more force is applied to the string, it is obvious that the volume or amplitude is greater. Additional force applied to a string causes it to move in a bigger arc, but the frequency of vibration remains fairly constant. Figure 6.7 may help to clarify this concept.

Figure 6.7
Waveform diagram: same pitch or
frequency, two levels of amplitude
or volume.

One of the things I first learned when designing sounds using analog synthesizers is that it is important to start with an appropriate waveform. Attempting to create a bright sound using a sine wave is beating the proverbial dead horse. The concept is still true today: It is usually best to select (or sample) an appropriate waveform before applying modifiers to a sound source.

NOISE GENERATOR

Most analog synthesizers provide one or more noise generators in addition to traditional VCOs. A noise generator may generate *pink* or *white noise*. White noise consists of random frequencies with equal energy in all audible frequencies and sounds similar to a waterfall. Pink noise, which is filtered white noise, is similar, but the perceived effect is that there is more low end—pink noise sounds similar to thunder. Pink noise is used by engineers to test frequency response in a system.

MODIFIERS

Though the quality and variety of sound sources available on a synthesizer (analog or digital) is the primary ingredient for good sound, modifiers provide a way to manipulate these sounds. If you are considering investing in a sound-design synthesizer (hardware or software), it is important to evaluate the types of modifiers provided. You should also evaluate the ways that these sound modifiers can be controlled. (For example, is it possible to control filter cutoff using note velocity, an envelope, and/or a data slider?) As with sound sources, a look at common analog modifiers will provide a good foundation for learning how to use modern-day digital, analog, and software synthesizers.

Filters

Filters are an important component of sound synthesis. As a vocalist uses the shape of the throat and oral cavity to affect timbre, filters provide the synthesist with a means of modifying the timbre of a sound. Though there are many types of filters available, I will focus on three of the most common filters: *high-pass*, *low-pass*, and *band-pass*.

Voltage-controlled filters (VCFs) work by cutting or attenuating a range of frequencies while letting other frequencies pass through. This is the essence of *subtractive synthesis*—filters are used to remove harmonics, thereby altering the timbre of one or more oscillators. Filters are fun to use because they provide the ability to control or alter the timbre of a sound in real time.

A *high-pass filter* is a common filter found on analog synths. As the name implies, a high-pass filter lets high frequencies pass while setting a cutoff point for lower frequencies (see Figure 6.8).

Figure 6.8
High-pass filter graph.

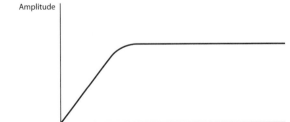

153

It is important to note that frequency cutoff represents the frequency range where filtering is evident to the listener; it is not an abrupt boundary. A related concept, *roll-off curve*, is an important consideration. For example, a 24 dB/octave roll-off is fairly steep when compared to a more gentle roll-off of 12 dB/octave (see Figure 6.9). When a gentle roll-off is used, more harmonics are present in the sound, producing what might be described as a less affected filter.

Figure 6.9
24 dB/octave roll-off versus 12 dB/ octave roll-off.

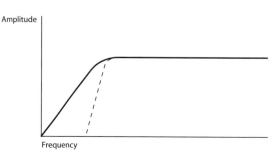

A *low-pass filter* provides a complement to the high-pass filter. Again, as the name implies, a low-pass filter lets lower frequencies pass unaffected while setting a cutoff point for higher frequencies (see Figure 6.10).

Figure 6.10
Low-pass filter graph.

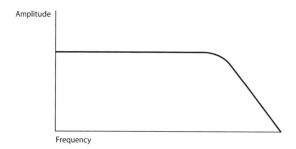

If you combine a high-pass and a low-pass filter you have a *band-pass filter*. A band-pass filter lets a range of frequencies pass while setting both an upper and lower cutoff boundary (see Figure 6.11).

Figure 6.11
Band-pass filter graph.

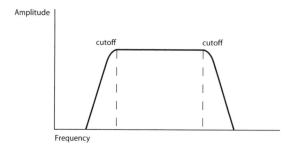

Filters can be used for all sorts of interesting effects such as "wah-wah" sounds or more subtle timbral variations. As with analog waveforms, the best way to get a sense of how filters work is to experiment with them. You may want to consider purchasing one of the excellent analog-emulation software synthesizers to explore this aspect of synthesis.

Filter Resonance

Many synthesizers provide a filter *resonance* or *peak* control. A resonant filter loops a portion of the output of the filter back to the input. The result of this loopback is that frequencies near the cutoff range are accentuated. Through careful control of the filter cutoff and the amount of resonance, many wonderful filter feedback effects can be achieved. A fun experiment is to resonate low-pass filtering of a sawtooth or triangle wave. By fine-tuning the amount of resonance and adjusting the filter cutoff point, you can actually hear each of the partials as they are resonated. This type of timbral change can be very effective when controlled by a real-time controller such as a data slider or keyboard velocity.

Amplifier

As Samuel Pellman points out in his excellent book, *An Introduction to the Creation of Electroacoustic Music* (Wadsworth, 1994), most *voltage-controlled amplifiers* (VCA) do not amplify a signal, they attenuate it. In other words, as a signal passes through a VCA, either it will continue through at its highest level, or the signal will be attenuated, or lessened.

As with the other modules of an analog synthesizer, more than one VCA may be used in the signal chain. A common use of the VCA is to control the attack and release of a sound. An *envelope generator* (see below) is often used in conjunction with a VCA to automate the attack and release of a sound, but it is also common to control a VCA using a knob or foot pedal.

Control Voltage and Signal Flow

The concept of control voltage is at the heart of analog synthesis. Control voltage is used to control a sound source or sound modifiers, but control voltage sources do not, by themselves, create any sound. The most common control-voltage source is a control-voltage keyboard. In the following example, control voltage from a keyboard is used to control the frequency of a voltage-controlled oscillator. The output of the oscillator module is then routed through a voltage-controlled amplifier (VCA) that finally sends the signal to a loudspeaker or other output destination (see Figure 6.12).

Figure 6.12
Keyboard control voltage, VCO, VCA, loudspeaker.

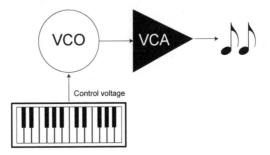

Although it is most common to use a control-voltage keyboard to control pitch, the voltage output of the keyboard may also be used to control a modifier such as a filter or VCA. *Keyboard tracking* is a term used to describe the application of a control-voltage keyboard to a filter or other modifier. As the performer plays higher notes on the keyboard, control voltage can be used to simultaneously increase the frequency cutoff of a low-pass filter so that the filter cutoff responds in a more natural way—the filter cutoff point increases for higher pitches, resulting in a more brilliant tone.

ENVELOPE GENERATOR

Envelope generators are an important tool for synthesists. An envelope generator provides a specific control-voltage shape or contour. This shape can then be used to control another module such as a VCO (voltage-controlled oscillator), VCF (voltage-controlled filter), or VCA (voltage-controlled amplifier). Most analog synthesizers provide a four-stage envelope generator that includes attack, decay, sustain, and release (ADSR). During the attack stage, voltage rises from zero to a peak level at a rate determined by the attack level. A larger attack level results in a slower attack. During decay, the voltage drops to the sustain level. If the sustain level is set to maximum, then no decay is heard. Releasing a key initiates the release stage and voltage falls back to zero at a rate determined by the decay level. Larger decay levels mean a slower decay. Figure 6.13 illustrates the four stages of a typical envelope generator.

Figure 6.13
Attack, decay, sustain, and release (ADSR).

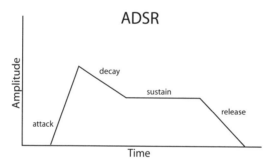

A common envelope generation (EG) function involves the application of the output of the EG to a VCA. In this scenario, the envelope generator begins its operation when the user presses a key on a control-voltage keyboard. This initial trigger initiates the attack portion of the envelope. As the key is held down, the envelope continues through the initial decay portion until it reaches the sustain stage. When the key is released, the envelope generator continues with the release stage where, if the envelope generator is used to control a VCA, the sound will fade out.

I have found that, in addition to careful selection of sound sources and filters, envelopes are one of the most important considerations when attempting to emulate traditional instruments. The *Switched-On Bach* recordings I mentioned earlier are a fine example. Though the early analog synthesizers used on these recordings were incapable of reproducing authentic sounds from the Baroque era, Carlos's masterful use of envelopes and other sound-design techniques makes these recordings much more natural and musical. Figure 6.14 demonstrates how an envelope might be applied to a VCA.

Figure 6.14
An ADSR envelope applied to VCA.

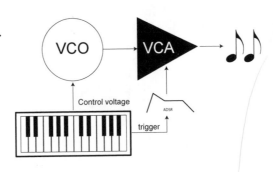

Many other options for sound design are available when you use an envelope to control a modifier such as a high- or low-pass filter. Consider using an envelope generator whenever you want to automate a particular characteristic such as a changing filter cutoff or a scoop (a note that starts flat and "scoops" up to another pitch). Figure 6.15 shows how an envelope generator might be used to control cutoff of a low-pass filter.

Figure 6.15
An ADSR envelope applied to a low-pass filter.

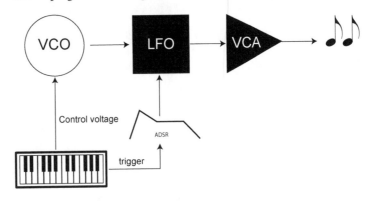

LOW-FREQUENCY OSCILLATOR

I remember when I purchased my first analog synthesizer many years ago. I spent many hours learning how to manipulate sounds using the *low-frequency oscillator* (LFO). An LFO can be used to create striking effects such as a siren or laser gun, or it may be used for subtle effects such as vibrato. Like an envelope generator, a low-frequency oscillator provides a source of voltage control that may be applied to a sound-source or modifier module. Where the envelope generator provides a voltage shape or contour, a low-frequency oscillator provides a series of slow-moving oscillations.

Though an LFO is similar to a traditional voltage-controlled oscillator, the frequency rate is generally slower than the range of hearing (i.e., LFO is *only* used as a control-voltage source, not a sound source). Again, like a traditional oscillator, most LFOs provide several types of waveforms. These low-frequency waveforms can then be used to control another synthesizer module such as a VCO (to control pitch), VCF (to change the timbre of a sound), VCA (for fading types of effects), or any number of other modifiers. In addition to the choice of waveforms, an LFO also provides a frequency or rate control as well as an amplitude control. When the output of an LFO is applied to a VCO, the frequency of the LFO determines the rate of pitch fluctuation of the VCO, and the amplitude of the LFO affects the range of pitch fluctuation. One use of LFO is to create an oscillating siren-like effect (see Figure 6.16).

Figure 6.16
LFO applied to VCO to create a siren effect.

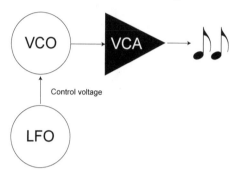

As with other control-voltage sources I have talked about so far, an LFO may be applied to any other sound source or modifier (e.g., you might use an LFO to control both pitch and filter cutoff frequency).

Other Tidbits

Most of us are familiar with the term *sample*. In a moment I will discuss the concept of digital sampling, but it is interesting to note that many analog synthesizers also had a form of sampling. A *sample-and-hold* circuit was used to measure the voltage of a waveform at a given point in time and "hold" the sample as an output until another sample was taken. In an analog synthesizer, a clock source, in the form of a modulation generator, can be used to trigger the rate of sampling. A common use of sample and hold is to sample white or pink noise as an input source and route the output to a voltage-controlled oscillator. In Figure 6.17, a sample-and-hold generator is used to control the frequency of an oscillator in this way. The song "Karn Evil 9" on the Emerson, Lake & Palmer album *Brain Salad Surgery* demonstrates an effective use of sample and hold.

Figure 6.17
Sample and hold (sampling white noise and routing the output to a VCO). A modulation generator controls the rate of sampling.

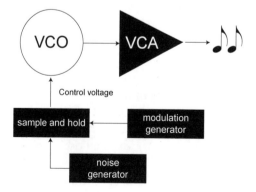

A *ring modulator* is another interesting circuit available on some analog synthesizers. A ring modulator is a form of *amplitude modulation*. The concept of amplitude modulation is as follows: When an oscillating voltage (above 30 Hz) is used as the control voltage of a VCO, and the VCA is passing an audio signal, new frequencies called sidebands will exist in the output of the VCA. A ring modulator multiplies the voltages of two input signals. The output of the ring modulator is a combination of the sum and the difference of the two frequencies. The original signals are not a part of its output. When complex waveforms are used as input to a ring modulator, interesting bell-like sounds result.

Now review what you have learned so far regarding analog synthesis.

▶ An analog synthesizer consists of modules that may be connected or "patched" in a variety of ways.

▶ The three types of modules available on an analog synthesizer are sound source, modifiers, and voltage-control sources.

▶ Voltage-control sources may be used to control a sound source or modifier, but voltage-control sources do not produce an audible signal.

▶ Filters such as a high- or low-pass filter are used to affect the timbre of a sound source and form the basis for subtractive synthesis.

▶ Resonance accentuates the cutoff point of a filter.

▶ Voltage-controlled amplifiers are used to modify or attenuate a given input source.

▶ The shape or contour of an envelope generator (often a four-stage ADSR generator) is typically used to control amplitude, frequency, or filter cutoff.

▶ Another control-voltage source, the low-frequency oscillator, may also be used to control an oscillator, filter, or amplifier.

This would be a good time to reiterate that, though synthesizers have grown in complexity since the days of analog synthesis, the basic concepts such as application of modifiers to a sound source and the use of various controllers to modify and modulate in real time or through automation is still at the heart of modern synthesis design. Modern synths may provide tens (if not hundreds) of modifiers, and envelopes may provide eight or more stages. However, the basic signal flow and modular approach of analog synthesis is still germane.

Case Study: Navigating Around a Synthesizer

In this section I will apply the concepts presented in the last section to a popular software synthesizer. For this example, I elected to use the Subtractor synthesizer, one of the virtual synthesizers that comes with Reason (Propellerhead). However, I would point out that these concepts could just as easily be applied to software or hardware synthesizers from any number of vendors.

Take a look at the screen shot in Figure 6.18. All of the components described in the last section (and a few more) are provided by the synthesizer.

Figure 6.18
Reason's Subtractor synthesizer.

We will use the primary components of this synthesizer to create a sound from scratch. A good first step is to select a waveform for one or both oscillators. In Figure 6.19, notice that the oscillator section provides controls for the octave and coarse and fine tuning, as well as a mix button to mix the level of the two oscillators. As is common on most analog synths, a noise generator is also provided in the oscillator module.

Figure 6.19
Oscillator module.

The primary filter provides all of the common options including high-pass, low-pass, band-bass, and notch (a filter that cuts out a band of frequencies). As is evident in Figure 6.20, a frequency slider is available to set the cutoff frequency for the selected filter, and the resonance knob can be used to accentuate the cutoff point of the filter.

Figure 6.20
Primary filter.

Several four-stage envelopes are provided. As discussed in the last section, envelopes can be used as a source of control voltage to control any number of modules. In the Subtractor, an amplitude envelope is automatically connected to the amplifier. In Figure 6.21, a gentle fade-in is created by turning up the attack stage of the amplitude envelope.

Figure 6.21
Creating a gentle fade-in using an amplitude envelope.

The filter envelope can be used to automate the primary filter. The filter envelope level knob controls the level to which the envelope has an effect on the filter. In a similar way, the modulation envelope can be routed to modulate the pitch of either oscillator, the amount of frequency modulation, phase of the oscillator waveforms, or relative level of the oscillators. For example, the "scoop" effect mentioned previously can be created by turning up the modulation envelope level and setting the envelope to control the pitch of oscillator 1 as shown in Figure 6.22.

Figure 6.22
Using an envelope to control pitch of an oscillator.

The Subtractor provides two low-frequency oscillators. Six waveforms are available for the primary LFO, and this oscillator can be routed to control many other components such as an oscillator, filter cutoff, or the amount of frequency modulation. In Figure 6.23, the primary LFO is used to control oscillator 1 in order to create a siren effect.

Figure 6.23
Using an LFO to create a siren effect.

Although there are a few additional parameters such as sections for keyboard tracking and modulation-wheel routing, the primary components as described above form the basis for sound design on most modern synthesizers. The primary variations in other synthesizers come in the form of other types of sound sources and synthesis methods, and the type and routing flexibility of modifiers.

Creating Sounds from Scratch

One of the best methods of learning how to design and manipulate sounds is through experimentation. If you are using a hardware synthesizer, consider backing up your user banks prior to doing extensive editing. Once you have backed up your sound banks you will be able to enjoy the process of editing and creating new sounds without worrying about trashing existing sounds. If your experimentation goes awry, it is then a simple process of reloading your previous sound banks. I would also caution you to keep your monitors or headphone volume at a low level while creating new sounds. This is particularly true if you experiment with algorithms such as the numerous signal routings provided on the Kurzweil 2500/2600 series instruments. Depending on the algorithm you choose, it is very easy to overdrive the system and create a nasty wall of sound.

Although there are as many ways to design sounds as there are synthesists, I have found the following steps helpful when creating sounds from scratch.

1. **Start with the sound source.** The goal is to use a waveform that best matches your vision for the final sound. An example would be to select white noise if your goal is to create the sound of wind, waves, or a waterfall. A less obvious example might be to select a square wave to represent the nasal quality of an oboe, or a sine wave to represent a flute. Many synthesizers allow you to select a sample or physical model as the sound source. Depending on the sound you wish to create, this can open up an exciting array of possibilities for sound sources.

2. **Adjust the amplitude envelope.** As I mentioned previously, amplitude contour can be an important component of a sound design. For example, a car backfire and shotgun are distinctive when heard back to back, but the similarity in sudden attack and decay might cause us to mistake one sound for another. Of course, context is also important: White noise might be a perfectly acceptable substitution for a snare drum if the listener expects to hear a snare and the amplitude envelope closely matches that of a real snare drum. This type of substitution can be wonderfully effective when designing sounds. Why not use a sample of a slamming door or other percussive effect as a percussive instrument?

3. **Apply filters to modify timbre.** After completing the first two steps, you should have a sound that is beginning to take shape. I find that this is usually a good point to begin to tweak the filters. As with amplitude envelopes, filters can go a long way in creating a convincing sound (if your goal is to mimic a traditional instrument). Because of their effect on timbre, filters can also be wonderfully effective for designing non-traditional sounds. As an example, you might want to try routing your signal through a low-pass filter to create a convincing bass drum (turn down the cutoff point until you find a frequency range that works well to

your ear). Conversely, you might consider using a high-pass filter to cut out low frequencies when designing a synthetic snare drum.

4. Apply real-time modifiers. To my ear, the most musical sounds are often those that change over time. Vocalists, woodwind, and brass players almost always use a touch of vibrato to add more expression to a musical passage. Real-time modifiers can be an equally expressive tool for synthesists. For me, tweaking a sound with real-time modifiers is one of the most creative parts of the sound-design process. Some examples are as follows: A touch of low-frequency oscillation (LFO) might be used to control the pitch of an oscillator for a vibrato effect; use an envelope generator or data wheel to control filter cutoff or resonance; or use LFO to sweep a filter and assign a slider or modulation wheel to control the rate of low-frequency oscillation. Of course, I am only scratching the surface of sound-design concepts, but the important thing to remember is to experiment. I am the first to admit that some of my most successful designs were the result of experimentation.

Here is one last bit of advice regarding sound design: Pick out a few of your favorite patches on a synthesizer or sound module and take some time to study the signal flow of these sounds. These sounds are often created by professional designers who have vast experience with getting the most out of any synthesizer. I often learn many new tricks when studying the sound designs of other musicians. It can also be helpful to listen to a sound and ponder how you would create such a sound. Consider the probable parameters such as sound sources, filters, modulators, and the like, and then study the sound to see how it was actually created. You will probably be surprised at the innovative methods used in many of these patches.

Digital Synthesis

Just as the transistor had a huge impact on the design and availability of synthesizers to the mass market, the introduction of inexpensive microprocessors set the stage for a revolution in the field of digital synthesis. Although analog synthesizers provided many new sonic possibilities for composers and performers, analog synths were plagued by several deficits: a limited number of basic waveforms to choose from, a tendency of oscillators to drift out of tune, limited or no ability to store and retrieve patches, and limited polyphony (many synthesizers from this era were monophonic).

One of the first commercially available digital synthesizers was manufactured by Yamaha in the early 1980s. The Yamaha DX7 was a huge success and set the stage for the decline of analog synthesizers. The relatively inexpensive cost of this instrument combined with the mind-boggling array of sounds (by 1980s standards) ensured its success. It is interesting to note that, in hindsight, many musicians consider the sound of the DX7 and other early digital synthesizers to be dated. In my estimation, many musicians prefer older analog gear, but I would point out that instruments such as the DX7 do provide extensive sound design capabilities.

Where an analog synthesizer uses voltages analogous to a sound wave, a digital instrument uses numbers to represent sounds. Such numbers may represent a *sample* of an acoustic instrument—much like CD playback technology—or digits may model traditional oscillators, filters, and the like. Digital synthesizers provide many benefits such as tuning stability and the ability to store and retrieve patches. Some digital synthesizers provide more extensive editing capability than analog synthesizers.

Synthesis Methods

There are a wide variety of digital synthesizers. In most cases, you will find both hardware and software synthesizers available in the following categories. Note that many of the synthesis methods listed in this section are not unique to digital synthesizers. For example, frequency modulation can be achieved on an analog synthesizer, as can a primitive form of additive synthesis.

SUBTRACTIVE SYNTHESIS

You have already learned about *subtractive synthesis*. This form of synthesis is the heart of classic analog synthesizers, and the architecture is still evident in most digital synthesizers. In a subtractive synthesizer, filters are used to remove or subtract overtones from a sound source, thereby changing the timbre of the sound source.

ADDITIVE SYNTHESIS

Where filters are used to remove partials from a sound, an *additive synthesizer* functions by summing the output of multiple oscillators. The idea behind additive synthesis is that any waveform, even a complex one, can be created by combining sine waves of varying amplitudes and envelopes. For example, a sawtooth wave can be constructed by combining sine waves such that each sine wave is a multiple of the fundamental and the amplitude is a fraction of the fundamental (see Figure 6.24).

When you consider that each sine wave can have a unique amplitude envelope and that these envelopes cause a change in timbre over time, it is evident that additive synthesis can be a deep and powerful form of synthesis.

Figure 6.24
Creating a sawtooth wave from sine waves.

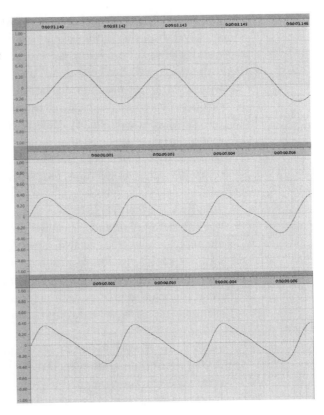

FREQUENCY MODULATION

Some early digital synthesizers such as the Yamaha DX7 utilized a synthesis method called *frequency modulation* (a technique still used in some synthesizers). The concept of frequency modulation (FM) synthesis is similar to how a low-frequency oscillator can be used to modulate an oscillator, but, unlike LFO, the modulating wave is in the audible range. When a nonharmonic modulator is used, bell-like sounds and other complex waveforms can be created.

GRANULAR SYNTHESIS

Granular synthesis is an interesting method of synthesis that is similar to the concept of digital sampling. With a sampler, a given waveform is stored as a series of digital "slices" (often at a rate of 44.1 kHz). On playback, the slices reproduce the sound of the original waveform. A granular synthesizer uses tiny slices, or *grains,* of sound, but the grains can be played back and combined in many ways. For example, the order of the grains can be changed, as can the playback speed of each grain. Grains can be produced by mathematical formulas or from sampled sounds, and grains can be combined to create many interesting sounds. Conceptually, a granular synthesizer can be visualized as a sampler in which each sample (often a few milliseconds in length) can be independently controlled and looped.

PHYSICAL MODELING

A *physical modeling* synthesizer uses mathematical algorithms to simulate the physical properties of an instrument such as a violin or guitar. Often, properties such as embouchure can be controlled in real-time, yielding very expressive possibilities. One of the most interesting uses for physical modeling is to combine physical properties not ordinarily used with traditional instruments. For example, a model of a woodwind mouthpiece might be combined with physical characteristics of a brass instrument, creating an unusual hybrid instrument. Physical models often include parameters to control the type of material and amount of dampening. Note that physical modeling is often used in reverb and amplifier plug-ins to model the physical characteristics of a room, amplifier, or even a classic microphone.

WAVETABLE SYNTHESIS

In a *wavetable synthesizer*, samples are stored in a lookup table. One sample might be used for the attack portion of a sound while one or more samples, such as an interesting morphing sound, might be achieved by combining and looping samples during the sustain of a note. In this way, wavetable synthesis offers a more efficient method of storage and playback of samples than traditional sample playback methods.

RECONSTRUCTIVE PHRASE MODELING

Two of the demonstration recordings on the accompanying CD utilize a software synthesizer called "Synful Orchestra," which is developed by Synful, LLC. Synful Orchestra utilizes a promising technique called *reconstructive phrase modeling*. With this method of synthesis, the synthesizer maintains a database of musical phrases. When MIDI input is received, the synthesizer evaluates incoming data to determine the type of phrasing and articulation used in the phrase and splices together fragments to form a representation that includes musical elements such as slurs, bowing, portamento, and the like. In my estimation, this method of synthesis shows great promise in recreating the sound of traditional instruments such as strings, brass, and woodwinds because, unlike traditional sample playback methods, the synthesizer responds to performance nuance in a way that is more natural and responsive.

SAMPLING AND SAMPLE PLAYBACK

One of the most common forms of digital synthesis is the sampler. As with the sample-and-hold circuit common in analog synthesizers, digital samplers use an analog to digital converter (ADC) to take a periodic snapshot or sample of the amplitude of a given input signal. The resulting collection of samples provides a numeric representation of the input source. I should point out that the term sample is typically used to refer to both the individual snapshots as well as the collection of samples. For example, a one-second sample of a piano key might actually contain 44.1 thousand samples (providing it was recorded at the standard CD recording rate). Though this recording contains thousands of tiny samples, we still refer to the collection of individual samples as a sample.

A truism in the digital domain is that the higher the sample rate, the more accurately a digital audio converter (DAC) will convert an analog signal to its digital representation. An important consideration here is that, to accurately sample a given frequency component, two samples are required for each of the frequency cycles. If you combine this with the knowledge that the range of human hearing is roughly 20 Hz to 20,000 Hz, it is evident that a sample rate of at least 40,000 samples per second is required to accurately represent frequencies within the range of hearing. The Nyquist frequency (named for Harry Nyquist, a theorist who developed the theoretical basis for these concepts in the 1920s) is the frequency that is half that of the sample rate. The Nyquist frequency represents the highest frequency that may be accurately represented by a given sample rate.

One of the problems associated even with high sample rates is that frequencies higher than the given Nyquist frequency may become audible as an *alias* (i.e., an overtone of a high note may become audible as a new (and usually unwanted) frequency. To deal with the problem of aliasing, many digital devices use a low-pass filter to remove frequencies from this range. Since a low-pass filter does not provide an abrupt boundary between filtered and unfiltered frequencies, the actual sample rate must be slightly higher to account for this discrepancy. As it happens, the sample rate of a compact disc is 44.1 kHz. This rate provides a "buffer" for the hardware to filter unwanted aliases while still providing a Nyquist frequency that is at the upper limits of the human hearing range.

The other important factor associated with analog-to-digital conversion is bit depth. In short, the greater the range of numbers that are used to represent a given amplitude, the more accurate the conversion will be. An 8-bit number (11111111 binary) provides a maximum of 255 levels of amplitude. In contrast, compact discs use 16-bit numbers to represent levels of amplitude. A 16-bit number (1111111111111111 binary) provides a whopping 65,536 levels of amplitude. Even when converting with a 16-bit number, an undesirable process called quantization still occurs. Simply put, a given amplitude must be quantified to the closest numeric value in the range provided by the bit depth. In an 8-bit system, quantization error is very evident—a numerical range of 0–255 is simply not accurate enough to provide a quality sample. Though a 16-bit analog converter is very good, many feel that the resulting signal-to-noise ratio of 96 dB is still not sufficient. Many studios are now moving to 32-bit numbers (0–4,294,967,295) and sample rates of 96 kHz and higher.

Sampling Concepts

Before delving into sampling concepts I would like to take a moment to point out that, though extremely useful, samplers are not an end-all for synthesists. One of the inherent problems with samplers is that, while they provide useful snapshots of sound, the resulting sounds are just that—snapshots. An analogy would be to compare samplers to photography. A camera can be used to provide a useful and even artistic "sample" of a musical performance. The resulting photograph may conjure up emotions or even provide an insight into the human experience, but a photograph, as with a musical sample, lacks the perspective of change over time. A sample of a complex sound such as a piano provides only a snapshot of a given note at a given velocity. The sounds of a real piano, however, are constantly changing as vibrations from one string interact and cause sympathetic vibrations in another. Velocity also has an effect on the timbre of a note. As you work with sampling synthesizers you may want to consider this limited aspect of the technology. As with the photography analogy, a musical snapshot can be either a poor substitute for the real thing or a wonderful opportunity for creativity. As I get off of my soapbox let me also mention that, in practical terms, samplers can be very useful. Let's face it, most of us do not have the luxury of writing for a studio orchestra every day. The reality is that many commercial productions, for obvious financial considerations, utilize samplers to mimic the real thing. I would encourage you to explore sampling technology for both its ability to mimic as well as its potential for more creative pursuits.

Taking a Sample

Before you attempt to sample a traditional instrument such as a piano or guitar it would be helpful to do some preplanning. As with any recording, your sample will only be as good as the gear you use. High-quality microphones and preamps are essential if you wish to accurately sample an acoustic instrument. As with any audio recording, the characteristics of the room are also an important consideration. Unwanted background noise or reverberations will end up in the recording if your sampling environment is less than pristine. You may also want to consider purchasing commercially produced sample libraries if your goal is to sample something as complex as a piano.

Consider the characteristics of the instrument you intend to sample: How does the timbre of the instrument change at various dynamic levels? Will it be necessary to capture special nuances such as fret or breath noise? Will the sample be static, or should it change over time (e.g., asking a wind player to add some vibrato to the end of a note can add a wonderfully natural quality to an otherwise static-sounding sample). You should also consider how you intend to sonically use the sample. A sample of a saxophone that includes much room ambience may sound awkward when mixed with relatively dry or synthetic-sounding backing tracks. A final consideration is memory. Keep in mind that a stereo sample at the standard rate of 44.1 kHz will take up 10 megabytes of memory per minute! If you consider that an accurate sampling of a grand piano requires a variety of samples (at varying velocities) for every couple of notes across the keyboard, it is evident that memory soon becomes a precious commodity.

If you plan to record a sample from an analog source, be sure to take a minute to adjust the gain of the input source. As with any recording, the goal is to get the strongest possible input signal while still remaining under the 0 db threshold. Look at the level meter on the sampler and adjust your levels until you have optimized the signal. If you have not had much experience with recording it might be helpful to point out that, though signal clipping will most certainly wreck your sample, recording at a volume that is too low will be equally problematic: When you sample a weak input source, the ratio of background noise to signal level is lessened and the resulting sample will be less than pristine. Also be sure to select an appropriate sample rate. Most samplers will let you set a rate of between 22.05–48 kHz. It is important to remember that your sample rate must be at least twice as high as the highest frequency to be sampled.

After taking a sample you will need to assign the sample on a specific key or range of keys. In most cases, if you have sampled a pitched instrument you will want to place this sample at same key represented by the pitch of the instrument. It is always a good idea to name your samples with a descriptive name. Most musicians include the key name as a part of the sample name—for example, "MyPiano_C3." You will also need to set a sample range. The sample range might be a single key for a percussive sample or two or more adjacent notes for a piano or other pitched instrument. As I mentioned before, you may need to sample every other note to get an accurate sample of some instruments. Some instruments such as an electric bass will sound passable by sampling in thirds or fourths.

Multi-Samples

Most effective sampled sounds are actually multi-samples. A multi-sample is a collection of individual samples mapped across a range of notes. More than one set of multi-samples are often used to account for a variety of timbres or effects. Typically, you will set up these groups of sounds to respond to changes in velocity or other controller data. Using samples in this way provides more expressive capability—the timbre of your samples may change as a result of an increase or decrease in key velocity levels. Multi-samples are also essential if the sound you intend to record changes over time (e.g., a saxophone with vibrato). In this instance, the rate of vibrato changes as you play the sample at various pitches. For best results you will need to plan on sampling six or more notes for every octave.

Truncation

It will usually be necessary to truncate both the beginning and end of a sample. Simply put, truncation cuts the unwanted portion of a sample from both ends of a sample. Some synthesizers will attempt to automatically truncate a sample, but in any case, you will probably need to make some manual adjustments.

Normalization

Normalization is often used to equalize the dynamic level of one sample to another. A normalization algorithm is actually quite simple. The highest peak of a given sample signal is raised to 0 dB. All of the other samples are raised by this same proportion. Note that some samplers allow you to set a level other than 0 dB (if you wish to normalize to some lesser level for contextual reasons).

Looping

Sample looping is used for a variety of reasons. A sample loop can provide the ability to sustain a note that would ordinarily decay (e.g., a sustained snare or other percussive sound). Sample looping is also used to conserve memory. A case in point: If you strike middle-C on a piano at a dynamic level of forte, you will find that you would need about 20 seconds (or over three megabytes for a stereo 44.1 kHz recording) to capture the entire attack and decay of the note. If you consider that it would take at least 44 samples (sampling every other note) of at least two dynamic levels, the resulting 88 samples would require about 293 megabytes of sample memory. With sample looping you could save a great deal of memory by simply looping the first 2 to 4 seconds and adding a shortened decay of another several seconds. Though the resulting sample will not be entirely accurate, looping is often necessary in order to conserve memory. Most samplers allow you to set separate points for looping, attack, and decay.

One of the tricky things you will need to consider when setting a loop point (see Figure 6.25) involves finding an appropriate boundary between the end of the loop and the start of the loop. Without editing, loops will generally emit an audible pop if the start and end amplitudes of the loop do not match. Many samplers provide tools to help you match the start and end of a loop.

Figure 6.25
Setting a loop point.

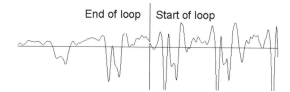

End of loop | Start of loop

Crossfade

An effective sampling technique involves splicing two samples together. You might wish, for example, to splice together the sound of an amplified guitar with the sound of a guitar feeding back. Simply splicing the two samples together will result in a sudden change of timbre that may be too abrupt. A crossfade allows the samples to be gracefully spliced together. Depending on the amount of time you allow for the crossfade, the transition from one sample to the next can be very subtle. Crossfading is covered in more detail in Chapter 5 (see Figure 5.21).

Pitch Shifting

It is often necessary, for intonation purposes, to adjust the pitch of individual samples when creating a multi-sample. Keep in mind that gross adjustments in pitch will alter the quality or timbre of the sound. An almost comical version of this effect can be heard on some sample playback synthesizers that use a limited amount of RAM: A sample of a flute sound that contains vibrato will sound very unnatural if the pitch is shifted more than a semitone or so. Wind players rarely (if ever) increase the rate of vibrato as they play an ascending scale, but this is an effect I have heard on more than one synthesizer! Pitch shifting can also be used for special effects. For example, a human voice might be pitch shifted to a lower register to create an unusual special effect.

Gain

It is often necessary to change the level of one or more samples in a multi-sample. As with adjustments in pitch, gain can be used to equalize the levels of samples in a multi-sample so that key velocity, when applied equally across the keyboard, will result in the same output level.

Using Sample Libraries

There is no question that sampling can be a challenging and tedious process. In my own work, I have found that sampling is most useful when I want to create new instruments based on a limited number of samples such as auxiliary percussion instruments. For practical reasons, commercial libraries are useful in many situations. For example, sampled string and piano libraries are available for a reasonable price and with a sound quality that would be virtually impossible to create in a typical home studio. Commercial libraries can be loaded into a hardware sampler via a CD-ROM drive. Software samplers have provided new opportunities such as the ability to store huge sample libraries on an external hard drive. Some of these instruments load samples on the fly (much like multi-track audio playback in a DAW), so huge samples can be effectively played in real time without the need for massive amounts of RAM. For example, some new piano libraries require 8 gigabytes of disk space—an amount of sample data that was unheard of in the days of hardware-based samplers.

Archiving and Loading Samples—The SCSI Connection

Depending on the sampling hardware you use, it will usually be neces-sary to archive or store your samples to some type of storage media such as a hard drive, floppy disk, or other removable media. Because samples require a great amount of memory, floppy disks are useful for storage of only the most minimal samples. Most professional samplers provide an interface to connect to an external storage device such as a Zip disk. Samplers often utilize a SCSI bus which can be used to con-nect the instrument to an external hard drive or CD-ROM drive. SCSI is an acronym for *small computer system interface* and is a fast parallel interface that allows you to link together up to eight devices such as hard disks, optical disks, or other storage devices. Though SCSI is rather ubiquitous in the music synthesizer industry, the use of SCSI devices can be tricky. You will certainly want to take time to read your manual regarding the types of devices that may be connected to your SCSI chain and, more importantly, to learn about some of the dangers associated with connecting SCSI devices. In short, you can cause serious damage to your synthesizer or computer if you attempt to connect these devices with the power on: Always turn off the power to your synth, computer, and any other SCSI devices before hooking up SCSI cables.

SCSI uses ID numbers to differentiate between different devices on a SCSI network. Be sure to set each of your SCSI devices to a different ID number before powering up your system. Just remember that each device *must* have its own unique number. Some devices such as your synthesizer or computer may have a fixed ID number that cannot be changed. Again, it is important to read your manuals before connecting these devices.

Before you purchase SCSI cables or devices, you will want to find out what type of cables are required. Two types of SCSI cables are common: DB25 and 50-pin Centronics. Depending on the equipment you intend to use it may be necessary to purchase a special adapter.

When hooking up a SCSI chain remember that the total length of the chain should not exceed 15 feet. If you can get by with shorter lengths, do it; the shorter the length of cables, the less likely you will have problems with transmission errors. You will also need to consider the issue of termination. Terminators are resistors that you add to both ends of the SCSI chain. Some devices include internal terminators, but these resistors may also be added in the form of a termination block that is plugged into the SCSI device.

It is sometimes helpful to connect your sampler directly to a computer using SCSI. The benefit here is that you can use your sampler to record the samples, and special software can be used to edit and manipulate the samples. An added benefit is that you can use the storage devices on your computer to archive your samples.

If you experience problems getting your SCSI network to work properly it may be helpful to consider the following solutions.

▶ Use high quality, shielded SCSI cables.

▶ Ensure that your SCSI chain is as short as possible and that it does not exceed 15 feet in total length.

▶ Ensure that each device is set to a unique ID number.

▶ Be sure to mount the drives (you will find a menu option or button on the sampler to initiate the mounting procedure). You may need to remount the drives after removing and inserting new media in a removable SCSI device.

▶ Check for termination on both ends of the SCSI chain.

▶ Find the problem. Power down, disconnect a device, and power up again. Repeat this process until you find the offending device.

▶ Change the order of devices in the chain. You may need to experiment to find a sequence that works. Note that the device ID numbers *do not* need to reflect the order of the device in the chain—ID numbers are simply used to determine what data belongs to which device.

Sound Design Tips and Practice Techniques

The process of editing sounds and designing custom sounds from scratch can be rewarding. Hardware and software synthesizers often provide vast editing capabilities that can be used to create an almost infinite number of interesting timbres. With all of the choices, it can be a daunting task to begin the process of custom sound design, so the following tips and practice techniques are provided to facilitate the process.

- ▶ Set an oscillator to produce a triangle or sawtooth waveform. Use the peak or resonance control to accentuate the cutoff point of a low-pass filter. Slowly change the filter cutoff and listen as each overtone is resonated.

- ▶ Apply an amplitude envelope to pink or white noise to create a snare drum. Apply filtering to change the timbre of the instrument.

- ▶ Set two oscillators to the same octave. Detune one oscillator slightly to create a natural chorusing effect.

- ▶ Use crossfading to combine two dissimilar sounds (e.g., a duck quack that turns into a vocal "ah" sound or a violin that blends into an organ.

- ▶ Create a patch using several layers—for example, an electric piano layered with the sound of a muted electric guitar and an organ.

- ▶ Use an envelope generator to control filter cutoff of a low- or high-pass filter. Use a low-frequency oscillator on the same filter and compare the results.

- ▶ Use an amplitude envelope to modify a nontraditional sound—for example, a stringed instrument with a sudden and percussive attack or a drum with a gentle attack.

- ▶ Use a low-frequency oscillator to create a siren sound. Route a data slider or wheel to control the rate of oscillation.

- ▶ Use sample looping to loop a portion of a percussive sound—for example, an infinitely decaying gong sound.

- ▶ Use velocity scaling to control a multi-layered sound—for example, an electric piano that sounds more percussive the harder you strike a key.

- ▶ Create an interesting drone texture. Drone or ambient sounds usually change over time such as with automated filter sweeping, amplitude modulation, or another real-time modifier.

- ▶ Create a new sound based on a sample in an unusual range such as a bass flute or soprano contrabass.

- ▶ Use dopplerization to create a "moving" voice. Try to emulate left-to-right as well as front-to-back movement.

▶ If your instrument supports it, create a sound that utilizes non-tempered tunings such as Werkmeister.

▶ Use a filter envelope to create a wah-wah guitar sound.

▶ Design a sound using a new algorithm (e.g., Pitch > Low-Pass Filter > Shaper > Band-Pass Filter > Amplifier).

▶ If you have access to a physical modeling synthesizer, create a sound that utilizes a traditional physical model for a nontraditional sound—for example, breath and embouchure control of a stringed instrument.

▶ Create a groove patch by sequencing a bass and drum groove and sampling the output of the synthesizer.

▶ Edit the previous example to create a time-expanded groove.

▶ Edit the previous example to create a pitch-shifted groove.

▶ Create a snare drum-map where snare samples are placed on consecutive keys at slightly different pitches (to create natural sounding rolls and fills).

▶ Assign the modulation wheel to crossfade between two multi-samples such as an electric guitar and electric guitar feedback.

▶ Use a low-frequency oscillator to control pitch and assign the modulation wheel to control LFO amplitude (for a vibrato effect).

▶ Create a keyboard split (bass in left hand, piano in the right hand).

▶ Use a data slider to control two or more modifiers at the same time—for example, control filter cutoff frequency and filter resonance.

CHAPTER 7

Loop-Based Production

Loop-based tools offer many benefits in a production environment such as the ability to quickly create backing tracks or flesh out a sketch for a song or commercial project. This chapter explores two of the popular looping tools and discusses the process of creating music with these tools as well as how to create loops in a number of formats. Not only are these tools useful in creating new music, but many electronic musicians generate income by creating and selling finished loop libraries. This chapter covers the following looping concepts:

▶ Software tools for loop-based production

▶ Creating music with ACID and GarageBand

▶ Editing techniques

▶ Track effects and automation

▶ Recording audio tracks

▶ Recording MIDI tracks

▶ Bouncing to disk

▶ Creating your own loops in the ACID, Apple, and REX formats

▶ Common loop file formats

Overview

Most looping tools use a similar paradigm: The user selects prerecorded audio, MIDI, or hybrid MIDI and audio loops and uses a mouse to draw the loops into a track view (see Figure 7.1). It is interesting to note that Live, a program by Abelton, uses a somewhat different approach to building loop-based music.

Figure 7.1
ACID (Sonic Foundry).

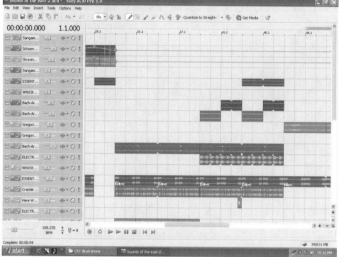

As with MIDI and audio programs, the lines have blurred in recent years, and all of the major DAW applications now support the ability to import loops. Likewise, popular looping tools like ACID provide at least a minimal amount of MIDI sequencing capability.

Software Tools for Loop-Based Production

Several popular looping tools are available on the PC and Macintosh platforms. On the PC side, ACID (made by Sonic Foundry, a division of Sony Music) has long been a favorite among electronic musicians. On the Macintosh platform, GarageBand is a capable looping and sequencing tool that comes free with new Macs. GarageBand projects can be loaded and edited with Apple's flagship DAW program, Logic Pro. As mentioned previously, Abelton Live, a cross-platform application, features a unique approach to creating music from loops. Although I would consider Propellerhead's Reason to be a sequencing and software synthesis application, the program provides a REX loop player and thus is a good choice for users who want to use REX loops in a sequencing environment on either the PC or Mac platform. Fruityloops is an inexpensive loop-based program used by many musicians on the PC platform. On the Macintosh platform, Soundtrack is a program that features audio editing and looping capability and can synchronize audio to video in programs like Apple's Final Cut Pro.

Several tools are available for musicians interested in creating their own loops: Propellerhead's ReCycle is a cross-platform tool for creating MIDI/audio hybrid loops in the REX file format, a format supported by many DAW applications. Sonic Foundry's ACID and Sound Forge provide the ability to edit ACID-format loops. Apple's Logic Pro and Soundtrack provide a loop-editing tool called Apple Loops Utility that can be used to edit loop files for GarageBand or Logic.

Creating Music with ACID Pro

A first step in creating new music with ACID often involves selecting and importing loop files. ACID Pro comes with a number of loops, and commercial libraries are available from a variety of vendors. Since ACID can be used to create music solely from preexisting loops, the only requirement is a good ear and artistic sensibility. For this reason, ACID is a good choice for people who don't play an instrument. With that said, many professional musicians also use ACID because it provides an efficient method of creating music. For example, backing tracks for a jingle or similar project can be developed in a matter of minutes by selecting loops from a library. Loops can be purchased from many vendors, including Sony Media Software.

The file explorer window, usually visible at the bottom of the track window or available from the View menu is used to navigate and select prerecorded loops (see Figure 7.2). Once a file has been selected, it can be dragged to a track or double-clicked to create a new track that links to the selected file. While in the explorer view, clips can be previewed via a single click on the filename.

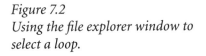

Figure 7.2
Using the file explorer window to select a loop.

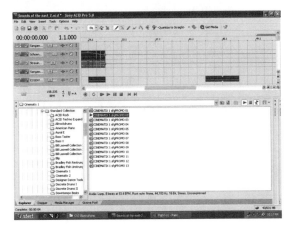

Once a track has been created, use the Draw tool to draw the loop into a track. Use the horizontal zoom button to create an insertion grid of increasingly smaller values. For example, loops can be drawn into the track view a measure at a time, a beat at a time, or some smaller value. Figure 7.3 shows several loop fragments being drawn in the track view.

Figure 7.3
Drawing a loop in the track view.

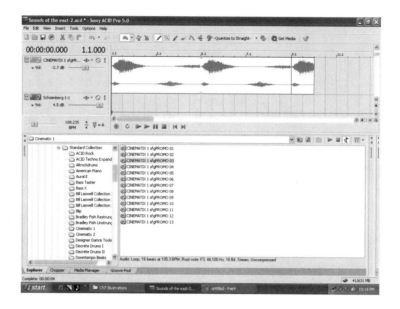

Each track provides a slider that can be toggled between track volume and pan. To automate a mix (such as for a fade-out), right-click on a loop and select the "add volume envelope" or "add pan envelope" option from the context menu. Once volume or pan has been inserted into a track via the context menu, double-click the mouse to insert a volume or pan keyframe. As with most DAW programs, volume and pan envelopes can be adjusted by dragging a node with the mouse (see Figure 7.4).

Figure 7.4
Adjusting volume envelopes in the track view.

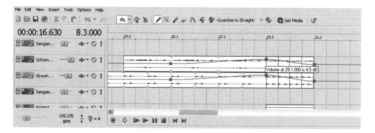

Pitch shifting is also available from a context menu. To change the pitch of a clip, right-click on the clip and select the pitch shift option to raise or lower the clip by a semitone (half step). Note that extreme pitch shifting will cause noticeable audio artifacts, a type of unwanted distortion.

One of the amazing things about ACID is that the tempo and rhythmic feel of audio loops can be freely edited. For example, global song properties including the key, time signature, and tempo of the piece can be selected via the tuning fork, time signature, and beats per minute (bpm) icons respectively (see Figure 7.5).

Tempo, key, and time signatures can be added at any point in a composition via the Insert menu. To add an event such as a tempo change, use the mouse to place the insertion point at an appropriate place in the song and select the "Tempo/Key/Time Change" option from the Insert menu. These events will be visible at the top of the track view just like a conductor track, as discussed in Chapter 4, "Sequencing Concepts."

Figure 7.5
Setting the global song key property.

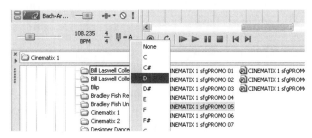

Unlike many programs, the playback of audio loops can be quantified to conform to any number of grooves. To change the groove of a clip, open the Groove Pool tab and drag the groove so that it overlays an existing clip. Although audio artifacts are sometimes audible, many interesting grooves can be created from an existing audio clip. For example, a straight-eighth drum groove can be made to swing using a groove template. As you can see in Figure 7.6, the relative position of beats can be adjusted using the groove editing tool.

Figure 7.6
Applying a groove to an existing audio loop.

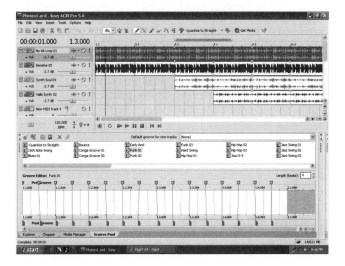

ACID Pro also supports the ability to record and edit MIDI or software synthesizer tracks. Use the "Insert > MIDI Track" menu option to insert a MIDI track. To use a software synthesizer, use the Insert menu to create a software synthesizer plug-in. Click the Device Selection button to select a software synthesizer as a track insert (see Figure 7.7).

Figure 7.7
Using the Device Selection button to select a software synthesizer.

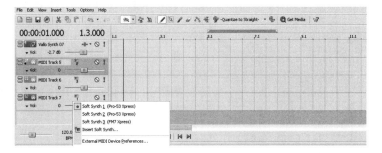

Once a software synthesizer has been selected, click the record button, type a filename, and select a destination location to record MIDI data that can, in turn, be drawn into the track view just like prerecorded loops.

When mixing, it is often desirable to add plug-ins such as reverb, delay, or equalization to a track. Plug-ins are available via the Plug-In Chooser button on each track or from the main mixer. A plug-in *chain* can be created by combining multiple plug-ins, as in Figure 7.8. These types of plug-ins can be used to add a wah-wah effect to a guitar track or to equalize, compress, or otherwise alter the sound of a track.

Figure 7.8
Creating an effects chain for an audio track.

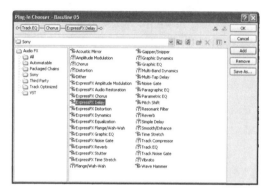

ACID Pro also provides the ability to record audio data. The process is similar to recording MIDI data except it is necessary to first adjust the input level to an optimal level. Depending on your hardware configuration, input levels can be adjusted from the Sound Manager in Windows or via an audio card properties application. Once the input level has been adjusted to an appropriate level (just below the clipping level), audio can be recorded and a new track will automatically be created to store the audio clip. As with MIDI clips, custom audio clips can be freely drawn into the track view. Alternately, some users prefer to record and edit audio in a dedicated application such as Sound Forge and then import the files into ACID.

Since loop-based production will, by definition, involve a large number of audio loops, it is a good idea to develop a storage strategy. For example, I like to keep my own custom loops in a separate subfolder, and I often find it convenient to use the root note of the clip in the name (e.g., "my_bass_line_E2"). It can be difficult to keep track of hundreds or thousands of loops, so consider placing all loops in a single location and use subfolders to organize loops into logical groupings (e.g., vendor, style, tempo, etc.).

ACID provides a useful beat-mapping wizard for editing custom recorded loops (or to change prerecorded loop mapping). Note that beat mapping does not change the underlying audio data—you might think of a beat map as a virtual beat overlay that tells the program how to interpret and play back the underlying audio data. You will see the process for creating ACID loops later in the section "Rolling Your Own Loops."

Creating Music with GarageBand

Although GarageBand does not have all the bells and whistles of a professional-level application, the program offers an attractive feature set for a program that comes free with most Macs. The program provides a convenient method of creating rough sketches, so I often gravitate to the program when I am experimenting with a new idea for a song.

As with ACID Pro, GarageBand provides a track view in which audio or MIDI loops can be dragged to create a composition. Click on the eye icon to open the Loop Browser window (see Figure 7.9). Loops are organized according to instrument and styles. Once an instrument or pattern has been selected, click the Reset button in the loop browser to make all of the instrument groups available for another selection. To add the loop to a project, simply drag the file to the track view, and a new track will be created.

Figure 7.9
Using the loop browser.

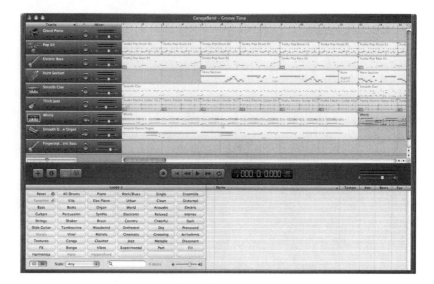

Several properties are available for each track, such as a mute and solo button and track pan and volume. Click on the small arrow to view a volume or pan curve (envelope) for the current track. As with most DAW programs, a volume or pan event can be created by clicking on the volume or pan line (see Figure 7.10).

GarageBand provides two convenient views for editing MIDI and audio data. Click on the Track Editor icon and then select the graphic or notation views to view MIDI data in a piano roll or notation view, respectively (see Figure 7.11).

Figure 7.10
Creating a volume envelope.

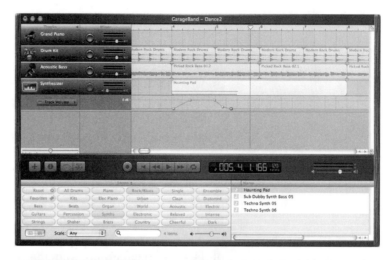

Figure 7.11
Editing MIDI data in the piano roll
view.

As with sequencing applications, the pitch and duration of notes can be adjusted with the mouse, and one or more notes can be cut, copied, or pasted by lassoing a region of notes (see Figure 7.12).

Figure 7.12
Lassoing a region of notes in a
notation view.

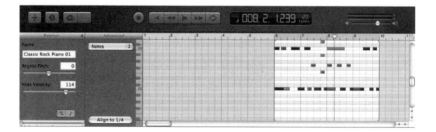

The Track Editor view is also used to adjust the pitch of a loop. To change the pitch, select one of the loops in the track view and then adjust the pitch via the Region Pitch slider. The slider will only have an effect on the currently selected loop, so multiple transpositions are possible on a single track. Of course, global pitch can be changed via the master pitch button. This is useful if you paste a portion of a song and want to create a global modulation.

MIDI and audio loops can be edited in higher resolution by zooming in. In Figure 7.13, a loop has been truncated so it plays for a single quarter note.

Figure 7.13
Editing the length of an audio loop
in the track view (use the zoom
slider for finer resolution).

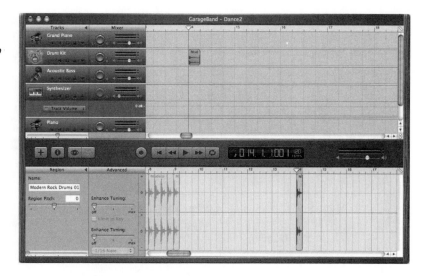

GarageBand provides a number of useful software synthesizers. To record a MIDI passage using a software instrument, select "New Track…" from the Track menu. A dialog box will present several software instruments. Once the software instrument track has been created, MIDI data can be recorded by clicking the record button. To quantize or tighten the rhythm of a passage, select the graphic or notation view and select one or more notes. Depending on the settings of the zoom slider, the Align To button will provide a quantization level in the range of a quarter note to 64th note (see Figure 7.14). Note that triplet values are available from the notation view.

Figure 7.14
Quantizing a grouping of notes in
the graphic view.

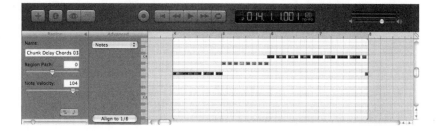

Although GarageBand does not provide the same editing options as a professional-level program, several continuous controllers are available from the advanced drop-down menu to edit or insert pedal events, pitch bend, modulation, or expression (see Figure 7.15).

In terms of signal processing, click the Track Info icon to set track parameters such as reverb, delay, chorus, and the like (see Figure 7.16).

Figure 7.15
Editing continuous controller data
in GarageBand.

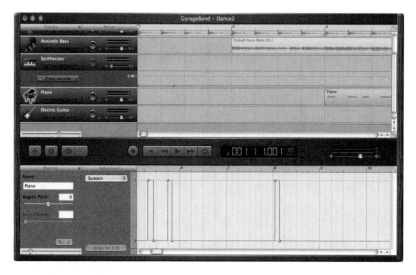

Figure 7.16
Adjusting track effects.

GarageBand provides a music typing keyboard that is available from the Window menu (see Figure 7.17). Although the typing keyboard is a poor substitute for a real MIDI keyboard, this virtual keyboard is useful if you don't have access to a MIDI keyboard or are stuck on a airplane. It's helpful to know you can record an idea when the muse strikes!

Figure 7.17
Music typing keyboard.

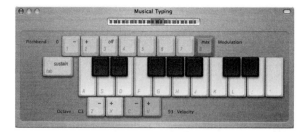

To record audio tracks for a vocal or acoustic instrument, select the "New Basic Track" option from the Track menu. Click the Track Info icon to select an input source as well as processing options such as compression (see Figure 7.18).

Figure 7.18
Selecting an input source prior to
recording an audio track.

Split and join commands are available from the Edit menu for basic cutting and pasting of audio data. Although it is not evident from the file menu, it is interesting to note that audio files (including ACID loops) can be dropped into an available track in GarageBand.

Once you complete a GarageBand project, select "Export To iTunes" from the File menu. You will find the finished master in your iTunes library and can then use iTunes to burn this (and other audio files) to a CD.

Rolling Your Own Loops

Loop-based tools are fun and efficient to use, but, as with most things musical, it can be rewarding to have complete control over a project. The composition and recording of custom loops can add an exciting dimension to the music making process and may yield commercial opportunities as well. This section will look at the techniques involved to create loops in three of the most popular formats: ACID loops, Apple Loops, and REX loops.

CREATING AN ACID LOOP
ACID Pro provides a helpful beat-mapping wizard. Beat mapping involves analyzing a file to determine transients (periodic audio spikes that represent beats) and tempo. Once an audio file has been mapped in this way, it can be used like any other loop in ACID, and the audio will automatically adjust to tempo changes or the application of beat-mapping grooves.

To use the wizard, record (or import) an audio loop and click the Beat Mapper Wizard button (see Figure 7.19).

The Beat Mapper will determine the starting beat (which you can confirm or adjust in the Beat Mapper dialog box). Next, adjust the length of the blue line at the top of the "Step 2" dialog so that the region conforms to a single measure and aligns with the click track (see Figure 7.20).

Figure 7.19
Starting the Beat Mapper Wizard.

Figure 7.20
Configuring the length of a measure in the Beat Mapper dialog box.

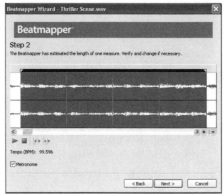

In the next dialog box, double check that each measure is properly aligned. You can make adjustments with the measure start and end tabs. If the loop sounds good, be sure to select the option to "Save beatmapper information with file" before saving the loop to disk. That's it! The file is now ready to be used in a loop-based project.

CREATING AN APPLE LOOP

The process for preparing an Apple Loop is similar to preparing a loop for use in ACID. There are two common ways to proceed. If you own Logic, loops can easily be created within the program. First, record or import an audio file into the program. For example, you might bounce to disk a few bars of a groove created with the Ultrabeat drum machine or other software synthesizer and then import the audio file into an audio track in Logic. Double-click the audio clip to load it into the sample editor. Adjust the start and end points of the file and turn on loop playback (within the sample editor) to check that the start and end points loop properly (see Figure 7.21).

Depending on the file, you may wish to save a region as a new file. Once the file has been trimmed, consider normalizing the file to optimize the level of the file and apply any additional edits such as with the Groove Machine or Audio Energizer. Save your work and close the sample editor.

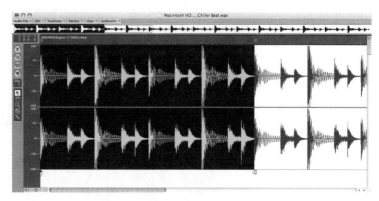

Figure 7.21
Adjusting the start and end points
of an audio file in the sample editor.

In the track view, select the audio loop and select "Open In Apple Loops Utility…" from the Audio submenu. This function will load the Apple Loops Utility, a program that allows you to configure tags such as the loop style as well as adjust transients for beat mapping.

A first step is to configure the loop parameters such as turning on the "loop" option, entering the number of beats, base key, tempo, author credits, and style parameters. Figure 7.22 shows settings that might be used for a typical loop.

Use the "Transient division" and "sensitivity" options so that transients align with the beats in the audio file. If necessary, select the Transients tab and make manual adjustments so that transients align properly with beats, divisions, and subdivisions (see Figure 7.23).

Figure 7.22
Configuring file tags in the Apple
Loops Utility program.

Once you are happy with the loop, save the file to disk. I find it helpful to reserve one or more folders for custom loops so I don't have to search through my hard disk for loops. One of the fun things about creating loops on the Macintosh platform is that loops can be imported into the global Apple Loops library for use in programs like GarageBand and Logic. To import the loop into the global library, run GarageBand or Logic Pro and drag the loop into the loop browser. The loop will be automatically added to the global loop library and can be found via the category settings you selected when using the main page of the Apple Loops Utility.

Figure 7.23
Adjusting transients in the Apple Loops Utility program.

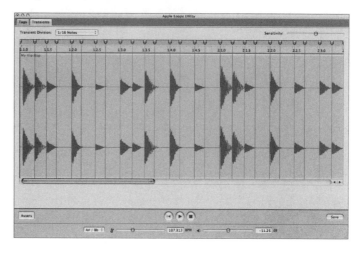

CREATING A REX FILE

REX files are used by programs such as Reason. The program ReCycle is used to convert audio files into the REX file format. A REX file is an audio file in which each "beat" in the loop is stored as a separate sample or slice. The benefit of this approach is that each slice retains its original timbre when played back at a new tempo. This contrasts with the process of audio-file time stretching used in other loop formats.

The first step in creating a REX file is to import an existing audio file into ReCycle. (You can use a DAW or audio editing program to create such a loop.) Once the loop has been imported, drag the left and right locators to an appropriate place in the file (see Figure 7.24). I usually record an extra beat or bar so that it is easier to determine the right locater (just drag the locater prior to the first transient of the extra bar or beat).

Figure 7.24
Setting the left and right locaters in ReCycle.

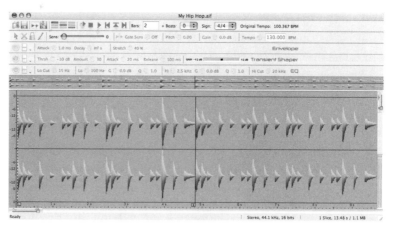

Next, adjust the sensitivity slider so that all (or most) of the transients are selected. You can lock selected transient markers prior to turning up the sensitivity and then delete any extraneous markers (see Figure 7.25).

Figure 7.25
Locking transient markers and
adjusting the sensitivity slider in
ReCycle.

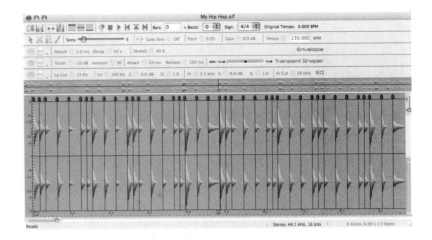

Select the "Crop Loop" option and enter the number of beats at the top of the editing window. You may also want to normalize the file prior to saving your completed REX file. To adjust EQ and other parameters such as attack and decay, toggle the Preview Play button and these options will be enabled. When your loop is edited to your satisfaction, save the file as a REX file.

Using a REX File

To use a REX file, you must import the file into a program such as Reason that supports this file format. The following paragraphs detail the steps necessary to load and use a custom REX file in Reason.

Start Reason and create a mixer and any effects you wish to use. Next, select "Create Dr. REX Loop Player" from the Create menu. Use the Browse Loop button to load your newly created REX loop into Dr. Rex and click the Preview button to check if your REX file loops properly. Set the left and right locator and click the To Track button to paste the REX loop to the current track (see Figure 7.26).

Figure 7.26
Pasting a REX loop to a track in
Reason.

Once REX data is pasted into a track, select the Edit Mode button to view the raw REX data. Adjustments can be made to the velocity of each slice, and the slices can even be used to play back a new drum kit or other sound in the Dr. Rex Loop Player.

Summary

Although it takes some time to create custom loop files in the ACID, Apple Loops, or REX file formats, you may find the process to be liberating. I have found it useful to develop bass and drum loops in a variety of styles and also enjoy using this technology to bring new life to some of my older analog gear. For example, classic analog synthesizers can be used to create unique bass lines and other types of audio loops. As I mentioned previously, some electronic musicians make an income from developing these types of custom loops.

CHAPTER 8

Music Notation

In a professional music environment, few things are as important as clearly notated music. A clean score and parts save rehearsal time and allow players to more quickly interpret your musical vision. Written music is used in many facets of the industry including film scoring, live performance, commercials, and just about any other situation where time is at a premium. In the past, music copyists labored with pen, ink, and vellum to prepare professional-quality scores. Today, professional scores can be prepared by anyone with a modest computer system and musical know-how. This chapter will look at the process of notating musical scores.

Although major music publishers around the world use music notation software, the tools, without human guidance, are incapable of producing quality scores, so a primary focus of the chapter will be to develop an understanding of notation techniques that can help your scores look more professional. Having been involved with recording sessions, shows, orchestral concerts, and the like, I can attest that notational clarity will make or break a session. In these types of environments, it is customary that the musicians might have a single rehearsal to prepare for an entire show, so anything the composer or arranger can do to clarify the music will be advantageous.

This chapter is not a tutorial on how to use notation software. Rather, the chapter focuses on strategies that will help you to efficiently utilize the software to create professional-looking scores and parts. To use an analogy, word-processing software can help to facilitate the writing process, but the software can't help you with punctuation and form—that part of the process still requires a knowledgeable writer. The comments in this chapter are based on problems I have encountered in professional and academic settings, and the discussion is intended to provide a link between learning how to use the software and utilizing the software to produce professional results. The following concepts will be emphasized:

▶ Selecting a music notation application

▶ Creating professional scores

▶ Data entry methods

▶ Enhancing workflow

▶ Case studies: creating scores in Finale and Sibelius

Picking the Right Tool

Digital audio workstation software such as Digital Performer, Logic Pro, and Cubase provides at least a basic level of notation capability. These tools are primarily intended to render a MIDI performance into notation for purposes of editing or to quickly generate a rough score. Surprisingly, I have found that sequencing applications such as Logic actually do a better job of translating a performance into notation than most music notation programs, but at the end of the day, DAW software will generally not provide the same editing capability as a notation-specific program, so these applications are generally not appropriate for serious music notation tasks.

CHOOSING A NOTATION APPLICATION

Currently, the two primary notation applications are Finale and Sibelius. Notion, a new product by VirtuosoWorks, features an interesting mix of notation and sample playback technology and shows great promise as an alternative to the two "big players." Students and colleagues often ask for recommendations on how to select a notation application, and I typically suggest the following.

▶ **Download demos.** The best way to select a notation application is to spend time learning to use the program. Output quality and overall stability are excellent in applications from each of the major software vendors, so the most important issue will likely be to determine which program provides the most comfortable interface for your work style.

▶ **Download manuals.** Online manuals and tutorials are available from each vendor. These references provide an excellent look at how each application approaches typical notational tasks.

▶ **Create a variety of projects.** Each program has strengths and weaknesses that may not be evident until you have worked on a variety of projects. For example, you might use the case studies at the end of this chapter as a good point of reference. Create a lead sheet and a short orchestral score to see how each program handles part extraction, chord entry, and other tasks.

▶ **Visit user forums.** Online user forums can provide an excellent insight into the strengths and weaknesses of each program.

A few subjective comments are in order. I own and use Finale and Sibelius extensively and am impressed with both products. If ease of use is a primary concern, I would suggest Sibelius. The Sibelius user interface is elegant, easy to use, and requires very little use of the mouse. I also give Sibelius an edge when it comes to entering notes without the aid of a MIDI keyboard and for choral writing. I gravitate to Finale for orchestral and jazz ensemble projects because Finale provides several tools such as staff lists and custom staff styles that are very useful when dealing with large scores. I have also found Finale's "Mass Edit" tool to be a great help in copying slurs and articulations in large orchestrations.

LEARNING HOW TO USE NOTATION SOFTWARE

Finale, Notion, and Sibelius provide manuals with excellent tutorials. I encourage you to spend some time working through the manuals; in a few days, you should be quite comfortable handling typical notational tasks. The two case studies later in the chapter provide helpful insights into the notation process, but again, this is not intended to be a substitute for a thorough tutorial.

The following tips will help you get started with basic note entry should you wish to download a demo of either application.

Getting Started with Finale

▶ Use the Setup Wizard to start a new project.

▶ Visit the MIDI > Midi Setup menu and make sure a valid MIDI device is selected for input and output.

▶ Select the MIDI > Midi Thru menu and select the "Smart" option (a good default setting).

▶ Select the Speedy Entry tool and click on a measure where you would like to add notes.

▶ If you plan to use a MIDI keyboard for note entry, make sure "Use MIDI Device for Input" is selected in the Speedy menu.

▶ Hold down a note or chord on a MIDI keyboard and press a number on the keypad representing the value of the note or chord: 4 = eighth note, 5 = quarter note, and so on.

▶ Look in the Speedy > Speedy Edit Commands menu to learn other helpful entry commands.

Getting Started with Sibelius

▶ Use the New Score Wizard to start a new project.

▶ Visit the Play > Devices dialog box and set input and playback devices to a valid MIDI device. Also select the "Thru" option.

▶ Click on a whole rest in a measure where you would like to start adding notes.

▶ Press the appropriate rhythmic value as shown on the floating numeric keypad (4 = quarter note, 5 = half note, and so on).

▶ Press a note or chord on a MIDI keyboard to insert one or more notes at the current rhythmic value. Or press a letter name on the keypad representing the note you wish to enter.

▶ Press the Escape key twice to exit note-entry mode.

Music Notation Concepts

Although tools like Finale and Sibelius are wonderfully advanced notation programs, you will likely need to do some tweaking to achieve the best results. This section is intended to provide an overview of notation principals that you should consider when preparing scores. Differences of opinion exist when it comes to "norms" of music notation, but the following concepts are used by many professionals and will help your scores look better and be more easily read. Most of the problems I see in music notation are the result of users who are passive about the choices made by a notation program, so consider the suggestions in this section as you work your application of choice.

RHYTHMIC NOTATION

A common problem involves rhythms that do not reflect the underlying beat. Take Figure 8.1 as an example: Although 6/8 can be written as three groups of two eighth notes, it is generally better to present the underlying beat (dotted quarter note), so two groupings of three eighth notes is preferred:

Figure 8.1
Eighth notes in 6/8: unclear and clear.

Similarly, a subdivision is much easier to read if rhythms are beamed according to the underlying beat (see Figure 8.2).

When notating syncopation, it is best to reflect an imaginary bar line in the middle of a bar of common time. As with beaming of division and subdivisions, syncopation should reflect the underlying beat. Notice how the second measure of Figure 8.3 is much easier to read than the first measure because the beat is evident in the notation.

Figure 8.2
Sixteenth notes in 6/8: unclear and clear.

Figure 8.3
Notating syncopation (imaginary bar line).

COURTESY ACCIDENTALS

Courtesy accidentals can be useful in preventing reading errors. Without a courtesy accidental, most players would miss the E-flats in the second bar of Figure 8.4. A courtesy accidental is essential in this context, but take care that you don't use them too liberally—a score can become hard to read if many unnecessary accidentals are used.

Figure 8.4
Using courtesy accidentals to avoid performance errors.

When preparing parts, utilize accidentals that enhance readability—even if the accidentals don't make sense from a theoretical standpoint. The second measure of Figure 8.5 is easier to read than the first measure—even though the D-sharp does not make good theoretical sense in relation to an E-flat chord. Depending on context, F-flat to E-flat might be an even better choice.

Figure 8.5
Enhancing readability with enharmonic equivalents.

CHORD SPELLING

If a given chord is based on tertian harmony (built in thirds), it often makes sense to reflect the underlying interval of a third when spelling these chords. Students often ask why double sharps and flats are used, and chord spelling is a great example: The first bar of Figure 8.6 is awkward to read because the accidentals do not reflect the fact that these structures are triads. As you can see, the second measure is somewhat easier to read.

Figure 8.6
Chord spelling: unclear and clear

CHORD SYMBOLS

The primary problem I see with chord symbols are situations where parentheses are missing from an altered chord. For example, it is unclear if the first measure of Figure 8.7 is a B-natural chord with a lowered fifth or a B-flat "power chord" (often used in guitar music). The second chord more clearly indicates a B-flat "power chord" and the third example indicates a B chord with an altered fifth. If the chord contains a seventh, it is not usually necessary to place alterations in parentheses. Also, depending on typeface, it is often a good idea to use "mi" or "min" for minor instead of a single "m" character since upper and lowercase characters can be difficult to differentiate in some fonts.

Figure 8.7
Chord symbols.

MUSIC SPACING

Programs such as Finale and Sibelius provide quite a bit of flexibility when dealing with music spacing. In many cases, it is a balancing act to space a score so that notes and ties are easy to read but there is not an inordinate number of pages. In practice, I have found that proportional spacing provides the best results. With proportional spacing, a measure containing a single whole note would require much less horizontal space than a measure containing 16th notes (see Figure 8.8). Similarly, you may want to avoid specifying or "locking" a specific number of measures per system in order to optimize music spacing. Vertical spacing is also important—a range of about 8 to 10 staves per page will have a "cleaner" look and be easier to read than parts with too many staves. I find that it is best to let the software space music as you enter notes, dynamics, chords, and other items. Don't worry if spacing looks cluttered at this point in the process—once all of the elements have been entered it is easy to manually override computer-generated spacing in order to perfect the spacing of your score. Some programs have a reformat feature that respaces the music to different proportions. For example, in Finale, allotment libraries for loose or tight spacing can be loaded in order to override the default note spacing proportions.

Figure 8.8
Proportional spacing.

I often see computer-generated parts with a final page consisting of one or two bars. A more professional look can be achieved by "forcing" measures from previous pages in order to fill in the final page. Sometimes, page reduction or enlargement can be helpful in finding a more natural flow of measures.

PAGE TURNS

It is best to lay out pages so that players have a few bars of rest prior to a page turn. Of course, this is moot if a part is only two pages long. However, musicians will have no recourse other than to miss notes if they are required to turn pages in the middle of a phrase. Along these lines, it is helpful to signal the end of a piece with a *fine* mark. You should also consider using the text "V.S." (which stands for stands for *volti subito*: turn the page suddenly) in cases where players might inadvertently think they have reached the end of a work. Figure 8.9 shows the final two systems of a part preceding a page turn. Notice how the multimeasure rest provides ample time to turn the page.

Figure 8.9
Placing multi-measure rests prior to a page turn.

REHEARSAL LETTERS AND MEASURE NUMBERS

Measure numbers and/or rehearsal letters are essential on any project involving more than a few measures. Thankfully, this is simply a matter of selecting an option within a notation program, and the computer will take care of the hard work. It often makes sense to include double bars in places that a rehearsal letter is used since this will provide another visual clue to help the reader (see Figure 8.10).

Figure 8.10
Using measure numbers and rehearsal letters.

PICKUP BARS

A common notational error involves pickup bars. Since notation programs usually insert a whole rest for any empty measure, empty pickup bars usually look like a full measure of rest (see Figure 8.11). This will create confusion in a rehearsal or recording session, so be sure to insert an appropriate amount of rest to avoid this situation.

Figure 8.11
Missing pickup rests.

MULTI-MEASURE RESTS

Multi-measure rests are useful because they reduce page count and make it easier for players to count rests. Be sure to add double bars at important structural points in the score prior to extracting parts so that multi-measure rests will reflect the form of the music. Also, check that time or key signatures are not hidden in a multi-measure rest. In Figure 8.12, notice how an eight-bar rest is broken into two smaller multi-measure rests so that the player can see the change of key.

Figure 8.12
Breaking a multi-measure rest into smaller units.

REPEATS

I am sometimes forced to read charts with extensive instructions such as *"play four times then D.S. for solos and take the second ending and play two times."* These types of instructions are impossible to follow in a reading situation. Since it is so easy to use the computer to copy and paste music, it is generally better to write out a repeat that would be inordinately complex. Strive for instructions that are clear. For example, *"Play four times"* seems clearer than *"Repeat three times,"* and *"To Coda 2ⁿᵈ Time"* alleviates any question as to when to take a coda. Also, consider writing out the first bar of any new system if using single or double bar repeats as in example 8.13.

Figure 8.13
Single bar repeat.

STYLE AND TEMPO MARKINGS

A tempo or style marking is always a good idea in the first bar of a composition. A descriptive style marking can help players more readily interpret your intentions. For example, *"Slow Gospel 12/8 Feel"* is much more helpful than a generic *"Moderately."* This is particularly important in situations where players will question if eighth notes are straight or "swung."

DYNAMICS, PHRASING, AND ARTICULATION

Dynamics, phrase marks, and articulations are a necessary part of any score. At the very least, a dynamic marking in the first bar is essential. Dynamics are also prudent when a part re-enters after a period of rest. With regard to articulations, it can be difficult to find a balance between too few and too many. A good rule of thumb is that any note that might be interpreted in more than one way should have an articulation. Notes that are "played as usual" don't need an articulation. Phrase marks are most often used to indicate to brass or woodwind players that a passage should be slurred (no tongue). Figure 8.14 shows the type of markings found in a typical part.

Figure 8.14
Dynamics, articulations, and phrase marks.

VOCAL NOTATION

When writing vocal parts, use a slur and underscore (also referred to as a lyric extension line) to indicate a melisma (more than one note sung on a single syllable). It is also customary to use hyphens to break multi-syllabic words (see Figure 8.15).

Figure 8.15
Notating melismas and multi-syllabic words.

Data Entry

Music notation software provides several data entry methods. Each method has advantages and disadvantages, so you will want to consider the method that best suits the project at hand. The following section details the common methods of data entry in a modern notation application.

REAL-TIME NOTE ENTRY

The Holy Grail for music notation software is to be able to sit at a MIDI keyboard, press a record button, and generate a perfectly notated score. Although software has come a long way in this regard, music of any complexity will likely have an abundance of transcription errors. This is due to several factors: Music is a complex notation system that deals with many abstract concepts such as "interpretation" that are not well suited to computer algorithms. Since there are several ways to notate a given note, chord, or rhythm, computers must make an educated guess (but computers lack the context to always make the best decision). Performance inaccuracies will manifest themselves in rhythmic and note errors. Although real-time entry can be convenient in some situations, I feel strongly that step-time entry is faster and less prone to error (see below). Notation programs provide options to specify a quantization value and desired interpretation of tuplets, so it is a good idea to consider these settings prior to transcribing a real-time performance.

It is sometimes necessary to notate a "freely" recorded sequence—a performance that has been captured without a click track. Most modern sequencing applications provide the ability to create a custom beat map in order to tell the sequencer how the performance should be interpreted in relation to measures and beats. The common method is to use a foot controller or MIDI note to "tap" the beat in performance. Once a free performance has been mapped in this way, it is possible to save the performance as a standard MIDI file and import it into a notation application in order to transcribe the performance. Beat mapping will be an essential step should you wish to notate such a performance—music that has been transcribed without a clear beat reference will be impossible to read.

STEP-TIME NOTE ENTRY

With the step-time entry method, notes or chords are added a "step" at a time. For example, to add four C-major triads in Finale, press and hold the triad on a MIDI keyboard and press the number 5 key four times while in "speedy" entry mode. (Sibelius functions in a similar way.) Having transcribed, arranged, or engraved many thousands of pages of music for publication, I feel confident in saying that step-time entry is the most accurate and efficient form of notation data entry. By way of illustration, consider the prospect of entering 60 quarter notes in a composition with a tempo of 60 beats per minute. Of course, it would take an entire minute to enter the notes using real-time entry. In a non scientific test, I was able to accurately enter 60 notes in about 12 seconds with step-time entry—clearly a more efficient method!

MOUSE AND KEYPAD NOTE ENTRY

In lieu of a MIDI keyboard, a mouse and computer keypad can be used for smaller projects. I would give Sibelius an edge over Finale in its support for keypad input: Sibelius provides many helpful key commands that make it efficient to enter notes and build chords without the use of a MIDI keyboard. Since note-entry keyboards can be purchased for about $100, I would encourage the use of such a keyboard for any moderately sized project—chords are particularly time-consuming to enter without the aid of a MIDI keyboard. Alternately, an Electronic Wind Instrument (EWI), Malletkat, or other MIDI controller may be used for note entry. Some programs provide the ability to transcribe monophonic passages via a microphone.

IMPORTING A STANDARD MIDI FILE

Modern notation applications can transcribe a performance from a standard MIDI file. As with real-time entry, the process is prone to errors and usually requires a fair amount of manual tweaking to produce a quality score. To transcribe a MIDI file, first save the file in Format-1 so that each part is saved as a separate track. (This is in contrast to Format-0 files in which all parts are stored in a single track.) The file can then be opened in a notation program via a File > Open or File > Import command.

CHARACTER RECOGNITION

Character recognition offers the potential of scanning a page of sheet music and converting the digital image into notes and rhythms in a musical score. My experience has been that the technology has not developed to the point that it is very useful. This feature will work better on simple music. In several tests, it was faster for me to simply enter notes using the step-time method than spend time fixing numerous errors resulting from the scanning process. One tip is to try scanning uncompressed TIFF files using a black and white (line art) scanner set to 300 dpi. Companion MOCR scanning programs (such as ScoreScan) are available that can add more functionality, such as text and lyric recognition.

Enhancing Workflow

As I mentioned earlier in the chapter, the best way to learn notation software is to work through the tutorials. Once you feel comfortable entering and editing notes, chords, articulations, and other types of data, it is time to consider techniques that will help you to work more comfortably and efficiently. I have found the following techniques to be helpful in creating a more efficient workflow.

TEMPLATES

All of the major notation software packages provide the ability to load and save score templates. Although using templates might seem like an obvious choice, I have noticed that many students choose to start a project by selecting individual parts in a score setup wizard. Preexisting templates for everything from jazz band to orchestra and hymnals are provided and can be a great timesaver. If you plan to do your own publishing, custom templates provide a great way to create a consistent look and feel in every new project.

CUSTOM LIBRARIES

Libraries are used to store custom chord symbols, spacing allotments, performance symbols, and other kinds of custom data. Libraries, when combined with custom templates, provide the most efficient environment because you only need to design these custom elements once. For example, I once spent an hour designing a large library of chord symbols in Finale, and it is now a simple matter to import the library into a new project in order to gain access to the large palette of symbols. Instrument patch libraries can also be useful when using non-General MIDI synthesizers, particularly when notating certain styles of music such as marching percussion or jazz ensemble.

CUSTOM KEY COMMANDS

In general, key commands are more efficient than using a mouse. For example, "metatools" (a type of key macro in Finale) can be assigned to articulations and other score elements. These types of key commands can be saved in a template and are a huge timesaver. Sibelius offers similar functionality via the numeric keypad and the Preferences > Menus and Shortcuts menu. In general, any repetitive task will be more efficient with keystrokes, so it is advantageous to learn the default commands and to create customized commands as needed.

EXPLODING PARTS

When writing vertical parts such as a five-part sax soli, part "explosion" can be a great timesaver. To take advantage of the technique, enter complete chords in one part and use the software to explode each note to the respective part. In Sibelius, this functionality can be achieved by using the "filter" command to select the bottom note in a series of chords. Once selected, the notes can be copied and pasted into individual parts. Finale provides an "explode" function that is available from the Mass Edit tool. This technique is even more effective if you add slurs and articulations prior to exploding a phrase as in Figure 8.16.

Figure 8.16
Exploding parts in Finale.

Part implosion can also be useful. For example, implosion can be used to create a two-stave piano reduction of an orchestral passage.

COPYING SLURS AND ARTICULATIONS

It is often a time-consuming process to enter slurs and articulations. One trick that I have found to be effective is to add slurs and articulations in one part and selectively copy these markings to other parts. In a soli section, for example, it is likely that ten or more parts might share the same set of slurs and articulations, so the technique can save a great deal of time. Figure 8.17 shows a Finale dialog box used to configure the selective copying options.

Figure 8.17
Setting up the Mass Edit tool to selectively copy.

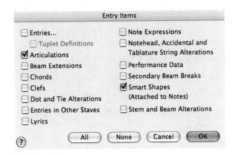

Figure 8.18 shows how the Mass Edit tool is used to selectively copy slurs and articulations from one part to another.

Figure 8.18
Copying slurs and articulations in a soli.

USING MIDI

Chapter 3, "Introduction to MIDI," provides an overview of MIDI technology that will allow you to enhance any modern notation application. For example, a knowledge of bank select and program change messages will allow you to configure notation software to work seamlessly with a keyboard that does not support General MIDI. An understanding of MIDI also provides the opportunity to customize playback, as shown in Figure 8.19. In this instance, a program change message is attached to the text "To Flute" to change the playback sound of a line of music from saxophone to flute at a given point in the score.

In Sibelius, MIDI commands can be added (and hidden) directly in a score by inserting "Technique" style text. For example, the text "~C1,64" would insert a hidden control change #1 (modulation) message with a value of 64. These types of MIDI messages can be helpful in providing more realistic playback.

Figure 8.19
Using a custom MIDI message.

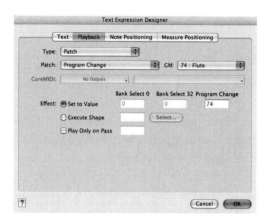

Finale and Sibelius both offer plug-ins that can add greater versatility such as the ability to check the range of instruments, apply cues, double or halve rhythmic values, and a host of other options. If you have some programming experience, you can even create your own custom plug-ins for Finale or Sibelius.

Case Studies

The following section demonstrates the process of creating a score in Finale and Sibelius. This section is not meant to be a tutorial but to provide a look at the process of creating scores in two modern notation applications. Readers who already own one of the products may be interested to see how scores are created in competing products. New users will find the discussion to be a helpful overview of the production process. I will illustrate two common tasks: creating a lead sheet in Sibelius and creating a score and parts in Finale.

CREATING A LEAD SHEET IN SIBELIUS

The goal of the Sibelius project is to demonstrate the creation of a lead sheet containing lyrics and chord symbols. The project will also be useful in demonstrating basic page layout and formatting.

Setting Up the Score

Sibelius provides numerous templates as well as an intuitive Setup Wizard. For this project, I elected to use the default "Lead sheet" template (see Figure 8.20). The Setup Wizard guided me through the process of selecting a default time and key signature as well as selecting an eighth note pickup for the first bar. Of course, these elements can be changed after the score has been created, but the wizard provides an easy method of establishing default values.

Entering Notes

The first step to entering notes is to select an insert position. This is achieved by selecting a rhythmic entry (usually a whole rest) in the bar where you intend to enter notes. After the insert point has been selected, the numeric keypad is used to select a rhythmic value and the keypad or MIDI keyboard can be used to enter notes. The Enter key (the bottom-right key on the numeric keypad) is used to enter ties. Figure 8.21 shows the first few bars of note entry.

Figure 8.20
Selecting a template.

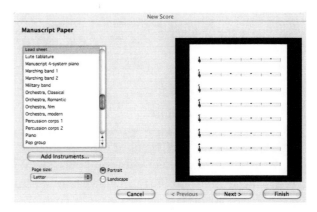

You will probably notice that some notes may be spaced too tightly, and lyrics and other items may collide. As I mentioned in the section on note spacing, I find it is best to simply enter notes and fix any spacing problems once everything has been entered.

Figure 8.21
Entering notes.

Adding Lyrics

Lyric entry is similar to note entry. Click on a note and select the Create > Text > Lyrics menu option and begin typing. The minus key is used to add hyphens and the spacebar will move the insertion point to the next note in the current voice. One convenient feature provided by Sibelius is that underscores are automatically added if you press the space key on two (or more) consecutive notes. It is customary to use both an under-score and slur for any melismas. Slurs are added by selecting the first note in a slur group and pressing the "S" key. While in slur entry mode, the spacebar will extend a slur to the next note in the current voice.

Figure 8.22
Entering lyrics in Sibelius.

Adding Chords

To add chords, select a note or rest to establish the insertion point. Then select the Create > Text > Chords menu option. Chords are entered by typing and, like lyric entry, the space key is used to tab from one rhythmic entry to the next. For a flat symbol, type a lowercase "b," and use the "#" key to enter sharps. While in chord entry mode, chords can be selected from a list by clicking the right mouse button.

Figure 8.23
Entering chord symbols in Sibelius.

Page Layout

The final step is to adjust the overall layout of measures and staves and fix any collisions or other problems. To force a measure to the next system, select a barline and press the Return key. Multiple measures can be forced into a single system by "shift-clicking" a range of measures and selecting the Layout > Format > Make Into System menu option. Vertical staff spacing is achieved by selecting a system and dragging it up or down with the mouse. Note that all of the entry modes described in this section can be selected by pressing a predefined key command. As I mentioned previously, key commands are much more efficient than selecting menu items with the mouse.

Although I didn't cover the entry of dynamics, crescendos, and other elements, these (and many other score elements) are available from the Create menu. In general, adding items to a Sibelius score simply involves selecting a note, rest, or barline with the mouse and selecting an appropriate option from the Create menu.

The final version of the lead sheet is shown in Figure 8.24.

CREATING A SCORE AND PARTS IN FINALE

The goal for the Finale project is to demonstrate the creation of a transposing score and the extraction of parts from the full score.

Getting Started

Finale comes with many helpful templates, which are located in the templates subfolder. However, since this project involved a nonstandard orchestration, the Setup Wizard provided the best starting point. The wizard functions in a similar way to the Sibelius wizard described in the previous section.

Entering Notes

It is generally more convenient to enter notes in concert pitch instead of transposing them "on the fly." Select the Options > Display In Concert Pitch menu item to toggle transposition on and off. Notes can be efficiently entered via the Speedy Entry tool. Select the Speedy tool and click a measure to begin entering notes. Finale note entry is slightly different than Sibelius: In the default entry mode, select a measure, then hold a note or chord on a MIDI keyboard and press a number to define the duration of the entry: number 5 = quarter note, 4 = eighth note, and so on. Finale provides a "hands-free" mode that is similar to Sibelius entry—press the Caps Lock key to enter hands-free mode. In this mode, durations are entered first and any number of notes can then be entered via a MIDI keyboard. A list of speedy commands is available via the Speedy > Speedy Edit Commands menu. This is a handy way to learn the commands for common functions such as entering ties, enharmonic equivalents, and dotted notes.

Figure 8.24
The finished lead sheet.

One thing that I found to be confusing when I first learned Finale is that menus appear and disappear depending on the current tool selection. This makes sense when you consider the large number of menu items but it can be confusing at first. Figure 8.25 shows notes being entered via the Speedy Entry tool.

Adding Slurs

Slurs are added with the "Smart Shape Palette." Select the slur tool from the palette, double-click and, without releasing the second click, drag the shape to the destination note and release the mouse. All of the "Smart

Shapes" work in a similar fashion—double-click and hold; then drag and release. Figure 8.26 shows a slur being added to a group of notes.

Figure 8.25
Entering notes in Finale.

Figure 8.26
Adding slurs in Finale.

Adding Articulations

The Articulation tool is of course used to add articulations such as accents and staccatos. Finale provides a method of assigning hot keys called "Metatools" that can be a real timesaver when doing repetitive tasks such as entering articulations. To assign a metatool, hold the Shift key and press a hot key, then make a selection from the resulting dialog box to "wire" the hot key to the articulation. Many metatools are preprogrammed. For example, to add an accent to a note, select the Articulation tool, hold the "A" key, and click on a notehead. In Figure 8.27, the "meta" commands are the letters in parentheses.

Figure 8.27
Assigning a meta command.

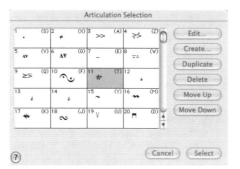

Adding Dynamics

Dynamic entry is similar to articulation entry. Select the Expression tool and double-click to insert an expression in the score. Expressions can be selected from the resulting dialog box (see Figure 8.28). Click the Create button to make a new expression.

Finale provides a powerful tool called "staff lists" that is available any time an expression is added to a score. Once a staff list has been created, dynamics can be entered in any number of staves with a single click. Notice how a saxophone staff list has been created in Figure 8.29.

The "Score" column indicates that an item will be drawn on the given score staff, and the "Parts" column is used to specify that the item should be included in the given part.

Figure 8.28
Selecting an expression.

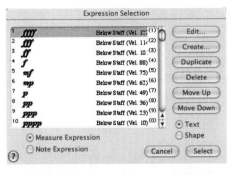

Figure 8.29
Creating a staff list to facilitate efficient entry of dynamics.

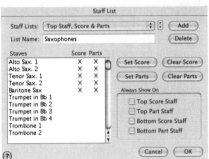

Adding Chord Symbols and Slash Notation

Chords are entered via the Chord tool. Select this tool and click a note to begin typing chords into the score. The "Type Into Score" option may first need to be selected from the Chord menu. Since chords must be assigned to a note or rest, it is often necessary to insert "dummy" rests into the score. In Figure 8.30, a series of quarter-note rests was added prior to entering chord symbols in the first bar. The "rhythmic notation" staff style was created by selecting the Staff tool and right-clicking on the second bar. Custom styles, such as a combination of slash notation and traditional notation, can also be created with this tool.

Figure 8.30
Chord symbols and slash notation.

Extracting Parts

Once a score has been prepared and edited, select the File > Extract Parts menu item to create individual files for each part. Notice how the piano, which is a multi-stave part, is selected from the group list, and individual parts are selected from the "staves" list in Figure 8.31.

Figure 8.31
Selecting parts to extract.

Page Layout

Page layout in Finale is usually achieved by using a combination of the Mass Edit tool and the Page Layout tool. The Mass Edit tool can be used to force a measure to the next or previous system (select a measure and press the up or down arrows). As you can see in Figure 8.32, the Page Layout tool can be used to adjust the position and margins of systems within a page.

Figure 8.32
Using the Page Layout tool in Finale.

Figure 8.33 shows a finished page of the score. The "Display In Concert Pitch" option was toggled to off so that each part will be shown in its normal transposition.

Figure 8.33
The transposed score.

Part II

Musicianship

Practical Music Theory

This section of the book considers many theoretical concepts that will aid the creative process. The chapters on practical music theory, chord and scale relationships, linear process, composition, orchestration, and arranging will provide a thorough grounding in "real world" concepts that will serve to support, enhance, and even invigorate the process of creating original music.

How Theory Can Be Helpful

I feel that some introductory comments are in order because theory can be a hot topic both in and outside of academe: On the one hand, some traditional theorists are reluctant to embrace concepts such as popular chord symbols and progressions. On the other hand, some self-taught musicians are reluctant to consider the benefits of traditional concepts such as musical form and voice leading. One thing I have noticed in teaching music technology is that students often have an easy time learning how to use a sequencer or digital editor but have trouble making the leap of using the technology to create original music. In many cases, students may have a good handle on traditional music theory but may not know how to effectively create original music because theory is often taught in the abstract, not the practical. Similarly, I have also noticed that many excellent self-trained musicians have trouble moving "out of the box." Again, this is where theory can be useful, and it is in this spirit that I present this section of the book.

Conceptually, I find it helpful to think of theory this way: Theory should rarely come first in the composing process (exceptions might include using a concept such as a tone row as the basis for a composition or considering a predetermined formal structure at the start of a work), but theory should be available to guide the intuition as needed. I remember a teacher talking about the relationship between intuition and intellect—he made the point that intuition, without intellect, is like a ship without a navigator. In a similar way, knowledge of theoretical concepts can help to guide the intrinsically intuitive process of creating music.

In my opinion, theory provides the following primary benefits to musicians:

▶ Theory provides an efficient means for communicating ideas and concepts.

▶ Theory provides a means for understanding, on a structural level, the work of other composers.

▶ Theory can help musicians to assimilate new musical vocabulary and concepts.

▶ Theory can aid the creative process.

▶ Theory can help musicians to learn and interpret music.

This chapter, "Practical Music Theory," will provide a foundation for several concepts that will be developed throughout this section of the book. The primary focus of the chapter will be to develop an understanding of popular chord symbols, melodic organization, and formal structures. Other related topics such as non-tonal concepts, harmonic progressions, and music composition will be developed in related chapters. This chapter focuses on the following building blocks:

▶ Chords

▶ Chord groups

▶ Extensions

▶ Altered chords

▶ Vertical structures

▶ Melody and unifying elements

▶ Phrase structure

▶ Melodic contour

▶ Musical form

Chords

Most popular music revolves around chords, so an understanding of these structures can be a great asset. By way of example, consider that you are composing a progression of chords to support a melody and, at one point, a whole-note "G" in the melody requires a particular chord (which you are having trouble finding by ear or trial and error). Assuming that the "G" is a chord tone, a knowledge of triads would reveal that the "G" could be used with the following chords: C, Cmin, C♯ diminished, Dsus4, E♭, Emin, Edim, F2, G, Gmin, C♭ aug. (see Figure 9.1). Similarly, an understanding of seventh chords and extensions provides exponentially more options. I use this example simply to make a point: Fluency with chords can enhance and expedite the process of composing chord progressions.

Figure 9.1
Triads that contain the note "G" as a chord factor.

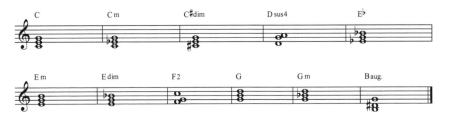

Note that in this chapter, chords are always presented in root position (the root of the chord on the bottom) so that the construction of the chord is clear. I will consider ways to combine and arrange the notes in a more pleasing way in the chapters on music composition, contemporary keyboard techniques, arranging, and orchestration.

TRIADS

The discussion of chords begins with triads. Triads can be defined as a chord containing three notes. Although triads are most often built in thirds from an associated scale, for our purposes, we will use the term triad to describe any chord containing three notes.

Figure 9.2 shows the four primary triads. The major and minor triads each contain an interval of a perfect fifth with a major and minor third, respectively. An augmented triad can be created by raising the top note of a major triad one half step. Similarly, a diminished triad can be constructed by lowering the top note of a minor triad by a half step. Note that by convention, an "o" symbol is used to indicate a diminished triad and a "+" symbol is used to indicate an augmented triad.

Figure 9.2
Primary triads.

In popular music, augmented and diminished triads are infrequently used because, in many contexts, they tend to sound dated. Two nontraditional triads are used extensively in popular music: Sus2 and Sus4 chords are interesting in that they do not contain a third (see Figure 9.3). The third of a chord is the note that provides what might be described as the "effect" of the chord—in simplistic terms one might think of major as happy and minor as sad. Since suspended chords do not contain a third, they have the advantage of providing a sonority that is more elusive. Of the two, Sus4 chords are less frequently used because they sound more unstable than Sus2 chords.

Figure 9.3
Suspended second and suspended fourth chords.

Suspended chords get their name from traditional music theory: When a dissonance is held over another note and then resolves, the dissonance is said to be suspended (see Figure 9.4). In this example, the interval of a fourth creates a dissonance that resolves to a major third. Sus chords are similar except that they often do not resolve.

Figure 9.4
Suspension (4th–3rd).

Any chord, triad or otherwise, can be inverted. To invert a chord, move the lowest note of the chord up an octave (or the highest note down an octave). There are three possible positions for a triad: root position, first inversion, and second inversion (see Figure 9.5).

Figure 9.5
Inversions of a triad.

In popular chord notation the inversion is not usually specified. It is up to the player to select an inversion that is appropriate for the given musical context. If a note other than the root is prominent in the bass, the bass note is indicated with a slash following the chord symbol. In Figure 9.6, the third of a G-major chord (the note B) is used in the bass.

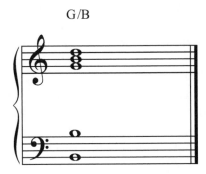

Figure 9.6
G-major triad with the third in the bass.

In popular music, it is always understood that the denominator of such a structure refers to a single note, not an entire chord. If you really intend to indicate a true *polychord*, it is best to specify this by writing a complete description of each chord (e.g., A major/C-major or C/E7).

Most triads are constructed by building chords in thirds from a given scale. When chords are constructed in this way, Roman numerals are used to describe the function of the chord within the key. In Figure 9.7, we would say that the first chord is a "I" chord since it was constructed on the root or tonic of the scale. The second chord, a D min, is a "ii" chord since it was constructed from the second degree of the scale, and so on. By convention, upper case Roman numerals indicate major or augmented chords, and lower case Roman numerals usually indicate a minor or diminished chord.

Figure 9.7
Using Roman numerals to describe the function of chords found in the key of C.

Although Roman numerals are less useful in describing music that is heavily chromatic, Roman numerals are frequently used by musicians to quickly communicate a diatonic progression such as " I vi ii V" (see Figure 9.8).

Figure 9.8
"I vi ii V" progression in the key of C.

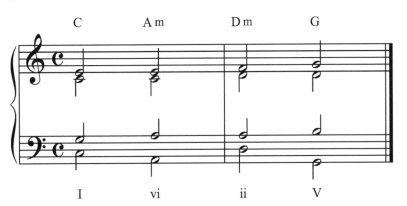

As you will see in Chapter 10, "Chord and Scale Relationships," nontraditional and synthetic scales can also be used to create some truly interesting vertical chord structures and progressions.

SEVENTH CHORDS

Seventh chords are constructed in the same way as triads except that an additional tone (the seventh) is added. Figure 9.9 lists the four primary seventh chords: major seventh, minor seventh, "dominant" seventh, and minor-major seventh.

Figure 9.9
The four primary seventh chords.

The naming scheme used in popular music can be confusing, so I would describe it in this way: In traditional music theory, a chord containing a major triad and the interval of a major seventh is called a "major, major seventh" chord. Since both the third and seventh are major, the name is shortened in popular notation to just "major seventh." Minor seventh chords work in a similar way; these chords contain a minor triad and minor seventh interval, so the chord name is shortened to "minor seventh." Of course, no shorthand notation is used for a "minor-major seventh" chord—the chord symbol reflects the type of triad and type of seventh chord.

The "dominant seventh" chord requires a few additional comments: This chord contains a major triad and an interval of a minor seventh, so you might think of it as a cross between the major and minor seventh chords. It gets its name from the fact these chords often function as "V" in a given key—the dominant. To this point, I have used quotes on the term "dominant" because, strictly speaking, unless the chord functions as "V" in a given key, the term dominant is not accurate. Having said that, you will often hear musicians talk about a chord as being a "dominant seventh," so I will occasionally use the term in that broad sense.

When constructing seventh chords, it may be helpful to consider how the seventh relates to an octave. For example, the interval of a major seventh is just a half step "shy" of an octave, and a minor seventh is a whole step below an octave. For most people, it's much easier to visualize half-steps than intervals of a seventh.

In terms of function, the major and minor seventh chords are used in many popular music genres. The dominant seventh is also common but rarely used in the voicing shown—it sounds too old-fashioned. The minor-major seventh chord is relatively rare but can be used to great effect as a suspense chord (and sometimes in minor blues).

ADDING EXTENSIONS

Extensions (9th, 11th, 13th) are used to add color to chords. Although many styles of music (such as old-school country and rockabilly) rely primarily on triads and seventh chords, many musical genres utilize extensions for the interest and color provided by these structures. Extensions can be added by continuing the process of building a chord in thirds (see Figure 9.10)

Figure 9.10
Adding extensions by building a chord in thirds.

In terms of popular-music chord nomenclature, the 9th and 13th will always be "major" intervals and the 11th will always be a "perfect" interval. Exceptions will generally be listed in parentheses, as in C7(♯9). Fortunately, this naming scheme follows the process previously described in the section on seventh chords—the only difference being that the highest numbered extension will be listed *in place of* the seventh. For example, a C9 chord is just a C7 chord with an added major 9th. A Cmaj9 is a Cmaj7 chord with an added major 9th, and so on. The higher the extension number, the more potential chord tones that can be included. A Cmin13 chord could, for example, include the following chord factors: root, 3, 5, 7, 9, 11, 13. In common practice, however, the 11th is only used on minor triads because it is too dissonant when used with chords containing a major third. Figure 9.11 lists several extended chords and their associated seventh structures.

Figure 9.11
Adding extensions to seventh chords.

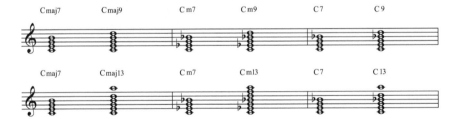

ALTERED TONES

If the 5th, 9th, 11th, or 13th of a chord is raised or lowered, the chord is said to be an "altered" chord. For example, a C13 chord containing a lowered 9th would be written as C13(♭9) or C13(-9). Similarly, a C-major seventh chord containing a 9th and a raised 11th would be written as Cmaj9(♯11) or Cmaj9(+11). Note that a plus or minis sign refers to raising or lowering a note, not adding or omitting the note. Figure 9.12 shows several examples of altered chords. (Remember that the quality or type of the underlying seventh chord is determined by the chord qualifier—e.g., a Cmin11 is a Cmin7 with a 9th and 11th added.)

Figure 9.12
Several examples of altered chords.

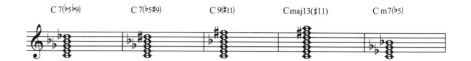

DIMINISHED CHORDS

Diminished seventh chords can be either *half diminished* or *fully diminished*. In a half-diminished chord, only the fifth is diminished—the seventh is a minor seventh. For this reason, it is helpful to visualize half diminished chords as an altered minor seventh chord (see Figure 9.13). Note that this chord can be indicated with a circle and line or by writing min7♭5.

Figure 9.13
Half-diminished chord (minor seventh chord with a lowered fifth).

To construct a fully diminished chord, build a diminished triad and add a diminished seventh. It is interesting to note that the diminished seventh chord consists solely of intervals of a minor third (see Figure 9.14). For this reason, it is often not clear which note should function as the root (e.g., a Cdim7 shares the same notes as an Adim7). This ambiguity was exploited by many composers in the Viennese and Romantic eras (and even still today). For example, an Adim7 chord can function as vii in the key of B♭ or as an *enharmonic* vii chord in D♭, E, or G.

Figure 9.14
Fully diminished chord.

Chord Groups

Since extensions do not ordinarily affect the function of a chord, it is helpful to visualize each triad, seventh, and extended chord as a group of related chords. In this way, it is easy to experiment with subtle changes in "color" when composing and arranging. Just as a painter might add a dab of yellow to bring out depth in background foliage, a composer might use extensions to emphasize or color a musical passage. In the following section, chords are presented in groups of related chords.

Thinking of chords in this way makes it easy to experiment with varying levels of color. For example, for a major triad, a sus2, major 9th, or any number of other options would be suitable replacements. I should point out that this is not the only way to think of chords—alternate approaches might include using nontraditional structures, polytonality, or relying on the linear process. With that said, this is a process that I have found to be extremely useful in composing and arranging many forms of tonal music. To illustrate the point, consider that you are arranging keyboard or horn parts for a blues progression. The "stock" options are to add a 7th, 9th, or 13th. Sometimes, an uncommon option (such as an augmented ninth chord) is the best choice—but knowing the stock options is a great timesaver because you can quickly determine if the best choice is (or isn't) one of the stock chords.

MAJOR CHORDS

Figure 9.15 lists a major chord with all of the common extensions and color tones. Most pop music utilizes the major triad and "Sus2" chord although occasional 7ths and 9ths may be heard. The 9th and/or 13th is almost always added to major seventh chords in jazz and jazz-related styles.

I did not list an 11th chord in this group because, as I mentioned earlier, the 11th is not added to major chords in common practice. However, a raised 11th is a very pretty chord; these chords are often used when the altered 11th is naturally found in the key. For example, in the key of C, a major chord built on the subdominant (F) could naturally contain a raised 11th because the note "B" is found in the key of C. Note that, in each illustration in this section, chords on the left are least colorful and those on the right are most colorful.

Figure 9.15
Major chord group.

TONIC MINOR

I use the term *tonic minor* to describe minor chords that often function as a tonic (or subdominant) such as in a minor blues. These chords are relatively dark—a minor 6 or minor 6/9 is often used in place of the very dissonant sound of a minor-major seventh. Note that this group of chords is exactly like the major chord group except that all of the chords are minor. The seventh and extensions are the same for both chord groups (see Figure 9.16).

Figure 9.16
Tonic minor chord group.

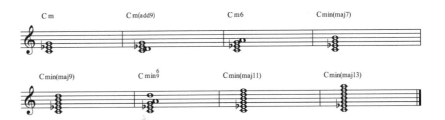

MINOR SEVENTH

Minor seventh chords are found in most genres of popular music from pop to jazz and fusion. When extensions are added, these chords tend to sound similar to the major-chord group—this is by virtue of the fact that a major seventh chord is found within an extended minor seventh chord: In an Amin9, the notes C-E-G-B form a Cmaj7 chord. Unlike chords based on the major triad, a perfect 11th is often added to minor seventh chords (see Figure 9.17). Although these chords may function as tonic or subdominant, they are also used as a "ii" chord—often as part of a "ii-V-I" progression.

Figure 9.17
Minor seventh chord group.

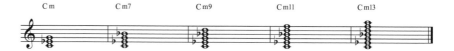

HALF DIMINISHED

A half-diminished chord can be constructed by lowering the fifth of a minor seventh chord. Functionally, these chords work in a similar way to the minor seventh chord group—often as a "ii" chord in a minor key. For this reason, the 9th may not be a good choice. Consider, for example, a Dm7($\flat$5) chord in the key of C minor. The ninth of a Dm chord is an E-natural—a note not found in the key of C minor.

An 11th is frequently added to this chord and may even replace the third. Figure 9.18 lists chords in the half-diminished chord group. Half diminished chords can be very effective when utilized in nonfunctional progressions such as an ascending third progression (see Figure 9.18 B).

Figure 9.18 A
Half-diminished chord group.

Figure 9.18 B
Ascending third progression.

DOMINANT SEVENTH

As the name implies, dominant seventh chords can function as the dominant or "V" in a given key. Without alteration, only three options are possible: 7, 9, or 13 (see Figure 9.19A). These chords can also function as a tonic or subdominant in blues or in many non-traditional ways. For example, Debussy and Ravel used extended 9th and 13th chords to great effect in many compositions—a striking use being Ravel's use of symmetrical or planing chords in *Pour le Piano* (see Figure 9.19 B).

Figure 9.19 A
Dominant seventh chord group.

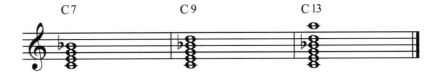

Figure 9.19 B
Pour le piano.

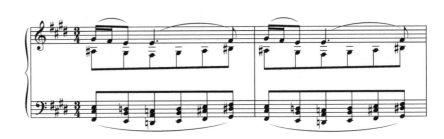

ALTERED DOMINANT

Altered dominant chords are most frequently found in jazz, but you will occasionally hear them in pop music, rock, funk, and other styles. These chords come from altering the 5th or 9th of a traditional dominant seventh chord (see Figure 9.20). Altered dominant chords are most often used to strengthen motion to a tonic (or temporary tonic) chord. For example, in the progression G7–C, it would be common to alter the fifth and/or ninth of the G7 in some styles of music. If you need to add more "zing" to a V–I progression, experiment by raising or lowering the 5th and/or 9th of the dominant chord. I find the augmented ninth chord to be particularly fascinating—this chord, which comes from an *octatonic scale* (see Chapter 10), was used as a tonic by composers as diverse as Claude Debussy, Igor Stravinsky, and Jimmy Hendrix.

Figure 9.20
Altered dominant chord group.

LYDIAN DOMINANT

The so-called Lydian dominant chord group is a variation on the dominant-seventh chord group but the raised 11th (or Lydian tone) is added for extra color (see Figure 9.21). (I will talk about Lydian and other modes in the next chapter.) A good rule of thumb is to use these chords anytime a dominant chord does *not* function in the traditional manner. For example, a raised 11th is a good choice for the first chord in the progression G7♯11 Gbmaj7.

Figure 9.21
Lydian dominant chord group.

Vertical Structures

To this point, all of the chords you have seen are based on *tertian harmony*; tertian chords are constructed in thirds. Around the turn of the last century, composers started to utilize new vertical structures such as *quartal* and *quintal* chords—built in fourths or fifths—and *clusters* or *secundal harmony*—chords built in seconds. Figure 9.22 illustrates a few of these structures.

Figure 9.22
Quartal, quintal, and secundal structures.

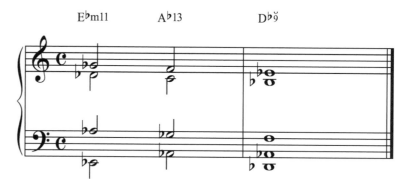

Non-tertian structures are very useful in many musical contexts—particularly if the goal is to minimize the sound of traditional tertian harmony. In the 20th century, composers utilized these structures to "blur" the sound of tertian harmony to an extent, but they can be very effective in traditional harmonic progressions. In Figure 9.23, quartal and quintal structures are combined to create an interesting variation on an otherwise ordinary progression.

Figure 9.23
Using quartal and quintal structures to voice a traditional progression.

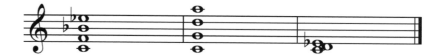

Similarly, a cluster or secundal structure, while useful in nontraditional applications, also has an amazing potential to subtly imply tertian structures. Note the many possible functions of a single cluster in Figure 9.24. When used in this way, clusters are often called *chords of omission*, because just a few notes are used to imply a more complex structure.

Figure 9.24
Implying tertian harmony with a cluster chord.

Along these lines, I can't resist inserting a quote from Debussy because I feel it illustrates a healthy approach to chords that does not place an overreliance on a purely theoretical use of these concepts:

"No one's ever really pointed out how few chords there are in any given century! Impossible to count how often since Gluck people have died to the chord of the sixth and now, from Manon to Isolde, they do it to the diminished seventh! And as for that idiotic thing called the perfect triad, it's only a habit, like going to a café!" (*Composers on Music*, edited by Josiah Fisk, Northeastern University Press, 1997).

USING THE CHORD GROUPS

The following example shows how chord groups might be useful in the process of composing and voicing a progression of chords. Consider the following progression: All of the chords in this progression are found in the key of G and, as written, contain no extra color (see Figure 9.25).

Figure 9.25
Basic diatonic chord progression in the key of G.

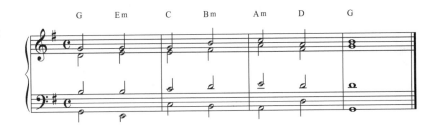

Although the progression could work fine as written, it is interesting to consider how chord groups could be utilized to spice up the harmony. I elected to demonstrate a pop-music version of the progression—largely to show that an understanding of chords and extensions is not the exclusive realm of jazz musicians. In the updated version (see Figure 9.26), a second or ninth was added to each of the major chords in order to create a more modern sound. Color tones were added to the minor triads in the form of a 7th or 11th. Those particular choices were guided by my ear—again, my goal is to let theory support the creative process, not drive it! Many other variations are possible, but this illustration shows how the chord groups can be utilized in most any situation.

Figure 9.26
Pop-music version of a basic chord progression.

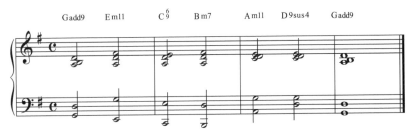

Creating Convincing Voicings

When voicing chords, several concepts are helpful to consider. First, avoid large gaps (more than about a 5th or 6th) between any two voices. (One exception is between the bass and tenor voice—large gaps are often necessary between the bottom two voices.) Second, close-position voicings do not work well in the mid to low register. In these cases, use a larger interval such as a perfect fifth, seventh, octave, or tenth in the lowest two voices. Figure 9.27 illustrates several common bass structures. Notice how gaps are minimized between the upper voices.

Figure 9.27
Common bass structures.

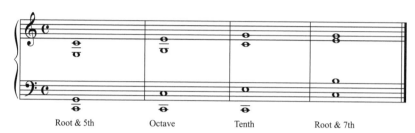

The following steps can be useful in creating convincing voicings.

1. Place the melody in the top voice.

2. Select a common bass structure for the bottom two voices (root and seventh, tenth, etc.).

3. Fill in other notes between the melody and bottom two voices while avoiding intervals larger than a fifth or sixth.

Of course, many other options are possible, but I have found these steps to be useful in many situations. Figure 9.28 demonstrates how these steps can be used to create several voicings for a given chord and melody note.

Figure 9.28
Several voicings for a single melody note.

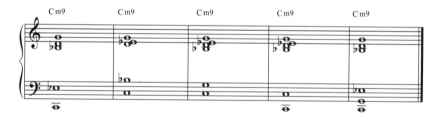

Another concept to consider is that, though a voicing might sound good by itself, the voicing will lose its effectiveness if it doesn't flow in a natural way to the next chord in a progression. Voice leading is a big topic, but I have found the following tips to be helpful:

- ▶ If two chords share a common tone, it often makes sense to share the tone between two or more chords in a progression.

- ▶ The leading tone of a key tends to want to ascend.

- ▶ The fourth degree of a key tends to want to descend.

- ▶ When possible, avoid parallel movement of fifths and octaves.

- ▶ Avoid simultaneous parallel motion in all voices.

I would point out that parallel motion is not always undesirable—parallelism has been effectively used by many composers. However, if the goal is to create a rich chorale-style harmonization, the tips mentioned above will be helpful to consider. Figure 9.29 is an excerpt of a chorale arranged by one of the undisputed masters of voice leading: J.S. Bach. I would highly recommend picking up a copy of his four-part chorales (available in the U.S. from Associated Music Publishers). Through studying his chorales, I have learned many things about voicing chords that directly translate to writing for orchestral, choral, and other settings. In the following example, note how smoothly the inner voices flow ,as well as his use of "open" bass structures as described above.

Figure 9.29
Excerpt from a J.S. Bach chorale arrangement.

Figure 9.30 illustrates a jazz version of the same chorale. Although more modern structures are used, the voice-leading principles are the same (though parallel motion is more "permissible"). In this example, awkward jumps are avoided in the inner voices and tendency tones are handled in a natural way. Note that I will talk in greater detail about voicings in Chapter 15, "Real-World Arranging."

Figure 9.30
Jazz version of a Bach chorale.

Melody

In my own writing, I have found it helpful to take a step back and analyze a melody from a theoretical perspective. Often, a melody might be close, but intuition tells me that something is amiss. Theoretical tools are often helpful in such a situation. This section will introduce several terms and concepts that are useful in the context of writing and analyzing melodies.

UNIFYING ELEMENTS

Most successful melodies share one common characteristic: There is an identifiable melodic or rhythmic element that serves to unify the melody. In Figure 9.31, a strong rhythmic motive provides a strong sense of "purpose" to the melody. Try singing or playing the melody but change each rhythm so that no clear rhythmic motive is present—you will notice that the melody loses much of its effectiveness.

Figure 9.31
Rhythmic element.

A recurring interval or grouping of notes can also provide a clear sense of direction. Notice how an interval of an ascending sixth provides a strong melodic motive in Figure 9.32.

Figure 9.32
Melodic element utilizing the interval of an ascending sixth.

CONTOUR

The term *contour* is used to describe the overall shape of a melody. A melody might start on a low note and work toward a penultimate note near the end of a phrase. In other instances, a melody might start with a high note and descend to an arrival point. There is certainly no right or wrong contour, but a melody will be less successful if it "fights" against its natural tendency. Sometimes I even find the concept of contour to be helpful in the initial stages of writing a melody. For example, folk-like melodies tend to exhibit minimal variation in contour—that's one of the reasons folk melodies are so easy to sing. On the other hand, a melody that is meant to cause a sense of agitation might have many extremes in contour. In both cases, analyzing the melody from the perspective of contour can yield helpful information.

Figure 9.33 demonstrates a melody that gradually ascends. This type of melody often has an uplifting quality that relates directly to the underlying melodic contour.

Figure 9.33
Ascending contour.

Figure 9.34 exhibits a contour in which ascending motion is balanced by descending motion. The penultimate note is near the middle of the phrase.

Figure 9.34
Climax in the middle.

A third example, illustrated in 9.35, demonstrates a more dynamic approach to contour. This melody exhibits an extreme range from the lowest to highest tone, and the descending motion to a low climax provides a sense of foreboding.

Figure 9.35
Extreme melodic contour.

MELODIC CADENCE AND PHRASE STRUCTURE

In the context of melody, it is helpful to visualize a cadence as a type of musical punctuation. Phrases are analogous to sentences that might be punctuated by cadences in the form of musical commas, semicolons, question marks, or periods. A cadence occurs when there is a relative point of rest in a melodic line, rhythmic figure, harmonic progression, or some combination of the three. Without cadence points, music will sound restless or unsettled. For some compositions, restlessness may be an important consideration, but in most genres of music cadences are essential.

A common grouping of phrases, called a *period*, has the characteristic of an initial phrase that ends in a musical question mark, followed by one or more phrases that "answer" the question. Musical theorists often use the term *antecedent* and *consequent* to describe a question and answer relationship evident in a periodic melody (see Figure 9.36). As technical editor, Dr. Bruce Frazier points out, English grammar can be used to illustrate the antecedent–consequent relationship: "On the way home from the gig, we stopped for pizza."

Figure 9.36
Two phrases that form a musical period.

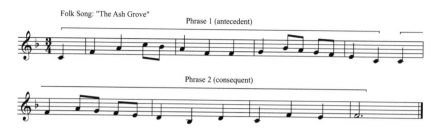

Some melodies do not exhibit a strong periodic relationship between phrases. In this case, the phases are still delineated by cadences, but the phrases don't happen to form an antecedent and consequent relationship. Figure 9.37 demonstrates a melody comprised of three phrases that form a phrase group.

Figure 9.37
Three phrases that form a phrase group.

Form

Just as phrases can work together to form a complete melody, sections of a composition combine to form a piece in its entirety. The sections of a work can be determined aurally by a number of phenomena such as cadential activity, change of key, change of tempo, change of register, dynamics, contrast of prevailing rhythm, and new orchestration.

As with other aspects of theory, a decision about the form of a work should not necessarily be made in the initial stages of the composition process. However, an understanding of musical form often provides insights into potential directions that a composition might take. Musical forms provide a way of looking at the big picture: Where does a composition start, how does it develop, and where does it end?

The formal designs presented in this section have been utilized by many composers, but it is important to note that a composition need not exhibit characteristics of one of the traditional forms to be effective— many outstanding compositions have utilized a more freewheeling approach to formal design.

BINARY AND TERNARY

The two elemental musical forms are *binary* and *ternary*. A binary form consists of two primary sections: AB. In many cases, a binary composition starts in the tonic key and moves to a new key at the end of the A section, but other elements such as a change in orchestration or rhythm may signal the start of a new section. The sections in a binary composition often exhibit a complementary relationship—as with a musical period, the sections of a binary composition often form an antecedent–consequent relationship. In its classic form, a binary piece moves back to the tonic at the end of the B section (see Figure 9.38).

Figure 9.38
Binary form.

As the name implies, a ternary composition is comprised of three sections: ABA. Ternary contrasts with binary in that each section of a ternary composition is usually a complete or "closed" unit. The B section may modulate, or other musical elements may indicate the start of new section (see Figure 9.39).

Figure 9.39
Ternary form.

SONATA ALLEGRO

The term *sonata* can be confusing. On the one hand, a sonata refers to an instrumental composition. On the other hand, *sonata form* or *sonata allegro* refers to a musical form that was developed in the Viennese period. A sonata allegro may exhibit characteristics of both binary and ternary. Although a sonata has three primary sections—*exposition*, *development*, and *recapitulation*—a sonata typically exhibits the antecedent and consequent relationship found in many binary compositions. In a traditional sonata allegro movement, the development section starts in a contrasting key from the exposition and modulates back to the tonic for the restatement in the recapitulation (see Figure 9.40). Two (or more) primary themes will be presented in the exposition, but the second theme is usually in a new key. These themes provide the basis for the development section and are restated (in the tonic key) in the recapitulation.

In terms of modern-day usage, the idea of presenting themes in an exposition, transforming themes in an unstable developmental section, and restating thematic material in a recapitulation can provide a powerful model for a large-form composition. The sonata allegro might be thought of as an idealized form. Even in the classical period, composers like Mozart and Beethoven didn't always stick to the "stylized" form shown below. For example, a sonata allegro may exhibit characteristics of both a rondo and a traditional sonata allegro—many variations are possible.

Figure 9.40
Sonata allegro.

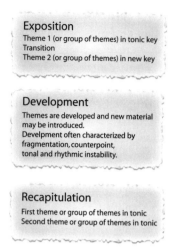

Exposition
Theme 1 (or group of themes) in tonic key
Transition
Theme 2 (or group of themes) in new key

Development
Themes are developed and new material
may be introduced.
Develpment often characterized by
fragmentation, counterpoint,
tonal and rhythmic instability.

Recapitulation
First theme or group of themes in tonic
Second theme or group of themes in tonic

RONDO

In a *rondo*, the primary theme returns again and again. Theorists use the terms *refrain* and *episode* to describe the primary and contrasting themes in a rondo form. Some of the more common forms are: ABACADA, ABACA, and ABACABA. As you might imagine, rondo form is most successful if the A section is truly interesting! In modern day usage, the refrains may be embellished and developed.

POPULAR SONG FORM

I use the term *popular song form* to describe hundreds of American popular songs that utilize an AABA song form (see Figure 9.41). In most cases, the second A section modulates to the key of the bridge (B) although a closed A section is also possible. Many popular songs modulate to a closely related key in the bridge (e.g., the subdominant or relative minor), but more distant key relationships are also used and can be quite striking.

Figure 9.41
Popular song form.

THEME AND VARIATION, CONTINUOUS VARIATION

In theme and variation, an initial theme is presented and transformed in many ways such as being embellished, being set to a new meter, being set to a new modality, and the like. Although many theme and variation compositions were written in the classical era, continuous variation is more common today. A repeating bass line (ground bass or bass ostinato) or progression of chords provides the basis for a composition based on continuous variation. This type of music evolves over an ever-present bass line or repeating chord progression (e.g., Pachelbel's "Canon"). Many popular tunes and short jazz pieces are based on the concept of continuous variation (e.g., Miles Davis' "Blue in Green").

THROUGH-COMPOSED AND NARRATIVE MUSIC

In the 19th century, composers experimented by writing songs in which new material was used for each stanza. The benefit of this approach is that the music can be changed to better support the words. You might think of a through-composed composition as a planned improvisation. In a similar vein, a narrative composition attempts to tell a story. Though some wonderful symphonic works have been written that can be described as narrative, a narrative composition can be difficult to pull off because of the absence of an overarching formal structure. In such a composition, the presentation and transformation of motives provides a unifying element. Another concept, called a *leitmotif*, is helpful to consider. Wagner often used musical themes to represent characters and actions in his operas. The technique can still be heard in feature films such as *Star Wars* and *Harry Potter*.

Using Forms

If find it helpful to approach the concept of forms in an abstract way. Even if I haven't started a composition with a well-defined form in mind, most compositions will naturally fall into one of these categories. If a composition seems to wander or gets overly repetitive, an evaluation of formal structure will often yield a solution that better clarifies the composition. Of course, forms can also be a great source of inspiration: It is often helpful to start a composition with a well-defined form such as a rondo or ternary in mind.

With larger works, the idea of a *composite form* is often helpful to consider. For example, imagine writing a 15-minute composition consisting of three primary movements or sections. One movement might be in ternary form, another movement a sonata allegro, and so on. In the ternary movement, each of the three sections might be further divided into binary units (or some other form). Suddenly, the daunting task of writing a 15-minute composition has been structured into more manageable units. Although there is a tendency to view forms as inhibiting, I find that this type of "big picture" approach can be very liberating. Forms can provide a sense of cohesiveness in much the same way that chapters, paragraphs, and sentences are used to organize the content of a book.

Summary

In this chapter you have learned about chords, chord groups, voicings, melody, and musical forms. Although theory is a vast topic, the concepts I elected to present in this chapter will be useful to most modern-day musicians. The threads of harmony, melody, and form will be developed in other chapters in the book. As these threads are developed, many complementary concepts will be presented such as non-tonal approaches to composition, arranging, orchestration, and a variety of linear techniques.

CHAPTER 10

Chord and Scale Relationships

Jazz musicians have long understood the need for a way to categorize and relate linear sounds (scales) to vertical structures (chords). What many commercial musicians don't know is that chord-scale relationships have also been utilized by composers of art music. As you will see in this chapter, scales are not used solely for improvisation. Scales can also be immensely helpful in voicing chords, composing melodies, and creating interesting harmonic progressions. This chapter will explore the following concepts:

▶ Using scales

▶ Modes

▶ Chord and scale relationships

▶ Applications of the melodic minor scale

▶ Major-scale tips

▶ Blues scales

▶ Diminished scale

▶ Whole-tone scale

▶ Pentatonic scales

▶ Synthetic scales

▶ Using chord scale relationships

▶ Scale–tone chord concepts

Using Scales

In Chapter 9, I talked about how extensions can be used to provide color to a chord. Scales can be used in a similar way, but unlike extensions, the "color" of a scale can be applied to a passage of music or an entire composition. For example, film composers often utilize modes to create a special mood in a scene (more on this in a moment). Some composers start a new piece by designing or choosing a *synthetic scale* and then use the scale to create interesting chords, melodies, and progressions.

On the melodic plane, scales provide a palette of notes upon which a melody or improvisation can be based. In any chord and scale relationship, the notes of a related scale will function in a unique way, so as you explore the concept of scales, keep an ear open to the way that each tone works against a related chord. When a major scale is played over a major chord, for example, the fourth degree of the scale is very strong—it has a tendency to move. In contrast, the fourth degree of a major scale is stable when played over a the "ii" chord (see Figure 10.1). I encourage you to explore chordscale relationships in this way—listen for the *potential movement* of each note in a scale. As you sensitize your ear to these potentials, scales and modes will become even more useful.

Figure 10.1
Potential movement or "strength" of notes over major and minor chords.

On the harmonic plane, scales provide a rich framework for exploration. In Chapter 9, I showed how triads and seventh chords can be constructed from a major scale. Triads and sevenths can just as easily be constructed from exotic scales. Note the many interesting vertical structures created by building chords in thirds based on the scale in Figure 10.2.

Figure 10.2
Building chords in thirds from an exotic scale.

Another use of scales involves moving chords such as triads or seventh chords in parallel within the scale. In a major key, the triads

formed by building chords in thirds can be used to give a sense of the modality without the necessity of using a functional chord progression. Theorists often use the term *scale-tone triads* or *scale-tone seventh chords* to describe this concept. In Figure 10.3, Beethoven uses inverted triads based on a major scale. Incidentally, first- or second-inversion triads often sound best in this context.

Figure 10.3
Beethoven's use of scale-tone triads (Opus 2, No. 3, Allegro Assai).

A more modern approach to scale-tone structures can be heard in Debussy's *La Cathédrale Engloutie*—The Sunken Cathedral (see Figure 10.4). Here, quartal and quintal structures are used to imply a major tonality. Although this piece was written for piano, the technique is just as effective when writing for orchestra or a collection of synthesized sounds.

Figure 10.4
Debussy's use of scale-tone structures (La Cathédrale Engloutie).

I should point out that, while scales are useful in many situations, they can also be inhibiting; a tremendous amount of music (both popular and classical) has been written that does not follow traditional scale relationships so, like any other technique, scales should be utilized for their usefulness but not overused to a disadvantage. To better illustrate this point I will show you a trick. A teacher once told me, *"You can use any note over any chord. As long as it makes melodic sense, it will work."* In Figure 10.5, every possible chromatic tone is used over an F9 chord—even the "bad" ones. This phrase is a good example of how embellishments such as changing tones and neighbor tones can be used to expand the function of a traditional chord–scale relationship.

Figure 10.5
All 12 tones used over an F9 chord.

Modes

A useful category of scales, called *modes* or *church modes,* is based on theoretical concepts developed in the Middle Ages. In a major scale, each of the tones in the scale can potentially be a *tonic* note. In the key of C major, the note "C" is the tonic. In the same scale, if the note "D" is emphasized in such a way that we start to hear "D" as the tonic instead of C, the sound of the C-major scale is replaced by one of the modes of the scale (D Dorian in this case). Figure 10.6 demonstrates the difference between a C-major scale and D Dorian scale.

Figure 10.6
C major versus D Dorian.

The seven modes of a C-major scale are listed in Figure 10.7. To describe a mode, use the tonic note of the mode along with its qualifier such as "D Dorian" or "F Lydian." In order to visualize modes based on other major scales, I find it helpful to visualize the mode in the key of C and work backwards. For example, in the key of C, the Lydian mode is based on the fourth degree of the scale (the note F in this instance). Therefore, to find the Lydian mode of a given major scale, find the fourth degree of the scale. In the key of G, for example, the note C is the fourth degree of the scale, and if you play a G-major scale but start on C, you will hear the notes of the C Lydian mode.

Figure 10.7
Modes of C major (Ionian, Dorian, Phrygian, Lydian, Mixolydian, Aeolian, Locrian).

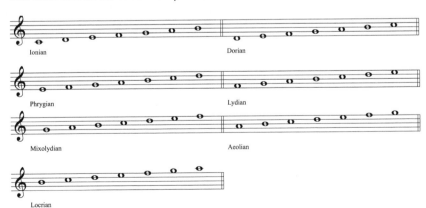

A good way to explore modes is to compose or improvise short melodies that imply a given mode. At first, it may be difficult to break away from the major tonality, but you will find that placing an emphasis (through repetition) on the tonic will help imply a mode. Melodies that contain notes from the tonic triad are also useful in implying a given mode. As you explore modes from a melodic standpoint, you will hear that, in each mode, certain tones work in special ways. In the Lydian mode, for example, the fourth degree of the mode provides a unique sound: In contrast to a major scale, the fourth degree of a Lydian mode is raised. Other modes have a similarly unique quality, and developing a sensitivity to these sounds can be very beneficial.

Modes can also be useful when creating chords and progressions. Unlike traditional major and minor scales, modal progressions have a distinctive sound because the chords often function in a unique way. In Figure 10.8, a progression of chords based on the tonic, subdominant, and dominant is shown in D harmonic minor and D Dorian. The D Dorian mode provides a distinctive sound when compared to the progression based on a D harmonic minor scale.

Figure 10.8
Progression of chords in D harmonic
minor and D Dorian.

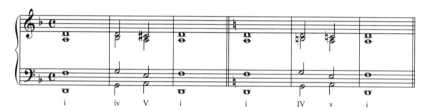

One of the advantages of using modes is that each mode can provide a unique "flavor." This concept is not lost on film composers—I hear modes used to underscore many movie scenes. By way of example, the Lydian mode is often used for joyous or tender scenes. When combined with careful use of orchestration (such as an oboe or piano melody with string accompaniment), a powerfully poignant effect can be achieved. In the following excerpt, transcribed from *Forrest Gump*, starring Tom Hanks, the Aeolian and Lydian modes are used to underscore a tender moment when Forrest learns that he is a dad (see Figure 10.9).

Figure 10.9
Piano reduction from Forrest
Gump, *composed by Alan Silvestri.*

In his book *Twentieth-Century Harmony* (W.W. Norton, 1961), Vincent Persichetti, describes an approach to finding "primary and secondary chordal materials" from a mode. He defines the primary triads as the tonic triad and the "major or minor triads that include the characteristic scale step which produces the principal flavor of the mode." For example, since the Lydian mode is characterized by the unique sound of the raised fourth, the I, II, and vii chords can be utilized to establish the unique flavor of the mode. Figure 10.10 shows the primary chords in F Lydian.

Figure 10.10
Primary chords in F Lydian (I, II and vii).

Similarly, the lowered seventh provides the unique characteristic of the Mixolydian mode. In this mode, the two major or minor chords that contain the lowered seventh degree are based on the fifth and seventh degrees of the scale and provide the primary chords that help to establish the mode (see Figure 10.11).

Figure 10.11
Primary chords in G Mixolydian (I, v, vii).

A helpful way to experiment with the concept of modes is to use an *ostinato* as the basis for a composition or improvisation. An ostinato is a repetitive pattern that can be played in the left hand on a keyboard or sequenced in DAW software. Since ostinati are repetitive, they can help to establish the tonic of the mode. In Figure 10.12, a simple ostinato is used as the basis for an improvisation. Experiment with a variety of melodies and chord structures in the right hand and try the technique in each mode—you will find that such exploration will yield many benefits.

Figure 10.12
Using an ostinato as the basis for an improvisation or composition.

Chord and Scale Relationships

This part of the chapter looks at the relationship between scales and chords from the common chords groups. As with modes, these concepts are useful both from a melodic and harmonic perspective. The first three scales all derive from a major scale and can be described using modal terminology: Ionian, Dorian, and Mixolydian.

When exploring the relationship between scales and chords, I find it helpful to think in terms of static tones and moving tones. A static tone is a note that does not sound as if it needs to move (e.g., the first, third, or fifth degrees of a major scale). A moving tone is one that implies motion or tension. Try to develop a second sense regarding static and moving tones; most great melodies use a combination of moving and static tones. In contrast, a melody that uses primarily moving tones will tend to sound haphazard, while a melody that uses only static tones may sound "rambly."

MAJOR SCALE

One of the more obvious chord-scale relationships is the major scale. This scale is used over any chords that derive from a major triad or major seventh chord (see Figure 10.13).

Figure 10.13
Major scale for major chords (C6, Cmaj7, Cmaj9, etc.).

(Also used for C6, Cmaj9, Cmaj13, etc.)

DORIAN SCALE

The Dorian mode is most often used for chords from the minor seventh chord group—for example, G Dorian for a Gmin7 (see Figure 10.14). Although I use the term Dorian to describe this scale, it might be convenient to think of this scale as a major scale down one whole step from the root of a given chord (F major for Gm7, A major for Bmi7, and so on). Remember that chord and scale relationships imply a palette of useful notes; there is no specific starting note or ordering implied by the chord and scale relationships.

Figure 10.14
Dorian scale for minor-seventh chords and extensions.

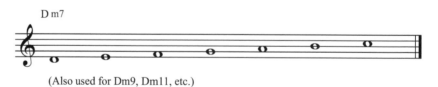

(Also used for Dm9, Dm11, etc.)

MIXOLYDIAN SCALE

The Mixolydian scale is typically used for chords based on a dominant seventh (e.g., G7, G9, G13). As with the major scale and Dorian scale, the Mixolydian scale represents a linear version of a dominant seventh chord along with the chord extensions. It is helpful to note that, since the 4th or 11th is usually too dissonant to use as a chord factor, this dissonance is also in effect as a melodic tone. In Figure 10.15, the note C is very strong when played over a G7 chord. However, the strength of that note to lead to another tone such as B can be effectively utilized.

Some jazz theorists would call the note an "avoid" note. I prefer to think of the note as a *tendency tone*.

Figure 10.15
Mixolydian scale for dominant seventh chords (using the fourth degree as a tendency tone).

(Also used for G9 and G13)

In many situations, it is helpful to visualize a single scale that can work over several chords. This is particularly true when a chord progression is derived from a single key center. In Figure 10.16, all of the chords are found in G major, so a G-major scale is a good choice over the entire progression of chords. Although it would not be wrong to use an E Dorian over the Emin7 chord, an E Aeolian scale is probably a better choice in this context. Again, it is more important to hear the melodic potential of a note over a given chord than to start a scale on a particular note.

Figure 10.16
Using a single scale for a diatonic progression in G major (I-vi-ii-V).

APPLICATIONS OF THE MELODIC MINOR SCALE

The melodic minor scale is one of the most useful scales for dealing with contemporary chords. If you have ever taken a traditional theory course, you may have learned that a melodic minor scale uses different notes in the ascending and descending versions of the scale (see Figure 10.17).

Figure 10.17
Melodic minor scale (ascending and descending).

This scale is the result of developments in tonal music. It was common for composers to use a leading tone when approaching the tonic or *final* in a mode such as Dorian or Aeolian. In the key of C minor, for example, the resulting interval from A♭ to B was awkward to sing, so composers often used a raised sixth degree (A♮) for ascending melodic passages. The traditional form of melodic minor scale developed as a result of this tendency to use the raised sixth and seventh scale degrees on an ascending passage and natural minor for a descending passage. In popular music, the ascending form is often used in both directions.

An easy way to construct a melodic minor scale is to visualize a major scale with one "wrong" note. The wrong note is the third degree of the scale. To use this trick, simply play a major scale that includes a minor third instead of a major third. This is an easy way to find the ascending version of a melodic minor scale (see Figure 10.18).

Figure 10.18
Constructing a melodic minor scale
(major scale with a minor third).

This simple scale can be used to handle four of the more complex chords found in popular music: tonic minor, half-diminished, altered dominant, and Lydian dominant.

Tonic Minor Chords

The melodic minor scale is useful over a tonic minor chord. For example, the major seventh and major sixth intervals found in this scale can sound wonderful when used over a minor blues progression. Note that the root of this scale is the same as the root of the given chord, as shown in Figure 10.19.

Figure 10.19
C melodic minor scale for a
C-minor(maj7) chord (tonic minor
chord group).

Half-Diminished Chords

A melodic minor scale can also be used over a half-diminished chord (also called min7(♭5). To find the appropriate melodic minor scale, base the scale on the third of the chord (see Figure 10.20).

Figure 10.20
C melodic minor scale for
Amin7(♭ 5).

Altered Dominant Chords

Altered dominant chords are often found in jazz, pop, and other styles of music. A melodic minor scale can sound great when applied to an altered dominant chord (see Figure 10.21). To find the appropriate melodic minor scale, construct a melodic minor scale a half-step above the root of the chord (e.g., C melodic minor for a B7 altered chord). The altered scale includes all of the altered tones (raised and lowered fifth and ninth) as well as the primary chord factors (root, third, and seventh).

Figure 10.21
C melodic minor scale for a rootless voicing of B7alt.

Lydian Dominant Chords

The melodic minor scale can be a good choice for a Lydian dominant chord (a Lydian dominant is any dominant seventh chord that includes ♯4 or ♯11). A melodic minor scale built on the fifth of any Lydian dominant chord provides an elegant solution to this complex chord (see Figure 10.22).

Figure 10.22
C melodic minor for an F7#11 chord.

To recap what you have learned so far about melodic minor scales, a melodic minor scale has four common applications: It can be used for chords from the tonic minor, half-diminished, altered dominant, and Lydian dominant chord groups. Table 10.1 provides a way to visualize the four common applications of a melodic minor scale.

Table 10.1 Common Applications of a Melodic Minor Scale	
Chord	**Scale**
Tonic minor	Melodic minor scale based on the root of the chord.
Half-diminished	Melodic minor scale based on the third of the chord.
Altered dominant	Melodic minor up one half step from the root of the chord.
Lydian dominant	Melodic minor based on the fifth of the chord.

Major-Scale Tips

Each of the scales explored to this point can be constructed by relating the scale to a simple major scale. For example, the Ionian, Dorian, and Mixolydian modes (used for maj 7, min7, and dominant7, respectively) can be visualized by finding the relevant major scale, as shown in Table 10.2.

Table 10.2 Using Major Scales to Find Modes		
Chord Group	**Example Chords**	**Relevant Major Scale**
Tonic major	Cmaj7, C6, Cmaj9, etc.	Major scale on the root of the chord.
Minor seventh	Dmin7, Dmin9, etc.	Major scale down one whole step from root of chord.
Dominant seventh	G7, G9, G13	Major scale up a perfect fourth from root of chord (or major scale with a lowered seventh).

The ascending form of a melodic minor scale is easily constructed by changing the major third of a major scale to a minor third. In this way, major scales can be used as the basis for constructing scales for several complex chords (see Table 10.3).

Table 10.3 Application of Melodic Minor Scales		
Chord Group	**Example Chords**	**Relevant Major Scale**
Tonic minor	Cmin(maj7), Cmin6, etc.	Melodic minor based on root of chord.
Half-diminished	Cmin7♭5, Cm11♭5, etc.	Melodic minor built on third of chord.
Altered dominant	B7alt.	Melodic minor scale up one half-step from root of chord.
Lydian dominant	F7#11, F9#11, etc.	Melodic minor build on fifth of chord.

Other Scales

In this section I will consider several useful scales that range from the blues scale to pentatonic scales and "customized" synthetic scales.

BLUES SCALE

Blues melodies and improvisations often contain *blue notes*—notes such as minor third that are slightly raised (not quite a minor or major third). The blues scale provides one way of visualizing this type of melodic vocabulary. The "standard" blues scale contains a minor third, raised fourth, and lowered seventh. However, it is rare to hear players use the scale solely in that form. A more common approach is to add what I like to call the "other good tones." These tones (root, second, fifth, and sixth) are often used as the basis for *riffs* (repetitive phrases) and other types of blues-related vocabulary (see Figure 10.23). This hybrid scale provides many sounds used on recordings of blues-based genres.

Figure 10.23
Blues scale with "other good notes."

Many common riffs use these four notes.

Many blues performers utilize notes from the underlying harmonic progression. Consider, for example, the tonic chord of a I-IV-V blues. The tonic chord in a C blues is usually a C7, C9, or C13. The third of this chord is an E natural, a note not found in the basic blues scale. Clearly, chord tones are always available as potential melodic notes, so the E-natural could be included in a melody over the I or V chords (although this tone should be avoided over the IV chord since it clashes with the seventh of that chord). If you consider adding all the chord tones found in a blues progression as potential melodic notes, it is clear that almost any note from the chromatic scale can be used in a blues melody or improvisation. Figure 10.24 illustrates the concept. This version of a blues progression utilizes several secondary dominants (a major-minor seventh chord that precedes a given arrival chord and provides a temporary dominant-to-tonic function) and is commonly heard in many jazz-based blues progressions.

Figure 10.24
Visualizing the use of chord tones in a blues progression.

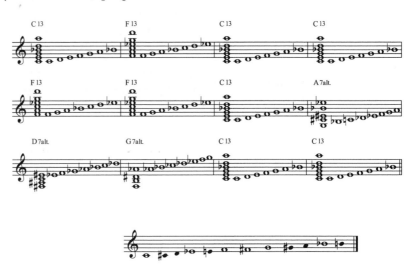

To get a sense of some of the variations possible when playing over a blues progression, play through the blues solo shown in Figure 10.25. Note that, though this example relies heavily on the basic blues scale and riff notes, many chord tones and embellishments are also evident. As always, your ear should guide you as to how best to use these concepts. Experiment with the sounds and listen to recordings—that is always the best way to develop a convincing vocabulary for any style of music.

Figure 10.25
Twelve-bar blues solo using blues scale, riff tones, chord tones, and embellishments.

DIMINISHED SCALES

Diminished scales are useful primarily in two situations: as a resource for diminished chords and when applied to altered dominant chords. The diminished scale gets its name from the fact that it is constructed from two fully diminished chords placed one whole step apart from one another (see Figure 10.26).

Figure 10.26
The diminished scale consists of two diminished seventh chords.

If you analyze the series of half and whole steps in this scale, you will find that the scale is symmetrical—it consists of alternating half and whole steps. This scale is sometimes called the *half-whole scale* or *octatonic scale* (see Figure 10.27).

Figure 10.27
Half and whole steps of a diminished scale.

The most obvious application of this scale is for fully diminished chords. To construct the scale, use a series of whole and half steps starting with the root of the given diminished chord (see Figure 10.28).

Figure 10.28
Diminished scale applied to a fully diminished chord.

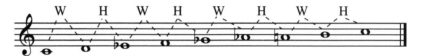

The diminished scale can also be helpful when applied to altered dominant chords such as a C13♭9. Figure 10.29 illustrates the relationship between a diminished scale and an altered dominant chord. Note how the interval ordering is alternating half and whole steps, not whole and half steps as in the diminished chord example.

Figure 10.29
Diminished scale applied to a C13♭9 chord (alternating whole and half steps).

PENTATONIC SCALE

A pentatonic scale is a scale that consists of only five pitches. Although any collection of five pitches can qualify as a pentatonic scale, the most common approach is to use 1-2-3-5-6 in a major key. These same tones also work well when applied to a relative minor as in Figure 10.30.

Figure 10.30
Pentatonic scale for a major key and its relative minor.

The pentatonic scale is particularly well suited for compositions that have a world music quality. I say this because the pentatonic scale is found in folk music in many parts of the world. Figures 10.31 and 10.32 illustrate the use of a pentatonic scale in a negro spiritual and Peruvian folk song.

Figure 10.31
Negro spiritual: "Trampin."

Figure 10.32
Peruvian folk song: "Blow on the Sea Shell."

Pentatonic scales are also used in many other genres. Many composers of 20th-century art music have used pentatonic scales because they provide a good way of establishing a major tonality while minimizing the traditional dominant and tonic relationship. This is due to the fact that the traditional pentatonic scale omits the two "functional" notes in a major key—the fourth and seventh. Pentatonic scales are also used in many styles of pop music including blues, rock, and rhythm and blues. Many musicians utilize the scale as in Figure 10.33.

Figure 10.33
Pentatonic blues excerpt.

SYNTHETIC SCALES

Twentieth century composers often create specialized scales that do not follow a recognizable pattern of half and whole steps found in "natural" scales such as a major or minor scale. These types of *synthetic scales* can be useful in creating unique thematic material as well as providing a fresh palette of chords.

Whole-Tone Scale

One synthetic scale, the whole-tone scale, was brought into vogue in the early 20th century. This scale is unique in that it does not include any semitones; it is constructed entirely of whole tones (see Figure 10.34). This scale is useful when applied to an altered dominant chord (e.g., C7♯5). The scale may also be used as a melodic or harmonic resource when your goal is to obscure any sense of functional harmony. The whole-tone scale often has a "dreamy" quality when used in this context.

Figure 10.34
Whole-tone scale.

Composing a Synthetic Scale

Figure 10.35 illustrates the type of synthetic scale that might be created by a 20th-century composer. There is no right or wrong way to compose such a scale. In this case, I experimented with half and whole step patterns until I was pleased with the results.

Figure 10.35
Composing a synthetic scale.

This scale, which has elements of the octatonic or diminished scale, was created to illustrate how synthetic scales can be useful in the composition process. Figure 10.36 shows how the scale might be used as the basis for a simple two-part composition.

Figure 10.36
A two-part composition based on a synthetic scale.

An even more interesting use of such a scale is to create chord structures based on the given scale. Although some enharmonic spellings were used, Figure 10.37 illustrates how triads could be constructed from the scale presented in Figure 10.35. In this example, ascending triads are placed over a descending bass line (which is also based on the scale).

Figure 10.37
Deriving chords from a synthetic scale.

Using Chord–Scale Relationships

If you have made it this far, you are now familiar with most of the common chord and scale relationships. These chord and scale relationships will help you find good notes for any harmonic setting, but most great music does not easily fit into well-defined chord–scale paradigms. One of the difficulties you may encounter is using scales in a musical way. It is one thing to understand the theory of chord–scale relationships, but it is sometimes difficult to apply these concepts in real time. The following suggestions will help bridge the gap between theoretical knowledge and functional application of these concepts.

THE WINDOW APPROACH

I often find it helpful to limit my choices as I explore a new musical concept such as chord–scale relationships. Pick a scale (such as a melodic minor scale) to experiment with. Play the scale and listen to how each note sounds when played over a given chord. Use a sequencer to record a one-chord vamp and paste or loop the vamp several times. Begin by improvising using only the first three or four notes of the scale. Try to pace your improvisation so that the minimal number of notes does not sound inhibiting (i.e., use lots of space and repetition). With this type of approach, you will quickly learn how to utilize the first half of any scale. When you are comfortable with the first three or four notes, repeat the exercise but focus on the next three or four notes. When this is entirely comfortable, allow yourself to use any of the notes of the scale. You will find that you can easily develop the facility to use a scale (even a complex one) in an effective and musical manner.

You may want to expand this technique to include a more complex harmonic progression. In Figure 10.38, a minor ii-V-i progression provides a useful way of exploring three of the possible applications of a melodic minor scale. Note how this melody uses only the first four notes of each scale.

Figure 10.38
Using the first four notes of melodic minor scales for a minor ii-V-i progression.

RUNNING EIGHTH NOTES

Another technique that can help you become more fluent with chord–scale relationships is to use a series of running eighth or 16th notes. For this exercise, try to gracefully move from one scale to the next (i.e., continue the moving line and start the next scale with a note that is close to the current note). Though this is a difficult technique to master, with a little practice you will find that you can move fluently through almost any harmonic progression (see Figure 10.39).

Figure 10.39
Moving eighth notes over a chord
progression.

DON'T ALWAYS START ON THE ROOT

We are creatures of habit. Though this is helpful when navigating a flight of stairs, habits can inhibit your ability to use a scale effectively. Most of us tend to start on the root of a given scale. One way you can get more comfortable with using scales is to start scales on different notes such as the third or fifth degree. Practice playing through a progression of chords and start on a particular note (such as the fifth) for each chord in the progression (see Figure 10.40).

Figure 10.40
Starting on the fifth degree of each
scale.

PATTERN PRACTICING

Another practice technique involves applying a pattern or "shape" to a scale. Select a series of pitches such as 1-2-3-5-3 and apply this same pattern to each scale over a progression of chords (see Figure 10.41). I have found this technique to be a great way to develop new vocabulary that might otherwise be uncomfortable to play (or difficult to hear).

Figure 10.41
Applying a pattern to a progression
of chords.

SCALE–TONE CHORD CONCEPTS

One of the most helpful practice techniques involving scales is the concept of scale–tone triads or seventh chords. Earlier in the chapter I mentioned that scale–tone triads and sevenths can be used when constructing chords. This concept can also be applied to single-note melodies. The idea is to use triads or other chord structures that are diatonic to a given scale. In a major scale, for instance, the scale consists of the triads shown in Figure 10.42.

Figure 10.42
Triads found in a C-major scale.

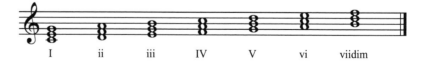

Diatonic triads (or any other structure) can be outlined to form any number of interesting melodies. Figure 10.43 illustrates the use of several scale–tone concepts applied to a chord progression.

Figure 10.43
Scale–tone triads applied to several scales.

Figure 10.44 illustrates how scale–tone seventh chords might be used in the context of a Dorian mode. Note how each of the melodic outlines in the example imply one of the seventh chords found in the D Dorian mode.

Figure 10.44
Scale–tone seventh chords (D Dorian mode).

THINGS TO TRY AND THINGS TO AVOID

As you explore the concept of chord–scale relationships, try to work past the academic nature of these concepts and internalize the sound of each note in a scale. As these sounds become familiar to your ears, many of the melodies and solos found on popular music recordings will become accessible. Also remember that, although scales are helpful, they can also be limiting. Avoid the temptation to stay only within the "appropriate" scale; many other options such as embellishments and passing tones (notes used to connect two chord tones) should be available to you as you compose and improvise.

Examples

The following examples represent the application of scales to a variety of harmonic progressions in several different styles. These excerpts are not meant to be comprehensive but will provide a useful starting point for further exploration.

Figure 10.45 illustrates the use of altered scale fragments in the context of a jazz progression. Note that many of the chromatic tones evident in this example are the result of melodic embellishments, chromatic passing tones, changing tones (a combination of upper and lower neighbor tones), and the like.

Figure 10.45
Using scales in a jazz context.

Figure 10.46 shows how blues scales and pentatonic vocabulary might be applied in a rhythm and blues piece.

Figure 10.46
Blues scale and pentatonic vocabu-lary.

In the next example, common chord–scale relationships, when combined with pentatonics, provide the basis for a solo in a pop style (see Figure 10.47).

Figure 10.47
Pop-style solo.

Figure 10. 48 illustrates how Dorian and Lydian modes might be utilized in a pretty fusion-style ballad.

Figure 10.48
Using modes on a fusion ballad solo.

In the next example, scale–tone triads are used as the basis for a keyboard fill (see Figure 10.49). This application of scale–tone triads is heard in many keyboard styles including blues, pop, and country music.

Figure 10.49
Keyboard fill utilizing scale–tone triads.

In the last example, several melodic minor scales are applied to a complex progression of chords (see Figure 10.50).

Figure 10.50
Application of melodic minor scales.

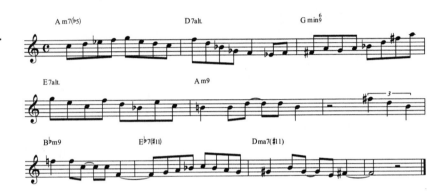

Summary

In summary, scales provide a useful way of looking at vertical structures from a linear perspective. Although scales are most often used as a resource for melodies and improvised solos, they are also useful in constructing chords and progressions. They can even be used as the basis for a composition. We will explore these concepts in other chapters, such as Chapter 14, "Music Composition," and Chapter 15, "Real-World Arranging."

CHAPTER 11

The Linear Process

This chapter looks at melody and harmony from a linear perspective. As the term implies, the linear process involves thinking of musical elements in terms of individual lines. A linear approach is helpful in nearly every aspect of making music from creating chord progressions to programming bass lines and drum grooves. It could be said that most great music—either art music or popular music—has a linear dimension, so this chapter considers practical concepts that will foster this useful approach to music making. The following topics will be emphasized:

▶ Brief history of the linear process

▶ Harmonic implications of a melody

▶ Guide tone lines

▶ Arrival points

▶ Bass lines

▶ Independent bass lines

▶ Imitation

▶ Additive formal process

▶ A linear approach to harmony

▶ Chord mutation

Brief History of the Linear Process

Historically speaking, the linear process is one of the "elemental" approaches. In medieval times, monophonic chants were embellished through the use of a secondary melodic line to form the first extensive use of *polyphony*—two or more independent melodic lines. Later, composers such as Palestrina used a linear process to create music with an amazing variety of textures and sonorities. In the Baroque era, composers such as J.S. Bach, an undisputed master of linear technique, used the linear process to push the boundaries of the tonal system we know today. In the 19th and 20th centuries the linear process continued to be an essential component of music composition. For example, Duke Ellington has long been admired for modern sounds that are largely the result of the linear process.

One of my favorite examples of linear process can be seen in a Bach harmonization of "Ich hab' mein' Sach' Gott heimgestellt" ("I leave my heart and soul to God"). In Figure 11.1, listen to the resulting vertical structure on beat two of the first full bar and beat four of the second full bar. Out of context, these chords have a sonority that, even by today's standards, sounds modern. In context one can only marvel at Bach's ability to utilize sonorities that are at once so modern and so appropriate for the piece.

Figure 11.1
"Ich hab' mein' Sach' Gott heimgestellt."

When you consider that Bach lived over 300 years ago it becomes evident that the linear process has much to offer to modern composers. For example, Bartók and Stravinsky are two of the many modern composers who used linear techniques to create music that is profoundly original. It is important to note that, though the vertical structures are very interesting in the Bach excerpt, he did not conceive of harmony in the purely vertical sense many musicians think of chords today. Although Bach did think in terms of chords and chord progressions—he even used an early form of chord symbols called *figured bass*—the linear process was always more important. An insight comes from J.N. Forkel's description of Bach's teaching methods (from *Composers on Music*, edited by Josiah Fisk) in which Forkel required his students

"To pay constant attention to the consistency of each single part, in and of itself, as well as to its relation to the parts connected and concurrent with it. No part, not even a middle part, was allowed to break off before it had entirely said what it had to say. Every note was required to have a connection with the preceding: did any one appear of which it was not apparent whence it came, nor whither it tended, it was instantly banished as suspicious."

Harmonic Implications of a Melody

In tonal music, a melody can be used to clearly imply harmony—even if no accompaniment is heard. Figure 11.2 comes from a J.S. Bach invention in D minor. As is evident in Figure 11.2, the first bar implies a D minor while the second bar implies a C♯ diminished chord.

*Figure 11.2
J.S. Bach, "Invention 4."*

In the next phrase, the tonic and dominant relationship is clearly implied by the countermotive (see Figure 11.3). A *countermotive* is a melodic line that provides a counterpoint to the primary motive.

*Figure 11.3
Countermotive: J.S. Bach, "Invention 4."*

As is evident in Figure 11.4, when the motive and countermotive are combined, they work together to imply the underlying harmonic progression (i-vii dim7-i-vii dim7).

*Figure 11.4
Melody and countermotive: J.S. Bach, "Invention 4."*

GUIDE TONE LINES

Some musicians use the term *guide tone line* to describe a series of notes that serves to imply an underlying harmonic progression. In many cases, the third and seventh are two of the most important notes that help imply a harmonic progression, but other tones are possible. The song, "All the Things You Are" provides an excellent example of a guide tone line. Most of the notes in this song are either a third or seventh and, when combined with a single bass note, are sufficient to clearly imply the underlying harmony (see Figure 11.5).

Figure 11.5
The first few bars of "All the Things You Are."

Guide tones are helpful when writing in a linear style because these notes can be utilized to imply a harmonic progression. For example, the melody in Figure 11.6 utilizes the guide tones from Figure 11.5. The harmonic implication of this melody is fairly clear, even without a bass line.

Figure 11.6
Melody based on the guide tones of "All the Things You Are."

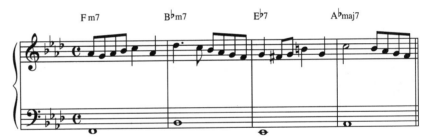

ESTABLISHING ARRIVAL POINTS

I use the term *arrival point* to describe a point at which a vertical harmony must be implied. In many musical genres, arrival points occur at each chord change; however, the concept is also useful in music that is *freely tonal* (see Chapter 9, "Practical Music Theory"). The concept can even be applied to atonal music when independent lines serve to lead to an arrival point that is accentuated with a rhythmic cadence. In Figure 11.7, two independent lines "arrive" at a chord tone at each chord change in the following progression. Note how nonharmonic tones serve to embellish and connect the chord tones in this example.

Figure 11.7
Two melodic lines that imply a
chord progression.

Figure 11.8 demonstrates a more modern version of the concept. This example is typical of music that is freely tonal. Although the lines are truly independent and no clear progression is heard, each part leads to a clear arrival point.

Figure 11.8
Freely tonal approach to an arrival
point.

Bass Lines

Bass lines have been an important part of the linear process throughout the common practice period. I find it fascinating to compare how Baroque composers like Bach utilized a *basso continuo* and how this concept is still with us in many forms of popular music. As you can see in Figure 11.9, the continuo part from Bach's second "Brandenburg Concerto" has many of the elements we associate with bass lines today: The continuo provides a steady pulse that "drives" the orchestra, roots help to indicate most chord changes, an emphasis is placed on primary chord factors (root, third, and fifth), and passing tones are occasionally used to connect chord tones.

Figure 11.9
Excerpt from J.S. Bach's
"Brandenburg Concerto No. 2"

When you compare Bach's use of a bass line with a more modern example, it is clear that the function of a bass line is still very much with us in the 21st century. Figure 11.10 is an excerpt from George Russell's

"All About Rosie" and demonstrates how a bass line might be used to drive a modern-day orchestra.

Figure 11.10
Excerpt from "All About Rosie," by
George Russell.

INDEPENDENT BASS LINES

Popular music and jazz often feature bass lines that provide traditional harmonic and rhythmic function while retaining an independent character. As with other melodies, as long as arrival points (usually a chord change) are clearly implied in the bass, these lines can be written in a highly linear and independent way. Figures 11.11 through 11.13 show several ways a bass line might be constructed. In the first example, roots and chord outlines are used.

Figure 11.11
Implying harmony with primary
chord tones.

Figure 11.12 develops the chord-tone idea presented in Figure 11.11. In this instance, chromatic approach tones and passing tones are used to embellish the primary chord tones.

Figure 11.12
A bass line featuring nonharmonic
tones.

In the next example the bass functions in an independent way—the bass descends to an arrival point at the end of the phrase. Although some vertical dissonances result, this type of independent bass line is quite effective.

Figure 11.13
Descending chromatic bass line.

Case Study

The next example combines the concepts of guide tones, arrival points, and independent bass line to create a linear composition for bassoon, viola, and flute. A first step is to look at the harmonic progression and consider guide tones and arrival points. Figure 11.14 shows the melody and basic harmonic progression for a pseudo-Baroque composition. As evident in this excerpt, the melody already contains several important guide tones.

Figure 11.14
Melody and chord progression for three-part composition.

Next, a linear bass line is constructed that helps imply the harmonic progression and provide rhythmic motion in places where the flute rests (see Figure 11.15).

Figure 11.15
Constructing an independent bass line.

The viola part was composed to complement the flute part. Notice how the viola melody is independent and often arrives at chord tones that help imply the underlying harmonic structure. As with the bass, the viola helps create a sense of rhythmic motion with occasional quarter- and eighth-note motion (see Figure 11.16).

Notice how the chord progression is implied by each melody in the previous example. Although it would be possible to determine the chord progression by listening to each independent line, the lines combine to form a fairly convincing presentation of the harmonic progression. Though this example is in a pseudo-Baroque style, the techniques work well in more modern applications. For example, the composition titled "Lullaby for Emily" on the accompanying CD features a very linear approach to a composition for flute, violin, and piano in a pop or new age style.

Figure 11.16
Composing an independent viola
line.

Imitation

Imitation is a powerful linear technique heard in many styles of music. As the term implies, imitation involves repetition of previously heard material in another voice. Two of my favorite examples come from classical literature. Figure 11.17 is an excerpt from a J.S. Bach prelude. In this example, a highly chromatic motive is placed over a chromatic bass line. In the second bar, the motive is repeated in the left hand under a chromatic countermotive in the right hand. Although it would be difficult to provide a traditional harmonic analysis of this passage, the strength of the chromatic motive makes the passage sound natural.

Figure 11.17
J.S. Bach, "Prelude XX" (from book
two).

In the next example, Béla Bartók uses a similar approach in his "Chromatic Invention." It is interesting to hear how the concept of imitative counterpoint can be effectively utilized in a 20th-century composition (see Figure 11.18).

On the accompanying CD you will find a piece titled "Scherzo" that was written to demonstrate linear technique. The primary motive of this piece (which is closely related to Bartók's "Chromatic Invention") is presented in the form of a *fugue*. In a fugue, the theme (or *subject*) is presented in each voice in turn throughout the course of a composition. Once the subject has been stated, the given voice continues with a *countersubject* while another voice presents a transposed version of the subject called the *answer* (see Figure 11.19).

As a fugue is developed, the subject is often fragmented, inverted, or otherwise transformed, or new material may be presented. The term *episode* is used to describe these sections. Figure 11.20 demonstrates one such section in the "Scherzo." In this example, fragments of the subject are used as well as new developmental ideas.

Although the concept of a fugue might seem inhibiting to a modern-day musician, the technique is capable of producing music with a profound range of emotions. Writing in a contrapuntal style can also provide a unique perspective on the composition process. In my experience, the process of composing music in this way often yields results that are refreshingly different from the vertical approach most of us are more familiar with.

Figure 11.20
Developing the fugue subject.

The Additive Formal Process

In *The Elements of Music, Volume Two* (McGraw-Hill, 1996), theorist Ralph Turek talks about an approach to formal process used by Debussy, Stravinsky, and others. With this approach, musical ideas are combined, juxtaposed, and transformed in many ways over the course of a composition or section of a work. Although the concept relates to a more freewheeling approach to form, the technique illustrates a powerful use of linear technique.

I like to think of the concept of *additive formal process* in terms of a musical collage. In a collage, various materials are glued to a surface and provide interesting variations in texture and color. In a similar way, musical elements such as a motive, series of chords, ostinato, or bass line can be combined to form any number of interesting combinations. Two of the many examples that come to mind are "Nuages" ("Clouds") by Claude Debussy and "Le Sacre du Printemps" ("The Rite of Spring") by Igor Stravinsky. When you listen to these works, identify primary "threads" that are presented, combined, and transformed. Although the concept is easy to visualize, the results can be profound. Since the modern-day ear is generally more tolerant of dissonance, disparate elements can be combined with little need for consideration of traditional harmonic structures.

A Linear Approach to Harmony: Connecting Chords

In the realm of tonal music, linear process provides a virtually limitless number of options for connecting arrival points. When using linear technique, consider the melodic tendencies of each of the voices in a progression of chords. Instead of relying solely on vertical chord structures, consider how each voice can work in an independent way to work toward an arrival point. Often a melody and/or bass line may help determine a linear choice. In Figure 11.21, a number of linear solutions are presented for a common progression of chords. Notice how each of the inner voices retains an independent quality. These voices might approach an arrival point using chromatic or diatonic motion, embellishment, or even a jump. The important thing to remember is that each voice retains melodic freedom. The resulting harmonies are often not easily recognizable using traditional analysis, but to the ears of the listener, linear motion can be very pleasing.

Figure 11.21
Linear solutions Fsus4 to Gsus2.

I would emphasize that a linear approach to harmony can work in *any* style of music. For example, many of the examples in Figure 11.19 would be suitable for a song in a popular style. The linear process can provide that elusive "something special" to even the most pedantic progression. In terms of practice, I would suggest composing linear variations of traditional progressions such as I-IV-V-I. Start by composing several linear bass lines and then focus on creating variations for each of the voices in the progression. There is no right or wrong way to implement linear technique—experimentation will yield many interesting results.

CHORD MUTATION

Chord mutation represents another linear approach to harmony. Consider a chord such as E minor. If the top note is raised to a C, the chord mutates into a C-major triad. The third of this chord (E) could be lowered to form a C minor chord and the fifth (G) could be raised to form an A♭ major (see Figure 11.22).

Figure 11.22
Mutating an E-minor chord.

A wonderful example of chord mutation comes from Chopin's "Prelude in E minor." In this example, mutation provides a series of chords that is much more interesting than a series of diatonic harmonies or a functional progression (see Figure 11.23).

Figure 11.23
Chord mutation in Chopin's "Prelude in E minor."

Summary

When exploring a linear approach to composition and arranging, focus on the melodic potential of each voice. In many cases, independent movement of voices in the context of a chord progression or bass line can provide results that are distinctive and difficult to achieve with a purely vertical approach to harmonization. When writing in a linear style, consider how each voice can help to imply the underlying harmony in an independent fashion and also consider primary arrival points. If a melody approaches an arrival point in a convincing way, the resulting vertical harmonies will usually be effective, even if the structures are nontraditional.

CHAPTER 12

Sequencing Bass and Drum Grooves

Much of today's popular music revolves around bass and drums. It could be said that bass and drum grooves are the building blocks for pop music. For many electronic musicians, establishing a good groove is the first step in creating a new composition. Because of the importance of bass and drums in many styles of popular and commercial music, I am devoting a chapter to these concepts. This chapter will focus on the following objectives:

- ▶ Function of instruments in a standard drum kit

- ▶ Traditional and nontraditional approaches to drum sequencing

- ▶ Using a matrix view to create derivative patterns

- ▶ "Weighting" a groove

- ▶ Creating drum fills

- ▶ Playing drum grooves in real time on a MIDI keyboard

- ▶ Drum substitution

- ▶ Linear drumming concepts

- ▶ Function of the bass

- ▶ Creating bass lines

- ▶ Anatomy of common styles

One of the best ways to learn about sequencing drum parts is to watch a live drummer in action. The primary goal of a drummer is to provide the rhythmic feel or groove, but when you listen closely to a good drummer you will find that there is much more to it than simple timekeeping. Good drummers often delineate the form of the music, they provide interesting textures and fills, they create excitement behind a soloist, and they may dynamically lead or react to the ensemble.

You may elect to use either a traditional or nontraditional approach to sequencing drum tracks. In a traditional approach, the goal is to mimic what a real drummer would do. In nontraditional drum sequencing, MIDI and audio technology is used to create drum parts not necessarily playable by a live drummer. Which approach is best? It all depends on what you are trying to accomplish with your sequence.

I once had the pleasure of playing a few concerts with Ralph Humphries from the Frank Zappa band. He spoke on the subject of sequencing drums, and I was surprised to learn that he does not always attempt to program "realistic" drum grooves. The example he described involved keeping an eighth-note hi-hat part going through a drum fill. Although this would not be possible using traditional drumming technique, it is easy to do with a sequenced drum part. His observation was that if a live drummer could play time on the hi-hat during a fill, he probably would. Since then, I have worried much less about creating drum sequences that sound like the real thing. If you keep the aesthetics of a tune in mind as you sequence, you will find an approach that works for you.

Traditional Drum Sequencing

When creating drum parts it is helpful to consider the traditional function of instruments in the drum kit. A basic kit will include a bass drum (kick), snare, hi-hat cymbals, ride cymbal, one or more crash cymbals, and one or more toms. Most drummers also use a variety of other percussion instruments such as woodblock, cowbell, tambourine, shaker, guiro, bell, or clave.

The instruments in a traditional drum kit can generally be divided into two groups: instruments that divide or subdivide the beat and those that provide the unique accent or weight that defines the groove. Table 12.1 shows common usage of the primary instruments listed above. It is important to remember that this is just one of many ways of using these sounds—many excellent drum grooves have been sequenced using the instruments in nontraditional ways.

Table 12.1. Traditional Usage of a Drum Set

Instrument	Common Function
Hi-hat	Division or subdivision of beat (eighth or 16th notes in 4/4 time). A drummer may also open and close the hi-hat using a foot pedal—typically on beats two and four in 4/4 time.
Ride cymbal	Same function as hi-hat cymbals. The ride cymbal is often saved for an important part of the song such as the bridge or an out chorus.
Snare drum	Often used on the backbeat (beats two and four in common time). Also used in conjunction with crash or toms for fills as well as for general rhythmic accompaniment (comping).
Bass drum	Used in conjunction with the snare to delineate the "weight" of a groove. Most often used on the strong beats (1 and 3 in 4/4 time) but may be heard on all beats or even a division or subdivision in some styles of music. Most drummers also add kick in conjunction with a cymbal crash.
Crash cymbal	Often used as part of a fill to set up an important structural point such as a bridge. Cymbal rolls are frequently heard during fermatas at the end of a tune, or they can be used to subtly build intensity to support a crescendo.
Toms	Usually used for fills but may also be heard on the backbeat or subdivision of the beat.

USING SOUNDS FROM THE TRADITIONAL DRUM KIT

The following section demonstrates how a wide variety of traditional grooves can be achieved by using the primary instruments in a drum kit: hi-hat, ride, kick, and snare.

Hi-Hat

When creating a traditional drum sequence, many musicians start with the hi-hat cymbals. Sticks or brushes may be used to play the hi-hats in a closed, half-open, or full-open position. The sound of the hi-hat being opened and closed is also an important component. By using these sounds in consort with well-placed accents, a virtually limitless combination of interesting pulses may be achieved. For more natural sounding patterns, any ringing notes should be stopped when the hi-hat closes. Many keyboards provide this functionality, but it can also be achieved through sequence editing by ensuring that the open-hi hat sound is turned off prior to receiving a closed hi-hat message.

The following examples demonstrate several of the common hi-hat patterns. Note that, in the examples in this book, the bass drum is represented on the bottom space of the percussion clef, snare on the third space, and cymbals above the staff. An "x" above the staff denotes closed hi-hat or ride, and a "o" over the note indicates an open hi-hat. Note that standard noteheads are typically used to denote drums with heads such as a snare or tom and an "x" is often used to denote "headless" instruments such as a cymbal or woodblock.

Figure 12.1 demonstrates a basic rock groove. In this example, the hi-hat is used to divide the beat, and the kick and snare provide a repetitive "anchor" to the groove.

Figure 12.1
Basic rock pattern.

Figure 12.2 is similar to the basic rock groove but the subdivision is emphasized in both the hi-hat and kick drum. Although this groove could be heard in rock and other styles of music, the 16th note syncopation is characteristic of many funk tunes.

Figure 12.2
Basic funk pattern.

The basic swing rhythm demonstrated in Figure 12.3 shows another use of the hi-hat. Here, the hi-hat opens on beats one and three and closes on beats two and four. Sticks or brushes are used to play a pattern of alternating quarter and eighth notes. Note that, in the swing style, the bass drum is sometimes used on each beat but is barely audible.

Figure 12.3
Basic swing pattern (snare "comps" freely).

In order to explore the process of creating a drum groove from scratch, try sequencing a groove such as the basic rock or funk rhythm shown above and configure the sequencer so that it loops in a matrix or drum editing view (see Chapter 4 for a discussion of these views). While the sequence plays back, alter the hi-hats to a shaker, tambourine, or other sound and experiment with a variety of velocities. I have found that this type of experimentation can yield many new and interesting derivative grooves. Figure 12.4 shows a drum matrix view in which a repetitive hi-hat pattern has been expanded to include several percussive instruments.

Figure 12.4
Using a drum matrix view to create a derivative pattern.

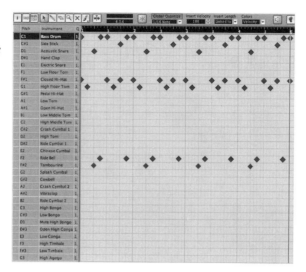

A common variation on the traditional hi-hat approach involves using auxiliary percussion or even nontraditional percussive sounds to provide basic division or subdivision of the beat. Shakers, maraca, tambourine, brushes on hi-hat or snare, or any number of sampled sounds can be used in a similar fashion to create some truly interesting grooves. In fact, many excellent grooves used in techno and other styles of music are based on traditional grooves but feature nontraditional percussive sounds.

Ride Cymbal

The ride cymbal is typically used to provide rhythmic division or subdivisions of the beat. Its function is similar to the hi-hat. Many drummers will include more than one ride cymbal in their gig bags: Chinese and inverted ride cymbals are just two examples. Although there are many examples of songs that use the ride during an introduction or first verse, ride cymbals are most often saved for an exciting part of the tune such as a last chorus, interlude, or bridge. When used in this manner, the ride cymbal can provide a refreshing change.

Most drummers are able to get a wide variety of sounds out of a single ride cymbal. The placement of the stick and the force used to strike the cymbal determine the specific sound or color that is achieved. In MIDI terms, just two sounds are usually available: "ringing" or "bell" sounds. The ringing sound comes from striking the ride near the edge of the cymbal, and the more percussive bell sound is achieved by striking the bell near the center of the cymbal. Figure 12.5 illustrates the use of the bell sound in a typical rock groove.

Figure 12.5
Rock groove: bell ride, kick, and snare drum.

Kick or Bass Drum

The kick or bass drum is almost always used in conjunction with the snare drum in popular music. For variation, drummers might use a stick on the rim of the snare or another percussive instrument in place of the snare. One way to create new bass and drum patterns is to sequence an eighth or 16th note hi-hat pattern. Loop the pattern and experiment with different kick and snare rhythms. In this way, a wide variety of grooves can be created. Drummers sometimes talk in terms of "weight" when describing a groove. Though the term is vague, you can get a sense of this concept by varying the position and frequency of kick and snare attacks. A groove that uses a snare only on beat four will provide a "lighter" weight than a groove that includes snare hits on beats two and four. Figure 12.6 demonstrates several types of "weighted" grooves. Often, listening to a bass guitar part may provide a hint as to how to weight a particular groove.

Figure 12.6
Four contrasting groove weights.

The bass or kick drum is most often used near the first and third beats in common time. I use the term "near" because, depending on the style of music, the kick may be offset by an eight or 16th note to imply an underlying subdivision of beats. The snare is usually placed near or directly on the backbeat—beats two and four in common time. Figure 12.7 demonstrate a few of the many common kick and snare patterns.

Figure 12.7
A few common kick and snare patterns.

Note that all of the examples are variations of a basic rock groove with snare on beats two and four. Experiment with different hi-hat and ride patterns—the possibilities are limitless.

It is sometimes difficult to play an active hi-hat or snare part using only one finger or alternating fingers on a MIDI keyboard. Because most synthesizers (and some software) allow you to map drum sounds to more than one key, a good way to overcome this problem is to assign a snare or hi-hat sound to two or more adjacent keys. For most players, it is easier to use two or three fingers on adjacent keys than trying to use alternating finger technique on a single note. With a little practice you will find that you can achieve natural sounding drum rolls, "flams," and fills. Figure 12.8 demonstrates a practice etude that can aid in the development of a natural-sounding snare and hi-hat technique. You can visualize flams as a grace note where one stick strikes the drum earlier (and softer) than the other stick. In this example, alternating sticks are shown as separate pitches. If your synthesizer supports the feature, try detuning each of the snare sounds slightly for an even more realistic effect. (The pitch of a snare will change depending on where it is struck and velocity with which the stick strikes the head of the drum.)

Figure 12.8
Two-finger drum etude.

DRUM FILLS

Drummers often use fills as a way of marking form, setting up a rhythmic figure, or adding an extra element of excitement behind a solo. One of the most difficult concepts to master when sequencing fills involves the function of each drum in a fill. Unlike the function of the hi-hat, ride, kick, and snare in a traditional groove, the function of these instruments is less clear in a fill. Although it is common to hear fills performed on just the snare or toms, most drummers use a combination of percussive instruments during a fill. A good way to experiment with fills is to record a traditional fill using the toms or snare. Use your sequencer to transpose some of the notes to other sounds such as a tom or hi-hat. Figure 12.9 illustrates one of the most common fills—the descending tom fill.

Figure 12.9
Descending tom fill.

By transposing some of the notes to other instruments in the drum kit, a more natural-sounding drum fill can be achieved. Experiment as in Figure 12.10: Many interesting variations are possible using the transposition method described above.

Figure 12.10
Variation of descending tom fill.

Step-time entry can be helpful when sequencing drum fills at a fast tempo. Use a step-time entry tool to enter a sequence of 16th or 32nd notes using a variety of percussive instruments such as snare, toms, and kick. Many interesting fills can be created that would ordinarily be difficult to play using traditional keyboard entry. A MIDI arpeggiator can also be useful for the purpose. For example, it is possible to mimic a fill by holding down three or four keys and running the track through a MIDI arpeggiator. An arpeggiator that supports randomized velocities can make such a fill sound even more natural.

It can be difficult to determine where to place a fill in a sequence. Good drummers tend to make very slight changes at the end of a phrase and save the "big stuff" for when it is really needed. One way to approach fills is to wait until a sequence is nearly complete before adding any fills. You can establish basic grooves and variation grooves to use while sequencing and then listen, with the ears of a drummer, to places that a fill could be effective. Once you have determined where fills need to be inserted, it is easy to cut out the underlying drum groove and insert appropriate fills in these places. Sometimes I will even retake the entire drum track when a sequence has taken shape because it allows me to respond and interact with the other sequenced tracks in a way that a real drummer might approach a piece in live performance.

Most drum grooves can be performed in real time on a MIDI keyboard by playing the hi-hat or ride in the right hand and using the left hand to cover the snare and bass drum. A good way to practice your "fill chops" is to play a groove for four or eight bars. In the last bar of the phrase (or even the last beat or two), perform a simple snare or tom fill. The goal here is to make the fill a natural extension of the groove, and you will find that, just like on a real drum kit, subtle gestures tend to work best. Figure 12.11 illustrates an example of a repetitive groove with a fill in the fourth bar.

Figure 12.11
Sample groove and fill pattern.

Nontraditional Drum Sequencing

It is interesting to note that in the early days of drum machines the goal was to achieve the most realistic drum sounds possible. Unfortunately, these machines were inept at reproducing drum sounds. We have since come full circle and early drum machines have become attractive because of how un-drumlike they sound. Drum machines and drum machine emulators are often used in techno, hip-hop, and other modern genres. This section considers ways that nontraditional grooves and sounds can be utilized.

DRUM SUBSTITUTION

I like to use the term *drum substitution* to describe an approach where nontraditional drum sounds are applied to traditional drum patterns in order to create new derivative grooves. With drum substitution, a variety of sounds, either traditional or nontraditional, can be substituted for instruments in the drum set. One way to experiment with this concept is to think of the quality or timbre of the original instrument and substitute another percussive sound with a similar timbre. Hi-hat cymbals, for example, are characterized by a mid-to-high frequency range and brilliant tone. The sound of a bell, shaker, lid of a pan, or even a toy cymbal could be suitable substitutes for the hi-hat. Similarly, the sound of a slamming door, gunshot, car horn, or other percussive sound might be candidates to substitute for a snare drum.

LINEAR DRUMMING

A relatively new approach to drumming involves thinking of the drum set as a linear series of instruments. To create a linear groove, two or more percussive instruments may work together to create a pulse that would have traditionally been established using only one instrument. A common example involves hi-hat subdivision. Instead of using only the hi-hat to produce a series of 16th notes, use a combination of hi-hat, shaker, tambourine, or other similar instruments to establish the subdivision. Figure 12.12 illustrates one such example.

Figure 12.12
Basic hi-hat subdivision and linear variation.

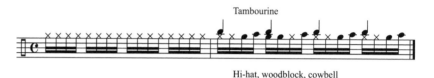

In Figure 12.12, the overall goal of providing a 16th note subdivision is met, but the variety of sounds used to produce this rhythm is more interesting. Note that the transposing drum fill presented earlier in this chapter is also an example of a linear approach to drum sequencing.

QUANTIZATION

Students sometimes ask if they should avoid quantizing drum parts. The question is not an easy one to answer. On the one hand, slight imperfections of time can be very important in establishing a realistic groove. On the other hand, too many rhythmic inaccuracies can undermine an otherwise good drum track. For most of us, the answer lies somewhere in the middle. It may be advantageous to quantize some component of the drums such as hi-hat or kick and snare and keep some subtle rhythmic inaccuracies in another part. However, if the goal is to create natural-sounding drum tracks, then the nonquantizing approach is often best. For some styles of music such as techno, quantizing of rhythms is the very essence of the genre: Techno wouldn't be techno without the heavily quantized and computerized sound.

GROOVE QUANTIZATION

Most professional sequencers now include groove quantization options that provide a more realistic result than simple quantization. With groove quantization, timing (and velocity) data is extracted from digitized audio or MIDI recordings. This "groove information" is then used to adjust a sequenced part to produce a more natural sounding groove. This topic is covered in more detail in Chapter 4, "Sequencing Concepts."

TECHNO AND DANCE GROOVES

The following tips may be helpful if you are interested in sequencing techno or other modern drum grooves. As I mentioned previously, techno or dance music is usually heavily quantized. Many of these recordings also rely on looping of audio and MIDI drum and bass riffs. Although these styles still use traditional drum functions such as snare on backbeat and hi-hat for rhythmic division, the sounds are usually not traditional and the orchestration is often thick. I have found good results by layering sounds from two or more drum kits. Start by recording a groove on one MIDI track and duplicate the track for simultaneous playback on another kit. This type of "thickened" sound can be useful in generating authentic grooves in the style. Another tip is to sequence a four- or eight-bar techno groove. Make a copy of the groove and paste it into an adjacent track. Extract the hi-hat, kick, and snare parts and experiment with a variety of transpositions so that the copied parts play in consort with the original drum sounds. I have discovered many interesting variations of using this simple trick. Samplers can be particularly useful: Import samples of nearly any percussive sound and map the sounds to keys normally assigned to kick, snare, and hi-hat. A simple change of timbre can bring new life to most any MIDI drum part.

Sequencing Bass Tracks

The bass has two important functions in popular music: to establish the harmonic progression and to provide appropriate rhythmic activity. This rhythmic activity will usually complement or even double rhythms occurring in the drum set. Though less common, the bass may also be used as a melodic instrument.

There are a number of traditional bass sounds provided on most synthesizers: plucked electric, picked electric, slap, fretless electric, and acoustic bass are common. The plucked and picked electric bass sounds are typically used for pop, rock, and country styles. Slap bass is often heard on pop recordings or in funk music. Fretless acoustic bass is used almost exclusively for jazz, Latin, and some styles of country. Synthesized bass sounds can be effective for many styles of dance and pop music.

When selecting a bass sound you may want to consider nontraditional sounds as well. If a patch has a full and slightly percussive low end it may function well as a bass instrument. Some patches I have used include the harp, electric piano, and a variety of synthetic voices. That is one of the great things about MIDI—there is no need to conform to the traditional function of instruments.

The bass provides the foundation tones for a given harmonic progression, usually the root and fifth of a given chord. As with the drums, it is generally a good idea to work with a clear and simple bass line. If the bass line is overly complex, it may get in the way of other tracks as you add new parts to a sequence. However, in some styles of music, bass lines are more intricate than in others—funk music being one such example. Although it is not a steadfast rule, the bass will usually play the root of a chord whenever there is a change in the harmonic progression. In the bossa nova shown in Figure 12.13, the bass revolves around the root and fifth with the root clearly stated on every chord change. Note that each of the bass examples in this chapter are written in the normal transposed range of the bass. A bass sounds an octave lower than it is written, so these examples will sound best if they are played an octave lower on a MIDI keyboard.

Figure 12.13
Bossa nova bass.

Of course, the bass is not limited to playing only roots and fifths of chords. A common variation involves the use of chromatic or diatonic passing tones. In Figure 12.14, note how chromatic approach tones are used to approach both the I and IV chords in a simple rock progression.

Figure 12.14
Chromatic approach tones.

Upper neighbor tones can also be useful. Experiment with tones either a half or whole step above the root or fifth as in the Figure 12.15.

Figure 12.15
Upper neighbor tones.

In some styles of music the bass may be rhythmically active. Note that though the bass line in Figure 12.16 is fairly intricate, the harmony is still clearly presented by a preponderance of roots.

Figure 12.16
Funk bass line.

To this point you have seen bass lines that rely heavily on the root and fifth of chords in a progression. For some styles, such as rockabilly or blues, all the notes of a triad might be used. Figure 12.17 demonstrates a triad-based line that might be suitable for rockabilly, blues, or other styles.

Figure 12.17
Rockabilly bass line (utilizing a triad).

The bass may also function as a harmonic pedal—a single note that remains under a variety of chords as in Figure 12.18. I hear pedal tones frequently used in pop music as well as other styles.

Figure 12.18
Bass pedal tone.

Octaves can be very effective in a bass line. In the 1970s, this sound was common in the much-maligned disco craze. I also hear it used in techno and other styles. Figure 12.19 illustrates a typical pattern based on octaves and chromatic approach tones.

Figure 12.19
Octave bass line.

For swing music, the bass typically plays a series of quarter notes with an occasional eighth or triplet figure inserted for variety. Note the use of chromatic approach tones and chord tones in Figure 12.20.

Figure 12.20
Walking bass line.

RELATIONSHIP OF BASS AND DRUMS

In popular music, the drums and bass maintain an important relationship. It is always a good idea to listen closely to your drum tracks when sequencing a bass line. In many situations, the bass and kick drum will have a sympathetic relationship. The bass line may double some or all of the rhythmic figures in the kick drum, as shown in Figure 12.21.

Figure 12.21
Relationship of bass guitar and kick drum.

277

Another approach is to use the bass to contrast the drums. Notice how, in Figure 12.22, the bass falls into the "cracks" of the drum track.

Figure 12.22
Contrasting bass and drums.

Creating Grooves: Anatomy of Styles

Although it would be impossible to list every style of bass and drum groove, the following examples will provide a helpful starting point as you start to create your own grooves. Notice the relationship between the bass and drum parts in the following figures: In nearly every instance the bass and drums complement each other.

ROCK

Figure 12.23 demonstrates one example of a rock pattern. The bass is centered on the root of the chord and provides some eighth-note motion. The snare provides a typical backbeat pattern while a bell-ride provides a steady quarter-note pulse.

Figure 12.23
Rock pattern 1.

Figure 12.24 provides another variation of a rock pattern. In this example, the bass provides a driving eighth-note pulse with an ascending chromatic line at the end of the pattern. The hi-hat also provides a division of the beat while the kick and snare are used in a backbeat pattern commonly found in the style.

Figure 12.24
Rock pattern 2.

COUNTRY

Figure 12.25 demonstrates a very simple country beat in a "two" feel. This example is definitely "old school" in that the pattern is more simplistic than would be heard commonly in "crossover" country and pop music.

Figure 12.25
Simple country pattern.

Figure 12.26 demonstrates a pattern that might be useful in the context of a country waltz or gospel composition. In a country waltz, it would be common to swing the eighth notes. This type of pattern is sometimes written in 12/8.

Figure 12.26
Country waltz.

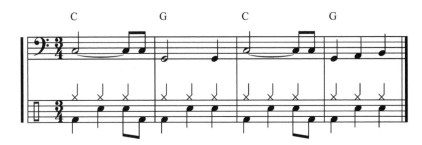

POP

Figure 12.27 is similar to an example presented earlier in the chapter. The bass and kick drum work together to provide a hint of a 16th note subdivision, and hi-hats (or a similar instrument) provide the division of the beat. The bass, as is typical in the style, revolves around the root of each chord.

Figure 12.27
Pop ballad.

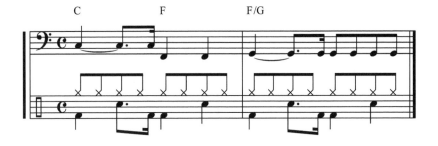

LATIN (BOSSA NOVA)

Figure 12.28 illustrates one example of bossa nova pattern. The bass plays the root and fifth of each chord and a clave is substituted for the snare drum. Notice how, once again, the bass drum and bass guitar are rhythmically very similar.

Figure 12.28
Bossa nova.

Substitute clave for snare

FUNK

The funk pattern shown in Figure 12.29 has many elements associated with the style: subdivision of the beat on the hi-hat, rhythmically active bass line, and kick and snare parts that are more intricate than many styles of popular music. Hi-hat accents are an important part of the style and can yield many interesting variations.

Figure 12.29
Funk pattern.

SWING

The swing pattern shown in 12.30 is typical of a moderate or fast swing tune in "four." The bass plays the root of each chord, and chord tones, passing tones, or chromatic approach tones precede each chord change. Ride cymbal or hi-hat may be used to provide the characteristic swing pattern and sticks or brushes are often used on the snare to provide a rhythmic "comping" pattern. Note that the kick drum is sometimes used to play soft quarter notes.

Figure 12.30
Swing pattern.

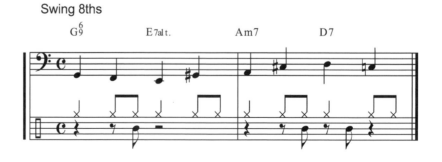

HIP-HOP

In Figure 12.31, shuffle or swing 16ths provide a groove characteristic of some forms of hip-hop. To my ear, the genre often contains elements of funk and Motown. In fact, funk and Motown recordings have been (and still are) used as the basis for some sampled grooves in many modern styles.

Figure 12.31
Hip-hop (shuffle 16ths).

Shuffle 16ths

Cm9

Summary

Hip-hop, techno, rap, electronica, and many other modern styles form a huge category of music based on what I would describe as derivative beats. I find it helpful to remember that beats created in each of these styles are derived from popular-music drumming concepts that have evolved for many decades. For example, in each of these styles of music, you will hear a snare-like sound used to provide backbeat and some form of a hi-hat providing a division or subdivision of the beat. In my estimation, the wide variety of grooves emanating from these genres has more to do with a creative use of timbre than a "new" approach to drum sequencing. With this in mind, it may be helpful to listen to these styles with an ear toward the "weight" of each groove as provided by the kick and snare, the use of new timbres that are substituted for traditional sounds, and a linear approach to sequencing as described earlier in the chapter.

As you experiment with sequencing bass and drum grooves, remember that many successful grooves are the result of nontraditional techniques. One of the great things about MIDI is the ease with which you can experiment. The examples listed above will get you started with some of the more common grooves, but the real fun comes when you use these concepts to develop your own patterns.

CHAPTER 13

Contemporary Keyboard Techniques

The keyboard, in all its variations from the early clavichord and organ to the modern piano and synthesizer, has attained prominence as a key ingredient of many musical genres. The reasons for this are simple: The keyboard has a range that approximates an orchestra, most keyboards are capable of a wide range of dynamics, and the modern synthesizer has an almost unlimited range of timbral possibilities. If you consider the great variety of popular music recordings that include keyboard or piano tracks, it is evident how important this instrument is to the contemporary computer musician. This chapter explores many keyboarding concepts that will allow you to enhance and expand your MIDI and audio projects. Although my goal is not to turn you into the next Liberace, you will find that a sufficient amount of keyboard facility will be an asset to almost any style of music you wish to create. This chapter will emphasize the following keyboard concepts:

► Function of keyboard instruments

► Chord voicing

► How to practice chord voicings

► Rhythmic concepts

► Scale tone concepts

► Keyboard styles and vocabulary

Function of a Keyboard

The keyboard (piano, organ, synthesized pad, etc.) has two primary functions in popular music: establishing or enhancing the harmonic progression and providing rhythmic activity. Of course, the keyboard may also be used as a melodic instrument. In some styles of music, the keyboard is used to provide a "pad" by establishing a sonic setting for music that may or may not include a clear harmonic progression or rhythmic pulse.

Before we delve into the details of keyboarding concepts, it might be helpful to consider several concepts that relate to the term *texture*. Although the term texture is vague, I use the term to describe the summative effect of a musical passage: how the elements of rhythm, harmony, voicing, register, dynamic, and timbre (sound color or quality) work together to create a specific texture. Most successful compositions use a variety of textures to retain the attention of a listener (although this is less true with some styles of music). And though textural changes are not solely the job of a keyboardist, most good keyboardists understand how to implement textural changes in an accompaniment.

When performing or recording keyboard tracks, I find it helpful to consider the following textural elements. Though each element is simple to implement, the combined power of these elements can be used to create effective textural changes at important structural points in a composition. As you explore the concepts presented in this chapter, consider how each of these elements can be used to expand the various techniques described below. Taking advantage of these types of textural elements can help keep music from sounding overly static or repetitive.

▶ Tessitura: How high or low a part is set (e.g., low "meaty" voicings versus high "pretty" voicings)

▶ Dynamics

▶ Complexity (or lack of complexity) of voicings

▶ Rhythmic activity (or absence of rhythmic activity)

▶ Density (the number of sounding parts)

▶ Timbre (e.g., changing from a piano patch to an electric piano or organ sound)

Chord Voicing

One of the most challenging keyboard concepts to master is learning to voice chords. By the term *voicing*, I mean the specific ordering of chord tones on a keyboard (or in an orchestration). If you consider that it is acceptable to double (or even triple) notes of a given chord and that these tones may be placed in any register and in any order or inversion, it is evident that the mathematical permutations of voicing a simple triad are staggering. Fortunately, there are several concepts that will be useful in developing the ability to voice chords. To get a sense of the many possibilities, play through the voicings of a simple seventh chord (see Figure 13.1).

Figure 13.1
A few of the many voicings of a C7 chord.

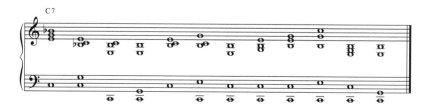

Although the variety of voicings is almost limitless, we can narrow the range of options by applying some general rules. The following tips can be a great help in exploring the concept of chord voicing. Keep in mind that these tips are just that—tips. As you will see later in this chapter, the tips may not be applicable in all situations.

Tip 1: Open structures work best in a low register.

Close position voicings work well in the mid and high registers, but these structures will tend to sound muddy in the low register. Often, this means that voicings must be "opened up" in order to work in a low register. Figure 13.2 illustrates several such voicings.

Figure 13.2
Open voicings in low register.

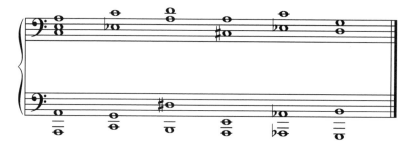

Tip 2: Avoid large gaps between the hands (i.e., a sixth or more).

In the first example of Figure 13.3, a large gap exists between the hands. Although this voicing isn't wrong, the second example resonates better—it might be said that the second voicing sounds more full.

Figure 13.3
Avoid gaps between the hands.

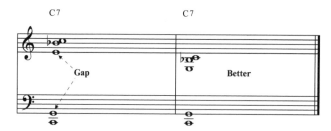

Tip 3: Avoid using a half step between the upper two notes of a chord.

Half steps can be effective in many voicings, but they tend to be less useful between the upper two notes (although such a sound can be useful for a special effect). I would subjectively say that the second and third voicings in Figure 13.4 sound better than the first example. Note that, in the third voicing, a half step us used between the second and third notes in the right hand.

Figure 13.4
Avoid a half step between the upper two notes.

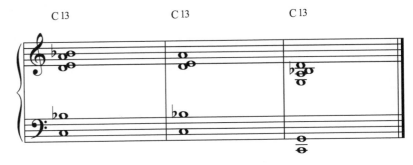

Tip 4: It may be helpful to omit a primary chord member when voicing complex chords.

The 5th of a chord is often omitted in complex voicings such as 9th or 13th chords. Strangely, the third is sometimes omitted when voicing half-diminished chords containing an 11th. Figure 13.5 illustrates these two common scenarios.

Figure 13.5
Omitting the 5th in a 13th chord and omitting the third in a half-diminished chord containing an 11th.

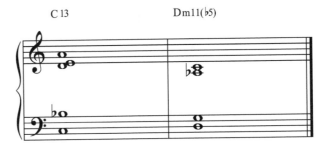

Tip 5: Consider voice leading.

It is rarely effective when voicings jump around in root position. In most cases, it is best to move smoothly from one voicing to the next. If a note is shared between two chords, it makes sense to keep the note in the same position. The smoothest voice leading will occur when each voice moves a minimal amount and tendency tones move in a natural way. Figure 13.6 illustrates relatively smooth voice leading. Notice how common tones are used and jumps are mainly found in the bass voice.

Figure 13.6
Voice leading using extensions and altered tones.

Tip 6: Consider common left-hand structures.

Wide structures such as an open fifth, seventh, octave, and tenth work best in the left hand—particularly in the lower register. Figure 13.7 illustrates the most common left-hand structures.

Figure 13.7
Common left-hand structures.

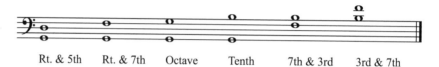

Rt. & 5th   Rt. & 7th   Octave   Tenth   7th & 3rd   3rd & 7th

Although there are many ways to approach the task of learning to voice chords, the following steps provide a chord-voicing method that will work in most situations. These steps are based on the common left-hand structures shown above.

1. Pick a chord that you wish to voice.

2. Select an appropriate left-hand structure.

3. Play the melody note in the right hand.

4. Add other chord tones in the right hand to complete the voicing.

5. As you add chord tones, keep in mind voicing tips 2, 3, 4, and 5.

With a little experimentation, you will soon find that you can create an appropriate voicing for most any chord. With a little practice, creating effective voicings "on the fly" will be easy.

Another common voicing scenario involves voicing complex structures such as extended and altered chords. As I mentioned in Tip 4, it is often helpful to omit certain notes from a chord in order to include color tones such as 9ths and 13ths. The goal here is to create a structure that best conveys the given chord quality while still retaining the texture of the moment (for example, you probably want to avoid using a seven-note voicing in the middle of a four-part texture). Although I'll explain the concept of chord voicing in more detail in Chapter 15, "Real-World Arranging," the following tips will get you started. These suggestions make it possible to voice any extended or altered chord with just four notes in either the right or left hand. Of course, a common bass structure can also be used, but this method provides a good starting point.

▶ To add a ninth, omit the root.

▶ To add a 13th, omit the 5th.

▶ To add an augmented 11th, omit the 5th.

▶ To add a perfect eleventh to a half-diminished chord, omit the 5th or the 3rd.

The next example can be found in most any jazz theory book. I include it here for two reasons: These voicings demonstrate an approach to using the rootless voicings listed in the previous section, and these examples also serve to show how smooth voice leading can be achieved. Notice how gracefully the chords flow in Figure 13.8.

Figure 13.8
Close position ii-V-I (two inversions).

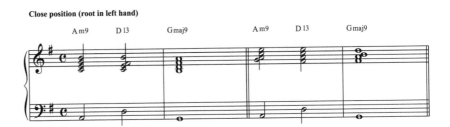

Figure 13.9 demonstrates an open position version of the previous example. Here, 3rds and 7ths are used in the left hand, and the 9th, 5th, or 13th are placed in the right hand. These chords are examples of "rootless" voicings.

Figure 13.9
Open position ii-V-I voicings (two inversions).

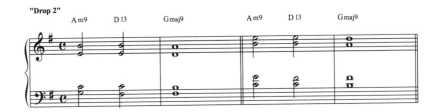

In the last example you might have noticed that the left hand utilized one of the common left-hand structures: the third and seventh (or seventh and third). These so called "drop-two" structures can be very helpful in situations where you wish to create an open sound. The term *drop two* comes from lowering the second note (from the top) of a close-position chord one octave as in Figure 13.10.

Figure 13.10
Drop-two voicings.

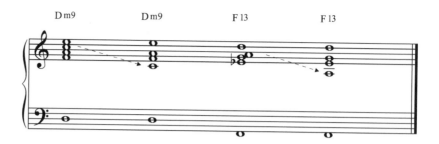

You can easily create a drop-two voicing for any chord using the following chord factors (from the bottom): 3-7-1-5 or 7-3-5-1. If you also consider the tips on adding extension tones, it is easy to use these structures as the basis for any complex chord structure. Of course, these rootless voicings tend to work best in situations where you allocate a bass track to play the root of the chord, but the voicings can also be used effectively without a root in the bass. Figure 13.11 shows several drop-two voicings for a variety of chords.

Figure 13.11
Drop-two voicing examples.

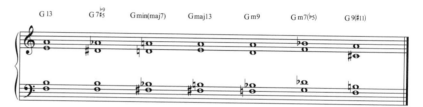

How to Practice Chord Voicings

Understanding the theory of good chord voicings in only half the battle. It is also essential to be able to use these structures in context. The following exercises are provided to aid in the process of developing harmonic proficiency. I would suggest practicing these exercises in all keys.

Figure 13.12 illustrates one way to develop proficiency with the primary seventh chords. Here, each common type of seventh chord is played in both hands through each key.

Figure 13.12
Primary seventh chords (descending half steps).

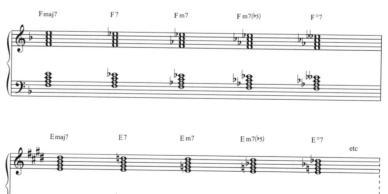

It is also helpful to practice each inversion of the primary triads and seventh chords as in Figure 13.13.

Figure 13.13
Triads and seventh chord
inversions.

Circle of fifth progressions (progressions in which the root descends by a perfect fifth) can be helpful in practicing voice leading. Figure 13.14 shows how a common tone can be utilized to create smooth voice leading in a circle progression. It is a good idea to start the exercise in the first and second inversions in addition to the root position version shown below.

Figure 13.14
Triads around the circle of fifths
(utilize common tones).

As with triads, circle of fifth progressions can be useful in developing smooth voice leading when playing seventh chords (see Figure 13.15). Practice this exercise with each of the primary seventh chords.

Figure 13.15
Seventh chords around the circle of
fifths.

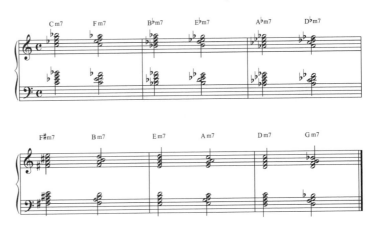

Figures 13.16 and 13.17 show common ii-V-I progressions in open and close position. These exercises are beneficial in developing proficiency for jazz-related harmony.

Figure 13.16
Close position ii-V-I exercise.

Figure 13.17
Open position (drop two) ii-V-I exercise.

Although this list of etudes is by no means comprehensive, these chord exercises will provide a solid foundation for further exploration. As voicings become more comfortable, muscle memory will alleviate the need to spell each chord from scratch. At that point, the ear can guide the hands and chord voicings really start to become second nature.

Rhythmic Concepts

Harmony is only one aspect of contemporary keyboard technique. To excel as a keyboardist, you will also want to develop a variety of rhythmic strategies. In this section, I will consider several rhythmic concepts applicable to a wide range of styles.

EXTENDED ALBERTI BASS

The term *Alberti bass* refers to a common 18th-century technique in which the left hand is used to arpeggiate the notes of a chord (usually a triad) as an accompaniment to a melody in the right hand. Domenico Alberti (1710–1740) was a composer who frequently employed this technique—hence the name Alberti bass. Figure 13.18 is an example of an Alberti bass from Mozart's "Sonata in C Major, K. 545."

Figure 13.18
Mozart's "Sonata in C Major, K. 545."

Although the Alberti bass can sound dated, you will occasionally hear this technique used in popular music—often in passages that are meant to sound quaint or charming. I use the term *extended Alberti bass*

to describe a more common variation. Instead of arpeggiating a triad in close position, open up the chord and place it in the bass register (e.g., root-5th-10th or root-5th-9th). Figure 13.19 demonstrates a common use of the "extended" Alberti left hand.

Figure 13.19
Extended Alberti bass.

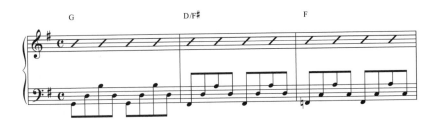

I have found the technique to be exceptionally helpful in a wide variety of styles, including jazz ballads, pop, new age, and country music to name a few. Figure 13.20 illustrates one possible approach. Notice how the right hand helps to fill in the harmony underneath the melody.

Figure 13.20
Extended Alberti bass excerpt.

OSTINATO

The *New Harvard Dictionary of Music* describes an ostinato as "a short musical pattern that is repeated persistently throughout a performance or composition or a section of one." Ostinati can be useful in a variety of styles. Entire compositions have been created that rely on a simple repetitive pattern in the left hand. An added benefit is that practicing ostinati can facilitate the development of independence between the right and left hands. Figure 13.21 lists a few of the many left-hand ostinato patterns.

Figure 13.21
Common left-hand ostinato patterns.

Try placing the ostinato under a single chord or simple progression (e.g., I-IV-V-I). Repeat the pattern until it is comfortable and then experiment with variations. Improvise by creating a melody in the right hand. Figure 13.22 demonstrates one such approach.

Figure 13.22
Ostinato excerpt.

PIANO PICKING

I use the term *piano picking* to describe a keyboardist's version of guitar finger-picking technique. If you have ever watched a guitarist finger pick, you know that the right hand is used to arpeggiate the notes of a chord held down by the left hand. In some cases, the arpeggiation will be repetitive, but more random variations are also common (e.g., a low note might be followed by a high note, then a middle tone, and so on). In keyboard terms, think of the instrument as being divided into three sections: low, middle, and high registers. The fifth finger of the left hand handles low tones and the fifth finger of the right hand handles high notes. The fun begins when you allow the first three fingers of the right hand and left hand to share in the role of arpeggiating or "picking" a chord. Notice how, in Figure 13.23, the right and left hands work together to create a sense of moving 16th notes.

Figure 13.23
Piano picking technique.

Figure 13.24
Piano picking variations.

To really master this technique, you need to develop the ability to vary the rhythms in real time. I suggest practicing the technique on a single chord with a focus on developing a wide variety of rhythms that imply a division or subdivision of the beat. The "piano picking" sound is a mainstay for many styles of popular music, including country, pop, and some styles of rock. You will see a related technique in the keyboard styles section of this chapter (the funky clavichord example). Figure 13.24 demonstrates a few variations based on the picking technique.

Scale-Tone Concepts

In Chapter 10 you learned about common chord and scale relationships. In addition to using scales as an aid to composition and improvisation, keyboardists often use scale-tone triads to enhance a passage of music. One of the great benefits of scale-tone triads is that they provide the keyboardist with a way of providing variations to a progression of chords without the necessity of using complex chord structures that might not be appropriate for the given musical context. For example, it might be inappropriate to use 13th chords in a "down and dirty" blues tune. Scale-tone triads provide a way of enhancing a harmonic progression while retaining an appropriate harmonic context. You will find that first and second inversion triads tend to work best. Figure 13.25 demonstrates the use of scale-tone triads over an F7 chord. In this case, the triads are derived from the appropriate scale (an F Mixolydian).

Figure 13.25
Scale-tone triads over an F7 (two inversions).

It is usually best to find a balance between chord tones and passing tones—strive for chord tones on longer note values and use passing tones (which do not imply a given chord structure) to move between arrival points. Once you have established arrival points, move the triads diatonically within the given scale. Note that this works for *any* scale. For example, scale-tone triads can be applied effectively to altered or diminished scales. In Figure 13.26, several chromatic passing tones are used to embellish a typical blues or gospel keyboard lick based on the concept of scale-tone triads.

Figure 13.26
Scale-tone triad excerpt.

Keyboard Styles

In this section I'll share concepts that will enable you to effectively play in a variety of styles. It goes without saying that an entire book could be written on each of the topics that follow. My intention is not to provide a comprehensive list of every technique in each style but rather to illustrate those techniques that help define the style. These concepts will provide a solid foundation for supplemental listening and transcription.

BLUES

Blue notes have always been an essential part of blues vocabulary. A *blue note* is a note that is slightly out of tune when compared to the modern Western European system of tuning. The most common blue tones fall between a minor and major third in a given key (called a *blue third*) and between the raised fourth and fifth of a key. Blues vocalists, saxophonists, guitarists, and others often use blue notes to great effect when performing. One of the limitations of traditional keyboard instruments is that the keyboardist can't bend the notes of a piano or organ. The workaround for blues keyboardists is to use grace notes to achieve a similar effect. Figure 13.27 demonstrates a few of the many common blues licks used by keyboardists. Often, a *pedal tone* is added in the right hand above the grace note figure.

Figure 13.27
Blues licks: grace notes and pedal tones.

Repetitive figures are also used in blues. Mature blues performers will often use a repetitive pattern for an entire chorus (or more) as a way of building tension and excitement in a solo. Sometimes a *cross rhythm* (a repeating three-against-four pattern) is used when performing a repetitive riff. Figure 13.28 demonstrates two common examples. These types of licks can be very effective when repeated over several measures.

Figure 13.28
Common repetitive blues figures.

Trills and tremolos have long been utilized by blues keyboardists. As with blue notes, a limitation of piano and electric piano is the inability to sustain a note. Trills and tremolos can be useful in providing a sustained or building effect. The most common use of this technique is to trill between two notes a minor or major third apart such as 6-1, 3-5, or 5-7 in a given key (see Figure 13.29).

Figure 13.29
Blues trills.

One other blues technique that relates specifically to the organ involves using a sustained note in the right hand. My favorite version of this lick is to perform an ascending gliss. At the top of the gliss, grab a note (often the tonic) and hold the note with the fifth finger. Use the other four fingers to continue to improvise (see Figure 13.30). I have found the technique very effective in building the last chorus of a solo.

Figure 13.30
Sustained note (organ lick).

Figure 13.31 incorporates many of the concepts presented in this section.

Figure 13.31
Hammond B3 blues excerpt.

COUNTRY CONCEPTS

Country music has evolved over the last decade to the point where there is much crossover between country, blues, and pop genres. If I had to pick one technique that best typifies country keyboard, I would present a concept perfected by Floyd Cramer. In this style, the quintessential country "twang" is achieved by the use of grace notes. In contrast to a blues grace note, the country grace note typically embellishes the third of the chord and is often diatonic. A good way to experiment with this technique is to play a series of major triads (e.g., I-IV-V-I). As you play through the progression, use the 9th or 2nd of the chord as a grace note leading into the 3rd of each chord. Figure 13.32 demonstrates a typical country piano phrase.

Figure 13.32
Country grace notes.

Note that you may want to include other tones such as the root as a part of the embellishment. As with all of the techniques listed in this section, the Floyd Cramer style can certainly be overused. On the other hand, few other licks so effectively convey the country twang.

Many country keyboardists incorporate an interval of a sixth in the right hand. This sound can be effective when used in the context of a solo or to complement a melody (see Figure 13.33).

Figure 13.33
Sixths in the right hand (country style).

Another common technique is similar to licks that you might hear on a mandolin or guitar. This "picking" style is often applied as an embellishment to a simple triad and is utilized by pianists such as Hargus "Pig" Robbins. In the next example, a chromatic approach tone is used to embellish the third of a major triad (see Figure 13.34). The repetitive nature of this lick nicely conveys the picking style that is characteristic of many country stringed instruments.

Figure 13.34
Fast country "picking" style.

ROCK KEYBOARD

Call me a traditionalist, but when I think of rock keyboard my heart is still with the early pioneers such as Keith Emerson and Rick Wakeman. Obviously, some wonderful rock music has since been recorded that utilizes keyboards, but the 1970s was certainly a time when keyboards were a key component of many rock bands. In contrast to some of the other styles we have looked at, my comments in this section will relate to more general concepts than specific playing techniques.

The function of a keyboardist in a rock band is varied. In the 1960s and 1970s groups such as Yes and Emerson, Lake & Palmer utilized keyboards in a variety of ways: melody, comping (accompaniment), textural (i.e., synthetic sounds), and as a solo or improvisational instrument. The arsenal of instruments traditional rock keyboardists utilized included Hammond B3, electric piano, acoustic piano, clavinet, and analog synthesizer.

Today the role of the keyboardist has changed—most of the rock albums that get airtime utilize keyboard as a textural device (e.g., synthesizer, piano, or organ pads that provide a change of texture behind a solo or at an important section of the tune) or as a melodic instrument to provide a synthesized "hook." In my estimation, the reason for this change has more to do with economics than with aesthetic reasons. The days of 15- or 20-minute "jam" tunes are largely over (with a big exception for bands such as Phish). For a band to reasonably expect to get airtime, songs must be presented in a concise format. If you spend some time analyzing rock tunes that are on the air today, you begin to realize that solo sections are usually short and much of the solo work is done with electric guitar.

One of the difficulties rock keyboardists deal with is what to play for a "power chord." Power chords are often used by guitarists and consist of an interval of a fourth or fifth played on the lower strings of the guitar (see Figure 13.35).

Figure 13.35
Guitar power chord.

Unlike traditional tertian structures (chords built in thirds), a power chord contains no third. The absence of a third results in a chord that is indeterminate—a power chord is neither major or minor. For keyboards, the goal is to find a voicing and rhythmic pattern to complement the sound of power chords. A common technique is to use open fifths to provide a background pad or rhythmic figure as in Figure 13.36.

Figure 13.36
Keyboard pad over guitar power chords.

Although the piano is used infrequently in heavier rock styles, keyboardists occasionally use a repetitive figure in the upper range of the piano as in Figure 13.37.

Figure 13.37
Repetitive keyboard figure over
power chord riff in guitar.

The sound of the classic Hammond B3 organ is still very much in vogue. When playing an organ sound on a modern synthesizer or virtual organ, it is helpful to remember that the original instrument did not have a sustain pedal. For pianists, it's tempting to play an organ like you might play a piano, but a more authentic sound can be achieved by avoiding the damper pedal.

A Leslie speaker is also an important part of the "B3" sound. These cabinets are unique in that they have a rotating horn that provides a characteristic *Doppler* effect. Since the rotating horn takes a few seconds to get up to speed, players often ride the tremolo on and off button in order to trigger the rotating effect at key points in a piece. The slowing and speeding up of the tremolo is a characteristic of many classic B3 recordings.

The timbre or an organ manual is controlled by adjusting one of nine *drawbars*. Each drawbar controls the volume of a partial. For example, the leftmost drawbar sets the level of the *suboctave* (an octave lower than fundamental) and the rightmost drawbar controls the *eighth harmonic* (the interval of a 22nd). The function of the nine drawbars is listed in Table 13.1.

Table 13.1. Function of Organ Drawbars

Drawbar	Interval
16′	Suboctave
5 2/3′	5th
8′	Unison (root)
4′	8th
2 2/3′	12th
2′	15th
1 3/5′	17th
1 1/3′	19th
1′	22nd

Choosing settings for the drawbars is largely a matter of personal taste, but a good starting point is to pull out the first three drawbars (suboctave, 5th, and unison) and experiment by adding upper partials. For example, Figure 13.38 shows settings on a virtual B3 that might be useful for a gospel or rock organ track.

Figure 13.38
Virtual B3 organ.

Volume changes are another important component of B3 technique. In the original B3, volume was controlled via a swell pedal. In modern synthesizers and virtual organs, an expression pedal or data slider can be used to create these types of effects.

In rock music, the B3 is typically used to provide harmonic "pads," but in some genres such as funk the B3 may take on a more rhythmic function. A common technique is to use sustained notes in the mid to upper register and to turn the Leslie effect on and off at key points in a tune; this is a distinctive sound that will add much to a bridge or interlude (see Figure 13.39).

Figure 13.39
Hammond organ accompaniment.

Another common technique is to use the organ to add fills that complement a vocal line or melody. These fills are often reminiscent of the Floyd Cramer grace notes presented earlier in the chapter (see Figure 13.40).

Figure 13.40
Hammond organ fills.

The piano is often used on rock tunes that have a more traditional harmonic progression (i.e., music that is not based on power chords). An effective way to use the piano in this context is to use octaves in the left hand with triads and octaves in the right hand. The goal is to provide a full sound with rhythms that complement the bass, drums, and guitar. The piano picking technique presented previously can be very effective for this style of music (see Figure 13.41).

Figure 13.41
Rock piano (full voicings with "piano picking").

A variety of synthesized sounds are also used by rock keyboardists. For example, analog sounds such as a square or sawtooth wave can really cut through a mix of guitars. Often, these sounds might be used for a melodic "hook" or to complement a prominent rhythmic figure. Judicious use of these sounds can enhance an important structural point in a piece. Figure 13.42 shows how an "aggressive" synthesizer patch might be used for a repetitive rhythmic figure.

Figure 13.42
An "aggressive" synthesizer patch providing a rhythmic complement to bass and drums.

FUNK

Though a variety of keyboard instruments are used in funk music, I will focus on the clavichord and organ. Keep in mind that many of the concepts presented in this section are applicable to other keyboard instruments such as electric piano.

Rhythm is the essence of funk music. When you listen to a great funk recording, such as cuts by Tower of Power, it becomes evident that the groove is a result of many layers of rhythmic activity. Since funk music has such a great sense of rhythmic energy, it is easy to overplay. My best advice is to remember that, although the overall groove may sound complicated, great funk grooves generally consist of layers of rhythms that are relatively simple and are typically very repetitive. As you experiment with repetitive patterns, try repeating the pattern with a slight variation at the end of a phrase or transition into the next part of a tune.

One of my favorite funk organ techniques is to use both the left and right hands to create a percussive rhythmic riff. Chester Thompson from Tower of Power often used the technique to great effect. Figure 13.43 illustrates how a repetitive organ groove can be achieved by utilizing a "two handed" approach. This technique can be heard on the tune titled "Funky Zone" on the accompanying CD.

Figure 13.43
Percussive organ riff.

The clavinet, a modern version of the clavichord (an instrument dating back to the 15th century) is used on many funk and pop recordings. One of the most famous is the Stevie Wonder recording of "Superstition." As with the organ, the clavinet requires a style of playing that is very different from traditional piano technique. The right and left hands often work together to provide a complex rhythmic groove. It is helpful to visualize the keyboard as being divided into three or four sections as in the piano picking examples discussed earlier in this chapter. Though it can work well to incorporate triads or other chords into this style of playing, many keyboardists use very sparse voicings (e.g., just roots and fifths). Figure 13.44 demonstrates an example of a funky clavinet groove that utilizes triads in the right hand over octaves in the left.

Figure 13.44
Clavinet excerpt: triad version.

In contrast, Figure 13.45 demonstrates a more sparse approach to a clavinet groove. In this example, roots and fifths are the predominant interval.

Figure 13.45
Clavinet excerpt: sparse version.

JAZZ

In the big band era, jazz reigned supreme in American pop culture. Though jazz has never managed to regain its prominence with the general public, the jazz influence is still evident in many areas of popular music. Jazz-derived harmonies are common in many styles of music from pop to funk. Because jazz music is often associated with a sense of sophistication and elegance, producers often elect to use jazz recordings in commercial and film productions.

One of the most important considerations for developing a convincing jazz sound is the use of extended and altered harmony. Mainstream jazz relies on sophisticated chord voicings and harmonic progressions. A general rule of thumb is to add extensions such as 9ths and 13ths when possible. Altered dominants are often used to create a heightened sense of motion at V-I cadences. Good jazz pianists spend years developing the ability to use good voice leading-techniques when playing through a harmonic progression. Figure 13.46 illustrates how extensions and smooth voice leading might be applied to a progression of chords. In this example, notice how jumps are mainly relegated to the lowest voice.

Figure 13.46
Jazz: chord progression with extended and altered harmony.

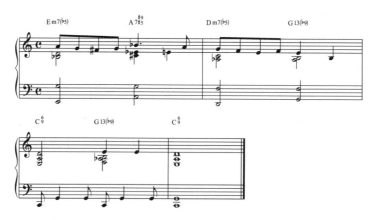

When playing a melody or improvising a solo, a common approach is to use colorful voicings in the left hand while the right hand maintains a "horn-style" approach. Some tips for developing a jazz-style right hand include using chord tones, chord-scale relationships, and common embellishments such as changing tones, chromatic approach tones, and turns. In Figure 13.47, a jazz, style right hand is placed over close position voicings in the left. The left-hand voicings are an example of rootless voicings presented earlier in the chapter. Note that in this style, the left hand functions very much like a guitar: The rhythms in the left hand complement the lines in the right hand.

Figure 13.47
Jazz: right-hand solo over close position voicings in the left hand.

When *comping* (accompanying) in a swing style, I find it helpful to visualize using a balance of on-beat and syncopated figures. Without off-beats, the music will not swing. On the other hand, too many syncopations may make the accompaniment sound chaotic. Figure 13.48 shows a few of the common vertical structures and rhythms found in a typical jazz keyboard accompaniment. In this instance, all of the voicings are examples of the "drop two" voicings presented earlier in the chapter. This style of comping is generally effective for any style of music based on extended and altered harmony.

Figure 13.48
Jazz: drop-two comping.

If your interests lie in the direction of solo jazz piano you may wish to explore some of the techniques associated with this genre. The masters of jazz piano—such as Bill Evans or Keith Jarrett—have developed a style of playing that transcends the two-handed approach common in some other styles of keyboard music. One way to visualize this technique is to rethink the traditional approach to the keyboard: Instead of thinking in terms of left versus right hand, visualize the keyboard as an orchestra. The left hand typically handles bass notes, the right hand usually covers the melody. Both the left and right hand may share in the function of harmony and rhythm. This "three-handed" approach is a mainstay of modern solo jazz piano. You will find that not only is this technique a powerful concept when applied to solo jazz piano, the technique is also useful in other styles of music and for orchestrating string, brass, and woodwind parts. Figure 13.49 is a transcription from a Bill Evans performance of "Lucky to Be Me." Notice how the right and left hands share in the harmonic and rhythmic role.

Figure 13.49
Excerpt from "Lucky to Be Me," Bill Evans's performance on Everybody Digs Bill Evans.

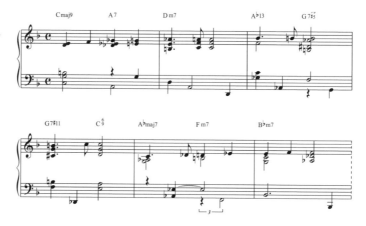

LATIN

As with funk music, rhythmic riffs are a primary ingredient in Latin styles. One of the most helpful keyboard techniques is the *montuno*. A montuno is sometimes used to describe an improvised section of a song, but, in piano terminology, the term describes a repetitive figure—a type of ostinato—that is central to many Latin styles. Figure 13.50 demonstrates a typical montuno pattern. In this example, the seventh of a minor seventh chord moves to the third of a dominant seventh chord.

Figure 13.50
Montuno example: ii-V progression.

When constructing a montuno, it is often helpful to look for potential moving notes—the notes that change from one chord to the next as in the previous example. Another approach is to visualize a counter melody—a secondary melody that accompanies the primary melody. For example, though the first two bars of Figure 13.51 consist of a single chord, the major seventh and major sixth are used for variety. Notice how the lowest notes of the right hand provide a melody of sorts—this type of countermelody can be effective in many situations.

Figure 13.51
Montuno for a Cmaj7 chord (using the major sixth and major seventh).

Another common Latin keyboard technique involves using both hands to arpeggiate the notes of a chord (see Figure 13.52). Latin keyboardists often utilize an interval of a 6th or 10th in this type of setting. Experiment with rhythmic variations and a variety of ascending and descending motion.

Figure 13.52
Arpeggiation in 10ths.

Another Latin keyboard technique you may wish to explore is to use both hands in rhythmic unison to provide a particularly strong groove (see Figure 13.53). This is very similar to the jazz comping example presented in the last section. As with funk music, it often works best to keep a pattern going for a while and implement variations at major points of a song such as a bridge or solo section.

Figure 13.53
Latin comping: two in rhythmic unison.

With regard to improvised lines, Latin keyboardists draw much of their vocabulary from jazz music. Horn-style right hand over left hand comping chords tends to work very well for this style of music. Figure 13.54 demonstrates a horn-style solo in the context of a Latin piano solo.

Figure 13.54
Latin (jazz) solo with left hand comping chords.

Note that the piece titled "Caliente," one of the tracks on the CD that accompanies this book, features all of the keyboard techniques presented in this section.

POP AND NEW AGE

A chapter on contemporary keyboard techniques would not be complete without a discussion of pop keyboarding concepts. I have already covered many techniques used in pop music such as extended Alberti, piano picking, and common left-hand repetitive patterns. Though pop keyboardists often use techniques that are common in mainstream rock or jazz, a key difference is the approach to harmonic vocabulary. Because we have already looked at many of the playing techniques associated with this style, I will focus on two harmonic elements that are common to pop music: suspended harmony and polychords.

Though much pop music revolves around traditional tertian harmony (triads and seventh chords), many pop tunes incorporate suspension chords. *Sus* chords are interesting in that they obscure the sound of traditional tertian harmony. Because these chords sound rather ambiguous, they can function in many ways. In Figure 13.55, notice how a simple sus-2 chord can be used over a variety of bass notes.

Figure 13.55
Sus-2 chord over a variety of bass notes.

A linear style of left hand is often used, in conjunction with the bass, to great effect in pop music. In this instance, the bass and left hand of the keyboard function as a melodic complement to the melody and harmonic progression. In rock and country, it is common for the bass to focus on the tonic of each of the chords in a progression. Though roots are used most frequently, it is also common to hear other bass tones such as a third or fifth. As you experiment with the concept, look for linear connections between the primary chords in a chord progression. I have found that a more linear approach can provide good results. (The piece titled "Homeward" on the accompanying CD contains several examples of linear bass movement in the context of a pop-style composition.) Figure 13.56 demonstrates the use of a linear bass line in an otherwise ordinary pop progression.

Figure 13.56
Pop progression with linear bass line.

Polychords are often utilized in pop music. Although I talked about polychords in Chapter 9, "Practical Music Theory," I will revisit the concept here because they are an important part of popular keyboard technique. Note that pop polychords generally consist of a triad over a single bass note (not two distinct chords as the term implies). One of the most common progressions found in many styles of music is a I-IV-V-I progression. Pop musicians often place this type of progression over a pedal point. The resulting structures are stylistic for the genre (see Figure 13.57).

Figure 13.57
Polychord excerpt.

In a similar vein, these chords are often used to tone down a more traditional progression such as a V-I cadence. Here, the subdominant (IV) is placed over V in the bass. The resulting chord is one of the most common structures found in pop music (see Figure 13.58).

Figure 13.58
Placing subdominant over dominant pedal point.

Figure 13.59 demonstrates many of the concepts described in this section on pop music. Some of the elements you may wish to study include the use of suspension and polychords, the linear bass line, extended Alberti, and incorporation of the piano picking technique from earlier in the chapter.

Figure 13.59
Pop excerpt: suspension chords,
linear bass movement, extended
Alberti, and piano picking.

Summary

Although it would be impossible to cover every keyboard technique in a single chapter, the vocabulary presented in this chapter will provide useful building blocks for further exploration. Supplemental listening and transcribing will be advantageous if you wish to explore a style in more detail, but I would also encourage the use of these concepts and techniques to foster the development of an individual playing style. I would also encourage non-pianists to experiment with this vocabulary—many of the concepts presented in this chapter require a modest amount of keyboarding facility and can easily be incorporated in a sequencing environment through the use of step-time entry or other methods.

CHAPTER 14

Music Composition

This chapter will focus on concepts that help support and initiate the process of composing music. The art of composing music can be a mysterious process—there is no correct way to approach composition other than perhaps to say that the end result should sound "convincing." Of course, the term convincing is subjective. In some instances, the term might be used to describe a composition that is convincingly dissonant. In other instances, the term might be applied to a piece that has an effective melody. In his book *What to Listen for in Music* (McGraw-Hill, 1957), noted composer Aaron Copland states:

> *"But whatever the form the composer chooses to adopt, there is always one great desideratum: The form must have what in my student days we used to call* la grande ligne *(the long line). It is difficult adequately to explain the meaning of that phrase to the layman. To be properly understood in relation to a piece of music, it must be felt. In mere words, it simply means that every good piece of music must give us a sense of flow—a sense of continuity from first note to last. Every elementary music student knows the principle, but to put into practice has challenged the greatest minds in music!"*

As I compose, I find it helpful to visualize the concept of *la grande ligne*. Do the components of melody, rhythm, harmony, orchestration, and form work together in a convincing way?

I will consider two primary approaches. The first part of the chapter is devoted to composing *tonal* music—the fundamental components being melody, rhythm, and the harmonic progression. Tonal principles are helpful for composing what might be generally described as popular music—the sounds we usually hear in songs, jingles, and related genres. The second part of the chapter will focus on techniques, tonal and otherwise, that have been utilized by composers of 20th-century art music. The following concepts are presented:

- ▶ The role of theory in the composition process

- ▶ How to practice music composition

- ▶ Descriptive composition

- ▶ Tonal concepts

- ▶ Writing a melody

- ▶ Lyrics

- ▶ Using motives

- ▶ Rhythmic concepts

- ▶ Common embellishments

- ▶ Practicing melody writing

- ▶ The relationship between melody and harmony

- ▶ Composing a progression of chords

- ▶ Chromaticism

- ▶ Other approaches to tonality and composition

- ▶ Free tonality

- ▶ Polytonality and polychords

- ▶ Atonality

- ▶ 12-tone technique

- ▶ Synthetic scales

- ▶ Cohesion

- ▶ Developing an idea

- ▶ Developing your own voice

- ▶ Composition starters and practice etudes

The Role of Theory in the Composition Process

I feel adamant that theory is a helpful (and often necessary) part of the composition process, but that is not to say that theory should be the most important part of the process. In an ideal world, a composer sits down to write and a piece flows naturally from the pen, notation application, or sequencer in the form of a convincing composition. Although every composer invariably composes some pieces in this fashion, in the real world, most of us agonize over many of the elements of a given piece. Questions might come into play regarding the overall form of a composition, the effectiveness of a melody, orchestration, or any number of related issues. This is where theory is helpful. Theory allows composers to take a step back and evaluate these types of questions. Theory can even be used to energize the creative process. For example, a knowledge of concepts such as bitonality and atonality can provide many interesting directions for a composer to explore. Through theory, we can also learn how to analyze and internalize the decisions made by other composers. I should stress that, in this context, theory is simply a way of clarifying the decision-making process. Critical listening is also an important part of the process of analyzing music and can yield many insights into the compositional process. Also, many musicians transcribe role models as a way to expand and develop musical vocabulary. My best advice is to follow your intuition but utilize theoretical concepts to support and enhance the composition process as needed.

How to Practice Music Composition

The process of composing music is all about decisions—what note comes next, how a motive is developed, the most effective instrumentation for a passage, and so on. It could be said that the process of composing provides an opportunity to practice the decision-making process. For this reason, the best way to develop as a composer is to practice the craft of composing. Ideally, composers write every day and the process of decision making starts to become second nature. A quote by Dmitri Shostakovich from *Composers on Music* (Northeastern University Press, 1997), makes a great point in this regard when he says:

> *"I'll admit that writing doesn't always come, but I'm totally against walking around looking at the sky when you're experiencing a block, waiting for inspiration to strike you. Tchaikovsky and Rimsky-Korsakov didn't like each other and agreed on very few things, but they were of one opinion on this: you had to write constantly. If you can't write a major work, write minor trifles. If you can't write at all, orchestrate something. I think Stravinsky felt the same way."*

Descriptive Composition

When the muse doesn't strike, I often find it helpful to utilize a technique that I call *descriptive composition*. This approach is probably the result of many years of working on writing assignments for publishers and commercial projects, but I have found the technique to be just as useful for art music. The idea is to reverse engineer a composition. Start by considering the intended audience: a recital hall, radio listener, or friend. Next, visualize the type of piece you would want to present—the approximate length of the composition, the instrumentation, number of movements, and general "feel" of the piece. Often, these types of general concepts will translate to specific musical elements that you can then start to explore. For example, an intense and dramatic work for string orchestra might include 20th-century vocabulary such as polytonality, while a pretty-popular song would likely incorporate a more traditional tonal approach. Since there is such a vast array of choices, descriptive composition can provide a method of lessening the choices to a more manageable level. I have also found the technique to be effective in exploring options for specific sections of a composition such as a development section or terminative section of a piece.

Tonal Concepts

This section will explore a *tonal* approach to music composition. There are any number of definitions of the term "tonal music," so a discussion is in order. In the context of this chapter, I will use the term tonal to describe music that is based on the Western European concept of major and minor tonality. Although chromatic elements may be used, such music has, at least temporarily, a well-defined key center or tonic. In contrast, many of the techniques described later in the chapter place less (or no) emphasis on establishing a tonic. To make a broad generalization, nearly all music on popular radio derives from tonal concepts, while much of the art music of the 20th century is derived from tonal and/or non-tonal concepts. Film music, particularly the dramatic type, often utilizes both tonal and non-tonal techniques.

WRITING A MELODY

Students often ask if they should write the melody of a composition before considering the harmony. There is no correct answer to this question. As simple as it sounds, the seed for a composition will be whatever happens to strike your fancy as you compose; it might be a melody, progression of chords, formal structure, rhythmic groove, interesting synthesized sound, or a theoretical concept. The point is that, whatever your original inspiration was, in order to mold this idea into the form of a complete composition, you must make a tremendous number of musical decisions.

A good melody is a thing of beauty. It speaks to us, conjures up an image or emotion, and draws us into the song. If you think about music that has stood the test of time (either classical or popular), it is clear how important a good melody can be. It could be said that our entire culture of popular music is based on melody: Songs drive the music industry, and songs are simply a vocal expression of a melodic idea.

In my estimation, humans are attracted to melodies in an almost physical way. I once had the pleasure of hearing a musical trio from southern India. Though the instruments sounded foreign to my ear, the rhythms were complex, and I didn't understand the words, I found myself captivated by the sheer beauty of the melodies. As humans, we are also attracted to rhythm. If you every have the chance to listen to music from other cultures, it becomes clear that melody and rhythm are the two most important ingredients of a musical composition. You will note that I didn't mention harmony. Our concept of harmony and even our system of well-tempered tuning is unique to music that derives from the Western European tradition. Harmony may or may not be germane to a successful composition. Again, if you think of melody and rhythm, it is clear that one of the reasons popular music is so, well, "popular" is that is speaks to the average listener on an almost physical level.

What are the elements that define a good melody? Part of the allure of a good melody comes from unexpected or intangible elements that can't be easily analyzed, but we can consider elements that exist in most memorable melodies. A good melody is often singable. Though many successful melodies have been written that are not singable, most listeners can't help but to be attracted to a melody that they can sing in their head. If you consider this concept you will find that singable melodies tend to share certain characteristics.

▶ Singable melodies generally avoid awkward jumps.

▶ The range is neither too high or too low.

▶ Diatonic melodies are easier to sing than melodies with many chromatic tones.

▶ Fast rhythms are hard to sing.

▶ Small jumps, passing tones, and intervallic or rhythmic repetition is often effective.

▶ Jumps are often balanced by stepwise motion in the opposite direction.

Singable melodies are not necessarily meant for the voice. A singable melody is also attractive to a listener when performed on an instrument such as a piano or violin. How can you tell if you have achieved a singable melody? Your voice can be your greatest asset. As you compose, if you find that you can sing or hum a given melody, you have achieved your goal. Figure 14.1 illustrates two singable melodies. The first melody is diatonic; the second melody uses some chromaticism (notes outside of the key center).

Figure 14.1
Singable melody: diatonic and chromatic versions.

Looking for a Unifying Element

In most successful melodies, there is a primary element that serves to unify the melody. Often, the unifying element is a repetitive rhythmic or melodic element. This can be a useful concept to consider in writing or evaluating a melody. For example, in Figure 14.2 a dotted quarter note and eighth note provide a strong sense of rhythmic propulsion that serves to unify the melody.

Figure 14.2
Unifying rhythmic element.

In a similar way, the melody in Figure 14.3 is unified by a frequent use of an ascending third.

Figure 14.3
Unifying melodic element.

Finding a Balance Between Repetition and New Ideas

A difficult concept to master when writing a melody involves the balance between repetition and presentation of new ideas. Though a predictable pattern of notes such as an ascending chromatic scale can be effective (listen to Duke Ellington's "Chromatic Love Affair"), you will tend to lose the listener if a melody is overly repetitive. On the other hand, melodies that sound random are generally not effective because there is nothing for the listener to latch onto. As you compose, try to find a balance between these two extremes. Of course, the style of music will have much to do with the approach you use: Classical and jazz composers often write melodies that take more listener attention than popular styles such as rock, pop, or country.

A Balance of Motion

It is helpful to consider the relationship of disjunct (skips) and conjunct (stepwise) motion as you compose a melody. Although many great melodies don't fall into this category, many melodies contain a balance of skips and steps. Often, a large ascending leap is followed by a stepwise descent. A descending leap is often followed by ascending motion. If your melody sounds too jumpy, consider adding some contrary stepwise motion to balance the effect of a jump. Similarly, a few well-placed skips can make a stepwise melody more interesting. Figure 14.4 illustrates a melody that contains a balance of skips and stepwise motion.

Figure 14.4
A jump followed by stepwise motion.

Using Cadences

In Chapter 9 I talked about the concept of musical *periods* and *phrase groups*. It is helpful to consider these concepts when writing melodies. One of the problems I see with some student composers are melodies that might be described as "rambling." In many instances, an absence of melodic cadences detracts from what might otherwise be an effective melody. Melodic cadences provide a sort of musical punctuation and can be used to fix the musical version of a run-on sentence. Figure 14.5 shows how a melody might be strengthened through the use of a melodic cadence. In my estimation, the second example works better than the first because cadences provide relative points of rest that serve to "punctuate" the melody.

Figure 14.5
Strengthening a melody with a melodic cadence.

Lyrics

When writing for voice, it is obviously important to consider the relationship between melody and lyrics. Although there is no right or wrong way to approach the issue, I have found that it is usually best to set a melody to lyrics (or write the melody and lyrics at the same time) instead of trying to fit words to an existing melody. In transcribing hundreds of songs I have noticed certain characteristics that are frequently used by good song writers.

▶ The melody usually follows the natural rhythmic flow of the words.

▶ Unimportant words such as "a," "the," and "of" are often used as part of a pickup rhythm or passing tone (e.g., not placed on a strong beat or note of long duration).

▶ Melodic contour tends to support and emphasize important words or phrases.

▶ Melodic cadences tend to coincide with implied punctuation of lyrics.

With these tips in mind, let's consider setting a lyric to music. For this example we will use the following text:

"I saw you there
looking out from the window
waiting for someone to call.
Could it be, that you were waiting
for me to come tonight?"

A helpful first step is to consider the natural cadence of the words. Speak the words out loud to get a sense of the rhythmic flow of the lyric. In the first line, the word "saw" is probably more important than the word "I" so it makes sense to consider this word as part of a pickup rhythm. Since the first and second lines make a complete utterance, it makes sense to include both of these lines of text in the first phrase. Figure 14.6 demonstrates one way that these words could be set to a melody. Notice that the musical line follows the implied punctuation between the first and second lines of the text. Some composers analyze the text in terms of the length and stress of syllables, marking each with symbols to indicate long (-) and short (.). The long stresses are associated with strong beats. Using this technique, the first phrase might look like this: (.---..-..--).

Figure 14.6
Using a pickup note and implied
punctuation (first two lines of text).

Since a fairly strong rhythmic syncopation has emerged in the first phrase, it makes sense to consider this rhythm in the consequent phrase as a unifying element. In this instance, the rhythm works nicely with the third line of text. A cadence serves to close the consequent phrase and helps to support the textual (and melodic) period (see Figure 14.7).

Figure 14.7
Using a rhythmic element to unify
the first three lines of text.

In the fourth line, the words *"Could it be"* work well with the rhythmic figure of a dotted eighth followed by a 16th note, so I elected to use that figure a third time. (This might also be a good point to consider a contrasting figure). Since the word *"that"* is less important than the word *"you,"* I decided to use the word as a melodic pickup to the next phrase in this phrase group. In a similar way, the word *"for"* is used as a pickup to the final and most important phrase. Notice how, in Figure

14.8, the final line of text is emphasized by longer note values and that the musical equivalent of a question mark leaves this phrase open in just the same way that the question mark implies more text is to follow.

Figure 14.8
Completing the final phrase.

There are many other valid ways to approach the text, but I trust that this discussion will provide an insight into the process of setting words to music. Incidentally, these lyrics were expanded into a complete demonstration song that you can listen to on the CD that accompanies this book.

USING MOTIVES

To this point I have focused on the concept of creating a melody or tune. The next several paragraphs deal with the concept of a *motive*. Whereas the *Harvard Dictionary of Music* describes a musical period as a "complete musical utterance," a motive represents a musical fragment. A motive should be easily recognizable by the listener, perhaps just two or three notes or a well-defined rhythmic figure. Motives can provide a powerful means by which a composition can be expanded. To a composer, a distinctive rhythmic and/or melodic motive is a sort of clay that can be transformed and manipulated in many ways. Two of the many examples that come to mind are Beethoven's Fifth Symphony and Shostakovich's Fifth Symphony (see Figure 14.9). Each of these compositions feature a short primary motive that provides the basis for a marvelous long-form composition.

Figure 14.9 A
Beethoven's "Symphony No. 5 in C minor."

Figure 14.9 B
Shostakovich's "Symphony No. 5, Op. 47."

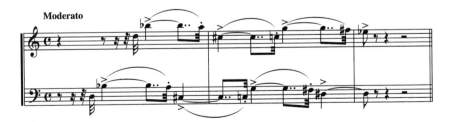

Conceptually, motivic transformation is used in much the same way that a good soloist might develop and expand a "lick." As a listener, you are aware that a particular idea is being presented and manipulated in many clever ways. In this sense, the effect of motivic development is much like that of an improvised solo. Influential composers throughout the history of Western European music have used motives as building blocks upon which larger works have been created. The following paragraphs detail some of the common transformations that can be utilized to develop motivic resources.

Rhythmic Shift

With rhythmic shift, an initial rhythmic motive is displaced either ahead of or behind the beat. In Figure 14.10, a five-beat pattern is placed on beats one, two, and three, respectively. Compare the written example with two or three repetitions of the motive starting on the same beat— the rhythmic shift makes an otherwise ordinary motive much more interesting.

Figure 14.10
Rhythmic shift.

Rhythmic Augmentation

Rhythmic augmentation involves expanding the rhythmic value of a phrase to twice (or more) of their original value. I often find that augmentation provides the basis for an interesting bass line or counter-melody. Although the listener may not be aware that a motive is being used in this way, these types of transformations can provide a sense of subconscious cohesion to a composition. The listener will subconsciously know that the parts of the composition seem to "fit" or "belong" when motives are utilized in this way. Figure 14.11 demonstrates the concept of rhythmic augmentation.

Figure 14.11
Rhythmic augmentation.

Rhythmic Diminution

In contrast to augmentation, diminution is a lessening of rhythmic values (see Figure 14.12). Diminution is often effective in developmental sections and is often combined with melodic fragmentation (see next paragraph).

14.12
Rhythmic diminution.

Fragmentation

As the term implies, fragmentation involves utilizing a subset of a motive. Often, a unifying element such as a repetitive interval of a half-step is used to develop a motive (see Figure 14.13).

Figure 14.13
Melodic fragmentation.

Melodic Sequence

Theorists use the term *sequence* to describe a phrase that contains repetition of a motive on successively higher or lower pitches. Though a sequence can be overused, sequential motives involving two or three repetitions are common. In a *tonal sequence*, the transposition of the initial motive remains diatonic to the key. A *real sequence* is simply an exact transposition of the original motive (see Figure 14.14).

Figure 14.14
Tonal and real sequences.

Common Embellishments

Motives are often embellished through the use of *nonharmonic tones*. In a sense, that term is less appropriate for music involving many extension chords—many of the "nonharmonic" tones can actually be considered as chord tones. However, these figures serve to embellish a given note and often do contain notes outside of the key or given chord structure. In each of the examples in Figure 14.15, it is assumed that the arrival tone is the last note in the measure. Note that, in most cases, embellishments such as a passing tone or neighbor tone can be either chromatic or diatonic.

Figure 14.15
Common embellishments.

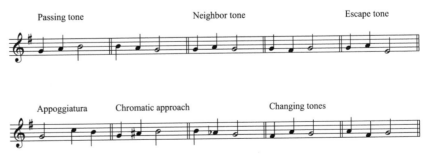

To see the power of such a simple concept, take a look at Figure 14.16. The motive certainly wouldn't win any awards for its inventiveness—the original idea is simply an ascending triad. Notice how, through the application of a few embellishments, the idea becomes more interesting (although somewhat contrived for the purposes of illustration).

Figure 14.16
Application of common melodic embellishments.

PRACTICING MELODY WRITING

When practicing melody writing, I often find it useful to limit choices in order to explore a window of well-defined parameters. To this end, the following list provides a few melody-writing exercises that can be useful in developing skill in this area.

▶ Write a melody based on a specific rhythmic element (such as a dotted quarter and two eighth notes). Use *any* notes.

▶ Write a melody based on two or three specific notes (use *any* rhythm).

▶ Write a melody that takes advantage of a specific melodic contour such as low-to-high.

▶ Develop a short motive using techniques such as rhythmic augmentation, displacement, and melodic embellishment.

▶ Write a diatonic melody—one that stays in a given key or mode.

▶ Write a chromatic or freely tonal melody—one that may not imply a specific key or modality.

▶ Set a poem or other text to music (experiment with several versions).

▶ Write a periodic melody that contains an antecedent and consequent phrase.

▶ Write a melody that contains phrases that do not form a musical period.

▶ Write a melody through the process of vocalization (away from an instrument such as a keyboard).

▶ Write a singable melody that stays within a small range such as a fifth or octave.

▶ Write a melody based on a pentatonic scale.

▶ Write a melody based on a synthetic scale.

AVOIDING TACTILE TENDENCY

If you think about it, nearly everything we do in our lives involves sub-conscious touching—when you enter a room and turn on a light switch or pick up a ringing telephone you are using subconscious physical movement. I use the term *tactile tendency* to describe the process of using subconscious physical movement when composing. In other words, most of us tend to play what our fingers know. Some people refer to this as *muscle memory*. Although muscle memory is desirable when swinging a golf club or playing tennis, it is counterproductive when composing. If you find that your compositions always sound similar to one another, you may be suffering from this malady. I have already presented a cure: Try to get away from the keyboard or guitar and use your voice. Most of us have lots of great melodies inside, and your voice is the best tool for getting to these ideas.

The Relationship Between Melody and Harmony

As discussed earlier in the chapter, there are many ways to approach music composition. Whether you start with a melodic idea, a progression or chords, or some other technique, the relationship between the melody and harmony is an important concept to consider in tonal music. This section will consider techniques for developing a harmonic progression.

Before you start experimenting with chords, it is generally advis-able to listen to the melody and try to determine a key center. Does the melody sound like it is in a specific major or minor key? Sometimes this is an easy question to answer. However, some melodies will not imply a specific tonality. In these cases it is a good idea to use the previously described concept of descriptive composition. Consider the type of effect or sound you wish to achieve: happy, sad, mournful, joyous, and so on. Each of these terms may help to determine the type of harmonic set-ting that is most appropriate for a given melody. It is hard, for example, to make a major triad sound particularly mournful. By describing the effect, it is often possible to zero in on potential choices.

Composing a Progression of Chords

A concept that I find helpful when composing a harmonic progression is to consider the wide variety of chord choices available for a given note. In short, any note can be harmonized as a chord factor of at least 12 differ-ent chords. When you start to look at progressions in this way, you will realize that a given chord can be used to move to any other key, even a distantly related key, in a graceful manner. Figure 14.17 illustrates how a single note in a melody can be harmonized with any bass note.

Figure 14.17
*Twelve of the many possible chords
that work with the note C.*

If you have a hard time finding just the right chord for a particular musical situation, experiment with a variety of roots, as in the previous example. You may or may not find what you are looking for, but at the very least, you will expand your ears to some new options.

We live in an era that is musically very tolerant. The modern audience can accept new ideas, sounds, and harmonies that are not traditional. Alas, with so many musical choices available to us, how do we narrow the choices to a manageable level? When dealing with harmony, I find it helpful to categorize musical choices into two categories: traditional and nontraditional. As you compose, you can save innumerable headaches by using descriptive composition as a problem-solving tool. As you experiment with chord choices, ask yourself if the chord you are looking for is "stock"—that is to say, should the chord sound natural or familiar to the listener? If the answer is yes, applying some simple theoretical principles can help you quickly find a possible solution. If the answer is no, descriptive composition can still be helpful in determining what chord to use in a given situation.

An example might be helpful at this point. Imagine that you are composing a new song and have run into a problem. You are currently in the key of C major and the melody note is a C. You would like to move to E-flat major but are having trouble finding a graceful way to move to the new key. By using the tip from Figure 14.19, you might realize that the note C could function as the fifth of an F minor chord. Because F minor is the ii chord in the key of E flat, a simple ii-V-I progression could provide one possible solution. Now let's say that you decide that the chord progression should move directly to a minor mode in order to provide a more suitable setting for the words. By describing the quality of chord (a minor chord in this case), you can narrow the choices to a more manageable level. What minor chords include the note C as a chord factor? Though an A minor, C minor, or F minor might not be the best choice for this situation, you have effectively used theory to begin the process of solving this musical dilemma. Of course, we have not considered the possibility that the note C might simply be a passing tone, anticipation, or some other embellishment, but the point is that descriptive composition can provide many *potential* solutions to a given problem.

DIATONIC PROGRESSIONS

Chord progressions can broadly be grouped into two categories. Progressions that stay within a given tonal center are considered *diatonic progressions.* The term *chromaticism* is often applied to music in which the tonal center is weakened through the use of harmonies outside of the key. Chromatic elements might include borrowed chords, frequent modulations, or the linear process. Figure 14.18 shows the chords found diatonically in a major and minor scale. Note that, in a minor key, the V chord is usually a major triad or major-minor seventh chord, and a leading-tone diminished chord is often used to strengthen harmonic motion towards the tonic.

Figure 14.18
Diatonic chords in major and minor keys.

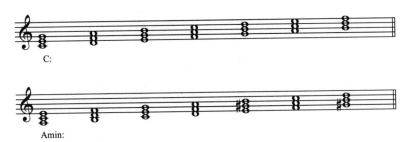

One way to visualize diatonic progressions is to be aware of a natural tendency for roots to descend by a fifth. For example, the ii-V-I progression and iii-vi-ii-V-I progression shown in Figure 14.19 are found in many popular tunes.

Figure 14.19
Example ii-V-I and iii-vi-ii-V-I progressions.

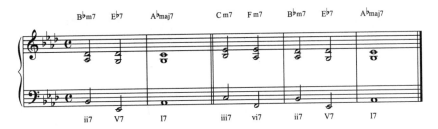

There is also a natural pull exerted by the tonic of the key. This effect can be heard in progressions such as I-IV-I (*plagal cadence*), I-vi-I, or IV-V-I. This tendency is often exploited through the use of *deceptive cadences* such as ii-V-vi. In this instance, the resolution of the V chord to the vi chord works because the vi chord shares two chord tones with the tonic, but the effect is surprising to a listener because of the strength of the tonic (see Figure 14.20).

Figure 14.20
Deceptive cadence.

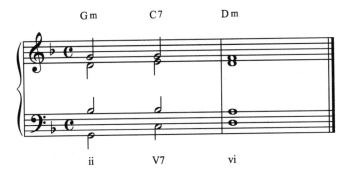

It is interesting to note that these concepts can also be applied to *modal* progressions. (See Chapter 10, "Chord and Scale Relationships," for a discussion of modes). For example, a I-IV-v-I progression in the Mixolydian mode sounds fairly exotic (see Figure 14.21).

Figure 14.21
Modal progression (I-IV-v-I in G Mixolydian).

It is also helpful to consider inversions when composing a diatonic progression of chords. For example, a first inversion I chord makes an interesting choice between the ii and IV chords in Figure 14.22. These types of alternate bass notes can open up many interesting possibilities in what might otherwise be an ordinary progression of chords.

Figure 14.22
Using an inversion in a diatonic progression.

CHROMATICISM

The common practice period (roughly 1600–1900) can be characterized by an increasing use of chromaticism and dissonance culminating around the turn of the 20th century with explorations in *atonality*, *bitonality*, and many other techniques. Chromatic elements such as borrowed chords and tonicizing chord groups are used in many popular songs as well as in traditional art music. In the next few paragraphs I will explore several of these interesting techniques.

Secondary Dominant (Applied Dominant)

Secondary or applied dominants can be used to strengthen the motion to a given arrival point. Since the motion of descending fifths is strong, a V or V7 can be used to *tonicize* nearly any arrival chord. For example, a "five of six" chord might be used to strengthen the motion to the relative minor in a I-vi progression as in Figure 14.23.

Figure 14.23
Using a secondary dominant in a I-vi progression.

In Figure 14.24, multiple secondary dominants are applied to a simple I-vi-ii-V progression. It is important to point out that this version is not necessarily better than the diatonic version of the progression—secondary dominants simply provide another choice. Incidentally, this progression (both the diatonic and chromatic versions) is often referred to as a *turnaround* or *turnback* progression. It's often used in the last few bars of a pop or jazz tune to lead back to the top of the form. In this example, I elected to use *altered secondary dominants* to make the circle progression even stronger.

Figure 14.24
Using secondary dominants in a turnaround progression.

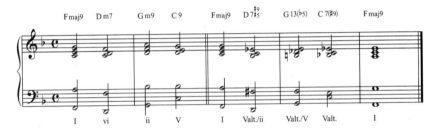

Tonicizing Chord Progressions

Tonicizing chord progressions function in a similar way to secondary dominant chords. In jazz, for example, the ii-V-I progression might be considered a building block of many tunes. Instead of using a "five of" relationship as in Figure 14.23, an entire progression of chords can be used to move to a given arrival chord. In Figure 14.24, a ii and V chord of A minor are used to enhance the movement from I to the relative minor (vi).

Figure 14.25
Using a tonicizing chord group to move to the relative minor.

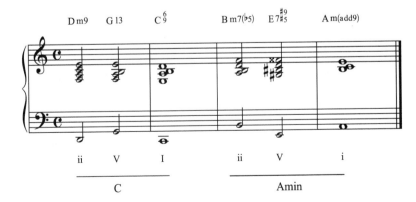

Tonicizing chord progressions can be a powerful tool: These progressions can be very effective in weakening the strength of a tonal center and have been utilized by many 19th- and 20th-century composers. When exploring this technique, just remember that the progression of chords leads to a given arrival chord—one that is often not found in the original key.

Modal Mixture

Theorists use the term *modal mixture* or *borrowed chords* to describe a technique where chords are *borrowed* from a parallel major or minor key. The most common use is to borrow a chord from a minor key for use in a major key. For example, the ii chord in C minor is D diminished or Dmin7♭5. Using this chord in C major is an example of modal mixture. J.S. Bach used the technique in some of his chorales, and modal mixture is still used in many popular songs and film scores today. The effect is so striking that I sometimes use the term *poignant chord* to describe the use of a borrowed ii or iv chord (see Figure 14.26).

Figure 14.26
Using a borrowed iv chord.

The Linear Approach

One of the most powerful approaches to developing a chord progression is to consider the linear process. In a linear approach, each of the voices in a chord moves in a melodic way to a given arrival point. Often, the resulting structures defy traditional analysis, but the results can be very effective. To utilize the technique, consider the movement of each voice as a melodic statement. If each voice moves in a natural way, the progression will work (even if it does not make vertical sense). Figure 14.27 illustrates one example. (This technique is described in more detail in Chapter 11, "The Linear Process.")

Figure 14.27
Linear approach.

Chromatic Mediants and Submediants

The terms *chromatic mediant* and *chromatic submediant* are used to describe an altered form of the mediant and submediant chords. In C major, E minor is the mediant, so E major, E♭ major, and E♭ minor are examples of chromatic mediants (these chords are outside of the key of C major). Similarly, A minor is the submediant, so A, A♭ major, and A♭ minor are examples of chromatic submediants. The concept can also be applied to minor keys. For example, E♭ major is the mediant in C minor so E♭ minor, E major, and E minor are examples of chromatic mediants in this key. A♭ major is the submediant, so A♭ minor, A, and A minor are examples of chromatic submediants. I mention this approach to chromaticism because these chords are often utilized in film music. The effect of a chromatic mediant or submediant is very striking—these chords are a good choice in places where a progression needs to sound dramatic. Figure 14.28 illustrates how these structures might be used:

Figure 14.28
Using a chromatic mediant and submediant.

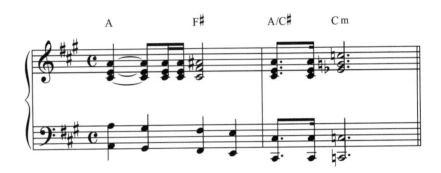

CASE STUDY: EXPERIMENTING WITH CHORD PROGRESSIONS

To this point I have covered many of the traditional techniques associated composing melodies and creating chord progressions. Let's consider how these concepts can be used to support the composition process. For this example, we will compose several harmonic settings for a short melodic fragment. The goal is not to demonstrate the "best" setting—that can only be determined in the context of a full composition. However, these examples will illustrate a process that can be useful in composing progressions. For each solution presented in this section, there are many other viable options, so I encourage you to experiment with each concept in order to find new solutions.

A good starting point is to consider a potential key center. The melodic fragment in Figure 14.29 could fit within a C major scale or any related mode such as D Dorian or G Mixolydian. The four notes in this example can also be found in a G major scale, so the seven modes of G are also available.

Figure 14.29
Melodic fragment.

A Diatonic Solution

One approach might be to use diatonic harmony to support the melody. I elected to start with an A minor chord and end with an F-major chord. The middle chord is the result of passing tones in the tenor and bass voices. Though the progression A minor–G major–F major works fine, I thought it was more interesting to keep the E in the tenor. Figure 14.30 shows one possible diatonic solution.

Figure 14.30
Diatonic chord progression.

Third Relationship

I talked about the concept of diatonic and chromatic mediants and submediants. A more generic way to think about those relationships is to use root movement of a third—often called the *third relationship* by theorists. In Figure 14.31, a third relationship exists between the first and last chord in the progression. A diatonic arrival point (A minor) would be another good option, but the relationship between F major and A major is interesting.

Figure 14.31
Using a third relationship.

Functional Harmony

The next three examples illustrate how a traditional chord progression such as ii-V-I can be utilized. In Figure 14.32, a ii-V-I progression in C major is used. Again, when you consider that the notes in this fragment can function as chord tones, extension tones, or altered tones, it becomes evident that there is a vast array of options in the realm of functional harmony.

Figure 14.32
ii-V-I in C major.

Figure 14.33 demonstrates the use of a ii-V-i in two minor keys: A minor and E minor.

Figure 14.33
ii-V-i in two minor keys.

Linear Process

In the next example, I elected to start with a C-minor chord in first inversion. The second chord, an enharmonic A♭ minor, provides another example of the third relationship. I decided to use a D major largely through the linear process—I liked the sound of contrary motion in the lower voices and thought the D major provided an interesting arrival point to match the third relationship between the first two chords (see Figure 14.34).

Figure 14.34
Chromatic submediant and linear
approach.

In Figure 14.35, I elected to start with an A♭-major chord because the notes C and D provide a hint of a Lydian mode when placed over this chord. This progression is yet another example of third relationship: A♭ major–F major–D major.

Figure 14.35
Descending thirds.

In each of the previous examples, theory was useful in support of the creative process, but it wasn't foremost in my mind. In exploring chords and progressions, I often find that intuition will bring me close to a solution—the descriptive composition process might help me to visualize the mood or effect of a passage. But theory can support the process by providing a gentle nudge to the intuition. When used in this way, theory becomes a great ally—often yielding results that would be difficult to achieve solely by ear or trial and error.

Other Approaches to Tonality and Composition

Although most popular music is based on tonal concepts, there are times when it is useful to consider other techniques. For example, film composers are often called upon to score scenes that might be described as too powerful to be effectively handled using a tonal approach. Around the turn of the century, composers of art music realized that, to an extent, the limits of tonal process and chromaticism had been reached, and they began to explore other techniques such as *atonality*, an absence of tonal center, and *polytonality*, concurrent tonal centers.

One of the many examples of powerful 20th-century works I like to use with my students is Penderecki's *Threnody to the Victims of Hiroshima*. What resources does a composer utilize when writing about an event in which more than 100,000 people died? Penderecki utilized micro-tuning, an element of indeterminism, nontraditional playing techniques, and what might be described as "sonorous counterpoint" to create a work that is at once powerful and disturbing. In this section I will look at several of the important techniques that have been developed by 20th-century composers. As with the discussion of melody and harmony, these techniques should be considered as a starting point for exploration. I mention this because there is a tendency to think that techniques such as 12-tone process should be used in a specific or "correct" way. As a composer, you should utilize these concepts in any way that best supports your artistic vision.

Free Tonality

In *freely tonal* music, a tonic is evident but traditional functional harmony is absent. In many cases, an ostinato or pedal point provides a sense of tonic while other voices move in a highly linear fashion. Figure 14.36 demonstrates the use of a pedal point in the context of a freely tonal passage.

Figure 14.36
Freely tonal excerpt (with pedal point).

Polytonality

The term *polytonality* is used to describe music in which two (or more) tonal centers are simultaneously implied. Béla Bartók used this technique to great effect in some of his compositions. Depending on the relationship of keys, polytonality can range from highly dissonant to exotic. In Figure 14.37, two distinct keys work together to produce an interesting sound.

Figure 14.37
Polytonal excerpt.

Polychords

When two distinct chord structures are stacked, one on top of the other, they are said to be *polychords*. In many cases, triads or seventh chords are combined but disparate structures such as a tertian chord and quartal chord can also be combined to form a polychord. As with polytonality, these structures can provide any number of interesting possibilities that go beyond traditional tertian harmony. Figure 14.38 illustrates how polychords could be used to create an effective harmonic cadence.

Figure 14.38
Polychord cadence.

Synthetic Scales

I talked about synthetic scales in Chapter 10. I will mention the concept again because the use of synthetic scales is such an important part of some 20th-century music. A synthetic scale such as a *whole-tone* or *octatonic* (half step/whole step) scale can be useful both for melodic vocabulary as well as chord structures. I find synthetic scales to be a great source of inspiration: A composer can devise a scale with a specific character and use the scale to derive harmonies and motives. Figure 14.39 demonstrates how an octatonic scale could be used as the basis for a musical passage.

Figure 14.39
Using an octatonic scale.

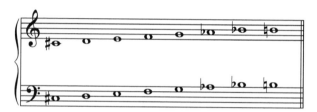

Atonality

In tonal and freely tonal music, the tonic takes on more prominence than other notes. In contrast, each note has an equal role in *atonal* music—no one tone is given special emphasis. It is surprisingly difficult to create a truly atonal composition because repetition of a note can easily imply a tonic. Listeners may also perceive a tonic if a succession of pitches implies a scale or mode.

In many cases, a group of pitches, called a *cell,* can provide a useful method of organizing material in an atonal or freely tonal composition. Cells usually consist of three or four notes and can be transformed in many ways such as backwards (*retrograde*), mirror *inversion,* fragmentation, re-ordering, or as a chord structure (*verticalization*).

"Scherzo," one of the tracks on the CD that accompanies this book, demonstrates extensive use of cellular organization. Although I would not describe the piece as atonal, I was very deliberate in using a cellular theme as the basis for the composition. Figure 14.40 shows common types of cellular transformation.

Figure 14.40
Common cellular transformations.

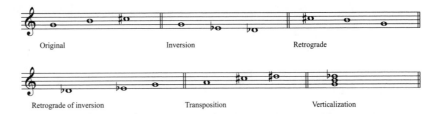

Twelve-Tone Technique

A related concept, called *12-tone technique*, was devised by Schoenberg in the early part of the century. I should point out that, while the term *atonality* is applied to much of Schoenberg's music, I understand that he did not conceive of his music as atonal. In his book *Structural Functions of Harmony*, Schoenberg states that "My school, including such men as Alban Berg, Anton Webern and others, does not aim at the establishment of a tonality, yet does not exclude it entirely. The [12-tone] procedure is based upon my theory of 'the emancipation of the dissonance.'"

A first step in using 12-tone technique is to order the pitches of a chromatic scale into a *tone row*. If the goal is to create an atonal composition, care should be taken that successive pitches do not imply a scale or mode. Next, a 12×12 matrix can be created from the original tone row. To create a matrix, place the original tone row on the top row of the matrix and create a mirror inversion of the row in the leftmost column. For example, if the interval between the first two notes is an ascending fourth, the first interval of the mirror inversion would be a descending fourth. Once the top row and leftmost column are created, inversions of the original row are placed according to the number of half steps between the first note in the given row and the starting note of the original row. For example, if the second row starts with an E and the original row started with a C, then the second row represents a transposition of a major third above the original.

The tone row and matrix can provide the basis for themes and thematic development in much the same way that a tonal motive might be exposed and developed. Figure 14.40 shows a 12-tone row and a completed matrix. The letters P, R, I, and RI stand for *prime, retrograde, inversion,* and *retrograde of inversion,* respectively. By convention, numbers are used to represent the number of half steps between the given transposition and the original row.

Figure 14.40
caption missing

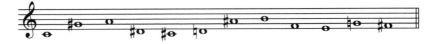

	I-0	I-8	I-9	I-3	I-1	I-2	I-10	I-11	I-5	I-4	I-7	I-6	
P-0	C	G#	A	D#	C#	D	A#	B	F	E	G	F#	R-0
P-4	E	C	C#	G	F	F#	D	D#	A	G#	B	A#	R-4
P-3	D#	B	C	F#	E	F	C#	D	G#	G	A#	A	R-3
P-9	A	F	F#	C	A#	B	G	G#	D	C#	E	D#	R-9
P-11	B	G	G#	D	C	C#	A	A#	E	D#	F#	F	R-11
P-10	A#	F#	G	C#	B	C	G#	A	D#	D	F	E	R-10
P-2	D	A#	B	F	D#	E	C	C#	G	F#	A	G#	R-2
P-1	C#	A	A#	E	D	D#	B	C	F#	F	G#	G	R-1
P-7	G	D#	E	A#	G#	A	F	F#	C	B	D	C#	R-7
P-8	G#	E	F	B	A	A#	F#	G	C#	C	D#	D	R-8
P-5	F	C#	D	G#	F#	G	D#	E	A#	A	C	B	R-5
P-6	F#	D	D#	A	G	G#	E	F	B	A#	C#	C	R-6
	RI-0	RI-8	RI-9	RI-3	RI-1	RI-2	RI-10	RI-11	RI-5	RI-4	RI-7	RI-6	

Figure 14.41
Twelve-tone row and matrix.

Although this process may seem overly complex and unintuitive, 12-tone technique was used by many composers in the 20th century—often in conjunction with other contemporary techniques. On the accompanying CD, 12-tone technique was used extensively in the composition of an orchestral piece titled "Thriller Scene." Although my goal was not to create an atonal composition, you will probably agree that the composition has a "bold" sound due in large part to the use of 12-tone technique. Note that my approach is different than the traditional approach to the 12-tone method. In a traditional approach, each tone is of equal importance so that no particular tone is emphasized as a tonic. When applying the technique in a traditional manner, notes may be repeated but all tones in the row are used before returning to a given note.

The Big Picture

I have covered many concepts relating to composition such as melody, motives, harmonic progression, tonal and non-tonal approaches. In this final section of the chapter I will consider techniques that can help you organize your work in the form of a complete composition.

COHESION
Earlier in the chapter I talked about the concept of la grande ligne. In order for a composition to work, the pieces must fit in such a way that they contribute to a unified whole. I find it helpful to visualize each part, section, and even an entire composition from the standpoint of cohesion—simply put, do the parts contribute or distract from the effectiveness of the piece? For example, an overly simplistic chord placed in the midst of lush harmonies can detract from the effectiveness of the passage. Similarly, a keyboard part that haphazardly oscillates between

three-note chords and six-note structures can be distracting, as can a random use of dissonance (or consonance). That is not to say that change and contrast—sometimes jarring in nature—are not an essential part of music. But it is beneficial to consider how each part contributes or detracts from la grande ligne. In looking for cohesiveness, I often find that I need to trim, cut, and pare certain elements. In this way, evaluating a piece for cohesiveness is often similar to the way a sculptor must use his tools to bring an image hidden in stone to its final form.

DEVELOPING AN IDEA

I suspect that most composers wrestle with the question of "what comes next?" As with other aspects of the composition process, I find that a descriptive approach to composition can be useful in dealing with this question. In their book, *A Practical Approach to the Study of Form in Music* (Waveland Press, 1988), authors Peter Spencer and Peter M. Temko discuss the four basic structural functions: *expository, transitional, developmental,* and *terminative.* As you compose, consider how a given section relates to one of the structural functions. For example, expository function is often characterized by melodic "clarity" and tonal stability. In contrast, a perception of movement is essential for transitional function. In terms of composition, you might ask yourself if a section is stating an idea, developing an idea, moving to a new idea, or finishing an idea. In answering the question you will have a better sense of how to approach the section.

The developmental function is one of the most powerful structural functions. In art music, a "developmental" section is characterized by presentation and transformation of preexisting motivic material. What this often means to me is that I look for themes, motives, and other elements *within* the piece in order to expand on these ideas instead of always looking for a new idea. For example, rhythmic augmentation of a melody might provide the basis for a bass line, and melodic fragmentation can be used to expand on a primary theme or motive. In my estimation, a piece that develops in this way will usually provide a stronger sense of cohesion than a piece in which most of the elements are unrelated. This is one of the things that astounds me with the music of revered composers such as Stravinsky, Schoenberg, Prokofiev, Bach, Debussy, and many more—the more you analyze the music of great composers of art music, the more you realize these composers often focused on developing and transforming material previously presented in a piece instead of constantly writing new material.

DEVELOPING YOUR OWN VOICE

One of the negative aspects of a formalized or academic approach to composition is that the process can take on more significance than the end result. A corollary exists in other aspects of music production such as mixing where, in many cases, the academic approach to mixing focuses on technology, not listening. By way of example, I was reluctant to embrace contrapuntal concepts because of the fairly rigid approach to species counterpoint that was commonly taught when I attended college. I have since learned that, since the time of Bach, counterpoint is used in a less dogmatic way, and I have come to embrace counterpoint as an integral part of my musical vocabulary. My hope is that these words will empower you to learn to use these techniques to your own advantage—not necessarily in the same way that other composers have used them. If the topic of music composition interests you, I suggest that you explore additional resources to learn about other compositional concepts such as serialism, impressionism, minimalism, leitmotivs, and the like.

Composition "Starters" and Practice Etudes

There may be times when the muse does not strike. Following is a list of tips to help get those creative juices flowing. The important thing to remember is to listen to music, perform with other musicians, develop a diverse musical vocabulary, and write every day. In this way, you will start to develop your own voice and become more proficient with the composition process.

▶ Create a melody to go with lyrics or a poem.

▶ Create a composition that conveys a specific mood such as joy, sorrow, or pain.

▶ Compose a melody or harmonic progression in a mode (Dorian Phrygian, Lydian, etc.).

▶ Compose a melody or harmonic progression based on a custom synthetic scale.

▶ Compose a melody that utilizes common melodic embellishments such as changing tones or chromatic passing tones.

▶ Compose a motive that uses only three or four notes (focus on rhythmic variations).

▶ Compose a motive using a simple one-bar rhythmic figure (focus on note variations).

▶ Create a melody that uses a distinctive element such as an interval or specific grouping of notes or rhythms.

▶ Create a new chord progression for a given melody.

▶ Create a composition using the pentatonic scale (i.e., the interval pattern of black notes on the piano).

▶ Create a musical setting or texture using quartal (chords built in fourths) or quintal (chords built in fifths) structures.

▶ Create a harmonic progression that modulates to a closely related key.

▶ Create a harmonic progression that modulates to a distant key.

▶ Create a harmonic progression that utilizes borrowed chords and other chromatic elements.

▶ Compose a melody to fit over an ostinato (a repetitive pattern).

▶ Create a contrapuntal composition using two or three voices.

▶ Listen to a recording and emulate some of the musical vocabulary from the album.

▶ Create a composition for an unusual collection of instruments or synthetic sounds—zither, flute, bagpipe, and koto, for example.

▶ Compose a *style* piece: a composition that sounds like a classical sonata, piano rag, or other such genre.

▶ Create a sequence that represents an element of nature such as a river, storm, or garden.

▶ Create a harmonic progression, then sing (and write) a suitable melody.

▶ Create a composition utilizing a form such as rondo, binary, ternary, or sonata allegro.

▶ Compose a piece utilizing the concept of leitmotivs (i.e., combine several motives that musically represent a character in a film, book, or opera).

▶ Use a sequencer to create a minimalist composition (i.e., start with a simple motive and cut, paste, loop, and offset to create a variety of permutations).

▶ Create a cellular motive and apply transformations such as retrograde and inversion.

▶ Create a composition based on a 12-tone row and/or matrix.

▶ Transcribe a piece by a composer who interests you and write a composition utilizing the musical vocabulary evident in the transcription.

▶ Create a freely tonal piece utilizing an ostinato or pedal point.

CHAPTER 15

Real-World Arranging

As computer musicians, a natural extension of our creative work often involves arranging material for both electronic and acoustic instruments. In fact, the very essence of sequencing involves arranging decisions: orchestration considerations, voicing of harmonic structures, stylization of melody and accompaniment, and elements of form such as introductions, interludes, and endings. When sequencing, the lines between composition, arranging, and orchestration become blurred. It is often advisable to rethink a sequence from the perspective of an arranger to come up with the best possible musical statement. Though there are many interpretations of the word *arrange*, in this context I will talk about ways to take an existing composition or sequenced idea and mold it into a complete musical statement. In the next chapter I will explore a related concept, *orchestration*, which involves the study of instrumental properties as well as the use of various combinations of instruments.

Ideally, a successful arranger must distance himself from details of the composition and consider the bigger picture. Most of the suggestions in this chapter will enhance the decisions you make while sequencing and recording. You will also find many techniques that will prove valuable should you be asked to provide an arrangement for traditional instruments or voice—a situation that most electronic musicians will find themselves in whether playing with a band or producing music for radio, television, or movies. In addition, you will learn many techniques that apply to playing keyboard instruments or guitar. On a personal note, I have found that as my arranging chops improve, these improvements apply directly to my playing. In a nutshell, the more solutions and concepts you can internalize, the more effective and efficient you will be. This chapter will focus on the following arranging concepts:

▶ The fine line between inventiveness and chaos

- ▶ Harmony: getting from point A to point B

- ▶ Voice leading

- ▶ Voicing techniques in two to five parts

- ▶ Nonharmonic solutions

- ▶ Chord substitution

- ▶ Stylizing a melody

- ▶ Introductions, interludes, and endings

- ▶ The big picture

The Fine Line Between Inventiveness and Chaos

I find it helpful to think of arranging in terms of choices. The more choices you have at your disposal as an arranger or composer, the better prepared you will be to find solutions to musical problems. It is easy to get caught up in thinking that the most interesting arrangements and compositions are the ones that utilize new material. In fact, the opposite is often true. I always like to relate music to other arts such as painting or literature. Consider some of the great American authors: Hemingway, Steinbeck, Faulkner, or James Cooper. None of these authors are well known for using obscure or obtuse words. What each of these authors was able to do was to put ordinary words together in an extraordinary and poetic way. As arrangers, our goal is often the same. Some of the best arrangers and composers of our time have used a fairly ordinary musical vocabulary. Does this mean you should avoid expanding the boundaries of your musical vocabulary? Of course not. As an artist you do need to find a balance between familiarity and inventiveness. How much inventiveness is too much? That is a question only you can answer.

Using Theory in the Arranging Process

Theory can be useful in the arranging process, but as with other creative pursuits, it's usually best to let your intuition guide your intellect. By way of example, the next section provides numerous theoretical techniques for voicing chords in two to five parts, handling nonharmonic tones, and establishing derivative chord progressions. When arranging, you will often find that one of these "stock" solutions is most appropriate—a knowledge of these concepts can help you work more efficiently. These concepts can also be a great stepping stone in finding your own unique approach to a given situation.

Getting from Point A to Point B

One of the most common tasks that we face as arrangers is the question of harmony. What chords to use, how to voice a melody in four parts, what to do if a note in the melody does not belong to a given chord? Let's begin by looking at some of the underlying harmonic concepts that are at work in most popular and classical music.

One of the most important concepts relating to popular music theory involves the relationship of tonic and dominant or dominant seventh chords. In any key, the dominant or V chord has a tendency to resolve to the tonic or I chord. To see how this works, play the sequence of chords in Figure 15.1.

Figure 15.1
Dominant-to tonic-relationship.

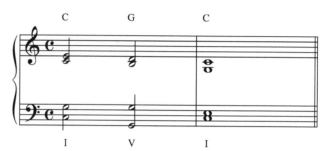

The tendency for dominant chords to want to resolve is even stronger when a seventh is added. Although you will find variations, a major-minor seventh (or altered dominant) is most often used as V in a given key. Play the progression in Figure 15.2 to hear how this progression differs from the previous one.

Figure 15.2
Dominant-seventh-to-tonic relationship.

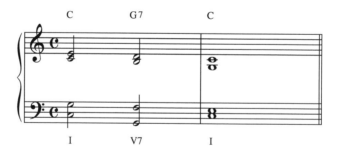

The important thing to remember is that root movement down a perfect fifth or up a perfect fourth is strong. Our ears tend to hear this as a natural progression. To see just how strong this progression is, play the progression in Figure 15.3, which utilizes a surprise resolution. Though the effect of this progression is unusual, it shows just how powerful the dominant-to-tonic relationship is.

Figure 15.3
Surprise resolution of a dominant
seventh.

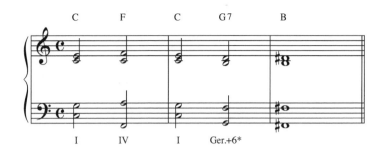

(Note: The German augmented sixth, spelled as a V7 in Figure 15.3, is a chord that was common in the Classical and Romantic eras. This example illustrates a typical use of this chord. In this context, the chord moves to a second inversion B chord.)

One way that these tendencies can be used in an arrangement or composition involves the process of *tonicization*. Tonicization involves using a dominant, dominant seventh, or leading-tone diminished chord to tonicize a temporary tonic. Bill Dobbins explores this concept in detail in his excellent book, *Jazz Arranging and Composing: A Linear Approach* (Advance Music, 1986). In many cases, it is possible to modulate from one key to another or move to a distantly related chord by simply inserting a temporary dominant before the chord you wish to arrive at. Say, for example, that you wish to move from an F-major chord to an A-flat major (a distantly related key). Within the context of your arrangement it may sound good to simply move to A-flat major without any preparation. If this progression sounds unusual, try inserting a temporary dominant or dominant seventh chord (see Figure 15.4).

Figure 15.4
Tonicization using a secondary
dominant.

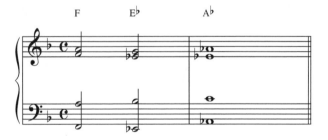

It is often possible to change keys using only a single tonicizing chord. It is even possible to tonicize a tonicizing chord, as in Figure 15.5.

Figure 15.5
Using two secondary dominants to
change key.

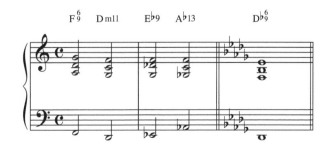

Although the dominant-to-tonic relationship is very strong, diminished chords can also be used to establish a temporary tonic. The diminished seventh chord built on the leading tone works as a tonicizing chord. To find the leading tone diminished, build a diminished triad or diminished seventh chord whose root is one half-step below the chord you wish to tonicize (see Figure 15.6).

Figure 15.6
Using a leading tone diminished to tonicize a given chord.

Another consideration involves the relationship of chords in a harmonic progression to the tonal center. A simple rule is that diatonic chords (i.e., all the tones of the chord are found in a given key or mode) tend to sound the most natural. Chromatic harmony (i.e., contains notes outside the key) will tend to sound foreign to the ear. I am not implying that you shouldn't use chromatic progressions; just be aware that chromaticism should not be treated haphazardly. To better understand the concept of diatonic or chromatic harmony, play through the progressions in Figure 15.7. In this case the A♭ would be considered to be a chromatic chord because it contains notes that are out of the key.

Figure 15.7
Diatonic progression versus chromatic progression.

Keep in mind that diatonic harmony tends to sound the most natural and chromaticism tends to "jump out" at the listener.

Voice Leading

Classical theorists often emphasize the importance of voice-leading. Though voice leading principles are not used rigidly in popular music, an understanding of these concepts can go a long way in making your music sound better. In a worst-case scenario, poor voice leading can actually wreck a good chord progression.

Although it is possible to devote years of study to the principles of good voice leading, most of the important "rules" can be summarized as follows.

▶ Avoid jumping around in root position.

▶ If two chords contain the same note, it often makes sense to keep that tone common to both chords.

▶ The seventh member of a dominant seventh tends to want to resolve to the third of a tonic chord.

▶ The leading tone in a key tends to want to resolve up to tonic.

▶ Avoid large leaps. If two tones are near one another in a progression, it usually makes sense to use minimal motion to connect the tones.

Although this list is by no means comprehensive, these simple suggestions will help you create pleasing voice leading in your compositions. A good rule of thumb is to sing each independent line. If the line is hard to sing or contains many awkward jumps it may indicate that voice leading can be improved. For example, in Figure 15.8 the voice leading is awkward because common tones and tendency tones are ignored.

Figure 15.8
Awkward voice leading.

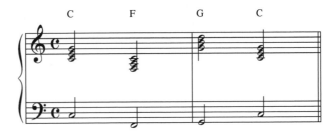

Figure 15.9 takes advantage of common tones and tendency tones to produce a progression that flows more smoothly.

Figure 15.9
Smooth voice leading.

Keep in mind that voice leading concepts should not be rigidly adhered to. It is often desirable to utilize parallel motion among voices or include large leaps if that best suits a given passage. However, voice leading concepts are often desirable when scoring a lush passage for strings or horns.

Voicing Techniques: Two to Five Parts

The following sections look at techniques for voicing a melody from two to five parts. These techniques are often used when writing for a group of brass and woodwind instruments with rhythm section accompaniment. In this situation, it may not be necessary to include chord roots since the bass can provide this note. There are a number of goals to keep in mind when doing this type of harmonization.

▶ The combination of voices should clearly imply the underlying harmonic progression.

▶ Each of the supporting voices should have a pleasing melodic contour.

▶ Harmonizations should be appropriate for the style of the music (e.g., extended and altered chords are not usually found in rock music).

Tip: A thorough understanding of chord groups and their related scales will be essential to effectively harmonize a melody in two or more parts. If you have not done so already, be sure to read the relevant chapters on popular music theory and chord-scale relationships.

TWO-PART HARMONIZATION

We will begin by looking at some simple two-voice harmonizations. Note that with each of the examples in this section, the melody will always be on top. Though it is possible to score a melody in a lower voice, the most common scenario involves placing the melody in the top voice. Keep in mind that these melodic harmonizations may not necessarily be the main melody of the song: These techniques are also useful for a counter-melody voiced in two or more parts or even a background horn riff.

One of the best ways to voice a melody in two parts is to derive the second voice from an appropriate scale. If the chord of the moment is an Am7, we know that one possible scale choice would be an A Dorian scale (or G major if you prefer to think that way). In Figure 15.10, the second voice is always a diatonic third below the melody. I use the term diatonic here in reference to the underlying scale—each of the notes in the second voice comes from an A Dorian scale. Note that this technique works well for *any* chord-scale relationship such as an altered scale synthetic scale.

Figure 15.10
Two-part diatonic harmonization using A Dorian.

It is also possible to arrange this melody in two parts using chromatic tones. Remember that when referring to chromaticism, we are not necessarily talking about half-steps. Any musical passage that contains notes outside of the key, mode, or underlying scale can be said to be chromatic. In this instance, we will start with the same interval (major third) as with the last example. The difference here is that this major third interval will remain constant. The E♭ in this example is chromatic; it is not found in the A Dorian mode. This passage does provide an interesting "bluesy" effect.

Figure 15.11
Chromatic harmonization in two parts.

In the previous examples, either a major or minor third interval was used for the second voice, but many other choices are possible. I find it helpful to think of intervals in terms of groups of related sounds. In the following example, the intervals are grouped according to function. Thirds and sixths have a similar quality or effect. Fourths and fifths are also similar. It is interesting to note that each of these groups is simply derived from inverting a given interval. If you invert a perfect fourth, you end up with a perfect fifth. It makes sense, then, that these groups of intervals would provide a similar type of effect to the listener. In Figure 15.12, the intervals progress from left to right with the leftmost intervals being most consonant and the intervals on the right sounding more dissonant. It is interesting to note that the term dissonance is subjective—many composers would place fourths and fifths before thirds and sixths in this diagram.

Figure 15.12
Interval groups.

When selecting an interval, consider the type of effect you are after. Thirds and sixths work well for "pretty" melodies. Fourths and fifths tend to sound more modern and "open." Seconds and sevenths can be helpful for creating dissonant or humorous effects. (Several examples of humorous intervals of a second can be heard on the composition titled "Hip Hop for Monk" on the accompanying CD.)

FOUR-PART HARMONIZATION

Four-part harmonization is perhaps the easiest of all melodic harmonizations. Why? With only four notes it is easy to imply any chord, even a complex one. As you will see, with a few simple guidelines it is possible to easily harmonize a melody in four parts.

One way to approach a four-part harmonization is to select chords from a related chord group. Figure 15.13 demonstrates this approach.

Figure 15.13
Four-part harmonization using the
tonic major chord group.

In this example, the chord of the moment is a C6. Our goal is to harmonize the melody (the top note) so that the harmonic implication of the measure retains a tonic-major quality. In this instance, the note B is not a part of C6 but is a note found in Cmaj7, one of the other chords in the group. Although this is not necessarily the best way to harmonize the passage, this approach can be very effective. I will discuss other approaches later in the chapter.

What if the given chord contains more than four notes, as with a C13 or C9 chord? One possible solution to this problem involves using rootless voicings (see Figure 15.14). Rootless voicings work because, in most cases, the root will be played by the bass. Even without a bass part, rootless voicings tend to work; the underlying harmony can still be implied by the musical context of the progression.

Figure 15.14
Rootless voicing of C9.

As I mentioned earlier, any chord (even a complex one) can be easily pared down to four parts. The following tips can help you to easily construct four-part voicings.

▶ To add a ninth, omit the root.

▶ To add a 13th, omit the 5th.

▶ To add an 11th, omit the 5th.

With these simple guidelines it is easy to voice a chord using only four notes. Note that these tips are also helpful for voicing chords on the keyboard or guitar. Figure 15.15 demonstrates how notes might be omitted in a progression of complex chords. Remember that our goal is to find a voicing that best implies the underlying harmony using only four notes.

Figure 15.15
Implying complex chords using four
notes.

What if you want to harmonize a melody or background line using four instruments or voices, but the underlying harmony is triadic? One possible solution is to double the melody in the lowest voice. Another option might be to use linear techniques—visualize one or more of the voices as an independent melodic line. Yet another solution is to place the root in the lowest voice. In Figure 15.16, the melody is doubled an octave lower. These types of voicings can work well for a brass section in the context of a funk or rock composition.

Figure 15.16
Four-part harmonization of a triad.

FIVE-PART HARMONIZATION

As with four-part voicings, five-part voicings are fairly easy to implement because almost any chord can be easily implied with just five notes. One common application of five-part voicings is for background pads (see Figure 15.17). It is common to use the root in the bass, but inversions can also be effective, as can the rootless voicings described in the previous section.

Figure 15.17
Five-part pad voicings.

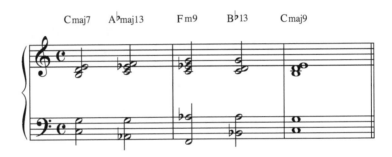

When voicing simple triadic structures in five parts, it is common to double the top note of the chord. It is also common to double the root when voicing these types of chords, but doubling of the third or fifth can also be effective.

Figure 15.18
Five-part harmonization of simple triads.

Another common five-part technique is "Supersax"-style voicings. To create a Supersax-style harmonization, start by creating a four-part voicing in close position. Simply double the melody note one octave lower for an effective five-part voicing (see Figure 15.19 A).

Figure 15.19 A
Supersax voicing.

Another common variation is closely related to the last example. After creating a close-position five-part harmonization, drop the second note from the top of each voicing down one octave and double the melody an octave lower (see Figure 15.19 B).

Figure 15.19 B
Supersax voicing (drop-2).

THREE-PART HARMONIZATION

I find that three-part harmonizations can be difficult to handle. On the one hand, many chords can be effectively voiced using only three notes. On the other hand, it is difficult to achieve voicings that are consistently full using only three voices. Before looking at examples of three-part harmony, it would be helpful to look at common three-part structures.

Three-Voice Chord Structures

There are three structures commonly used for three-part harmonizations (see Figure 15.20): tertian (voicings built in thirds), quartal/quintal (voicings built in fourths or fifths), and clusters (chords built using thirds and seconds).

Figure 15.20
Common three-part structures (tertian, quartal/quintal, and cluster).

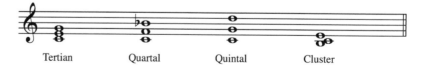

A helpful way to implement these structures is to visualize the great variety of chords that would contain the notes of the given structure. A C triad, for example, can be found in the following chords: C, Am7, Dm11, Bb7+11, Fmaj9, Eb13♭9, Gb7♭9, ♭5, Gm13, and Abmaj7+11. Though this list might seem a bit intimidating, I have found that, with a little experimentation, it is fairly easy to find suitable three-note voicings. The example in Figure 15.21 demonstrates a few such choices.

Figure 15.21
Various three-part harmonizations.

When creating a three-part harmonization it is generally advisable to be consistent with the approach to vertical structures (i.e., don't haphazardly mix quartal, tertian, and cluster structures). Notice how tertian structures are used to harmonize most of the following melody (see Figure 15.22). In this example, a quartal structure is used to provide a better vertical harmonization of the dominant.

Figure 15.22
Tertian harmonization (with quartal dominant chord).

Nonharmonic Tone Solutions

A common problem that arises when harmonizing a melody in three, four, or five parts occurs when one or more notes of the melody is not a chord tone. In the following figure, the note C does not belong to the tonic G-major chord group. In other words, it is difficult, if not impossible, to make this note "fit" as a chord tone of any of the chords found in this chord group. The following paragraphs detail a number of common solutions to this arranging problem.

TONICIZATION
Recall from earlier in the chapter that tonicization involves inserting a temporary dominant or leading-tone diminished chord to tonicize a given chord. Quite often, a nonharmonic tone can be harmonized as a tonicizing chord. Many options are available: dominant, altered dominant, leading-tone diminished, or even substitute chords, which I will talk about in a moment. In Figure 15.23, the nonharmonic tone C is harmonized as a tonicizing chord (F♯ diminished 7). You could also voice the nonharmonic tone as a D7 or D7 altered chord.

Figure 15.23
Voicing a nonharmonic tone using tonicization.

* Nonharmonic tone

Although the preceding tonicization example digresses significantly from the G6 chord symbol, the tonic-major quality is maintained. The diversion simply leads us back to the G6 chord on beat three. Remember that the key is to think of either a V7 or viidim7 of the chord you are attempting to harmonize: D7 or F♯-diminished tonicizes any G chord, A7 or C-sharp dim7 tonicizes any D chord, and so on.

There is one other consideration to keep in mind when tonicizing: This technique will not work if the tonicizing chord lasts for a substantial amount of time. Your ear will guide you in this case, but a general rule of thumb is that longer note values such as a half note or dotted half will likely need to be approached in a different way.

HALF-STEP SHIFT

A half-step shift can provide an interesting solution to a nonharmonic tone. To implement this technique, visualize a chord that is one half-step away from the given chord (see Figure 15.24). For example, if the chord of the moment is a G6, see if the given melody note will work as a chord factor of either A♭6 or F♯6.

Figure 15.24
Handling a nonharmonic tone with a half-step shift.

DIATONIC PLANING

Diatonic planing provides an elegant solution to a nonharmonic tone. To use this technique, carefully consider your arrival points (i.e., the notes that you plan to harmonize vertically). Once you have identified the arrival tones, simply plane each voice through the given mode (see Figure 15.25). Keep in mind that this technique will work for any type of chord such as an altered dominant or tonic-minor structure—it's simply a matter of planing structures through the appropriate scale for a given chord.

Figure 15.25
Diatonic planing.

CHROMATIC PLANING

Chromatic planing is similar to diatonic planing, but in this case, intermediate structures may include notes outside of the given key or mode. As with the diatonic planing example, be sure to identify melodic arrival points—this technique will work only if the underlying harmonic progression is still clear to the listener. Though chromatic planing can sound unusual, the technique can be very effective (see Figure 15.26).

Figure 15.26
Chromatic planing.

LINEAR APPROACH

I have already talked about linear concepts in Chapter 11, "The Linear Process," but it makes sense to revisit this concept as it relates to melodic harmonization. When approaching a harmonization with linear technique, consider each chord tone as an independent melodic unit. Providing each of the voices moves in an independent and melodically pleasing fashion, the harmonization will generally work (even if it does not make sense when analyzed vertically). Note that in Figure 15.27, the upper and lower voices move in contrary motion.

Figure 15.27
A linear approach to a
nonharmonic tone.

Chord Substitutions

Jazz musicians in particular have an affinity for using all sorts of interesting chord substitutions and reharmonizations. Though traditional chord substitutions are used less frequently in popular music, an understanding of these concepts can be a great aid in solving composition and arranging problems. You can hear examples of these chords used in a wide variety of styles.

In Chapter 14, "Music Composition," I presented the idea that any tone may be harmonized as a chord factor of at least 12 different chords. (You may want to review Figure 14.16 now.) This concept is central to substitute chords: For any melody note there will be several potential chords that would work with the given note. Though there are several common substitute chords, keep in mind that many of the most elegant solutions will not fall neatly into a substitution category. That is to say that these solutions depend on the musical context, not substitution "rules."

In my estimation, the goal of reharmonizing a chord progression is to accentuate a key note or phrase in an arrangement. Arrangers often reharmonize songs to provide a suitable setting for their concept of the tune. Though substitutions can be very effective, as with any musical device, substitutions will lose their effectiveness if used too frequently.

TRITONE SUBSTITUTION

One of the most common substitute chords is the so-called *tritone substitute*. In short, you can consider using tritone substitution for any dominant or temporary dominant seventh chord. The actual substitute chord is found by counting up three whole steps (hence the term tritone) from the root of the dominant. Tritone substitution works because the third and seventh of the dominant are enharmonically equivalent to the seventh and third of the substitute chord (see Figure 15.28).

Figure 15.28
Tritone substitution.

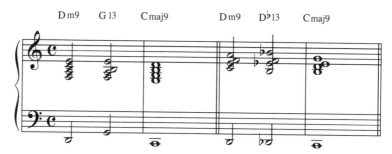

MINOR-THIRD SUBSTITUTION

Minor-third substitution is relatively rare. This technique will work only in places where the melody is appropriate for the substitution chords. A common implementation of this technique involves transposing both the ii and V chords up a minor third in a ii-V-I progression (see Figure 15.29).

Figure 15.29
Minor-third substitution.

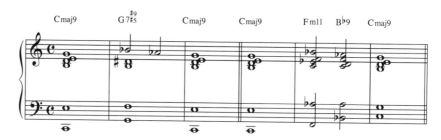

DIATONIC SUBSTITUTION

In a diatonic scale, alternate chords share two or more common tones. In a C-major scale for example, Cmaj9 and Em7 share four common tones. It often makes sense to make diatonic substitutions when you wish to retain the underlying function of a chord but vary the progression (e.g., use IV-V instead of ii-V, or iii-vi instead of I-vi as in Figure 15.30).

Figure 15.30
Diatonic substitution (turnaround).

SYMMETRICAL CHORDS

Symmetrical chords provide an interesting opportunity for chord substitution. For example, instead of using a series of tonicizing chords or tritone substitutions, consider a series of major seventh chords. Figure 15.31 demonstrates an interesting variation on the idea of tritone substitution. Instead of using a series of major-minor seventh chords, major seventh chords provide a very effective sound.

Figure 15.31
Variation on tritone substitution.

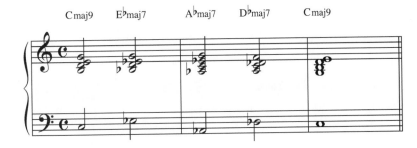

DIMINISHED CHORD SUBSTITUTION

Though diminished chords can sometimes sound dated, diminished chords are often used for a linear type of chord substitution. A common example involves substituting a diminished chord for a major-major seventh chord. This technique works because the inner voices move in a linear fashion—the resulting diminished chord is simply an embellishment of the underlying major chord (see Figure 15.32).

Figure 15.32
Diminished chord used to embellish a major-major seventh chord.

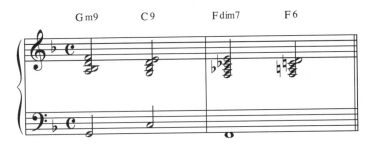

Tip: Diminished chords are also used as passing chords. They often function as passing chords between the ii and iii chords in a major key (either ascending or descending).

Stylizing a Melody

A key consideration when creating an arrangement is the treatment of the melody. Let's use something familiar such as "Twinkle, Twinkle, Little Star." I find it helpful to consider the underlying groove as a first step in stylizing a melody. Though the melody was written over 200 years ago, the piece could work fine as a stylized bossa nova groove, as in the Figure 15.33 A.

Figure 15.33 A
"Twinkle, Twinkle, Little Star"
stylized as a bossa nova.

In a similar vein, this tune could also work as a swing tune or even a funk melody. There are no steadfast rules, but do consider changing rhythms and articulations in a way that is appropriate for the given musical context. Figure 15.33 B demonstrates a not-too-serious swing version of the tune.

Figure 15.33 B
Swing version of "Twinkle, Twinkle, Little Star."

Striving for Consistency

When I arrange music, I find it helpful to evaluate the arrangement from the standpoint of consistency. Though the term is not easily defined when applied to music, a consistent arrangement might be said to be one that makes sense to the listener. Evaluate your arrangement on several levels: Does the harmony work in a convincing way? Do voicings relate to one another? Are substitutions used to accentuate the arrangement or do they distract the listener? Is the melody appropriately stylized for the given musical context? Do the introduction and ending make sense in context of the entire arrangement? Though it would be impossible to quantify these concepts into a set of rules, let your ear guide you when making these types of decisions. As you work, be sure that the various components of the arrangement, such as form, melody, dynamics, articulations, orchestration, and harmony work together to create a unified musical statement.

Considerations of Form

One of the most important considerations facing an arranger is the issue of form. Arrangements that tend to work best provide subtle variations of form that keep the listener interested. As you listen to music, evaluate the music from the standpoint of form. You will find that good arrangers are not afraid to use repetition. Arrangers will often use devices such as interludes or modulations to keep the music interesting. Arrangers often blur the boundaries between sections so that an arrangement does not fall into a predictable pattern. I have noticed that great arrangers such as Sammy Nestico, Henry Mancini, Bill Holman, and others often avoid relying on predictable 8- or 16-bar phrases. For example, you will often hear these arrangers break a 16-bar statement of a theme into smaller subphrases that are orchestrated with contrasting timbres.

INTRODUCTIONS

Though it is not always necessary to include an introduction in an arrangement, introductions can be helpful in that they help to set the vibe. An introduction may provide the arranger with motivic material that may be repeated later in the arrangement. Though there are as many introductions as there are compositions, most introductions provide the following characteristics.

► Introductions often set the mood of the arrangement.

► Introductions may draw the listener into the arrangement.

► Introductions often establish the tonal center.

► Introductions often provide motivic material that may be utilized in an interlude or ending.

The following list of ideas will provide a good starting point in exploring the concept of an introduction.

► Use a repetitive vamp based on a ii-V-I or turnaround progression (I-vi-ii-V or iii-vi-ii-V).

► Paraphrase the last few bars of the melody.

► Provide an introduction in a contrasting key and modulate to the starting key of the composition.

► Use a short melodic motive that helps to set the tone of the piece.

► Write a rubato introduction that culminates with a fermata prior to an *a tempo* section.

► Take snippets of the melody and combine them in a quasi medley prior to introducing the first theme.

► Use a functional chord progression such as #IV dim7-iv-iii-♭iii dim7-ii-V-I.

► Use a pedal point in the bass underneath a repetitive chord progression.

► Write a half-step vamp such as Fmaj9-G♭maj9-Fmaj9-G♭maj9.

► Use a symmetrical progression of chords such as Cm9-Ebm9-G♭m9-Am9 or Cmaj7-B♭maj7-A♭maj7-G♭maj7.

INTERLUDES

Interludes are often used to provide variation between the sections of an arrangement. Arrangers often insert an interlude between choruses of a song or to provide a vamp for a solo. I find that it is often helpful to create interludes that provide a textural change: If the preceding section of music is dynamically loud, a soft bass and drum vamp or stop-time section can be very effective.

ENDINGS

Your approach to the ending will have much to do with the success of the arrangement. Arrangers often utilize material from an introduction or interlude in the ending. This approach is helpful when you want to give a sense of symmetry to the arrangement. Though listeners might not be aware of it, they will appreciate the sense of order that comes from reusing material in the arrangement. In contrast, some arrangements benefit by the addition of new material such as a key change, tempo change, or ending riff. In most cases, you will want to set up the ending in a deliberate way so that the ending does not catch the listener unawares. When writing an ending, it is also helpful to consider the length of the ending as it relates to an arrangement in its entirety. For example, an ending might need to be drawn out to balance the length of long arrangement.

The following list represents several common endings.

▶ Repeat the last phrase of the tune two or three times as a *tag*.

▶ Write a *ritard* that culminates with a final fermata.

▶ Utilize a repetitive vamp such as ii-V-I or iii-vi-ii-V-I.

▶ Hold the final chord under a melodic cadenza.

▶ Use a symmetrical progression of chords such as Cmaj7, Fmaj7, B♭maj7, Ebmaj7 or Cmaj7, B♭maj7, A♭maj7, G♭maj7.

▶ Write a melodic riff (similar to a tag).

▶ Use minor-third substitution (e.g., Dm7-G7, Fm7-Bb7, Dm7-G7, Cmaj7).

▶ Paraphrase a motive from the introduction, interlude, or the tune itself.

▶ Modulate to a new key in the last phrase or section of a tune.

AVOIDING "CHUNKS"

Earlier in the chapter I stated that a consistent arrangement is one that makes sense to the listener. With that in mind, it is sometimes helpful to blur the boundaries between the sections of an arrangement. Though sudden changes can be very effective, you will probably want to avoid making the arrangement overly sectionalized. For example, imagine that you are sequencing a funk tune and wish to add a saxophone background figure on the bridge. Consider inserting the saxophones in the last bar or two of the chorus. An ascending scale or repetitive figure could help to connect these two sections of the piece.

Creating Interest

If your goal is to keep the listener's attention, you will want to evaluate the textures used in your arrangement. Static textures, while appropriate for some musical settings, will tend to tire the listener. Arrangers often utilize contrasting elements to keep the interest of the audience. For example, a soft soli for bass and piano can be effective after a full-ensemble "shout" chorus. Similarly, a change of orchestration from flute to trumpet and tenor sax can provide a welcome change for a bridge or interlude. Although the following list simply contains primary musical elements, it is easy to forget how effective these basic elements can be in the context of a musical arrangement. In a word, subtle changes are generally desirable as they create points of interest in an arrangement.

▶ Dynamics

▶ Voicing (complex versus simple)

▶ Rhythm (active versus static rhythms)

▶ Orchestration

▶ Range/Register

▶ Tonality (major versus minor, atonal, chromaticism, etc.)

▶ Harmony

▶ Articulations

▶ Texture

KEY CHANGES
Key changes can provide a refreshing change in an arrangement. Though key changes can easily sound trite, a change of key in the final chorus of a song can provide a new level of intensity. Arrangers often implement a key change in an unexpected place such as the last eight bars of the song or in the bridge.

REUSING MATERIAL
Consider creating a musical hook that can provide a unifying element in your arrangement. It is common for arrangers to use a well-defined bass line or rhythmic pattern in an introduction, interlude, and ending.

SOLO SECTIONS IN POPULAR MUSIC

Though most of us enjoy a jam, consider the audience as you compose and arrange. Though it is common to hear improvised solos on pop, rock, and country recordings, most recordings that get airplay generally do not include lengthy solo sections. Solo sections should be of a length that is appropriate for the genre.

Arranging versus Composing: Making a Statement as an Arranger

When arranging a cover tune, consider making a personal musical statement with the arrangement. There are many tools at your disposal, such as instrumentation, reharmonization, stylization, and the like. Consider doing a techno version of "Amazing Grace" or creating a "soundscape" of "Lush Life"—there are many possibilities. Creating new arrangements of existing pieces can provide an excellent opportunity to hone your skill as an arranger and develop your own unique voice.

Conclusion

There are many things to consider when arranging a song: harmonic progression, reharmonization, stylization of the melody, orchestration, groove, formal structure, introductions, endings, modulations, and the like. As you explore the many options available to you as an arranger, keep an ear open to the big picture: Most successful arrangements provide a sense of continuity—the various sections work together to provide a cohesive whole.

One final note: Consider working with other musicians. Collaboration can often yield new insights into the arranging and composing process. I also find it helpful to get feedback from friends and musicians as I work on a new arrangement or composition. This type of constructive criticism can go a long way in helping to refine a musical statement in the form of a successful arrangement.

CHAPTER 16

Electronic Orchestration

As computer musicians, the issue of orchestration is a dichotomy: On the one hand, synthesizers provide an almost unlimited palette of timbral possibilities. On the other hand, the use of synthesizers to realize traditional orchestrations sometimes provides marginal results. This chapter investigates the concept of orchestration from a traditional approach. Though the approach is traditional, I encourage you to explore the application of these techniques in a purely synthetic setting. Though synthetic orchestration and sound design can be very rewarding from an artistic standpoint, as computer musicians we are often called upon to create realistic orchestrations for jingles, industrials, and other commercial productions. Practicality of cost and expediency dictates that a significant portion of commercial productions are realized with synthesizers and computers. This chapter presents concepts that will enable you to write effective traditional orchestrations. These same concepts will also enhance the process of creating synthetic orchestrations. This chapter explores the following topics:

▶ Selecting sounds

▶ Orchestral choirs

▶ Using continuous controllers

▶ Emulating brass and woodwind instruments

▶ Breathing

▶ Range

▶ Articulation

▶ Dynamic contour

▶ Mutes

▶ Strings

▶ Percussion

▶ Putting it all together

▶ Foreground and background

▶ Sequencing orchestral parts

Are Synthesizers a Suitable Substitute for Acoustic Instruments?

When we listen to a live acoustic music performance, something magical happens: As listeners, we actually become physically connected to the music. As the performers use their instruments or voices to create sound vibrations, these vibrations interact with the hall, and our ears eventually translate these signals into something our brains recognize as music. The inevitable question that arises in a chapter on electronic orchestration is the validity of attempting to mimic acoustic instruments. I encourage you to ponder the validity of this question, but I would suggest two ideas: Although technology has improved to the point that synthetic instruments can be very expressive, synthesizers are not well suited to accurately mimic acoustic instruments. First, electronic instruments must be amplified, and amplification involves transduction—the conversion from electronic energy to kinetic energy or vice versa. For this reason alone, MIDI instruments face a distinct disadvantage. When a saxophonist blows into a mouthpiece and sets a reed in motion she is creating kinetic energy that connects, in a physical way, with the audience. A second disadvantage relates to the issue of real-time control. Though some synthesizers provide the means to manipulate a sound in real time by changing embouchure, air pressure, filters, and other parameters, a synthesizer that could accurately model a wind instrument would require dozens (if not hundreds) of real-time controllers. Such controllers would include not only parameters for embouchure and air pressure but parameters to control the position of the lips on the reed, type of reed, varying position of the tongue and teeth, shape of the mouthpiece, and a myriad of other features. Obviously, a MIDI musician with only four appendages and one mouth would be hard pressed to control such an instrument. As technology continues to evolve this gap may lessen. Does this mean that MIDI instruments cannot be used as artistic performance instruments? Of course not. But I would suggest that such instruments are better suited for production and performance of nontraditional timbres than replication of traditional sounds.

With regard to emulation of recordings of acoustic instruments, digital synthesizers are better suited to the task. Though most would agree that synthesized productions of symphonic music are not entirely accurate, synthesized orchestrations can be a suitable illusion of the real thing. For obvious financial reasons, this illusionary aspect of digital synthesis has been recognized by many film and record producers. I will leave the artistic debate of such practices to philosophers and conclude by saying that, with regard to music, the better prepared you are to handle both traditional and nontraditional orchestrations, the more marketable you will be as a computer musician.

Other Resources

It goes without saying that a single chapter of introduction to orchestration will not cover the topic in the type of detail of a dedicated text. If the topic interests you, I suggest that you study well-regarded texts on the subject by authors such as Samuel Adler, Walter Piston, and Cecil Forsyth. For symphonic work, the Adler text and accompanying DVDs, titled *The Study of Orchestration* (W.W. Norton, 1989), is a wonderful resource. I am also fond of the Henry Mancini book *Sounds and Scores* (Northridge Music, distributed by Cherry Lane Music, 1973). Though Mancini's comments and analysis are brief, the score excerpts and recordings are very helpful. Sammy Nestico's *The Complete Arranger* (Fenwood Music, distributed by Kendor, 1993), is also excellent and features many symphonic, commercial, and jazz excerpts along with an audio CD. Excerpts in this and other texts help not only in the understanding of range and sonic characteristics of the instruments, but can help you to develop an idiomatic style of writing that can lead to more convincing electronic realizations.

Background

In pre-Baroque eras, orchestration was not a primary consideration. Instruments tended to be used in an ad hoc fashion. Composers rarely indicated the instruments to be used in a performance, but left this up to the musicians. In the Baroque era, composers such as Bach and Handel began to write for specific combinations of instruments, though the approach was not refined in the sense that we think of orchestration today. Key developments in orchestration coincided with the invention of valved brass instruments in the mid 19th century. Prior to the invention of valves, valveless instruments such as the trumpet and French horn were often relegated to an accompanying role. With these natural instruments, it was impossible to accurately play chromatic tones— valveless instruments could only produce notes from the overtone series. The invention of valves (and coincident advancements in manufacturing technology) made it possible for composers such as Beethoven and Berlioz to utilize brass instruments as melodic resources on a par with the strings and woodwinds. By the mid to late 19th-century Romantic era, composers were writing for large orchestras, and orchestration was an integral part of the composition process. In the 20th century, composers continued to expand the concepts of orchestration to include new instruments and the use of extreme instrumental ranges and innovative playing techniques.

Selecting Sounds

One of the difficulties facing computer musicians is the relationship between orchestration and composition. In a typical sequencing environment one must consider not only the composition and instrumentation but the actual design of the sounds. If you have ever spent time designing sounds, you know that this aspect of synthesis can be a time-consuming task. Though there is no correct or incorrect way to approach this problem, I have often found it beneficial to separate these tasks. As you begin a new composition, select sounds that are close to your vision of the finished work. As the composition takes shape you may find it helpful to focus on the nuances of sound design.

It is also helpful to evaluate sounds from the standpoint of textural setting. Avoid the temptation to always select the most interesting synthetic sounds. In many cases, a combination of more subtle instruments can work together for a very effective composite effect. Also note that the goal of a synthesizer manufacturer is to sell synthesizers. I have noticed that, while default patches often sound great as solo sounds, many manufacturers create demonstration sounds that are artificially brilliant. Though these sounds may help to sell synthesizers, they are often less useful in the context of a complex orchestration.

Orchestral Choirs

The instruments in a traditional orchestra belong to one or more of the following orchestral choirs: percussion, woodwinds, brass, and strings. Though this classification system is not entirely accurate (a piano is both a stringed instrument and a percussion instrument, and a modern flute is not made of wood) this system is a helpful way to organize the instruments of a modern-day orchestra. In the next several pages I will discuss each of the orchestral choirs and consider some of the idiosyncrasies of the instruments in each group. Though this chapter deals primarily with traditional orchestral instruments, consider the application of these techniques to nontraditional sounds—for example, a square-wave synthesizer patch could be a suitable functional substitute for an oboe. Likewise, a synthetic string pad can provide similar functionality to a traditional string choir. By learning to mimic traditional sounds you can improve your approach to musical performance of nontraditional sounds.

Using Continuous Controllers

It takes a great deal of work to successfully mimic acoustic instruments. After all, orchestral players spend years leaning to master their instruments! When attempting to emulate these instruments, take time to configure your equipment to allow for the maximum amount of musical nuance. Synthesists often use a variety of continuous controllers simultaneously when doing this type of work. It is not uncommon for a MIDI musician to assign a breath controller for expression, modulation wheel or aftertouch for vibrato, data slider for timbral changes, and so on. Some physical modeling synthesizers even allow for control of elements such as embouchure, breath, tongue, and throat.

If your goal is to emulate traditional instruments, it is helpful to consider the idiosyncrasies of the instruments you are trying to emulate. To effectively emulate traditional instruments you must develop an idiomatic playing style. In a sense, you need to approach a passage of music in much the same way as the instrumentalist you are trying to emulate. For example, though woodwind players can usually execute fast arpeggiations quite comfortably, a similar passage might be very difficult on a brass instrument. Similarly, while it is easy for a saxophonist to play softly in a high register, a trumpet player will have a hard time controlling the dynamics of notes in the upper range of the instrument.

I am particularly excited by a new technology developed by Synful, LLC. The technology, called *reconstructive phrase modeling*, provides a level of expression and realism that can be more effective that, traditional sample playback technology. I have used their RPM software synthesizer for a few months and often find myself practicing a passage in order to perform articulations and phrasing with greater accuracy in real time. This is a welcome change from using sampled sounds that, in general, do not respond to these types of performance nuances. You can hear examples of the "Synful Orchestra" on the two string quartets on the accompanying CD: "Romance" and "Scherzo."

Similarly, sample-based products such as the Garritan Personal Orchestra provide the ability to control legato and detached articulations in real time. This type of expressive control can render much more realistic orchestrations than "static" samples. For example, the instruments heard on "Thriller Scene," a selection on the accompanying CD, were created using this reasonably priced software instrument.

Emulating Wind and Brass Instruments

Though it may be obvious, remember that brass and wind instruments are monophonic. To accurately mimic these instruments it is often advisable to sequence brass and wind parts monophonically. Though it may be tempting to sequence a trumpet section as a series of three or four note chords, this type of approach defeats the goal of playing in an idiomatic playing style. At best, such an approach misses the slight variations in dynamics and articulations that would be achieved through monophonic sequencing. In a worse case, this approach will sound like a keyboardist playing a brass or wind sound. As you work through the remainder of this chapter, consider how you can best emulate the playing style of each of the instruments in the orchestra and work on developing an idiomatic style of playing that accurately imitates the real thing.

BREATHING

One of the problems associated with keyboard sequence entry is that it is easy to forget about basic elements such as breathing and articulation. Obviously, a brass or woodwind player cannot hold notes indefinitely. Though it is easy to hold a 50-second high G on a synthesized trumpet, this type of passage will sound entirely unnatural to the listener. One of the techniques I use to overcome this tendency is to sing lines as I sequence them on the computer. A singable approach yields several benefits: Singing can help you to interpret a melody in a musical fashion (i.e., phrasing a melody with dynamic contours); singing can help you to articulate a melody in an appropriate way (you will tend to be more attuned to accents and, short and long notes); and, finally, singing will, out of necessity, help you to utilize a natural approach to breathing.

When approaching a passage of music in an idiomatic style, consider the size of the instrument you are emulating. Since low-pitched instruments necessarily require a greater length of tubing than high-pitched instruments, it is understandable that a low-brass player will need to move more air through the horn than for an instrument such as the trumpet or French horn. In general, you will need to phrase in smaller units when sequencing low brass or woodwind parts. In a similar vein, double-reed instruments such as bassoon or oboe can be more taxing to play than single reeds such as clarinet or saxophone. As with brass instruments, consider these idiosyncrasies as you sequence.

RANGE

Each instrument is unique with regard to range, but a general rule concerning brass instruments is that higher notes are more difficult to play than lower notes. If textural considerations dictate a soft passage, orchestrating a brass instrument in an extreme high register will not yield suitable results. Though it is easy to fix this type of problem with MIDI by scaling velocities or lowering channel volume, such a solution would not be entirely accurate. When orchestrating this type of passage, remember that a brass mute might be a potential solution. In a similar vein, it is very easy for a saxophonist to play high notes (within the traditional range). On the other hand, it is difficult for a saxophonist to play the lowest few tones of the instrument at a soft dynamic level. Note that the clarinet is unique in that most clarinetists are quite comfortable playing in the entire range of this instrument. Though the clarinet has three distinct timbres dependent on the given range, the instrument is often scored in any or all of the three registers: low (dark), mid (throat), and high (shrill).

When sequencing brass and woodwind parts I find it helpful to consider the "sweet range" of each instrument. The sweet range can be defined as the range in which the instrument can be played effortlessly and with a tone that is natural and pleasing to the ear. The easiest way to visualize the sweet range of brass and wind instruments is to consider the written (versus concert) pitch of the instrument. In general, the sweet range will fall in the staff in a transposed part. For example, though the range of a baritone and alto saxophone differs greatly, each of these instruments has a written (transposed) sweet range from around E4 (slightly above middle C) to G5.

When emulating acoustic instruments it is helpful to consider both the upper and lower limits of any instrument you intend to emulate. An instrument that falls grossly out of range will sound unnatural to an attentive listener. Of course, one of the great things about MIDI is that you can easily extend the range of a given instrument. Just remember that if your goal is to accurately create the illusion of a traditional orchestra, these types of inaccuracies can be a problem. Many years ago, I remember being very proud of one of my first synthesized orchestral pieces. I will never forget playing the recording for a percussionist friend: My friend heard only two notes before he informed me that my timpani sounded unnatural—the notes were far out of range! For this reason, a knowledge of instrumental ranges is helpful in developing natural sounding orchestrations.

ARTICULATION

A fundamental problem associated with most synthesizers is that it is difficult (and often impossible) to emulate articulations of traditional instruments. For example, it is difficult for brass and woodwind players to tongue extremely fast passages of notes. You should consider using a legato (connected) approach for these types of passages. Some synthesists will design a "composite" sound in order to activate or deactivate the tongued portion of the sample as needed. As I mentioned previously, new technology such as reconstructive phrase modeling provides greater control over articulation and phrasing, and I anticipate that these types of innovations will offer even greater expressive control in the future.

When articulating accents, note that accents generally produce a change in timbre when executed on an instrument such as a trumpet. (This makes sense when you consider that a brass player will need to increase the amount of air going into the horn when performing an accent.) In a sequencing environment, you may want to design your sounds to reflect this natural musical phenomenon: For example, try editing a sound so that higher velocities slightly increase the cutoff point of a low-pass filter. Even if you are not trying to emulate an acoustic instrument, these types of details will help your sequences to sound much more musical.

DYNAMIC CONTOUR

One of the best ways to create musical sequences (whether emulating traditional instruments or using synthetic sounds) is to implement the concept of dynamic contour. A clarinetist, for example, will rarely play a sequence of notes in a dynamically static fashion. It is natural for acoustic musicians to shape the dynamics of a passage in a musical way (even if the part is inconsequential). Though dynamic contour can be difficult to execute on a MIDI keyboard or guitar controller, the use of a dedicated volume pedal or aftertouch or a data slider can help you to naturally phrase a melody. Though dynamic changes are usually very subtle, they can provide very musical results. Note that it is also common for performers to add a touch of vibrato at the end of a long note or the climax of a melody. Again, the use of a modulation wheel can add much to the musicality of this type of passage. One technical solution is to invest in a relatively inexpensive breath controller. Note that many synthesizers provide a breath controller port. If your synthesizer does not support this feature you can still add this capability by purchasing a third-party breath controller interface. These devices are connected to an instrument via a MIDI cable and provide the ability to use breath to alter expression levels in real time. Another solution is to invest in a woodwind controller such as the Electronic Wind Controller manufactured by Akai or the Yamaha WX5. My subjective experience has been that woodwind players can effectively utilize these types of MIDI controllers to create a very expressive style of playing.

MUTES

Mutes are used almost exclusively for brass and string instruments. (An interesting exception is the rare saxophone bag mute.) Though most brass instruments utilize mutes on occasion, mutes are used most often by trumpet or trombone players. Mutes are used primarily for two reasons: Mutes can help fix dynamic imbalances between instruments, and mutes can change the timbre of an instrument. A few of the common mutes include the harmon, cup, bucket, and straight mute. In jazz styles, trumpet players and trombonists often use a plunger for wah-wah types of effects. When orchestrating, consider using mutes to add a unique color to a passage. For example, two trumpets in harmon and cup can be combined with a flute to create a distinctively "cute" timbre that is effective for a melodic unison. Similarly, a trombone section utilizing bucket mutes can provide a reasonable substitute for the softer tones of a French horn section. Since mutes generally have an effect on timbre, they can be useful in bringing a line to the foreground. This is often more effective than simply increasing the volume of a given part.

RANGES

Figures 16.1 through 16.5 list both the concert and written ranges for common brass and woodwind instruments. Transposition will not be an issue (unless, of course, you decide to prepare parts for acoustic instruments). I have included the transpositions for each of the instruments because the written range often provides a hint as to the "sweet range" of the instrument. In general, the sweet range will fall in the staff when a concert note is transposed for a given instrument.

Figure 16.1
B♭ clarinets.

Figure 16.2
Flutes.

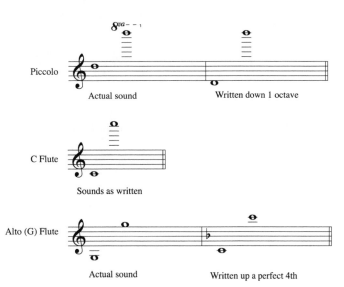

Figure 16.3
Double reeds.

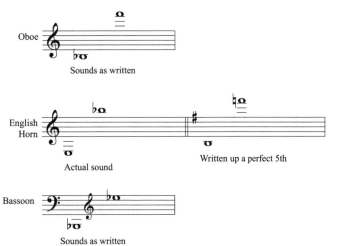

Figure 16.4
Saxophones.

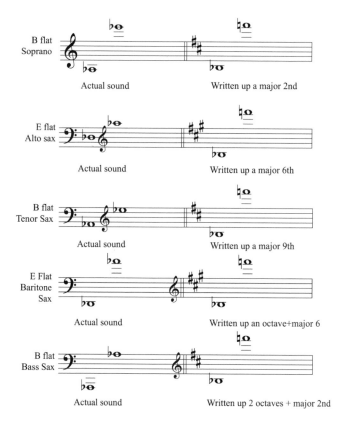

Figure 16.5
Brass.

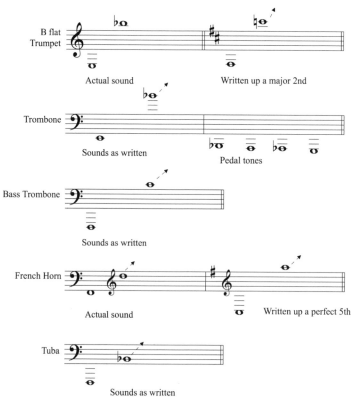

Strings

Strings have long been a mainstay of the symphonic orchestra. Strings are attractive to composers for several reasons: They are capable of great dynamic contrasts. The string choir is a largely homogenous group of instruments—the timbre of each of these instruments is very similar. Strings are also unique in that they can sustain notes indefinitely. Though strings are used for almost any musical situation, they often function as melodic instruments or to provide harmonic pads. Figure 16.6 illustrates the open tunings for each of the primary stringed instruments. I find it helpful to visualize the open tunings when writing string parts because the tuning of the string indicates possibilities for *double stops* (two simultaneous notes on adjacent strings). For example, since the cello is tuned in open fifths, double-stop fifths are available on all of the strings, but double-stop fourths can be problematic (e.g., C2-F2). Note that the range of each stringed instrument extends more than an octave beyond the highest string.

Figure 16.6
Range of stringed instruments.

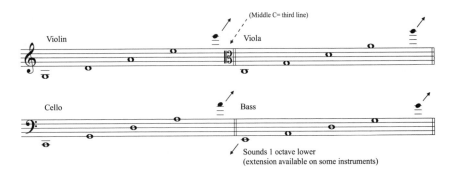

When sequencing string parts, it is helpful to consider the variety of bowing techniques common on these instruments (see Table 16.1). Though this list is not comprehensive, it should get you started with writing for most typical situations. Note that composers often indicate frequent changes in bowing technique in a composition. In MIDI terms, this means that you may need to set up a variety of string sounds to obtain an appropriate palette of bowing techniques for a given orchestral composition. For example, I set up four bowing patches for each of the stringed instruments in the "Thriller Scene" demonstration composition. In this piece, you will hear finger and bowed tremolo as well as several bowing styles. Although it is not necessary to be aware of all the bowing techniques when sequencing, a knowledge of these concepts provides an insight into the way string players produce sounds. By way of example, I had to practice several passages on the "Scherzo" recording in order to develop a reasonable representation of *spiccato* technique (off the string). I found it helpful to visualize the bouncing bow effect while practicing repeated notes on my MIDI controller.

Table 16.1. String Bowing and Color Techniques	
Term	**Description**
Détaché	The most common bowing stroke—player changes the direction of the bow for each note (i.e., non-legato).
Louré	A legato (connected) style but with slight separation between notes.
Staccato	Short notes played with one bow stroke.
Spiccato	A style of playing where the bow "bounces" on the string.
Pizzicato	The strings are plucked.
Sul Ponticello	Playing near the bridge to create a "metallic" sound.
Sul Tasto	Bow is placed over the fingerboard to create a soft tone.
Col Legno	The bow is turned backward and the instrument played with the wooden portion of the bow in a percussive manner.
Tremolo	Although string players utilize several types of tremolos, most synthesized tremolo sounds are unmeasured, bowed tremolos (as contrasting with a fingered or measured tremolo).
Con Sordino	Mute is placed on the bridge. Creates a softer sound and an interesting change in timbre.

In general, it's best to avoid playing string parts in an idiomatic keyboard style. In Figure 16.7, though the musical idea works well when performed on piano, the effect is unnatural when applied to a string ensemble.

Figure 16.7
Unnatural keyboard–string approach.

When orchestrating string (or brass or woodwind) music, consider using a more symphonic approach. Notice how, in Figure 16.8, each of the voices functions in more natural fashion. Though each line is simple, the combination of rhythmic elements produces the desired rhythmic feeling. You will find that this type of linear approach to orchestrating electronic instruments will yield outstanding results.

Figure 16.8
Linear version of a keyboard pattern.

Percussion

There are two categories of percussion to consider when creating a traditional orchestration: nonpitched and pitched instruments. Nonpitched instruments include the bass drum, snare drum, toms, triangle, cymbals, Latin percussion, tambourine, whip, whistle, anvil, wood blocks, and gong. Pitched percussion includes the xylophone, vibraphone, marimba, glockenspiel, chimes, and timpani. Of course many world and ethnic percussion are also available as sonic resources.

INDEFINITE-PITCHED PERCUSSION

A common mistake made by many MIDI musicians is an over-reliance on nonpitched percussion. Remember that, in particular, gongs and cymbals are generally used for grand musical gestures. As with any sound, percussive sounds lose their effectiveness if used too frequently. I have found that I gravitate to these sounds because percussion sounds are often some of the most accurate samples in my library. This makes sense when you consider that, unlike wind, brass, and string instruments, percussion sounds produce a fairly consistent attack and decay. This predictability lends itself to accurate reproduction in a sampling environment.

When sequencing drums, it is helpful to consider that, while the instrument may or may not produce a definite pitch, the pitch of the instrument will change depending on the force with which it is struck. Consider designing drum sounds that emulate this feature. One way to achieve this effect is to map velocity levels to pitch. As you increase the velocity of your attack, the pitch of the instrument will change in a natural fashion.

One of the more difficult techniques to master when sequencing percussion parts is the performance rudiments such as rolls and flams (the percussion version of a grace note). If you don't have access to a percussion controller such as a MIDI drum set, these rudiments can be comfortably performed using special keyboard mapping. One way to execute these types of passages on a keyboard is to map the same sound to several adjacent keys. By practicing a variety of trills and tremolos it is possible to achieve fairly natural-sounding drum rolls.

It is easy to forget the limitations of some percussion instruments when sequencing. Though drums and suspended cymbals have a large dynamic range, remember that crash cymbals are called crash cymbals for a reason. Using velocity scaling or volume changes to adjust a dynamic imbalance of a loud crash cymbal may produce artificial results.

I recently played an example of an electronic orchestration (one that mimics a real orchestra) for a friend who plays in our local symphony. He thought that the percussion parts sounded very realistic, but I found it interesting that he commented that the time feel was too relaxed. He mentioned that, in orchestral time, a percussionist must play slightly ahead in order to project the sound (which often emanates from the back of the orchestra) out into the hall so that it arrives with instruments placed closer to the edge of the stage. Although this makes perfect sense, it was an aspect I hadn't considered. When possible, ask professionals for feedback. I have certainly gleaned many helpful tips along these lines by asking for feedback on my work.

PITCHED PERCUSSION

Pitched percussion instruments are used for a wide variety of effects. The xylophone, for example, is often associated with comical musical effects. In contrast, the wonderfully mellow tone of a marimba can provide a beautiful accompaniment for a wind melody or as a featured solo instrument. Figure 16.9 lists common pitched-percussion instruments.

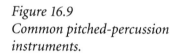

*Figure 16.9
Common pitched-percussion
instruments.*

When imitating pitched percussion instruments, it is helpful to visualize the playing technique common to these instruments. The xylophone is typically played with two hard mallets. When sequencing xylophone parts, consider using both hands just as a xylophonist would do. While it might be more natural to perform these passages using traditional keyboard fingering, a two-handed approach may help you to play in a more idiomatic style. Vibraphone and marimba performers generally use from two to four mallets when performing. When mimicking these instruments, consider the limitations of using two hands to control four mallets. Though marimba virtuosos can perform amazing feats of dexterity, there are limitations with regard to the independence of the mallets and execution of fast runs in a four-part mallet texture.

Depending on the tempo, marimba and xylophone players often use a roll (tremolo) technique to sustain longer note values such as a half or whole note. Though slow tremolos are usually comfortable to perform using a keyboard controller, you might want to consider temporarily slowing the tempo of a sequence in order to perform a natural-sounding marimba tremolo. As with snare rudiments, an arpeggiator can also be helpful. For single-note sustained passages, try setting your arpeggiator to repeat 24th or 32nd notes—the effect can be fairly natural. Step-time entry can also be effective in that it will allow you to implement slight variations of dynamic level while sequencing tremolos.

TIMPANI

Timpani are often used as an exciting percussive element in symphonic music—but note that the timpani can also be used as a melodic instrument. In orchestral music, four timpani are typically used. Each of the timpani can be tuned to a variety of pitches but, if your goal is to mimic a real timpanist, you must provide space in the score for the timpanist to re-tune the instruments should you want more than four pitches. Although some synthesized timpani sound fairly bombastic, these instruments have a huge dynamic range and can also be utilized in softer, lyrical types of passages. Timpani can also be used for interesting effects such as distant thunder. One of my favorite examples comes from a Debussy orchestral prelude titled "Nuages" ("Clouds"). The ranges of the four timpani are listed in Figure 16.10.

Figure 16.10
Timpani ranges.

Miscellaneous

Although you have now looked at ranges for most of the common orchestral instruments, there are several other instruments that you may want to use in an orchestration.

GUITAR

The guitar is similar to electric bass and double bass in that the instrument sounds an octave lower than the written pitch. When trying to mimic a guitar, remember that the tuning of this instrument makes some types of voicings awkward to play. In talking to many guitarists I have learned that "drop-2"-style voicings are common (see Chapter 15, "Real-World Arranging"). The common open-string tunings for six-string guitar are shown in Figure 16.11.

Figure 16.11
Open-string guitar tunings.

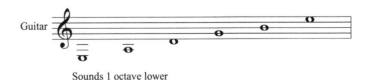

Sounds 1 octave lower

The piano picking technique presented in Chapter 13, "Contemporary Keyboard Techniques," lends itself well to guitar picking. Consider alternating between two notes in each hand to emulate the finger picking technique used by many guitarists. An example can be heard in the second half of "I Saw You There" on the CD that accompanies this book.

CELESTA

The celesta is a keyboard instrument that sounds very brilliant. The celesta is much like a piano in that notes can be sustained with a damper pedal. This instrument can be interesting as a solo voice or can be used to add a "metallic" quality when doubled with winds, brass, or string instruments. To my ear, the celesta often provides an appropriate sound for a magical or surreal passage—I hear the technique frequently employed this way in movie scores. Tchaikovsky's "Dance of the Sugar Plum Fairy" from *The Nutcracker* is a good example of an orchestral composition that features the celesta. The range of the celesta is listed in Figure 16.12.

Figure 16.12
Celesta.

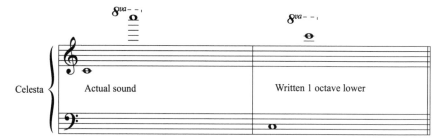

HARP

The harp has a range that is similar to a piano (see Figure 16.13). This instrument can be wonderfully effective as a melodic voice or when used as a backing instrument. The harp may also be used for glissando figures that serve to accentuate an important arrival point (several examples can be heard on the "Thriller Scene" and "Emerald City" orchestral demonstrations). When sequencing a harp glissando, you may want to execute a white or black note glissando on the keyboard. You can use your sequencing software to transpose the glissando to an appropriate key. For non-pianists, it may be helpful to temporarily slow down a sequence in order to successfully perform a stylistic harp glissando of a given chord. Note that the harp is a diatonic instrument and is tuned to a C♭ scale. Each note of the scale has a dedicated pedal that can be used to raise all notes of a given name one or two half steps.

Figure 16.13
Harp.

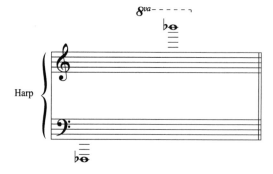

Putting It All Together

Now that you have learned about some of the common instruments, ranges, and playing techniques, it is time to consider using these instruments in an orchestral setting.

FOREGROUND AND BACKGROUND

It is often helpful to think of the concept of foreground and background when orchestrating music. An instrument may come to the foreground in several ways. An obvious example is volume—an instrument that is louder than other instruments will catch the ear of the listener. In computer-based music, however, a reliance on volume can be problematic. By adjusting note velocities or channel volume it is easy to make a flute sound louder than a full brass section. If your goal is to realistically mimic an acoustic orchestra, you will want to consider other methods for establishing a theme in the foreground.

Timbre

Timbre can be one of the most helpful elements in establishing a foreground voice. For example, doubling a flute melody with an oboe could help to make the melody stand out more effectively. This can be particularly helpful when trying to "bring out" an inner voice in a thick orchestral texture. (Several examples can be heard on the "Thriller Scene" recording on the accompanying CD). The modern symphonic orchestra provides an amazing number of timbral possibilities. My best advice is to listen to the masters and experiment—allow yourself to think across sections (i.e., various combinations of woodwinds, strings, brass, and pitched percussion). One of the things I love about creating music on a computer is the ease with which I can experiment with various combinations of instruments.

Rhythmic Motion

A line may also be heard in the foreground if it contrasts rhythmically with other parts. For example, if a viola melody consisting of quarter notes and eighth notes is set against cellos and violins playing whole notes, the motion of the viola part will tend to bring it to the foreground.

Register

In a homogeneous group of instruments such as five saxophones, the highest note will tend to be heard in the foreground. Similarly, a melody placed in a low register will tend to be heard in the foreground when placed against a group of homogeneous instruments in a contrasting register. Octave doublings (such as violin 1 an octave higher than violin 2) are also effective in bringing out a melody. (Listen to "Emerald City" on the CD that accompanies this book.)

Sequencing Orchestral Parts

Although modern orchestras often perform music with amazing complexity, time is never entirely accurate. For this reason, I find that it is usually best to avoid quantizing parts when I attempt to emulate an acoustic orchestra. Slight timing and phrasing imperfections can, in my estimation, yield a result that is much more natural and musical than the rigidly perfect time that can be achieved in a sequencing environment. Along these lines, it is often useful to work through an orchestration a phrase at a time, performing each independent part as though performing the part on an acoustic instrument. In this instance, an expression controller will provide the opportunity to phrase each line in a natural way. It's also helpful to consider turning off a click track—especially for passages that lend themselves to a *rubato* approach.

Dynamics can be particularly hard to control since it's difficult to gauge an appropriate dynamic level until several parts have been recorded. One technique that I find useful is to record any melodic lines first (such as an oboe solo). Once the melody has been recorded, add supporting parts and use your ear to adjust the volume of each supporting part to an appropriate level. This process mimics the process used by orchestral musicians. When mimicking a real orchestra, it is advisable to record each part using the patch (program) that will be the final intended timbre, rather than using a generic sound. Patches respond in different ways, and a passage input with one sound may have a different result when played on another patch.

Preplanning

Although it can be a time-consuming process, you will want to do a fair amount of planning before you attempt to sequence a traditional orchestration. You may even want to consider writing out the piece before you begin the sequencing process. "Thriller Scene" and "Emerald City" (on the accompanying CD) are two such examples. It would be difficult to create these types of orchestrations using a "bottom up" approach common to many popular music recordings. I find that taking the time to write and orchestrate before sequencing allows me to make better orchestration decisions.

"Snapshots"

In film music, "snapshot" electronic orchestrations are typically created as part of the approval process. Since it is very expensive to hire and record a large orchestra, producers want to hear a mockup of the cues in electronic form before scheduling a recording session. Many electronic musicians, specialists who excel in creating realistic orchestral mockups, are employed in the film industry.

Part III

Projects and Scores

CHAPTER 17

Anatomy of Styles: Recordings and Scores

This final chapter utilizes the concepts and techniques from the first 16 chapters to create original music in a variety of genres. I will provide a look at the production process from both the technical and artistic standpoint. Although not every genre is represented (and some of the pieces do not fall into a well-defined genre), I deliberately wrote pieces to demonstrate many of the challenges facing a contemporary musician, such as writing lyrics, horn parts, complex orchestrations, and a variety of bass and drum grooves. Some of the pieces, such as the string quartets and orchestral demonstration, utilize a classical approach to composition—each part was carefully composed and sequenced as written. Other pieces were based on lead sheets or "pony" scores. (A pony score often utilizes a grand staff for the strings, brass, and woodwinds instead of separate staves for each instrument.) I have always enjoyed the process of improvisation, so I elected to leave room for performers to improvise in many of the pieces.

I made a conscious decision to use a hybrid approach to many of the selections in order to model the resources available in a typical production environment. For example, I recorded live musicians in order to sweeten key components of several pieces but relied on a fairly modest sequencing environment for the bulk of the work. In working for a number of production companies, I have found that the hybrid electronic/acoustic model is commonly used given time constraints and production costs. All of the acoustic tracks were recorded in a modest home studio using inexpensive microphones and homemade cables.

After completing the final mix of each selection, I met with the owner of a production company who makes a living writing music for networks such as Fox and NBC. He listened to each of the selections, and I was pleased when he told me he wanted to license many of the compositions for use in their production library. I mention this because he made several helpful observations regarding the industry. First, a professional-sounding mix, is essential. They simply can't use music that doesn't have a clean mix no matter how good the underlying musical idea is. Second, they are generally not interested in music that is in a well-defined genre such as "Funky Zone." He was primarily interested in music that demonstrated my own personal style, such as "Emerald City," "Lullaby for Emily," "Caliente," and "Hip Hop for Monk." Third, real instruments are almost always preferable to MIDI tracks. And finally, musicality is important. For example, he liked all of the tracks that had an emotive quality. I will certainly take his comments to heart for future projects.

I would stress that this chapter is not intended as a definitive guide to the process of writing and recording original music. My goal is that the discussion will provide a behind-the-scenes look that will be useful in your own creative endeavors. I hope you enjoy listening to the compositions and that they will provide a good point of departure for your own work.

Thriller Scene

I wrote "Thriller Scene" in order to demonstrate how a 12-tone row might be used as the basis for a composition suitable for a sci-fi or thriller movie.

COMPOSITION NOTES

"Thriller Scene" is based on the following 12-tone matrix.

	I-0	I-7	I-6	I-1	I-2	I-9	I-8	I-3	I-11	I-10	I-4	I-5	
P-0	D	A	G#	D#	E	B	A#	F	C#	C	F#	G	R-0
P-5	G	D	C#	G#	A	E	D#	A#	F#	F	B	C	R-5
P-6	G#	D#	D	A	A#	F	E	B	G	F#	C	C#	R-6
P-11	C#	G#	G	D	D#	A#	A	E	C	B	F	F#	R-11
P-10	C	G	F#	C#	D	A	G#	D#	B	A#	E	F	R-10
P-3	F	C	B	F#	G	D	C#	G#	E	D#	A	A#	R-3
P-4	F#	C#	C	G	G#	D#	D	A	F	E	A#	B	R-4
P-9	B	F#	F	C	C#	G#	G	D	A#	A	D#	E	R-9
P-1	D#	A#	A	E	F	C	B	F#	D	C#	G	G#	R-1
P-2	E	B	A#	F	F#	C#	C	G	D#	D	G#	A	R-2
P-8	A#	F	E	B	C	G	F#	C#	A	G#	D	D#	R-8
P-7	A	E	D#	A#	B	F#	F	C	G#	G	C#	D	R-7
	RI-0	RI-7	RI-6	RI-1	RI-2	RI-9	RI-8	RI-3	RI-11	RI-10	R-I4	R-I5	

Twelve-tone technique is often used to devise music that does not have a tonal center, but I was interested to use the row to develop a piece that has a tonal center (albeit freely tonal). I experimented with the prime version of the row until I was pleased with the results and used a custom Java matrix calculator to calculate the matrix. Readers are welcome to a copy of "Brent's 12-tone calculator." Just send an e-mail and I would be happy to send a link.

For years I rebelled against the idea of using something as pedantic as a 12-tone matrix, but I have since come to realize that concepts such as matrices and set theory provide another way of organizing notes in just the same way as a major scale or mode. For this piece, the matrix provided a palette of notes that I used to devise the primary themes and harmonic structures. For example, the opening ostinato utilizes the prime version of the row (P0). The opening harmony in the strings contains the first four notes of the row, and the French horn and trombone theme is based on the second retrograde (R2). Similarly, the timpani is tuned to the first three notes of the row. Since an ostinato is used in the piano and timpani, the note D clearly emerges as a tonic.

The violins provide a counterpoint to the French horns and trombones starting in bar 15. This theme was based on P7. It is interesting to note that I didn't use the row exclusively. For example, the flute and harp flourishes in bar 22 come from a D-flat major scale, as do the polychords in bar 23. However, in the section starting in bar 24, the celesta and trumpets utilize P0, and the oboe is based on P9. Similarly, the pyramid chords starting with the French horns in bar 27 are based on P5.

PRODUCTION NOTES

I sequenced "Thriller Scene" in Logic Pro and utilized the Garritan Personal Orchestra, a reasonably priced orchestral library available from www.garritan.com. By default, the instruments in the Garritan Orchestra are mapped to the modulation wheel for expression (I suspect that this was a convenient way to utilize a high-resolution expression controller without any special configuration on the part of the user). I sequenced each part a layer at a time and used the expression controller to mimic the way a real orchestral musician might perform each phrase. One of the difficulties of layering parts in this way is estimating the overall volume of the finished piece. As expected, I had to scale the expression of some parts once the entire piece had been sequenced in order to balance the sound of the orchestra.

This piece really pushed the limits of my computer (an older Apple PowerBook). I ended up freezing a few tracks in order to free up processing power for effects. However, it is gratifying to know that it is possible to create such an orchestration on a machine that is not on the cutting edge of technology.

Hip Hop for Monk

"Hip Hop For Monk" features a disparate mixture of heavy electronic drum loops and bop vocabulary associated with the music of Thelonious Monk.

COMPOSITION NOTES

The melody features several "Monkisms," including an angular melody, interval of a second (bars 12, 14, and 17), whole-tone scale (bars 15 and 16), and rhythmic rhyming. The term "rhyming" is often associated with Monk's melodies. He often used repetition, cross rhythm, and accents to create melodies analogous to a poetic rhyme. Examples of rhyming can be heard in bars 13–16.

I considered formalizing the arrangement of this composition. Interludes and other devices could certainly be effective, but I decided that open solos best represented the spirit of the piece. (I remember hearing an interesting trio in Boston that featured a punk trio playing the music of Monk, so I'm sure that concept was in my mind as I worked on this piece).

Sometimes a drum loop can provide the seed for a composition, and that was the case with this piece. I selected a drum loop and sequenced several bass lines until I was happy with the underlying groove. At that point, I wrote the melody and began the sequencing process.

PRODUCTION NOTES

"Hip Hop For Monk" was fairly easy to produce since I relied entirely on prerecorded loops for the drum tracks. I added the bass part and fleshed out the chords using a virtual Rhodes keyboard. (The virtual Rhodes is one of the instruments included with Logic Pro.) Next, I recorded the trumpet and saxophone using a stereo microphone and punched in the saxophone solo using a condenser microphone. The guitarist listened to my scratch guitar tracks and recorded a similar groove using the Line6 Pod amplifier simulator.

One of the problems I ran into with the mix was that the original drum groove was too "wet." There was not much I could do since I really liked this particular groove. In the end, I tried to strike a balance by sweetening the horn and rhythm section tracks with a touch of reverb. I also added a touch of compression and EQ to the final mix in order to create an edgier sound.

Lullaby for Emily

My original intent was to write a piece to demonstrate a modal approach to composition. As with most compositions, my initial sketches led in a new direction, and "Lullaby for Emily" was born.

381

COMPOSITION NOTES

Although a hint of Lydian mode is evident in the initial statement (the B-natural over an F chord) and in the final bars (C Lydian), the piece is clearly in the key of C major. The piece is comprised of three sections that each contain two smaller sections alternating between solo piano and piano, flute, and violin.

Although some repetition is evident, the piece is largely *through composed* and does not follow a well-defined formal structure. The flute and violin parts are fairly independent and form a counterpoint of sorts. It is interesting to note that most of the composition is diatonic because chromatic elements would likely detract from the peaceful lullaby effect. However, a borrowed ii chord is used in bars 70–72 and serves to add a slightly poignant effect prior to the arrival at the final tonic chord. As mentioned previously, the C Lydian mode (the fourth mode of G major) is used for the final tonic chord.

PRODUCTION NOTES

I composed and engraved the piece using Sibelius notation software prior to beginning the sequencing process. Though it often works well to compose such a piece directly in a sequencing environment, I have noticed that my sketches sometimes sound too improvisatory, so I elected to write everything out in order to focus on the counterpoint between the flute and violin.

I recorded the piano track first using a software-based piano synthesizer called "Ivory," which is manufactured by Synthogy. I wanted the piece to flow naturally with a great deal of rubato, but in my experience, rubato is nearly impossible to achieve in a natural way by adding tempo changes to an existing performance. For this reason, I decided not to use a click track. I simply recorded the piano part using phrasing that felt natural for the piece. Once the piano track was complete, I added a scratch flute and violin part to double check that my ideas were sound. Although the synthetic flute and violin sounded fairly musical, I knew the piece would be better if I recorded acoustic performances, so I arranged separate sessions with a local flutist and violinist. In preparation for the session, I finalized dynamics and added bowings and articulations so that the players would have a sense of how I wanted them to interpret their parts.

The flute and violin were recorded using a large-diaphragm Rode condenser microphone in a fairly dead recording space. Although it was challenging for the players to match their performance to the rubato piano track, it took only a few passes for each player to get a feel for the piece. I elected not to fix the few slight timing imperfections in my digital audio workstation sequence because I feel that such slight imperfections are a natural part of a musical performance.

To achieve a reasonable facsimile of a live recording space, I used a single reverb on the main out of the DAW. In this way, each of the tracks interact with the reverb as if they were recorded in a live hall. Once I was pleased with the type and amount of reverb, I made some balance and panning adjustments and bounced the tracks to disk in the form of a stereo wave file.

Caliente

I wrote "Caliente" to demonstrate several latin piano concepts presented in Chapter 13, "Contemporary Keyboard Techniques." I understand that "caliente" means *warm* or *hot*. I'm not sure if "hot" is an appropriate term for the composition, but it was a fun piece to compose and perform.

COMPOSITION NOTES

The piece, which starts with a characteristic introduction with the right and left hands of the piano part in 10ths, is in a minor key. I arranged the melody for three horns and utilized tertian harmony for most of the piece. It is interesting to note that the trombone is particularly independent of the trumpet and saxophone in bars 12–14. Although this didn't sound very good when I played the parts back in my notation software, I was confident that it would work well when performed by live horns since each of the parts worked well in a linear fashion.

To break up the sound of the horns, I elected to use piano for the bridge (starting in bar 25). The form of the main theme is AABA—a form that is used on many popular songs. I elected to utilize the introduction as an interlude prior to the trumpet solo. I often find that an introduction can provide a sense of cohesion to an arrangement when it recurs in the form of an interlude or ending.

The trumpet solo is based on the same chord progression as the melody, but the saxophone and trombone "pads" provide a nice change during the bridge (alternating thirds and sevenths of each chord). My sense was that it might be too predictable to base another solo on the same set of chord changes, so I decided to develop a new section after the first eight bars of the piano solo. Here, the tenor sax and trombone provide a riff that expands on the chord changes heard previously in the melody and trumpet solo. Although the chords are not drastically different, they do provide a point of interest.

The final statement of the melody leads to a *montuno* section. Here, a characteristic piano vamp provides the basis for a short trombone solo. The trumpet and tenor saxophone are scored alternately in seconds and thirds and add to the repetitive effect of the montuno section. The introduction is restated once more in the form of an ending after eight repetitions of the montuno section.

PRODUCTION NOTES

Since I knew the piece would be performed live, I scored the entire piece using notation software and then sequenced scratch tracks for the rhythm section horn parts. I recorded the trumpet, saxophone, and trombone using a stereo microphone placed several feet in front of the performers. I debated recording each part individually but decided that the players would be better able to match articulation and phrasing if they played as a unit. For this reason, it was necessary to take extra time to make sure that the musicians were placed such that the microphone would pick up an optimal blend. We punched in solos using a large-diaphragm condenser microphone.

The drums were recorded after the horns (not necessarily an ideal situation). I had intended to use a stereo microphone over the drum kit and five individual microphones placed near each drum, but after experimenting with the position of the microphones, I realized that I liked the sound of the stereo microphone with a single dynamic microphone pointed at the snare and another on the kick drum. (The tom microphones only contributed ringing overtones from the toms and actually made the drums sound weak). This would certainly be different for another drum kit, but, in this instance, the combination of a stereo overhead and two close microphones worked well.

For the acoustic bass, I used a large diaphragm condenser microphone pointed at the "F holes." The sound was a bit too boomy, so on subsequent pieces I elected to run a separate direct line to blend the natural acoustic sound with the direct line in order to control the presence of the sound.

"Caliente" was a challenge for me to mix. I wanted a fairly live and reverberant sound, but the percussive nature of the piece tended to muddle the sound. In the end, I used separate reverb for the horn trio, solo horns, and drums. I used a touch of compression and EQ on the kick drum to get more presence while avoiding a "thumpy" sound. I suspect that I would make other changes to the mix should I revisit the piece in the future.

I Saw You There

I wrote "I Saw You There" to demonstrate the process of writing a popular tune with lyrics. My goal was to create the type of intimate sound associated with vocalists such as Norah Jones.

COMPOSITION NOTES

Although there is no correct way to write a melody and lyrics, the first phrase of the lyrics ("I Saw You There") came to me and provided the initial seed for the composition. In this instance, I wrote the melody concurrently with the text—each line of text provided a natural rhythmic cadence that I took advantage of as I wrote the melody. I also considered possible harmonies as I composed the melody, so when the melody was finished I had a good idea of how the melody and harmony would work together. (The process is described in more detail in Chapter 14, "Music Composition.")

I considered writing a second verse, but the tune seemed to lead to a simple interlude. The "floaty" middle section provides a point of rest between the two statements of the melody. As is typical of many pop tunes, color tones such as added ninths provide a nice variation when combined with simple triads.

PRODUCTION NOTES

Once I finished writing the tune, I met with the vocalist to determine an appropriate key. As it turned out, C major was the perfect choice to utilize the intimate sound of her lower register.

I sequenced the keyboard part first (using the sheet music version of the tune provided in the next section of the book). I then added a MIDI bass part and the scratch drum tracks. I elected to add a touch of shaker and MIDI acoustic guitar during the interlude. Once the sequence had taken shape, I re-recorded the piano tracks to remove the melody because I knew this would be distracting to the vocalist.

I asked the vocalist to record several takes so that I could create a composite track of the best phrases. However, the vocalist was a real pro, so this was hardly necessary. I used an inexpensive Rode condenser microphone placed about 12 inches away from the vocalist and experimented with the position of the microphone until I was happy with the sound. I would stress that it is important not to let technology get in the way when recording great musicians. In this instance the vocalist sounded great, had a wonderful dynamic range, and spot-on intonation, so it was not necessary to use compression, equalization, or any other type of processing other than reverb. Microphone placement and a good level were the only two requirements in capturing her performance.

Funky Zone

My goal with "Funky Zone" was to demonstrate some of the vocabulary associated with funk music such as percussive clavichord and organ as well as a horn section. I also decided to create all of the backing tracks in my sequencing environment to demonstrate the process of using and editing drum loops.

COMPOSITION NOTES

The piece is essentially a jam or groove tune that provides a vehicle for an improvised organ and guitar solo. The composition is in the key of E (a good key for guitar) and features several altered dominant chords—a sound I associate with groups such as Tower of Power. The horns are scored primarily in unison or tertian structures. Diatonic planing (as described in Chapters 10 and 15) was very helpful for realizing fairly complex harmonies with only three notes.

PRODUCTION NOTES

I started by sketching the tune in Finale. Once the basic sketch was complete, I sequenced the backing tracks in GarageBand. My original intent was to do the entire production in GarageBand, but it soon became evident that I would need more editing capability, so I imported the project into Logic Pro. Although drum and bass loops were used for a majority of the project, I found it necessary to record several sections using virtual MIDI synthesizers in order to accentuate rhythmic punches in the horn section. It was challenging to try to seamlessly alternate between drum and bass loops and MIDI tracks. I simultaneously used loops and MIDI drum tracks in a few spots such as the ride cymbal heard during the out chorus.

The horns were recorded with a stereo microphone as described in the production notes for "Caliente." All of the guitar tracks were recorded direct to disk using the Line6 Pod amplifier emulator mentioned previously. The lead guitar sound had a tremendous amount of background noise (an accurate representation of that particular amplifier), so I found it necessary to ride the faders on the lead guitar to minimize background noise during the solo and final riff. I wanted a tight sound and therefore used reverb and delay sparingly.

Homeward

"Homeward" is a lighter piece that features musical vocabulary typically associated with pop music.

COMPOSITION NOTES

The form is comprised of the main theme, an interlude, solo vamp, return of the main theme, and a coda. The first section is comprised of an AABA structure, but curiously, the first A is 10 bars long, whereas the second and final A is 8 bars in length. This is due to a cadential extension at the end of the first phrase. Though the harmony is simple, a linear bass line provides a point of interest to the chord progression. A similar device is used to set up the ending in the coda.

Some of my friends have described the theme as "catchy," and this is probably because the melody is singable—melodic contour is not extreme, and jumps are often balanced with stepwise motion. The interlude, which starts in bar 31, features a bass motive and helps to build intensity prior to the solo vamp.

PRODUCTION NOTES

Unlike some of the other selections in the book, I did most of the orchestration directly in my sequencing environment. I started by recording the keyboard and bass tracks and added a scratch drum track. I had planned on using drum loops, but unfortunately I didn't find a loop that was suitable for the swing 16th section during the interlude so I ended up recording scratch MIDI drum tracks so that the musicians would have a reasonable feel for the piece. For this reason, I try not to rely on drum loops in the initial stages of a composition. In this instance, the composition would have gone in a totally different direction had I started with a preexisting drum loop.

I prepared a lead sheet for the saxophonist and placed a large-diaphragm condenser microphone about 2 feet in front of the bell of his horn. Drums were recorded with a stereo overhead microphone, a dynamic microphone inside the kick drum, and another near the snare and hi-hat cymbals. The acoustic guitar was recorded with a large-diaphragm condenser microphone placed about 24 inches in front of the sound hole. The electric guitar was processed through a Line6 Pod that ran straight into the audio interface.

Although I was generally happy with the sound of the saxophone, the melody kept dropping out of the mix, so I applied compression to control the dynamic level. The acoustic guitar sounded great but was boomy when mixed with the bass and left hand of the keyboard part, so I found it necessary to insert a high-pass filter on that track. Finally, I used compression and EQ to bring the kick drum a bit more to the foreground.

I often find it helpful to check a mix using headphones. Although I was pleased with the sound coming from my near-field monitors, the headphones revealed that panning was somewhat unnatural, so I adjusted the position of the acoustic guitar and saxophone in the mix.

Techno Toys 2

"Techno Toys 2" is a purely synthetic piece based on a heavy drum loop and several software and hardware synthesizers.

COMPOSITION NOTES

The composition starts with a short vamp that is used to set the mood of the piece. The main theme and all of the supporting parts are in D Dorian. A secondary melody line follows the primary melody a diatonic third above—an example of diatonic planing. The piece is in ternary form (ABA) but a transitory interlude is used before and after the B section.

PRODUCTION NOTES

The bulk of the piece was recorded using a "bottom up" sequencing approach. I worked on the drum tracks and added a bass line, harmonic pads, pseudo-arpeggiations, and the melody. It was fun to use filters and other modifiers to tailor the sound of each synthesizer to the piece. I used an external synthesizer (a Yamaha EX5R) for some of the synthesizer parts, so it was necessary to record these tracks to an audio track prior to bouncing the mix to disk. To accentuate the transitory effect of the interludes, I used the mouse to draw panning controllers for each of the repetitive parts. The panning (which occurs at varying rates) heightens the sense of motion in these sections. I used step-time input (16th-note triplets) to enter the fast snare fills at the end of each of these sections—an effect that I have heard on many "techno" recordings.

Although it is not obvious, I also used an old analog synthesizer, a Korg MS-20, on this recording. (The Korg MS-20 and other vintage analog keyboards are available in virtual form as a part of the Korg Legacy Collection.) I recorded several sample-and-hold loops into a two-track editor and used ReCycle to convert the loops into REX files. I imported the REX files on an available audio track and used these loops during the interludes.

The piece was fairly easy to mix with one exception: It was difficult to gauge the level of the strident bass line and kick drum. I don't currently use a subwoofer in my studio, and it became clear that subtones from the bass and kick were too loud when I played the piece on a system with a subwoofer. I ended up using a high-pass filter on both parts to remove some of the unwanted frequencies below about 35 Hz. The bass and kick are still rather punchy, but I felt it was appropriate for the style so I kept the levels fairly hot.

Emerald City

"Emerald City" is a composition for orchestra and saxophone soloist that might be appropriate to underscore a *film noir* scene.

COMPOSITION NOTES
The piece is in D minor and makes use of many colorful extensions as well as altered dominant chords and substitutions. A minor ii-V-i progression is frequently used and the parallel major (D major) is used on the bridge. As with many orchestrations in this style, the strings are scored in a lush low register with occasional support by the French horns.

I wrote the theme first in lead-sheet format and then orchestrated the lead sheet in a pony score in Sibelius. The piece includes a lengthy improvised section, so I utilized a simple string background for variety during the piano solo. A modulation at the end helps the theme sound fresh for the final recap.

PRODUCTION NOTES
I sequenced all of the orchestral parts using instrument sounds from the Garritan Personal Orchestra and added MIDI bass, drums, and piano. I wanted the piece to sound as natural as possible so I made frequent use of the expression controller when sequencing the orchestral parts. I prepared a transposed part for the saxophone soloist and recorded with a large-diaphragm condenser microphone placed about 36 inches away from the bell of his horn. The bass was recorded with a condenser

microphone placed about 16 inches away from the bridge of the instrument and a direct line from his pickup. This allowed me to balance the natural sound of the instrument with a more present direct sound. The drums were recorded with a stereo microphone placed directly above the kit and a single condenser microphone located about 24 inches in front of the snare and hi-hat.

Piano Stomp

Many years ago I transcribed Dave Grusin's piano score for the movie *The Firm* for the Hal Leonard Corporation. "Piano Stomp" pays homage to this wonderful soundtrack.

COMPOSITION NOTES

I was primarily interested in demonstrating the "piano picking" technique described in Chapter 13, so the piece makes frequent use of a syncopated picking technique as well as many other concepts presented in that chapter such as scale-tone triads and blues riffs.

The composition is loosely built around a blues progression. Although the form is not a strict 12- or 16-bar blues, frequent use of the subdominant and dominant provides a characteristic blues effect. As with many pieces based on the blues, the theme is presented at the beginning and end of the tune with an improvised section in the middle.

PRODUCTION NOTES

I used Synthogy's Ivory virtual piano and sequenced each section in Logic Pro. I knew I would want to notate the performance for this book, so I elected to play to a click track to facilitate the transcription process. Although Logic is not a dedicated notation application, I am often surprised by how well the program does in terms of transcription of MIDI performances. I printed the Logic transcription and re-entered the notes in Sibelius. Although it is possible to import a MIDI file in Sibelius and Finale, neither of the programs produced a score that was usable—it was simply faster to re-enter the notes based on the score produced by Logic.

I added a touch of reverb via the Space Designer plug-in within Logic Pro and tweaked the stereo settings of Ivory until I was happy with the sound.

Seascape

"Seascape" features an interesting mixture of flute, acoustic guitar, drums, and synthesizers.

COMPOSITION NOTES

The introduction utilizes a lush synthesizer pad with improvised piano runs. After the introduction, the piano establishes the tempo and the primary mode of A Aeolian. The theme follows a common format of AABA and the introduction is used as an interlude prior to the piano solo. The chords in the piano solo are based on harmonies heard during the theme, and an ascending bass line in the second ending sets up the return of the theme.

PRODUCTION NOTES

As with many of the pieces on the CD, I sequenced a version of the composition with scratch drum tracks and a bass line and then recorded the piano part over the top of the bass and MIDI drums. Next, acoustic drums were recorded using a stereo overhead microphone and a dynamic microphone on the snare and hi-hats and a second dynamic microphone on the kick drum. The drums required a touch of compression and reverb to bring out the sound of a resonant side-stick. I equalized the kick drum to improve the blend of the drum with the other instruments.

The acoustic guitar was recorded with a large-diaphragm condenser microphone located about 24 inches in front of the sound hole. We focused on background comping for the first pass and made a second pass in order to double the melody during the bridge. The flute was recorded in a similar way, but I placed the microphone fairly close to the mouthpiece to pick up some of the natural breath sound.

It Was a Dark and Stormy Night

This piece was written for the Spokane Jazz Orchestra and is featured on the band's CD titled *It's About Time*.

COMPOSITION NOTES

I decided to approach the piece as a tone poem for orchestra—an approach used by Duke Ellington and many other orchestral composers. A primary feature is the repetitive bass line—an idea that came to me in the car one day. At the time, I wasn't sure what I would do with the bass line, but I wrote it down and it became the seed for this composition.

The piece features a series of tonal vignettes ranging from old-school Ellington to a more modern contrapuntal approach used by arrangers such as Bill Holman. Although the piece is largely through-composed, the first section is repeated at the end and provides a sense of symmetry to the composition.

Many of the brass voicings utilize close or open position structures as described in Chapter 15. The saxophone soli utilizes "Supersax"-style voicings as described in the same chapter.

PRODUCTION NOTES

The piece was recorded by Paul Brueggemeir and mixed by Dan Keberle. The final mix and editing were handled by Jaye Nordling. It is interesting to note that the piece was recorded with fairly primitive equipment: Each instrument was close miked with a Shure SM 58 and recorded with a linear 24-track digital tape recorder. Dan Keberle did the bulk of the mixing using the linear tape deck and 24-channel console sans automation. This meant he had to "perform" the mix in real time in order to print the mix to a two-track master.

Remix

I wanted to demonstrate the process of using Sony's ACID program to create a remix, and it occurred to me that it might be interesting to remix fragments of classical recordings. "Remix" is based on short samples from classical literature spanning a range of over 400 years.

COMPOSITION NOTES

In Chapter 11, I discussed the concept of the "additive formal process" used by Stravinsky and other composers. It was fun to apply the same techniques to music written by Stravinsky, Schoenberg, J.S. Bach, and others. Although some repetition is evident, the piece is largely through-composed, as the term additive formal process implies.

PRODUCTION NOTES

The first step was to extract audio fragments from several recordings. Next, I used the beat-mapping wizard in ACID to create beat-mapped loops. I then began the process of experimenting with the loop fragments over a variety of drum grooves. Once the piece began to take shape, I found it necessary to dice some of the loops in order to create fills that could be used to set up the second and third sections. These types of fills can be easily created by zooming in to a high resolution and drawing short fragments of the sample at a resolution such as a 16th or 32nd note. I thought it would be interesting to include computer-generated text, so I recorded a voice-over based on text from a book on artificial intelligence. (The text was originally "spoken" by a computer.) I used a vocoder to create the pseudo-electronic voice.

The final step involved working on the mix. Effects were inserted into some of the tracks, and I experimented with panning and track levels until I was pleased with the results.

Soundscape

"Soundscape" is a composition that combines music synthesis with sound effects.

COMPOSITION NOTES

Although some sustained notes and chords can be heard, I did not use traditional elements of melody, harmony, and rhythm—morphing synthetic sounds provide the basis for this piece. For this reason, no score is provided in the final section of the book. My concept was to blend synthesizers and sound effects in order to create the illusion of a virtual three-dimensional scene.

PRODUCTION NOTES

The synthetic tracks are based on a piece I composed several years ago. Envelope generators are applied to a variety of filters and provide most of the morphing effects heard in this composition. I utilized panning in some spots to create the illusion of three-dimensional movement. Once I finished the synthesized tracks, I added numerous sound effects such as wind, rain, a jungle, and thunder. It was fun to attempt to combine these distinct elements in a seamless way. Track automation and crossfades (covered in Chapter 5) were used extensively to bring sound effects in and out of the "scene" in an unobtrusive way.

You Are My Rock

It is interesting to hear how some gospel singers such as Marion Williams combine elements of blues and gospel in their music. "You Are My Rock" is in an "old school" gospel style—the piece contains elements of gospel, blues, country, and rock.

COMPOSITION NOTES

The harmonic progression is relatively simple and primarily revolves around the I, V, and IV chords. A V7/vi chord (C♯7) is used to set up a characteristic modulation to the relative minor (F♯ minor) in the bridge. For variety, I used a modulation of a major second for the solo section.

PRODUCTION NOTES

I met with the singer to determine the best key for her range. Once a key was established, it was then possible to sequence all of the tracks. I recorded the vocalist using a large-diaphragm condenser microphone placed about 1 foot directly in front of her. I asked her to sing three background parts (each of which was a note from a major triad) during the vamp at the end of the tune. We used a composite approach to the vocal part: I recorded several takes of each phrase and combined the best takes (although this was hardly necessary with this particular vocalist). After the vocal part was finished, I resequenced the piano track so that the part would interact with her track in a more natural way. The final step was to record the guitar parts and improve the sound of the drums. I used some compression on the snare and utilized separate reverbs for the vocal and drum tracks.

Romance & Scherzo

The two quartets ("Romance" and "Scherzo") were written to demonstrate concepts relating to string writing. Although the pieces were written for a string quartet, the concepts are equally applicable to a large string section.

COMPOSITION NOTES

"Romance" is a short piece in ternary form (ABA). The harmonic vocabulary is reminiscent of the Romantic era and linear technique was used throughout. "Scherzo," traditionally a light or humorous piece, is a vigorous and somewhat playful treatment of a "Bartokian" motive. I use the term "Bartokian" to describe a motive that is angular and highly chromatic. The primary motive is used as a fugue subject. In a fugue, the motive is successively introduced in each voice (often in transposed form). The piece uses a freely tonal approach to composition: The tonic is evident in places, but few traditional vertical structures exist. The fugue subject is developed through the process of fragmentation, and the fugue is restated prior to a playful ending.

PRODUCTION NOTES

Both string quartets were sequenced using Synful Orchestra, which provides a great deal of control over phrasing and nuances such as bowing and articulation. As I recorded each part, I used expression and note velocity to try to mimic the phrasing and bowing of a real violinist. One of the more challenging aspects was to try to blend with the other instruments as each part was recorded. Although I was generally pleased with the phrasing, the Synful Orchestra tended to add too much vibrato—an aspect that I feel is less successful. Once the parts were complete, I scaled expression values for some of the parts to produce a more balanced sound. Synful Orchestra provides a 1-second "look ahead" mode that can be used to render a more authentic sound, so I toggled this option on prior to bouncing the finished tracks to disk.

The Musicians

The following musicians can be heard on the audio CD. I am grateful to my friends and colleagues for their work in support of this project.

Dr. Philip Baldwin, violin
Joe Brasch, guitar
Brent Edstrom, keyboards/sequencing
Jennifer Edstrom, flute
David Fague, tenor saxophone
Angela Hunt, vocals
Eugene Jablonsky, acoustic bass
Dr. Daniel Keberle, trumpet
Dave Stultz, trombone
Rick Westrick, drums

THRILLER SCENE

Brent Edstrom

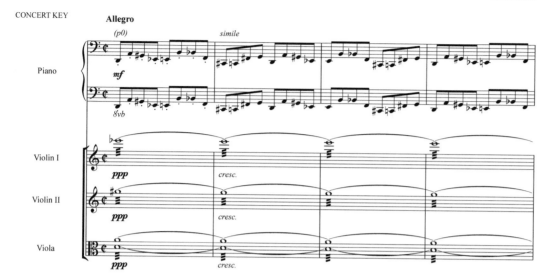

394

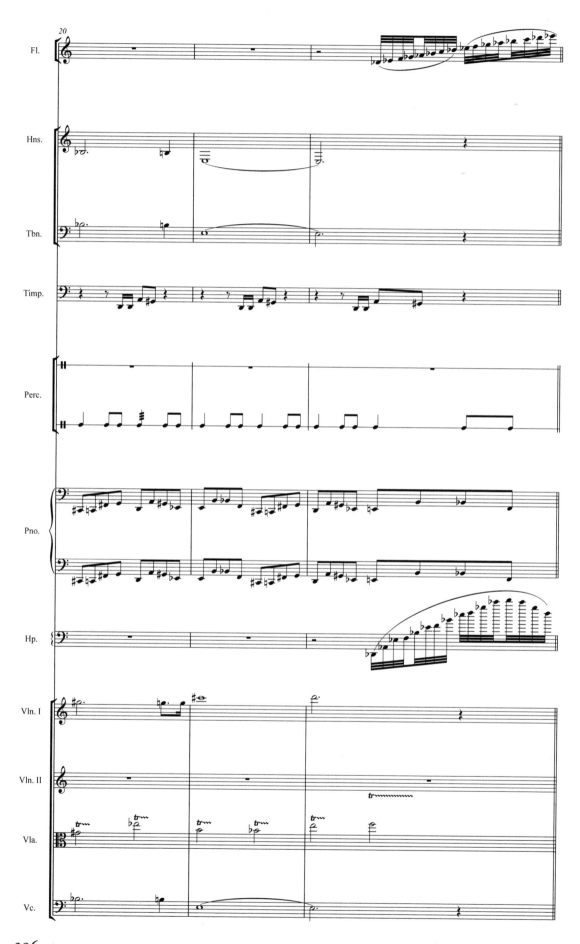

HIP HOP FOR MONK

Brent Edstrom

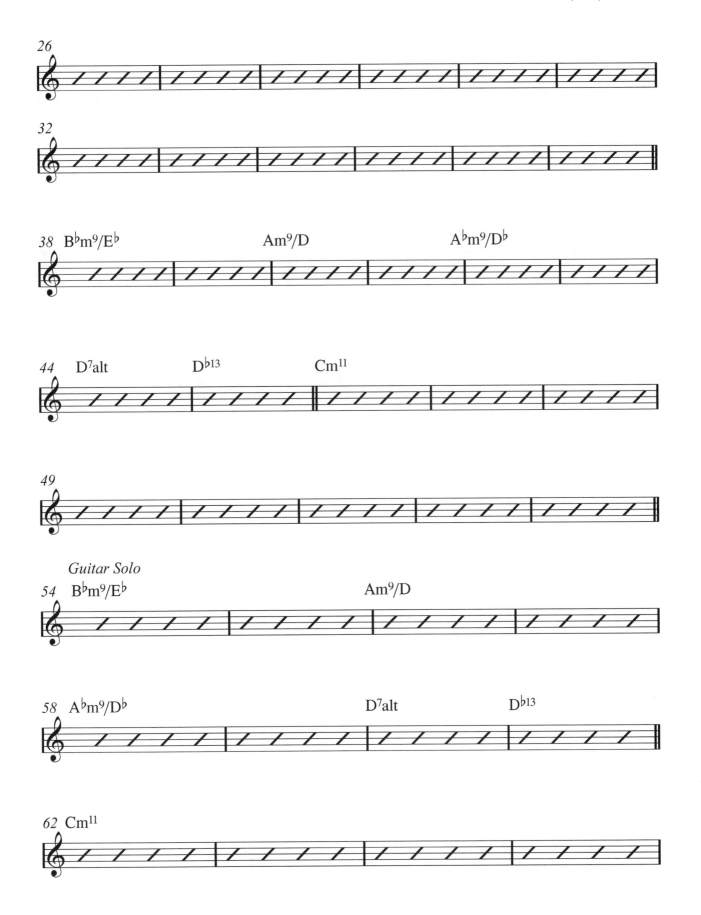

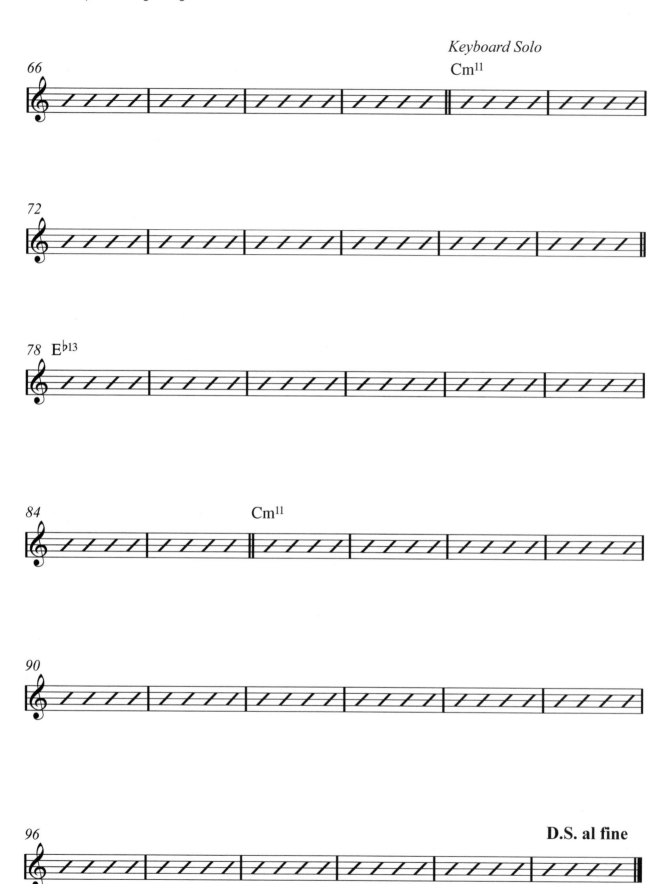

LULLABY FOR EMILY

Brent Edstrom

CALIENTE

CONCERT KEY

Bright Latin

Brent Edstrom

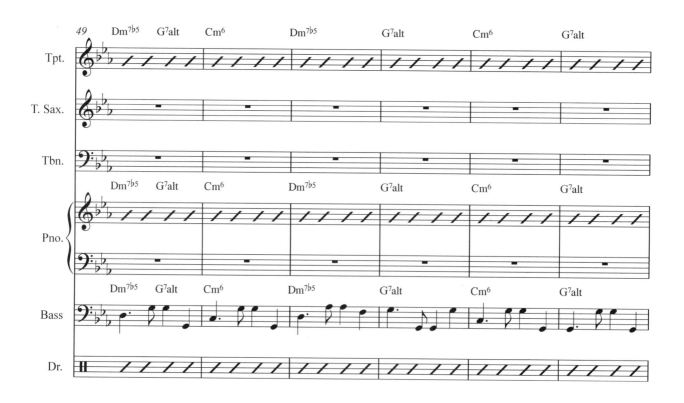

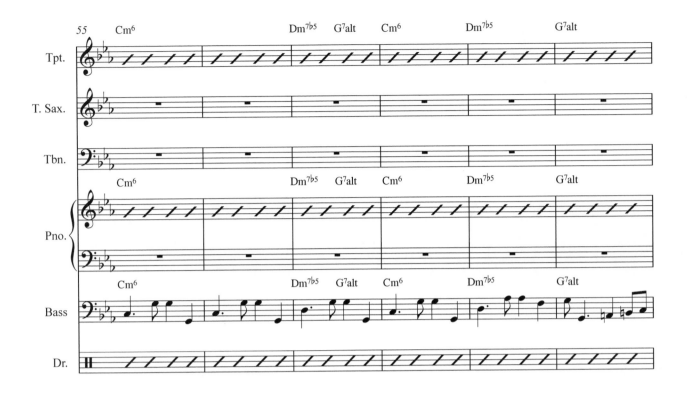

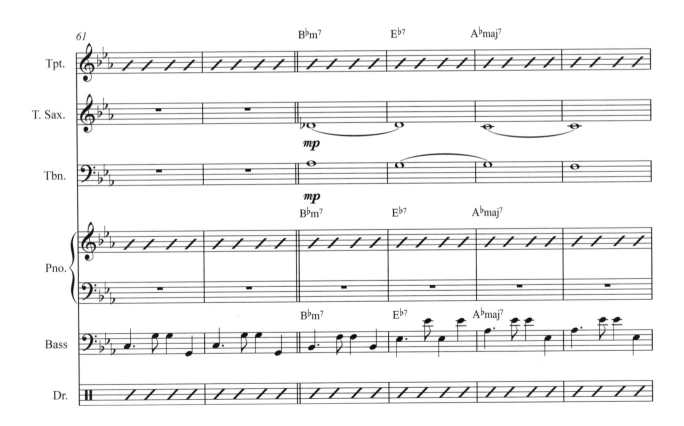

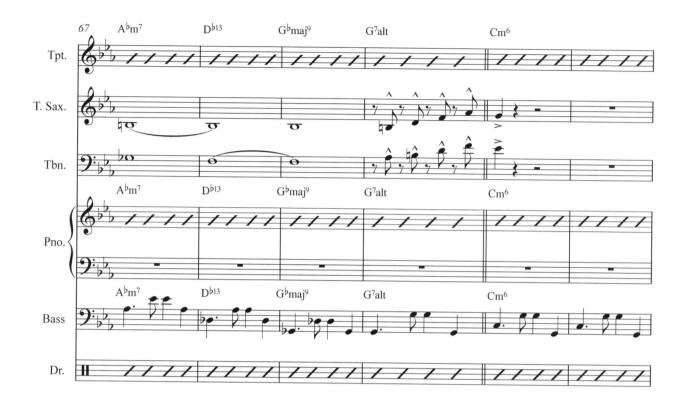

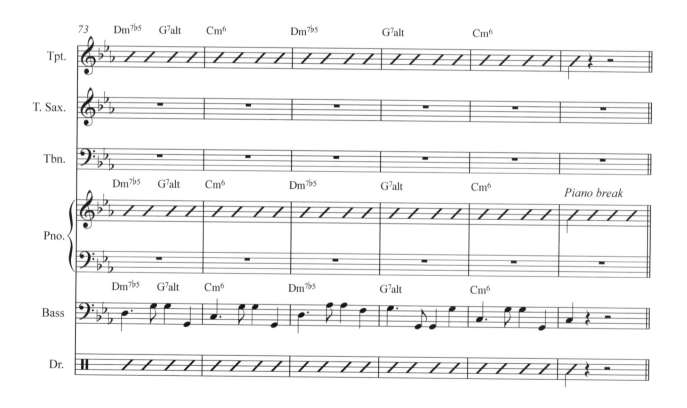

I SAW YOU THERE

Words and Music by
BRENT EDSTROM

FUNKY ZONE

Brent Edstrom

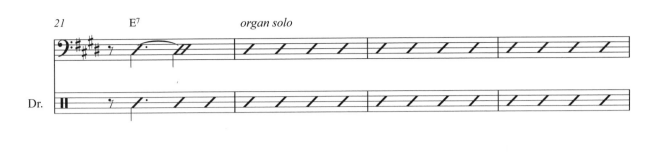

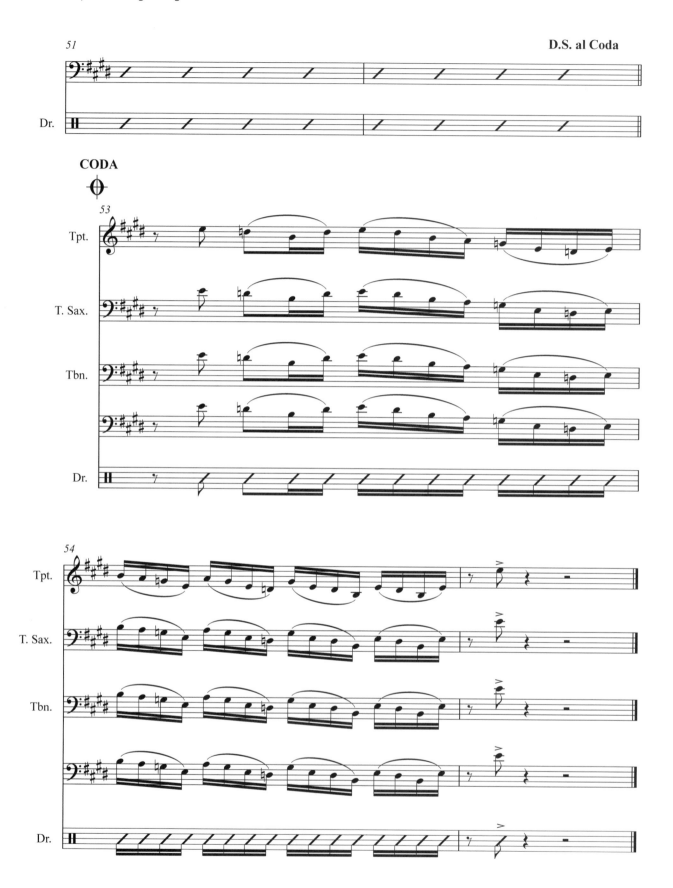

HOMEWARD

Brent Edstrom

TECHNO TOYS 2

Brent Edstrom

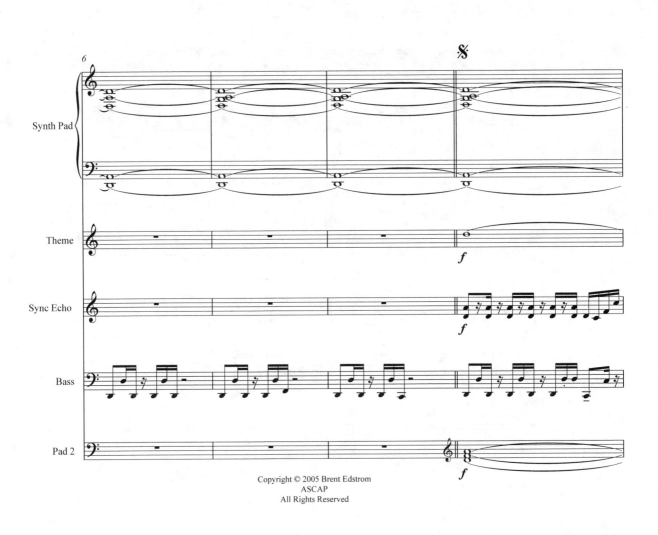

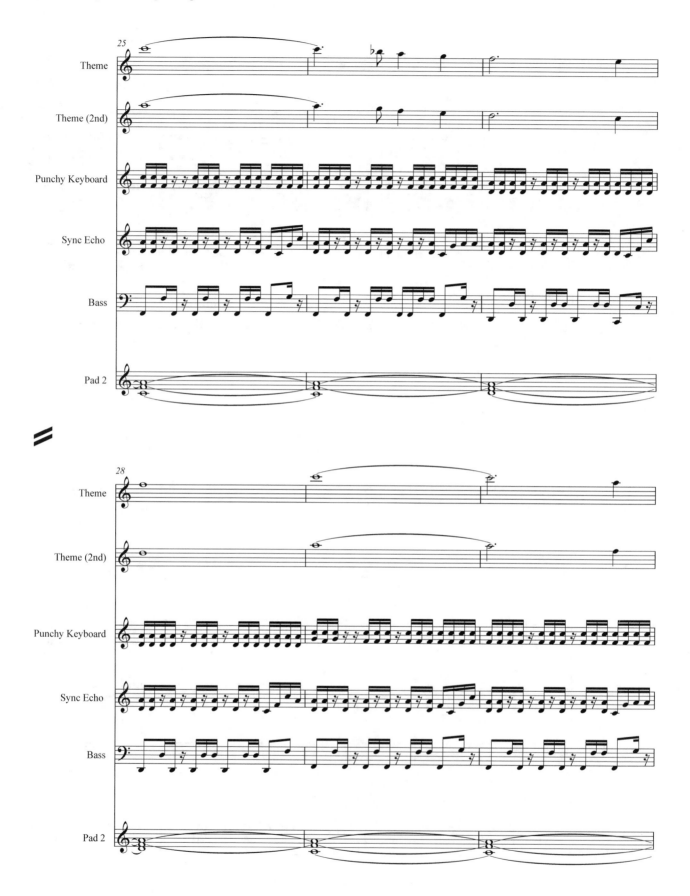

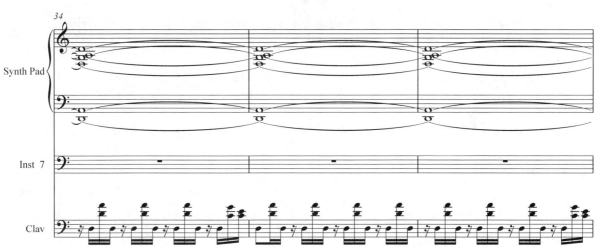

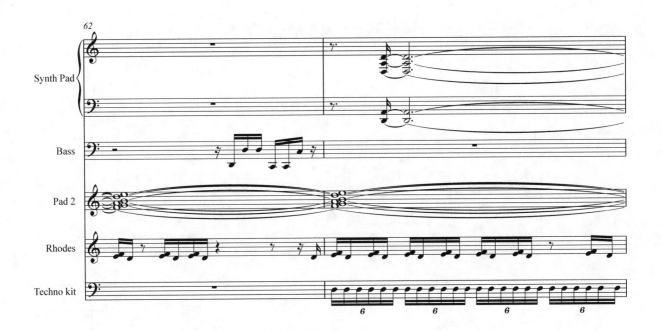

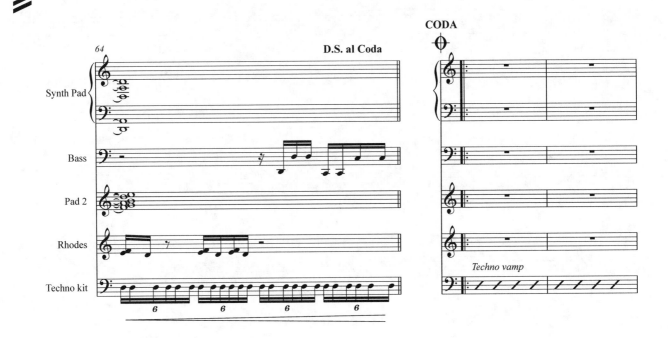

EMERALD CITY

Brent Edstrom

CONCERT KEY

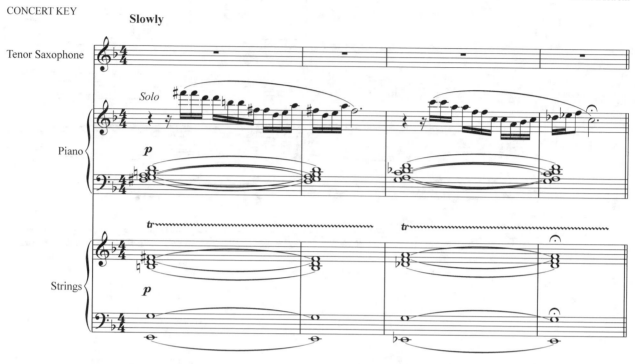

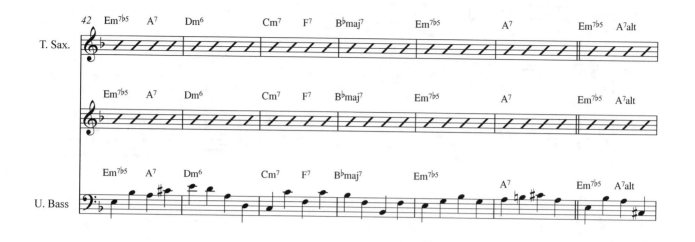

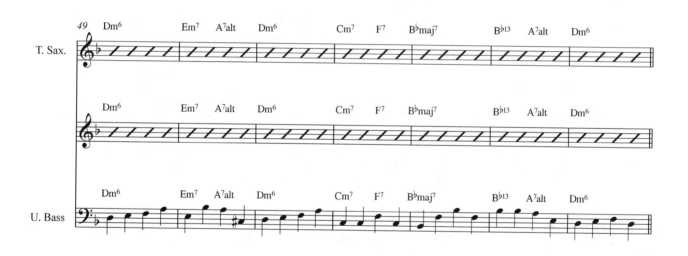

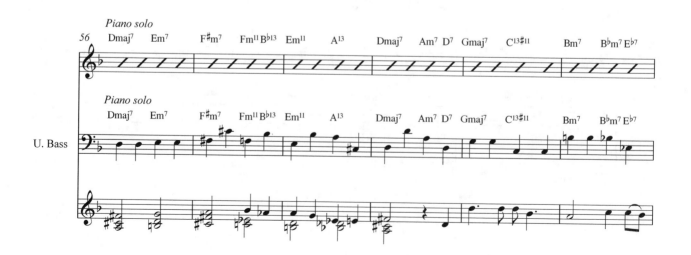

PIANO STOMP

Brent Edstrom

Medium Blues

8vb throughout

8vb throughout

SEASCAPE

Brent Edstrom

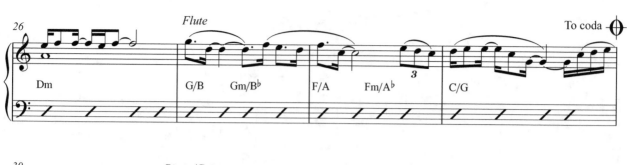

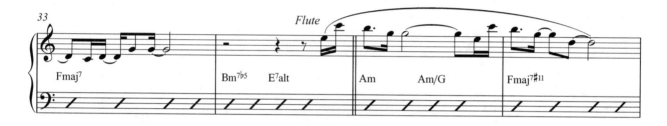

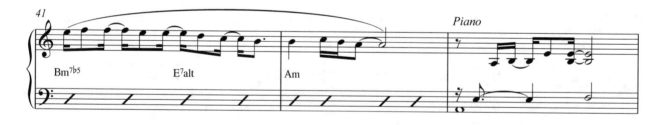

IT WAS A DARK AND STORMY NIGHT

For the Spokane Jazz Orchestra

Brent Edstrom

TRANSPOSED SCORE

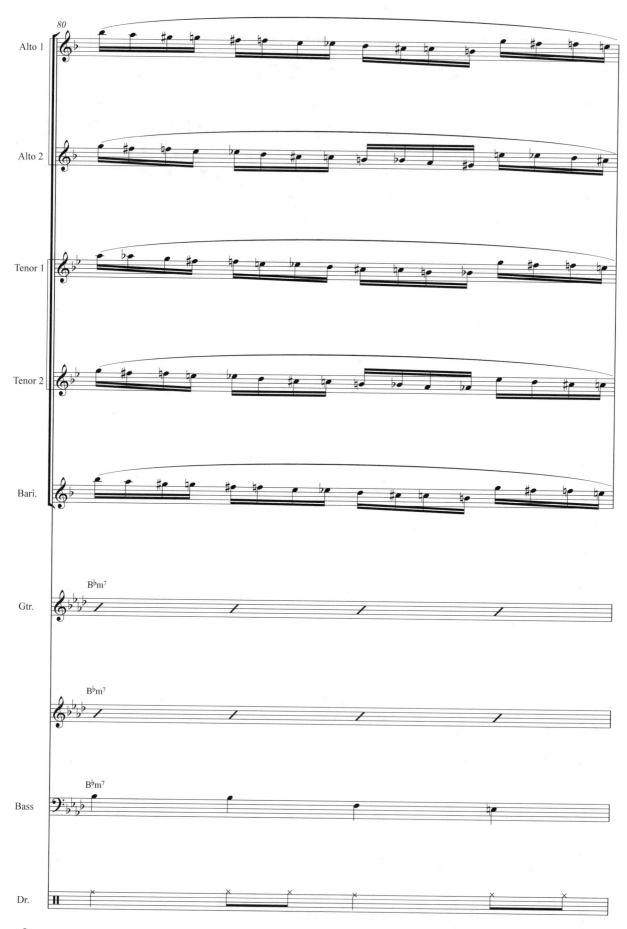

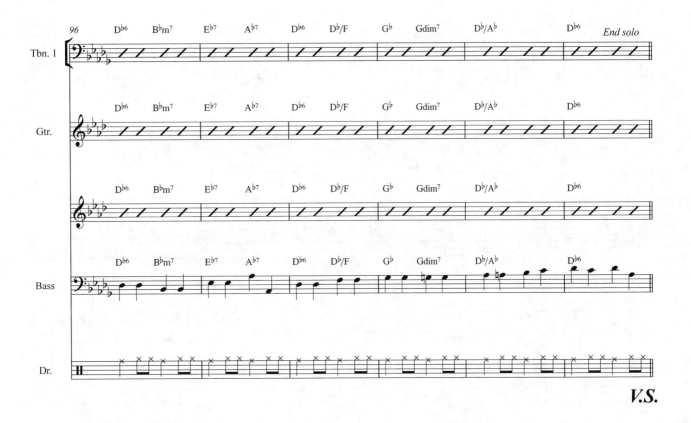

YOU ARE MY ROCK

Brent Edstrom

492

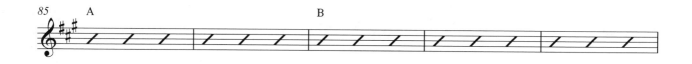

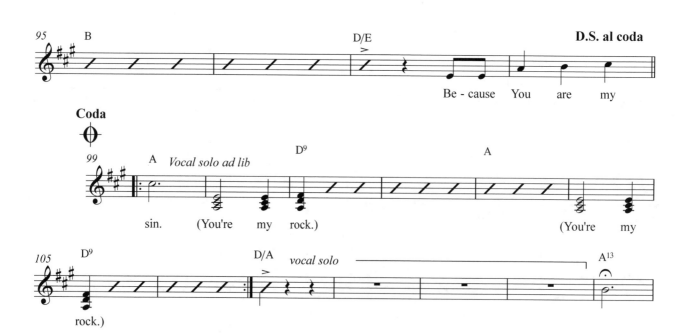

ROMANCE

Brent Edstrom

57.6"

SCHERZO

Brent Edstrom

Sources

Adler, Samuel. *A Study of Orchestration, Second Edition.* W.W. Norton and Company, 1989.

Alten, Stanley R. *Audio in Media: The Recording Studio.* Wadsworth Publishing Company, A Division of International Thomson Publishing Inc., 1996.

Benward, Bruce and Marilyn Saker. *Music in Theory and Practice, Volume 1 and 2.* McGraw-Hill Higher Education, 2003.

Burkholder, Peter J., Donald J. Grout, Claude V. Palisca. *A History of Western Music, Seventh Edition.* W.W. Norton and Company, 2006.

Charlton, Andrew and John M. DeVries. *Jazz and Commercial Arranging: Block Writing Techniques, Rhythm, and Melody.* Prentice-Hall, Inc., 1982.

Christopher, Felston W., Gilbert F. Close, Jr., Margaret G. Hummel. *Fun and Folk Songs.* The Westminster Press, 1949.

Copland, Aaron. *What to Listen for in Music, Revised Edition.* The McGraw-Hill Book Company, 1957.

Dallin, Leon. *Twentieth Century Composition: A Guide to the Materials of Modern Music.* WM. C. Brown Company Publishers. 1974.

Dobbins, Bill. *Jazz Arranging and Composing, a Linear Approach.* Advance Music, 1986.

Eckel, Bruce. *Thinking in C++.* Prentice Hall, 2000.

Fisk, Josiah, ed. *Composers on Music.* Northeastern University Press, 1956.

Forsyth, Cecil. *Orchestration.* Dover Publications, Inc., 1982.

Friend, David, Alan R. Pearlman, Thomas D. Piggott. *Learning Music with Synthesizers.* Arp Instruments, Inc., 1974.

Glinsky, Albert. *Theremin: Ether Music and Espionage.* University of Illinois Press, 2000.

Grout, Donald J. *A History of Western Music, Third Edition*. W.W. Norton & Company, 1981.

Guérin Robert, *MIDI Power!*, Muska and Lipman Publishing, a division of Thomson Course Technology, 2002.

Hindemith, Paul. *A Composer's World*. Anchor Books, Doubleday & Company, Inc., 1961.

Howe, Hubert S., Jr. *Electronic Music Synthesis*. W.W. Norton & Company, 1975.

Huber, David Miles. *Microphone Manual: Design and Application*. Howard W. Sams & Company, 1988.

Huber, David Miles. *The MIDI Manual*. Sams, A division of Prentice Hall Computer Publishing, 1991.

Huber, David, and Robert E. Runstein. *Modern Recording Techniques*. Sams, a division of Prentice Hall Computer Publishing, 1989.

Kennan, Kent. *Counterpoint: Based on Eighteenth Century Practice*. Prentice-Hall, Inc., 1959.

Mancini, Henry. *Sounds and Scores: A practical Guide to Professional Orchestration*. Northridge Music, Inc., 1973.

Nestico, Sammy. *The Complete Arranger*. Fenwood Music Co., 1993.

Pellman, Samuel. *An Introduction to the Creation of Electroacoustic Music*. Wadsworth Publishing Company, 1994.

Persichetti, Vincent. *Twentieth-Century Harmony: Creative Aspects and Practice*. W.W. Norton & Company, 1961.

Peterson, George, and Steve Oppenheimer. *Tech Terms: A Practical Dictionary for Audio and Music Production*. Hal Leonard Publishing Corporation, EM Books, 1993.

Piston, Walter. *Orchestration*. W.W. Norton & Company, 1955.

Pressing, Jeff. *Synthesizer Performance and Real-Time Techniques*. A-R Editions, 1992.

Randel, Don Michel, ed. *The New Harvard Dictionary of Music*. The Belknap Press of Harvard University Press, 1986.

Schoenberg, Arnold. *Structural Functions of Harmony, Revised Edition*. W.W. Norton & Company, 1969.

Schoenberg, Arnold. Translated by Roy E. Carter. *Theory of Harmony.* University of California Press, Belmon Music Publishers, 1978.

Spencer, Peter, and Peter M. Temko. *A Practical Approach to the Study of Form in Music.* Waveland Press,1988.

Taylor, C.A. *The Physics of Musical Sounds.* American Elsevier Publishing Company, 1965.

Turek, Ralph. *The Elements of Music: Volume Two, Second Edition.* The McGraw-Hill Companies, 1996.

Wright, Rayburn. *Inside the Score.* Kendor Music, Inc. 1982.

Index

CD TRACK LIST

1. Thriller Scene
2. Hip Hop for Monk
3. Lullaby for Emily
4. Caliente
5. I Saw You There
6. Funky Zone
7. Homeward
8. Techno Toys 2
9. Emerald City
10. Piano Stomp
11. Seascape
12. It Was a Dark and Stormy Night
13. Remix
14. Soundscape
15. You Are My Rock
16. Romance
17. Scherzo

License Agreement/Notice of Limited Warranty